AWS Certified Security – Specialty (SCS-C02) Exam Guide

Second Edition

Get all the guidance you need to pass the AWS (SCS-C02) exam on your first attempt

Adam Book
Stuart Scott

AWS Certified Security – Specialty (SCS-C02) Exam Guide

Second Edition

Authors: Adam Book and Stuart Scott

Reviewer: Naman Jaswani

Publishing Product Manager: Anindya Sil

Senior-Development Editor Name: Megan Carlisle

Development Editor: Shubhra Mayuri

Presentation Designer: Salma Patel

Editorial Board: Vijin Boricha, Megan Carlisle, Simon Cox, Ketan Giri, Saurabh Kadave, Alex Mazonowicz, Gandhali Raut, and Ankita Thakur

First Published: September 2020

Second edition: April 2024

Production Reference: 1150424

Published by Packt Publishing Ltd.
Grosvenor House
11 St Paul's Square
Birmingham
B3 1RB

ISBN: 978-1-83763-398-2

www.packtpub.com

Contributors

About the Authors

Adam Book has been programming since the age of six and has been constantly tapped by founders and CEOs as one of the pillars to start their online or cloud businesses.

Adam has developed applications and websites. He's been professionally involved in cloud computing and data center transformation since 1996, focusing on bringing the benefits of cloud computing to his clients. He's led technology teams in transformative changes such as the shift to Infrastructure as Code and implementing Automation.

As a distinguished engineer by trade, Adam is a cloud evangelist with a track record of migrating thousands of applications to the cloud and guiding businesses in understanding cloud economics to create use cases and identify operating model gaps. Adam ran the local AWS user group in Atlanta for over 6 years. He has been certified on AWS since 2014 and holds many of the AWS Certifications and the CISSP and CCSK security certifications.

Stuart Scott has an extensive career spanning over two decades in the IT industry; he has expertise across various technological domains, with a particular interest for Amazon Web Services (AWS). Currently serving as the AWS Content Director at Cloud Academy, Stuart has written over 250 courses, enriching the learning experiences of more than 1.3 million students. His instructional content covers a diverse spectrum of topics, ranging from compute to cutting-edge generative AI solutions. A focal point of Stuart's professional interest lies in AWS security, identity, and compliance, wherein he delves into the intricacies of implementing and configuring AWS services to safeguard and monitor customer data within AWS.

Beyond his role at Cloud Academy, Stuart is a member of the AWS Community Builder program which provides technical resources, mentorship, and networking opportunities to AWS enthusiasts and emerging thought leaders who are passionate about sharing knowledge and connecting with the technical community. Furthermore, Stuart has contributed significantly to the AWS community by delivering talks at AWS community events hosted by AWS User Group Leaders and making appearances on the AWS Twitch channel to discuss cloud education.

About the Reviewer

Naman Jaswani is a seasoned Cyber Security Senior Consultant with over half a decade of experience. He specializes in AWS Security and boasts proficiency in Cloud Security, Application Security, and other Cyber Security domains. Outside of his consulting role, he dabbles in programming, and is particularly intrigued by Blockchain technology. Naman is not only passionate about his professional pursuits but also enjoys indulging in his hobbies of reading, traveling, and photography.

Table of Contents

3

Understanding Attacks on Cloud Environments   55

6

Event Management with Security Hub and GuardDuty   131

Section 3: Logging and Monitoring   159

7

Logs Generated by AWS Services   161

8

11

Securing EC2 Instances   297

12

13

18

Securely Connecting to Your AWS Environment   499

19

Using Certificates and Certificate Services in AWS   521

20

Managing Secrets Securely in AWS   541

21

Accessing the Online Practice Resources   569

Other Books You May Enjoy   576

Index   581

Preface

This book aims to provide you with a comprehensive understanding of the *AWS Certified Security Specialty* exam services. It includes sample architectures and case studies of those sample architectures so you can visualize how AWS services work. There are also plenty of hands-on exercises to try out in your own AWS account. You will find some very helpful use cases and anti-patterns presented for the different services in the book. It's important to be aware of anti-patterns when preparing for an exam; an exam question may present a service as a potential solution, but that service may actually be an anti-pattern and should not be used. Knowing where a service fits best and where it doesn't will help you choose the right answers in the exam.

Many certification books assume you will read them once, pass the test, and then place them on your bookshelf or pass them on to a colleague, and both their content and structure reflect this. In contrast, this book has been put together in such a way that you can hopefully use it as a reference guide in your duties as a security professional working in an AWS environment. You will find that extra information that may not necessarily appear in the exam has been added to the book. Once you pass the exam, you will be expected to be able to practically apply the topics you have learned about in the real world. The extra information in the book will help you tackle real-world, high-pressure security events, which can sometimes be harder than cracking the exam.

Who This Book Is For

This book is for anyone who wishes to achieve the *Certified Security Specialty* certification offered by **Amazon Web Services** (**AWS**). Apart from that, this book will also be useful for security professionals looking to gain a more comprehensive understanding of the security aspects of AWS, as well as for AWS users looking to enhance the security of their offerings. The most common roles looking to achieve this certification are as follows:

- Cloud security consultant
- Cloud security architect
- Cloud security engineer
- DevSecOps engineer
- Cloud security specialist

This exam assumes you have some basic knowledge of security principles and concepts of information technology or cloud security or a background in IT security and governance.

The AWS Certified Security Specialty certification recommends a minimum of two years of practical AWS production deployment experience for the test taker. This requirement reflects the depth and technical proficiency expected from the candidate.

What This Book Covers

Chapter 1, AWS Shared Responsibility Model, discusses the different shared responsibility models that define where your responsibilities as a customer implementing, controlling, and managing security in AWS start and those of AWS itself, which controls the security of the cloud, begin.

Chapter 2, Fundamental AWS Services, briefly covers the core AWS services that will be discussed throughout the book. This chapter aims to ensure that you have a robust understanding of the core services before diving deep into the domains of the Security Specialty certification material.

Chapter 3, Understanding Attacks on Cloud Environments, shows you how the skills acquired from this book can translate into protecting you and your customers' environments from bad actors seeking to take advantage of unprotected environments. It discusses some of the top cloud-native attacks on software and infrastructure, as well as different AWS services that can be used to combat those attacks, are discussed.

Chapter 4, Incident Response, explains how you can prepare for and react to incidents manually and automatically. You will learn the value of using a separate security forensic account for quarantine and containment. You will also review several AWS tools designed to help in various incident response situations.

Chapter 5, Managing Your Environment with AWS Config, takes a deep dive into the AWS Config service. It will show you how to use automation to maintain compliance in your AWS environment, as well as how AWS Config can be used across multiple regions and accounts. You will also learn how to use Lambda functions to automatically remediate items that violate your compliance policies using Config's remediation feature.

Chapter 6, Event Management with Security Hub and GuardDuty, discusses threat detection and security management across one or more accounts with native tooling available in AWS, AWS Security Hub, and AWS GuardDuty. You will learn what types of data sources are ingested to provide threat detection and how you can enable services and trigger alerts for you and your team.

Chapter 7, Logs generated by AWS Services, discusses the different sources in AWS from which you can acquire logging data, as well as how to collect and search through these logs centrally. The different log types explained include S3 Server Access logs, VPC Flow logs, Load Balancer Logs, and CloudTrail logs.

Chapter 8, CloudWatch and CloudWatch Metrics, deals with the different monitoring aspects of the CloudWatch service. You will learn how to use and search CloudWatch Logs, install the CloudWatch Logs agent on an EC2 instance, use the basic metrics provided by CloudWatch, and create custom metrics. You will also learn about Amazon EventBridge and EventBridge Rules.

Chapter 9, Parsing Logs and Events with AWS Native Tools, explains the different storage options and their costs. It also takes you through the managed OpenSearch and Kinesis services and how they facilitate log aggregation. Finally, it teaches you how to parse logs with Amazon Athena.

Chapter 10, Configuring Infrastructure Security, aims to help you fully understand the **Virtual Private Cloud** (**VPC**) security features AWS offers to effectively secure your VPC environments. By the end of the chapter, you will be able to confidently build a secure multi-subnet VPC using internet gateways, route tables, network access control lists, security groups, bastion hosts, NAT gateways, subnets, and virtual private gateways.

Chapter 11, Securing EC2 Instances, covers securing your instance infrastructure using a variety of techniques. These include performing vulnerability scans using Amazon Inspector, securing your EC2 key pairs, and using AWS Systems Manager to effectively administer your fleet of EC2 instances.

Chapter 12, Managing Key Infrastructure, talks about **Key Management Service** (**KMS**), which stores and manages the encryption keys for the different services. You will learn about the differences between Amazon-managed keys and customer-managed keys. You will also learn about the CloudHSM service for companies that need more control over their encryption keys.

Chapter 13, Access Management, focuses on the core concept of **Identity and Access Management** (**IAM**) and the IAM service. You will learn how to provision users, groups, and roles in a single account, secure access to those users using **Multi-Factor Authentication** (**MFA**), and also look into multi-account access with the IAM Identity Center.

Chapter 14, Working with Access Policies, examines several different policies used to grant access permissions to resources. You will learn how to read, edit, and create IAM and S3 policies. You will also see examples of **Service Control Policies** (**SCPs**), which are key tools in providing security and governance to AWS Organizations.

Chapter 15, Federated and Mobile Access, provides comprehensive information on what federated access is. This includes explaining social federation and enterprise federation to your AWS account. You will see how to enable Single Sign On to your AWS account using SAML. You will also learn about the Amazon Cognito service, which allows federation with **Identity Providers** (**IdPs**) to your applications.

Chapter 16, Using Active Directory Services to Manage Access, explains the different types of Active Directory offerings in AWS and how to allow federated access from your on-premises system to your AWS cloud environment. You will review the differences between each offering and and explore scenarios in which a one-way or two-way trust would be useful.

Chapter 17, Protecting Data in Flight and at Rest, delves into the topic of encryption and, more specifically, how AWS handles encryption with different services. You will learn about Elastic Block Store encryption, Elastic File Store encryption, and options for encrypting S3 buckets from a filesystem and blob perspective. This chapter also covers database encryption, showing you how to encrypt the RDS and DynamoDB services.

Chapter 18, Securely Connecting to Your AWS Environment, teaches you how to connect securely to your AWS environment using AWS **Virtual Private Network** (**VPN**), AWS Direct Connect, and AWS CloudHub. It also presents an overview of VPN technology and the types of VPNs and AWS, as well as the different IPsec.

Chapter 19, Using Certificates and Certificate Services in AWS, covers the different types of secure certificates used in AWS. It then discusses the AWS Certificate Manager service and explains how it can generate public certificates and act as a private certificate manager. Finally, it shows you how you can use the certificates you generated with ACM with elastic load balancers in your account.

Chapter 20, Managing Secrets Securely in AWS, explains why you should store your secrets securely in a public cloud environment such as AWS. You will review the different service offerings available to help you perform this task: Secrets Manager and System Manager Parameter Store. Finally, it shows you how to tell which users actually used any given secret.

Chapter 21, Accessing the Online Practice Resources, presents all the necessary information and guidance on how you can access the online practice resources that come free with your copy of this book. These resources are designed to enhance your exam preparedness.

AWS Certified Security Specialty Exam

The AWS Certified Security Specialty exam was updated on July 11, 2023 and expanded from five domains to six. A new domain of Management and Security Governance was added. In addition to the additional domain, Domain 1 now includes threat detection.

The following table shows you the difference between the latest version of the exam outline and the previous one:

SCS-C01 (Applicable up to July 11, 2023)	SCS-C02 (Applicable from July 11, 2023)
Domain 1: Incident Response – 12%	Domain 1: Threat Detection and Incident Response – 14%
Domain 2: Logging and Monitoring – 20%	Domain 2: Security Logging and Monitoring – 18 %
Domain 3: Infrastructure Security – 26%	Domain 3: Infrastructure Security – 20%
Domain 4: Identity and Access Management – 20 %	Domain 4: Identity and Access Management – 16 %
Domain 5: Data Protection – 22%	Domain 5: Data Protection – 18%
	Domain 6: Management and Security Governance – 14%

Table 0.1: Comparison between the previous and updated version of the exam

Online Practice Resources

With this book, you will unlock unlimited access to our online exam-prep platform (Figure 0.1). This is your place to practice everything you learn in the book.

How to access the resources

To learn how to access the online resources, refer to *Chapter 21, Accessing the Online Practice Resources* at the end of this book.

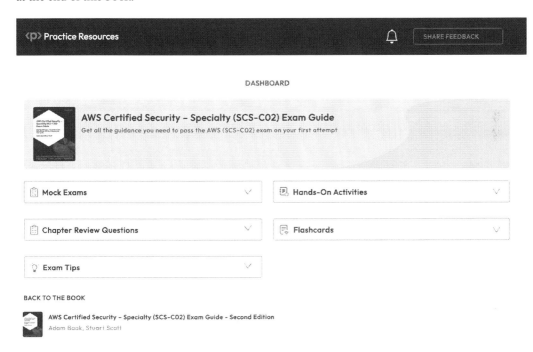

Figure 0.1 – Online exam-prep platform on a desktop device

Sharpen your knowledge of *AWS Certified Security Specialty (SCS-C02)* concepts with multiple sets of mock exams, interactive flashcards, and exam tips accessible from all modern web browsers.

Download the Color Images

We also provide a PDF file that has color images of the screenshots/diagrams used in this book.

You can download it here: `<https://packt.link/RzbVH>`

Conventions Used

There are a number of text conventions used throughout this book.

`Code in text`: Indicates code words in text, database table names, folder names, filenames, file extensions, pathnames, dummy URLs, user input, and Twitter handles. Here is an example: "You will use the `detect_labels` API from Amazon Recognition in the code."

A block of code is set as follows:

```
{
  "Effect": "Allow",
  "Principal": {
    "CanonicalUser": "b035577b325d98aa1e72ca0000EXAMPLE"
  },
  "Action": "s3:GetObject",
  "Resource": "arn:aws:s3:::abcuser-bucket/*"
}
```

Any command-line input or output is written as follows:

```
aws iam create-login-profile --user-name Packt --password Ch@ng3mE
--password-reset-required
```

Bold: Indicates a new term, an important word, or words that you see onscreen. For example, words in menus or dialog boxes appear in the text like this. Here is an example: "In **CloudWatch**, each **Lambda** function will have a **log group** and, inside that log group, many **log streams**."

> **Tips or important notes**
> Appear like this.

Get in Touch

Feedback from our readers is always welcome.

General feedback: If you have questions about any aspect of this book, mention the book title in the subject of your message and email us at customercare@packt.com.

Errata: Although we have taken every care to ensure the accuracy of our content, mistakes do happen. If you have found a mistake in this book, we would be grateful if you would report this to us. Please visit www.packtpub.com/support/errata, selecting your book, clicking on the Errata Submission Form link, and entering the details. We ensure that all valid errata are promptly updated in the GitHub repository, with the relevant information available in the Readme.md file. You can access the GitHub repository: <https://packt.link/L2aE6>.

Piracy: If you come across any illegal copies of our works in any form on the Internet, we would be grateful if you would provide us with the location address or website name. Please contact us at copyright@packt.com with a link to the material.

If you are interested in becoming an author: If there is a topic that you have expertise in and you are interested in either writing or contributing to a book, please visit authors.packtpub.com.

Share Your Thoughts

Once you've read *AWS Certified Security – Specialty (SCS-C02) Exam Guide, Second Edition*, we'd love to hear your thoughts! Scan the QR code below to go straight to the Amazon review page for this book and share your feedback.

https://packt.link/r/1837633983

Your review is important to us and the tech community and will help us make sure we're delivering excellent quality content.

Download a Free PDF Copy of This Book

Thanks for purchasing this book!

Do you like to read on the go but are unable to carry your print books everywhere?

Is your eBook purchase not compatible with the device of your choice?

Don't worry, now with every Packt book you get a DRM-free PDF version of that book at no cost.

Read anywhere, any place, on any device. Search, copy, and paste code from your favorite technical books directly into your application.

The perks don't stop there, you can get exclusive access to discounts, newsletters, and great free content in your inbox daily.

Follow these simple steps to get the benefits:

1. Scan the QR code or visit the link below:

https://packt.link/free-ebook/9781837633982

2. Submit your proof of purchase.
3. That's it! We'll send your free PDF and other benefits to your email directly.

Section 1:
AWS Security
Fundamentals

Before you start your journey into security with AWS, you first need to grasp a few fundamental concepts. This book begins with the AWS shared responsibility model, explaining the differences between security "in" the cloud and security "of" the cloud. The book also breaks down the responsibilities that you, the customer, hold regarding security compared with those AWS has as the cloud provider.

Next, the book dives into a quick review of AWS's essential services and discusses how they relate to security. The exam asks questions on many of these services. Having an understanding of the purpose and abilities of these is vital for your successful dissection of the question and the basis of its query.

This should be combined with a consideration of some of the pertinent reasons as to why security should be at the forefront when building your AWS environments. Finally, as we wrap up the section, we look at some of the top attacks our cloud environments can fall vulnerable to, and some ways to mitigate those risks.

This section comprises the following chapters:

- *Chapter 1, AWS Shared Responsibility Model*
- *Chapter 2, Fundamental AWS Services*
- *Chapter 3, Understanding Attacks on Cloud Environments*

1

AWS Shared Responsibility Model

Now that you are ready to begin your journey, the first step is to understand who is responsible for what when it comes to cloud computing. Security for both workloads and data stored in the cloud is separated into functions performed by both the customer and the cloud service provider (in this case, AWS). The shared responsibility model describes which duty belongs to whom.

From its very name, the **Shared Responsibility Model**, it is clear from the outset that more than one party is involved. This model defines where the customer's responsibility for implementing, controlling, and managing security within AWS starts and ends, compared to that of the cloud service provider – in this case, AWS.

The roles and responsibilities of managing security require a shared awareness between the two parties. The model itself is not a legal agreement in any way; it is simply down to you to be aware of the model and understand its importance so you can architect and protect your resources effectively.

AWS has three different shared responsibility models: infrastructure, container, and managed services. All these have varied levels of responsibility between the cloud customers and AWS. In this chapter, you will explore each model to help you understand their differences and how this affects security *in* and *of* the cloud.

The following main topics will be covered in this chapter:

- Understanding security in the AWS cloud
- The AWS shared responsibility model
- How different services require more or fewer security responsibilities from a customer standpoint

Making the Most Out of this Book – Your Certification and Beyond

This book and its accompanying online resources are designed to be a complete preparation tool for your *AWS Certified Security Specialty* exam.

The book is written in a way that you can apply everything you've learned here even after your certification. The online practice resources that come with this book (Figure 1.1) are designed to improve your test-taking skills. They are loaded with timed mock exams, interactive flashcards, and exam tips to help you work on your exam readiness from now till your test day.

> **Before You Proceed**
>
> To learn how to access these resources, head over to *Chapter 21, Accessing the Online Practice Resources*, at the end of the book.

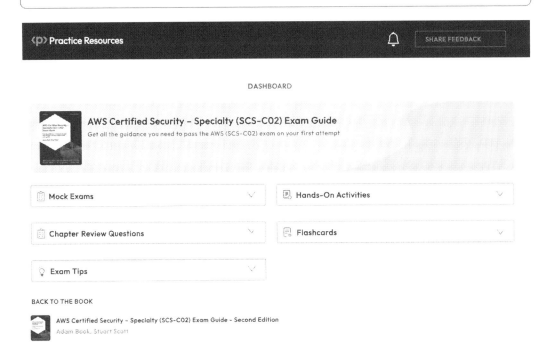

Figure 1.1: Dashboard interface of the online practice resources

Here are some tips on how to make the most out of this book so that you can clear your certification and retain your knowledge beyond your exam:

1. Read each section thoroughly.

2. **Make ample notes**: You can use your favorite online note-taking tool or use a physical notebook. The free online resources also give you access to an online version of this book. Click the BACK TO THE BOOK link from the Dashboard to access the book in Packt Reader. You can highlight specific sections of the book there.

3. **Chapter Review Questions**: At the end of this chapter, you'll find a link to review questions for this chapter. These are designed to test your knowledge of the chapter. Aim to score at least 75% before moving on to the next chapter. You'll find detailed instructions on how to make the most of these questions at the end of this chapter in the *Exam Readiness Drill – Chapter Review Questions* section. That way, you're improving your exam-taking skills after each chapter, rather than at the end.

4. **Flashcards**: After you've gone through the book and scored 75% or more in each of the chapter review questions, start reviewing the online flashcards. They will help you memorize key concepts.

5. **Mock Exams**: Solve the mock exams that come with the book till your exam day. If you get some answers wrong, go back to the book and revisit the concepts you're weak in.

6. **Exam Tips**: Review these from time to time to improve your exam readiness even further.

Technical Requirements

You need to have a basic understanding of AWS services and IaaS, PaaS, and SaaS cloud service models. Having a good understanding of **Infrastructure as a Service (IaaS)**, **Platform as a Service (PaaS)**, and **Software as a Service (SaaS)** will come into play as you learn about the nuances of the different models and how the responsibilities shift between the cloud provider (AWS in this case) and you, the customer.

You'll begin this chapter with a breakdown of which sections of security you, the customer, and AWS, the cloud provider, are individually responsible for, depending on the type of service you are using on the platform.

AWS Shared Responsibility Model

The more customizable your service or platform, the more responsibilities you hold as the customer. The AWS service that you choose to use dictates your responsibility based on the amount of configuration that needs to be performed in the service tier.

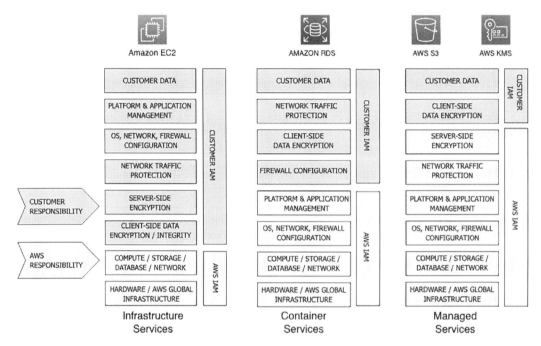

Figure 1.2: A comparison of shared responsibility models

Figure 1.1 shows that infrastructure services, which are presented as an IaaS platform, including services such as EC2, hold many more customer responsibilities regarding security. The trade-off you receive for this more significant burden of responsibility is the flexibility and customization you are allowed in the layer. You can see that each of the different models is labeled directly underneath, and each of the models will be discussed in detail in the following pages.

The basis for what AWS is responsible for remains the same—that is, the hardware, AWS global infrastructure, and the AWS foundational services. This security foundation is what AWS refers to as **Security in the Cloud** and is described in detail below:

- **AWS Global Infrastructure**: AWS provides security for the global infrastructure, including Regions, Availability Zones, Edge Locations, and Regional Edge Caches. This global infrastructure forms the physical data centers and point-of-presence locations that AWS uses globally to store your AWS resources physically. Customers do not have physical access to AWS data centers and are not allowed to turn up at the door of an AWS data center and ask to see their cloud resources. As a result, it is down to AWS to ensure that the physical security of their data centers meets stringent security controls and global security standards.

- **AWS Foundation Services**: AWS also provides foundation services, as defined in the model, covering compute, storage, database, and network components. This means it physically provides the hardware and underlying infrastructure to allow customers to create resources from the pooled hardware AWS provisions. Again, as a customer, you do not have access to these hosts, the physical infrastructure, or the underlying hypervisor software on each host. To ensure the separation of resources on a single host, all access is controlled and their security is managed by AWS.

The customer is responsible for the **Security of the Cloud**, which varies based on the service you are working with. As you will see in the following sections, the more control and customization you get with the AWS service, the more responsibility you have.

Shared Responsibility Model for Infrastructure Services

The shared model for infrastructure services is the most common model that AWS engineers and users are familiar with today. It is represented in *Figure 1.2* and covers IaaS services such as Amazon **Elastic Compute Cloud (EC2)**:

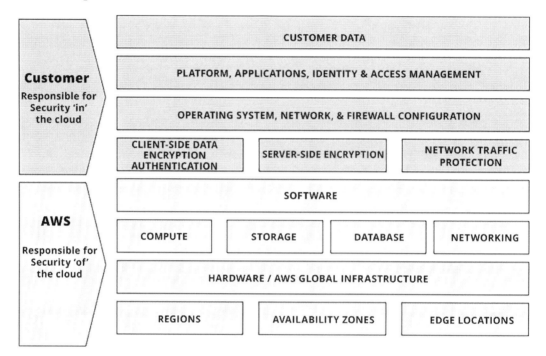

Figure 1.3: Shared responsibility model for infrastructure services

So, within this infrastructure, AWS provides global reach via various data centers and provides the underlying hardware and infrastructure required to allow its customers to create cloud resources from the AWS-provisioned and pooled hardware resources. These two components effectively make up the AWS cloud.

Essentially, customers have the ultimate security responsibility for anything they provision using AWS foundation services across the global infrastructure.

Using the EC2 service as an example, look at each point relating to the customer's responsibilities from the preceding diagram:

- **Customer data**: The customer has to maintain the security of the data they import into or create within their AWS environment—for example, any data stored on EC2 volumes, ephemeral or persistent.

- **Platform, application, and Identity and Access Management (IAM)**: Any platform or application installed on top of your EC2 instance must be secured and protected by controls configured and implemented by you, the customer. In addition to this, you are solely responsible for maintaining any access control to your EC2 instance and applications. AWS provides the IAM service to implement these controls, but it is down to you to implement adequate security measures using the features offered by IAM.

- **Operating system and network and firewall configuration**: As you saw in *Figure 1.2*, the responsibility of AWS ends at the hypervisor level. EC2 instances fall within the infrastructure model, so maintaining the operating system's security is the customer's responsibility. As a result, the customer must sustain and implement patching for the relevant operating system. EC2 instances are deployed within a **Virtual Private Cloud (VPC)**. Therefore, network configuration, including firewall restrictions such as security groups (effectively, virtual firewalls operating at the instance level) must be configured and associated appropriately to protect your EC2 fleet.

- **Client-side data encryption and data integrity authentication**: This relates to the protection of data generated by or stored on your EC2 instances via an encryption mechanism. If you plan to encrypt your data as a customer, you are responsible for doing so.

- **Server-side encryption (filesystem and/or data)**: Again, if you plan to use any form of encryption to protect your data using server-side mechanisms, (perhaps through the use of the **Key Management Service (KMS)**, which will be discussed in depth in a later chapter), it is down to you to use the service effectively for data protection.

- **Network traffic protection (encryption/identity/integrity)**: When network traffic is being sent to and from your EC2 instance, you can configure to encrypt the communication with a protocol such as SSL or HTTPS, where applicable. Using AWS Certificate Manager, which will be discussed in depth in *Chapter 19, Using Certificates and Certificate Services in AWS*, helps simplify the management and provisioning of secure certificates with AWS services.

Shared Responsibility Model Example for Infrastructure Services

When you spin up an EC2 instance in your AWS account, you are able to choose a region from all the available geographic regions AWS offers to have your instance come up in. There is no need to order a server or rack, stack it, secure it in the cage at the data center, and so on. Once that server spins up, it will have a base operating system and network connectivity based on the VPC settings that you have chosen or configured.

Once your instance is up and running, whether for minutes, hours, months, or even years, it is your responsibility as the customer to update (or remove) any packages that do not meet your security baseline. Suppose you add additional users; this falls under the Identity and Access Management category. In that case, it is up to you to ensure that these users conform to your organization's password or secure key policy. Similarly, if you decide to install any additional applications, keeping them up to date when security patches become available (either through the vendor or from the developers) is again your responsibility.

As you connect to this EC2 instance, creating a secure connection via SSL or TLS is up to you. Securing the data in transit to and from the instance falls under the customer responsibilities of the shared model for infrastructure security.

In summary, when working with services that fall within the infrastructure shared responsibility model, AWS is responsible for the security of the cloud, which includes everything in the hypervisor stack and levels below it. The customer is then responsible for security in the cloud, which starts from the operating system stack and levels above it.

Having an understanding of each of these models will help you define a more robust security strategy and strengthen your security posture across your AWS account. Fully understanding what you are responsible for and what AWS is responsible for will help ensure that you are not left open to any unexpected vulnerabilities.

Although infrastructure services constitute a large part of cloud computing (especially when it comes to AWS), the way the security responsibilities are handled for the customer and the cloud provider is not the same as that of packaged services. In the next section, you will learn about some of those differences of the shared responsibility model for container services.

Share Responsibility Model for Container Services

The second model this chapter will cover is the container model. The word container is frequently used to describe software packages containing code and all associated dependencies that can be run across various compute environments. Examples of standard container technologies are **Docker**, **Podman**, and **Kubernetes**. However, the word container refers to a slightly different concept when used in this context.

The container model focuses on services that reside on top of infrastructure services. This implies that the customer does not have access to some of the infrastructure-level components, such as the operating system. The following are some examples of services in the container model:

- AWS **Elastic MapReduce (EMR)**
- AWS **Relational Database Service (RDS)**
- AWS **Elastic Beanstalk**

Figure 1.4 shows the responsibility model for container services:

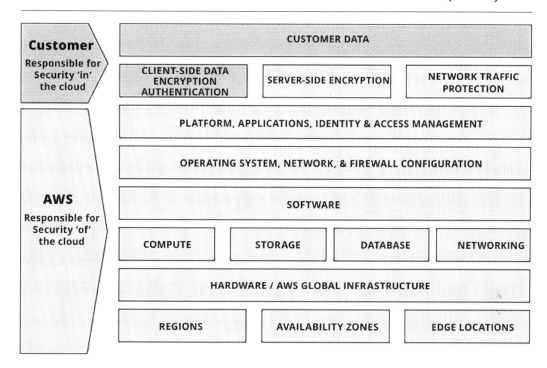

Figure 1.4: Shared responsibility model for container services

As is evident from the preceding figure, AWS still maintains the same level of security responsibility as it is retained from the infrastructure model, along with additional responsibilities. Platform, application management, operating system, and network configuration are now the responsibility of AWS in this model.

Shared Responsibility Model Example for Container Services

Consider the example of RDS. In this case, customers do not have access to the underlying operating system that the RDS databases are running on. As such, customers cannot patch the operating system. This security task has been shifted from the customer to AWS. In addition, platform and application management have also been passed to AWS. This is because RDS is a managed service, and as a result, all the application maintenance is undertaken by AWS. This takes a huge administrative burden off the customer but also simultaneously introduces a level of restriction, as they are only presented with the platform and everything above the stack.

Shared Responsibility Model for Abstract Services

The final model you will examine is the abstract shared responsibility model shown in *Figure 1.5*:

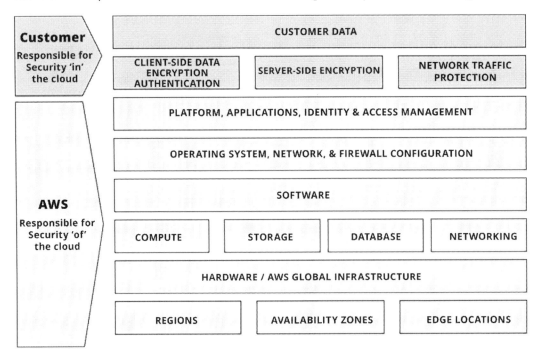

Figure 1.5: Shared responsibility model for abstract services

Right away, from a visual perspective, it is apparent that the shift in responsibility leans even more heavily toward AWS.

This model retains the level of security AWS must manage from the previous two models (infrastructure and container) and adds server-side encryption and network traffic protection. The following are some examples of services in the abstract model:

- Amazon **Simple Queue Service (SQS)**
- Amazon **DynamoDB**
- Amazon **Simple Storage Service (S3)**

These are defined as abstract services as almost all the control and management of the service is abstracted away from the end customer; you access these services through endpoints. Customers do not have access to the underlying operating system (infrastructure) or the actual platform running these services (container). Instead, the customer is presented with the service frontend or endpoint configured as required.

As a result, the customer is totally abstracted away from maintaining security updates for the operating system or any platform patches and security management. This also means that with services that fall in this model, AWS is responsible for implementing and controlling any server-side encryption algorithms, such as Amazon S3 **Server-Side Encryption** (SSE-S3). Therefore, the customer has no control over the access keys used for this encryption method—it is all managed by AWS.

Further, AWS will manage the secure transfer of data between the service components, for example, when S3 automatically copies customer data to multiple endpoints across different availability zones. As a customer, you have no control over this data transfer, so AWS must secure the traffic.

Shared Responsibility Model Example for Abstract Services

You have decided to store some static documents and data in multiple S3 buckets since S3 is both optimal for blob storage and cost-effective. AWS already manages the S3 platform and keeps the application and operating system patches up to date.

Once you decide to place one of the documents into a particular bucket, you need to refer to your organizational policies to see if encryption at rest is required. Your first decision is whether you will do client- or server-side encryption. If you decide to use client-side encryption, you will need to generate a pair of keys (if a pair is not already available), encrypt the document, and then upload the encrypted payload to the S3 bucket.

Suppose you decide to go with server-side encryption. In that case, you must either provide your own **Customer Managed Key** (CMS) using **Key Management Service** (KMS) or use the Amazon-managed key to encrypt the data once it is placed into the bucket.

Now that the data has been added to the bucket, you, as the bucket administrator, need to decide who will gain access to this bucket and how you will control this access. You can create an IAM policy if access is limited to internal users. If users from another organization need to access the data and documents, you will craft a bucket policy with the correct permissions.

To summarize this example, in the abstract services shared responsibility model, the customer manages their data, who has access to it, and the encryption settings.

With an understanding of the shared responsibility model for abstract services, you can now delve into how using and understanding these models can help you when dealing with audits or auditors.

Auditors and the Shared Responsibility Model

Many industries require you to show compliance in your cloud environment as it relates to industrial controls.

Using and understanding the shared security model will help you and your auditors understand which controls you, as the customer, are responsible for and which ones are the responsibility of AWS, the cloud provider.

Suppose your auditor is requesting information or evidence for something that AWS manages. In that case, you can refer the auditor to the specific shared responsibility model for the service to show how the cloud service provider maintains control of that particular standard.

Summary

This chapter discussed the three shared security models used for AWS services: infrastructure, container, and abstract services. You learned that, from a security perspective and depending on the service you are using, your responsibility as a customer and that of AWS as the cloud provider can change.

Understanding these models and being able to differentiate between them will be beneficial when you implement your security strategies across your solutions as it means you will clearly understand where your responsibility ends and AWS's responsibility begins. This will help ensure that you do not leave any vulnerabilities across your AWS infrastructure within your accounts.

You also examined how the shared security model can help you by clarifying which items you and your organization are responsible for when it comes to compliance and audits for your business.

Chapter 2, Fundamental AWS Services, will provide a brief overview of many of the services used in the AWS ecosystem that are not particularly focused on security. Even the services that do not have a specific security focus often play a significant role in the solutions we build for our systems and customers. The AWS Security Competency exam expects you to have a base knowledge of the services offered and how you can fortify them as a security engineer or professional.

Further Reading

For additional information on the AWS shared responsibility model and the underlying foundation of AWS security, please refer to the following resources:

- Introduction to AWS Security: `https://packt.link/yoltd`
- The shared responsibility model: `https://packt.link/JjZ65`

Exam Readiness Drill – Chapter Review Questions

Apart from a solid understanding of key concepts, being able to think quickly under time pressure is a skill that will help you ace your certification exam. That is why working on these skills early on in your learning journey is key.

Chapter review questions are designed to improve your test-taking skills progressively with each chapter you learn and review your understanding of key concepts in the chapter at the same time. You'll find these at the end of each chapter.

> **How To Access These Resources**
>
> To learn how to access these resources, head over to the chapter titled *Chapter 21, Accessing the Online Practice Resources*.

To open the Chapter Review Questions for this chapter, perform the following steps:

1. Click the link – `https://packt.link/SCSC02E2_CH01`.

    Alternatively, you can scan the following QR code (*Figure 1.6*):

Figure 1.6: QR code that opens Chapter Review Questions for logged-in users

2. Once you log in, you'll see a page similar to the one shown in *Figure 1.7*:

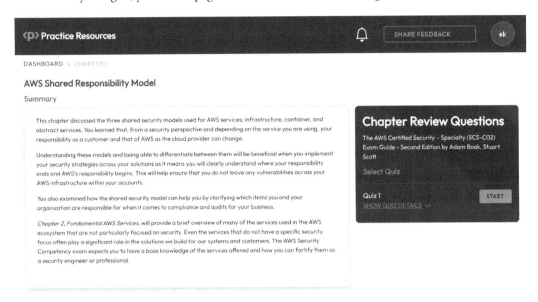

Figure 1.7: Chapter Review Questions for Chapter 1

3. Once ready, start the following practice drills, re-attempting the quiz multiple times.

Exam Readiness Drill

For the first three attempts, don't worry about the time limit.

ATTEMPT 1

The first time, aim for at least **40%**. Look at the answers you got wrong and read the relevant sections in the chapter again to fix your learning gaps.

ATTEMPT 2

The second time, aim for at least **60%**. Look at the answers you got wrong and read the relevant sections in the chapter again to fix any remaining learning gaps.

ATTEMPT 3

The third time, aim for at least **75%**. Once you score **75%** or more, you start working on your timing.

> **Tip**
>
> You may take more than three attempts to reach 75%. That's okay. Just review the relevant sections in the chapter till you get there.

Working On Timing

Target: Your aim is to keep the score the same while trying to answer these questions as quickly as possible. Here's an example of how your next attempts should look like:

Attempt	Score	Time Taken
Attempt 5	77%	21 mins 30 seconds
Attempt 6	78%	18 mins 34 seconds
Attempt 7	76%	14 mins 44 seconds

Table 1.1: Sample timing practice drills on the online platform

> **Note**
>
> The time limits shown in the above table are just examples. Set your own time limits with each attempt based on the time limit of the quiz on the website.

With each new attempt, your score should stay above 75% while your time taken to complete should **decrease**. Repeat as many attempts as you want till you feel confident dealing with the time pressure.

2

Fundamental AWS Services

Now that you understand the shared responsibility model, it's time to look at some essential services that are used throughout the environments and accounts in which you will be working. These essential services are compute services such as **Elastic Cloud Compute (EC2)**, the global **Domain Name System (DNS)** service of Route 53, database services such as RDS and Aurora, account management services such as Control Tower and AWS Organizations, and the advisory service of Trusted Advisor. This may seem like a review of services you already know if you have taken the Cloud Practitioner, Solution Architect (Associate or Professional), or other AWS certification. Although there is no need to take or pass any other AWS certification exams before attempting the Security Specialty certification by AWS, it's not a bad idea to get familiar with some essential services.

After reading this chapter, you should have a basic understanding of the AWS services that the exam covers. These services are also many of the core services that you use on a daily basis. There are plenty of opportunities to dig deeper into the topics presented using the links at the end of this chapter.

The following main topics will be covered in this chapter:

- Virtual private networking/Route 53 networking
- Compute services on AWS
- Cloud databases
- Message and queueing systems
- Trusted Advisor

Technical Requirements

You will need an AWS account to access the Management Console, and you need to have already set up the CLI.

> **Important Note**
>
> This book will not be going over AWS's geography, regions, Availability Zones, or edge locations. However, these are fundamental concepts you should fully grasp before you sit the Security Specialty certification exam. If you need a refresher on these topics, then please visit the following URL: `https://packt.link/7wY4v`.

Account Management in AWS

Whether you wish to set up a new environment or are on the path to growing an existing set of accounts, the Account Management tools can help you perform these tasks in an automated and systematic manner.

Control Tower

When you are looking for one of the easiest ways to secure and govern multiple accounts in AWS, AWS Control Tower is the best choice. With AWS Control Tower, you can implement best practices when creating new accounts using Account Factory. Guardrails can be put in place, offering governance and security across the entire organization. Control Tower also allows the use of blueprints that make it easy to set up a landing zone.

Control Tower is made up of four key components:

- **Landing Zone** – A landing zone is a standardized framework for managing an AWS environment and ensuring compliance with AWS best practices. Using AWS Control Tower to set up your AWS environment creates a well-architected, multi-account environment with, at a minimum, a master account, a security account (named audit by default), and a log archive account.

- **Controls** – These controls, also known as guardrails, define high-level rules that can provide governance and security for your accounts and AWS environment.

- **Account Factory** – This helps you provision new AWS accounts in your organization quickly and easily. Using Account Factory ensures the accounts are connected to the master billing account. The master billing account in a Control Tower or organization's structure is the account that receives the invoices for all subsequent child accounts. Each new account must have a unique email associated with the root account.

- **Dashboard** – A dashboard is a centralized user interface that lets your team of cloud administrators enable (or disable) policy enforcement, manage the organizational units for AWS Organizations, and even see non-compliant resources from a central location.

After you have completed the initial setup of your accounts using the Control Tower setup, then you will be shown a screen similar to the one in *Figure 2.1*.

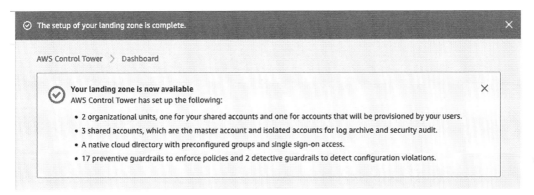

Figure 2.1: Control Tower dashboard after setup is complete

The following subsections dive deeper into the two **categories of controls**.

Categories of Behavior

The controls provided by AWS Control Tower are broken down into three distinct categories: preventative, detective, and proactive. These are called categories of behavior:

- Preventative controls disallow actions in your account that could cause it to be non-compliant and are implemented using **Service Control Policies** (**SCPs**).
- Detective controls look for and find compliance violations within your resources and are implemented using **AWS Config Rules**.
- Proactive controls scan your resources before they are provisioned and implemented using **CloudFormation** hooks.

Categories of Guidance

There are also three different levels of controls: mandatory, strongly recommended, and elective controls. These are called categories of guidance:

- Mandatory controls are always enforced throughout your accounts and cannot be turned off.
- Strongly recommended controls have been patterned after the AWS Well-Architected Framework best practices, especially in the case of multi-account environments, and should be kept in place.

- Elective controls are items modeled after rules commonly found in enterprise environments that allow you to lock down or track actions in your AWS accounts.

Security Considerations for Control Tower

Now that you know some of the basic elements of AWS Control Tower, you can consider some of the security responsibilities for which you, as an account holder, are responsible. Since this is regarding account-wide settings with Control Tower, the security is broken down into multiple sections as shown in the points below.

Data Protection

- Each account should have **multi-factor authentication** (**MFA**) enabled.

- Set up and enable AWS CloudTrail API for both user and system activity.

- When you communicate with AWS resources, do so via SSL/TLS.

Identity and Access Management (IAM)

- Once you create your root user, add MFA to the account and only lock it away for account management and service tasks.

- Use IAM roles to delegate access to services rather than provisioning long-term credentials from accounts, such as access and secret access keys.

- Use `aws:SourceArn` if you want only one resource associated with cross-service access.

- Use `aws:SourceAccount` if you want to allow any resource in the account to be associated with cross-service use.

Now that you are familiar with the Control Tower service, take a look at the AWS service that compliments Control Tower—AWS Organizations.

AWS Organizations

At its core, AWS Organizations provides you with a hierarchical way of organizing accounts in groups called **organizational units** (**OU**). These OUs can then be managed with specific controls from both the overall accounting structure level and the individual OU level.

Figure 2.2 shows an example of an organization with six accounts and four OUs. Two OUs, `Infrastructure` and `Security`, are nested under the parent OU, `Corporate`. This type of hierarchy allows cascading security policies and cost reporting for the child accounts. You can see this type of policy inheritance shown in *Figure 2.2*, where policies created are applied to specific OUs and cascade down. Separate policies have been applied to both the `North America` Ous, affecting the `Development` and `Marketing` accounts, and the Infrastructure OU is affecting the `Network` account.

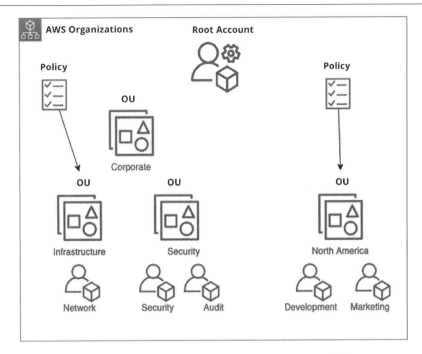

Figure 2.2: AWS Organizations structure with OUs and SCPs

Policy inheritance in AWS Organizations allows you to define policies at the root level of your organization, and those policies are automatically inherited by all member accounts in the organization. This means that you can create a policy once and have it apply to all accounts in your organization rather than having to manually apply the policy to each individual account. Overall, policy inheritance in AWS Organizations provides a way to centrally manage policies across numerous accounts, creating a continuous set of policies and governance standards across your organization.

There are some critical rules to understand when it comes to policy inheritance, which come down to the following three key concepts:

- Any policies attached at the root of the organization affect every account and OU in the organization, and this is the total cascading effect of the policies.

- If you attach a policy to a specific OU, then that OU, any accounts attached to the OU, and any child OUs and their subsequent accounts are affected by that policy. This also applies to future OUs and accounts added to this original OU that have this policy.

- A policy attached to a specific account only affects that account.

Next, take a look at one of the most powerful features of AWS Organizations, service control policies.

Service Control Policies

AWS gives you a tool in the IAM space to manage the permissions of that organization along with any child OUs when grouping your accounts into organizations and OUs. That tool is **Service Control Policies** or **SCPs**. SCPs allow you to provide a baseline of governance across the accounts they are applied to so that the rules are enforced at the organizational level regardless of the permissions set at the account, individual group, or role level.

The following are some points to note about SCPs:

- Once attached, SCPs are invisible to all roles in a child account. This includes the root account for that child account.

- The policies in the SCP are applied to all child account users, including the root account for that child account.

- The policies in the SCP are applied to all roles of the child account.

Using SCPs alone is insufficient to grant permissions to the accounts in your organization. Combining an organization's SCPs, the permissions boundaries are set, and the identity-based policy provides effective user, group, or role permissions.

> **Note**
>
> This book will go into much further detail about the verbiage of SCPs in *Chapter 14, Working with Access Policies*.

Security Considerations for AWS Organizations

The following list describes some of the specific security considerations and best practices when using AWS Organizations:

- Suppose you want to implement an SCP at the root level account/master billing account or any high-level OU. In that case, it is recommended that you test the effects of the SCP before implementing it so that your users and service roles don't run into unforeseen circumstances.

- SCPs are optimal for preventing users and roles from disabling security tools such as AWS CloudTrail, AWS Config, and Amazon GuardDuty.

SCPs can be used to prevent privilege escalation. To do this, you would deny any IAM administrative action and add a condition where the role was not like your account manager role name using the `ArnNotLike` key.

Now that you have a grasp of account management using tools like AWS Organizations and SCPs, you can move on to compute services in AWS.

Cloud Compute in AWS

Compute in AWS refers to many services, such as Amazon EC2, **Elastic Load Balancing** (**ELB**), AWS Lambda, AWS Batch, **Elastic Container Service** (**ECS**), and **Elastic Kubernetes Service** (**EKS**), along with AWS Fargate. The Fargate managed service allows you to run your containers with minimal overhead. AWS Compute even includes Lightsail, one of the quickest ways for customers to get their cloud up and running without needing to configure software or networking.

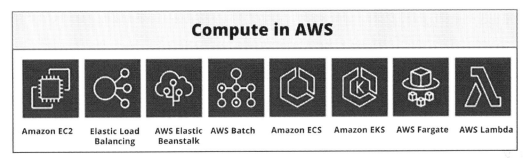

Figure 2.3: Compute services in AWS

You can see, as is shown in *Figure 2.3*, the myriad of services that fall under the classification of compute services in Amazon Web Services. These include not only the virtual instances of the **Elastic Compute Cloud** (**EC2**) service but also Lambda, which is a function-as-a-service offering, and even Elastic Load Balancing, the service that helps spread requests to multiple instances.

Although there are quite a few services that fall under the compute umbrella in AWS, the most foundational service is EC2. This is your virtualized instance in the Amazon cloud. While other services, such as Elastic Container Service, Elastic Kubernetes Service, and even Elastic Beanstalk can allow you to run containers in AWS, they run on EC2 instances at their core. Therefore, knowing the foundational elements of the EC2 service, such as how to select the correct instance type, how to use the optimal load balancer, and how to add volumes to an instance, is crucial both for processing questions for the Security Specialty exam and in your day-to-day duties as a professional.

Amazon Elastic Compute Cloud (EC2)

Amazon's EC2 allows you to create a virtual server to perform any number of tasks in the cloud, and EC2 allows a whole array of customization options. You can use many operating systems to meet your application needs, including both varieties of the Microsoft Windows operating system and multiple versions of the Linux operating system. Appropriating the correct amount of memory and processing power simply entails choosing the right instance type based on your workload's needs.

EC2 also has three distinct pricing models: On-Demand Instances, Reserved Instances, and Spot Instances. These different models provide flexibility, stability, or discounting to meet the needs of your workload or organization.

With a basic understanding of the EC2 service, you will next see how images of these virtual machines can be used via Amazon Machine Images.

Understanding an Amazon Machine Image (AMI)

Any time you launch an EC2 instance, it must start from an **Amazon Machine Image** (**AMI**) to contain the required information to launch. These images can be the base operating systems with clean slates, or they can be AMIs that you or some other entity has created as a valid checkpoint for a working system or systems running on a single instance.

These machine images can be provided by AWS itself, which is the default way to request an image for launching a new EC2 instance. If you create an AMI, then your account controls the image from which to launch more EC2 instances, or you could share that AMI with other accounts privately by designating the accounts that have access to the image. There are even AMI images that are available from the AWS community, and those that come with specialty software and a per-hour cost on AWS Marketplace.

Use Cases for AMIs

You can create your own AMIs to use in an Autoscaling group, a grouping of EC2 instances that scale up or down based on load, or to speed up the launch of complex instances that require multiple steps to download, install, and configure software on the instance.

In more of a security context, AMIs can be an excellent tool for creating a **golden image**, a preconfigured base image to be used as a template for creating new instances for your development teams and for members of your organization to use. This allows you to pre-install any software updates, patches, and security/monitoring software your organization deems necessary as part of its security posture before allowing another team member to use that instance. Using one or a set of golden images can help your technical support team by reducing the time needed to configure the software and services that need to be deployed into an environment.

Another use of AMIs in a security context is backing up applications, configuration settings, and user data to restore an outage quickly, either in the current region or by sharing the AMI image with another region or another account.

To give you some hands-on experience, the next section will guide you through the process of spinning up an instance and creating an AMI to be spun up at a moment's notice.

Backing Up Amazon EC2 Instances

If you want to back up your instance for either point-in-time recovery purposes or to use in a launch configuration with autoscaling, you need to create an AMI. Follow these steps to create an AMI:

1. Launch an EC2 instance. To do this, you must first ensure you have an instance to back up and create the AMI. You will need to find a public image from AWS to use as the base. An example AMI ID has been provided in the following example:

    ```
    $ aws ec2 run-instances \
    --image-id ami-0f3c9c466bb525749 \
    --instance-type t3.micro \
    --region us-east-2
    ```

> **Note**
>
> `image-id`, which is an AMI of Amazon Linux 2, is based out of the us-east-2 (Ohio) region.

Once it launches, it should return a JSON statement with the instance ID. You will need the instance ID for your next step to create the AMI. In this case, the instance ID that was returned was `i-0563e7e31aca9c89a`.

2. Create the AMI as the backup:

    ```
    $aws ec2 create-image \
    --instance-id i-0563e7e31aca9c89a \
    --name backup_ami \
    --no-reboot
    ```

    If the image is created successfully, then you should get a JSON return with the `ImageId` value:

    ```
    {
                "ImageId": "ami-046698ac2e320e8c6"
    }
    ```

3. Verify the image:

    ```
    $aws ec2 describe-images \
    --region us-east-2 \
    --image-ids ami-046698ac2e320e8c6
    ```

4. This should return a block of JSON with multiple values. However, the main value you are looking for is the line that says `State`. If the value says `available`, you have successfully backed up your EC2 instance and are ready to test your backup.

Here, you are going back to the command you initially executed in **step 1**; however, now you have your custom `ImageId` that you can substitute. Also, you will add the flag for an SSH key so that you can go in to verify any setting for the instance:

```
$aws ec2 run-instances \
--image-id ami-046698ac2e320e8c6 \
--instance-type t3.micro \
--key-name my-ssh-key \
--region us-east-2
```

You can see that with just a few simple commands, you have taken your running EC2 instance and not only backed it up but also created a launchable AMI. You could take this backup a step further and copy the AMI to another region, ensuring you remove any hardcoded region-specific values or settings from the image. If you do this, it should launch and run without issues.

Steps to Use AMIs in a Secure Manner

If you look in AWS Marketplace or even search from the EC2 Launch page, you will see that there are lots of AMIs to choose from. Many of these AMIs are provided by community members or third-party providers. How are you to know that the AMI that you are about to launch in your environment doesn't have a back door embedded inside of it for the creator to gain access to your network? The following are some steps you can take to use these types of AMIs in a more secure manner:

1. The first step, especially if you are working in a corporate or enterprise environment, is to test the AMI in a sandbox environment so that you, as a security engineer, can examine the AMI and run any necessary scans for malware or crypto miners on it before launching it in your primary working environments.

2. Next, you want to see if there are any previously stored public SSH keys on the image. If there are, you can disable or delete them. Not all keys will be stored in the `/root/.ssh/authorized_keys` file. Instead, use the following command to find any keys located on the image (run this command as the root user: `sudo su`):

```
find / -name "authorized_keys" -print -exec cat {} \;
```

This command should locate and print to screen any found on the image. If any appear that you don't recognize, you can remove them and create a new AMI image.

As an extra precaution with an image you have obtained from public sources, don't allow SSH access (port 22) from any IP address (0.0.0.0/0) in your security groups. Have a tightened list of IP ranges that are allowed access to prevent outside access.

3. The next thing to look for when using a public or community AMI is stored usernames and passwords. This is another way that someone could gain access to the instance and your network. Use the following command to help you find usernames and passwords that are stored on the AMI:

```
cat /etc/passwd /etc/shadow | grep -E '^[^:]*:[^:]{3.}' | cut
-d: -f1
```

If there is any output from the script, such as usernames you don't recognize, you can use the `password` command (still as the root user) to change the password or use the `userdel` command to delete the user.

> **Note**
>
> The scripts and steps presented here are for your information as you work as a security professional. Knowing the exact steps to sweep an AMI for planted keys is not a skill that's tested in the AWS Certified Security Specialty certification exam.

The next section will talk about how to configure EC2 instances automatically with the use of user data scripts.

Using User Data Scripts to Configure EC2 Instances at Launch

Although you can launch EC2 instances and then go and configure the software packages that you need on them manually, there are more efficient approaches. Following manual steps can lead to human mistakes and is a much more time-consuming process that can otherwise easily be automated.

User data scripts can also help you install and configure security patches and tools in an automated fashion as your EC2 instance is launching without the need to create an AMI, as discussed previously, in the *Backing Up Amazon EC2 Instances* section.

Example User Data Script

The following is an example of a user data script that can configure and set up an EC2 instance without user interaction. It can do so by adding items to the script that will perform tasks such as creating files from scratch, updating previously installed packages and software repositories, and even running commands:

```
#cloud-config
package_upgrade: true
repo_update: true
repo_upgrade: all
packages:
   - boto3
   - aws-cfn-bootstrap
write_files:
   - path: /test.txt
     context: |
            This is my file.
             There are many like it but this one is mine.
runcmd:
   - [ sed, -i, -e, 's/is/was/g', /test.txt
   - echo "modified my file"
   - [ cat, /test.txt ]
```

This example demonstrated how to implement a user data script to configure an EC2 instance at launch to create and manipulate files and update repositories. Next, you will look at networking interfaces on EC2 instances.

Elastic Networking Interfaces

Elastic Networking Interfaces (**ENIs**) work like virtual networking cards and can be associated with an EC2 instance or a load balancer to have a public IP address associated with that specific ENI. The main functionality of the Elastic IP is to provide a persistent public IP address that can be easily associated with and disassociated from resources. This is especially useful in cases where other systems are using that IP address or you need the instance to work on multiple security groups.

Since security groups are attached at the network interface level and not at the instance level, adding additional ENIs to your instances can allow you to join more than one security group for specialized purposes. If you have a web server that needs to access the public internet, you can attach an interface to the security group that serves this purpose. In the same instance, you may also need to SSH into the machine so that a team member can check logs or processes running on the server as shown in *Figure 2.4*. The security group attached to a particular ENI that allows access to the SSH port (port 22) can be locked in this manner.

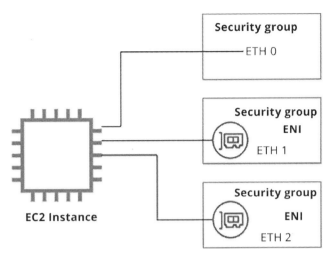

Figure 2.4: ENIs in separate security groups

Security Considerations for EC2

Now that you have gone through the EC2 service, you can examine the security best practices for Elastic Compute Cloud:

- Use the technique of least permissions when constructing the security group's ingress policy.
- For longer-running instances, have a plan to apply security patches and updates to the instance. Take advantage of System Manager's Patch Manager and Run Command for this purpose.
- Encrypt any EBS volumes that are attached to the instance.
- Always use a service role rather than adding an access key and a secret access key to the instance to access other AWS services.
- Use System Manager Session Manager to allow users to log in rather than having to manage SSH login credentials.

Elastic Block Store (EBS)

Although EBS and EC2 are closely tied together, it is important to remember that they are both separate services. EBS is a storage service that provides network-based storage allocated in the same Availability Zone as the instance and is then mounted for usage. The amount of instance storage allocated to an instance varies by instance type, and not all types of EC2 instances contain an instance store volume.

EBS is different from an instance store in some key ways. The instance store volume is the storage that is physically attached to the EC2 instance. It is best used for temporary storage since the instance store does not persist through instance stops or instance failures. In contrast, data stored on an EBS volume will persist.

EBS volumes can be allocated at the time of instance creation or created after the instance has been placed into services' additional storage. A key feature to remember about EBS volumes when allocating and restoring EBS volumes is that a volume must stay in the same Availability Zone as where it was created.

Types of EBS Volumes

The following are three main types of EBS volumes, all of which differ in performance, optimal use cases, and cost:

- **Solid State Drives (SSDs):** This type of drive is optimized for heavy read and write operations and where a higher number of IOPS is needed. There are two types of SSD EBS volumes that you can choose to provision for your EC2 instances, defined in the next section.

- **General-purpose SSDs:** These drives give you a balance of cost and performance and are best used in development and test environments.

- **Provisioned IOPS SSDs:** These are the drives you want to use for mission-critical workloads when performance is critical, especially in the case of databases.

Security Considerations for EBS

Now that you have a grasp of the EBS service, consider some of the security considerations to be kept in mind when using the service:

- When encrypting EBS volumes and snapshots, use KMS **Customer Managed Keys** instead of Amazon Managed Keys to retain control of the encryption and decryption of data.

- Enable encryption by default on EBS volumes. Use the AWS Config service to check that this policy is being adhered to across your organization.

- Make sure that all EBS snapshots that you create are encrypted.

Now that you have gone over the EBS service, the next thing to learn about is one of the most popular services—AWS Lambda.

AWS Lambda

AWS Lambda is a serverless compute service that allows you to run your code as a function without needing to set up or provision any servers or orchestrate any containers. Rather than being classified as the usual IaaS or PaaS, it falls under the category of **Function as a Service** (**FaaS**). It automatically scales up and down based on the number of requests it receives. Customers are charged based on the number of invocations and the amount of compute and memory they have allocated for their functions.

Any function being written and run on the AWS Lambda platform must be able to conform to the following parameters of the AWS Lambda service:

- 75 GB storage for `.zip` files

- 10 GB function size as a Docker image

- 250 ENIs per VPC

- Memory limitations of 128 MB to 10.240 GB

- Code must run and complete within 15 minutes

- Six vCPU cores

- 1,000 concurrent invocations

One of the primary reasons that Lambda has become so popular is that customers are only charged for the number of invocations performed per month rather than for the time the service runs. This is in direct contrast to the EC2 and ECS/EKS services.

Use Cases for AWS Lambda

Optimal use cases for function-based compute in place of an application running on an EC2 instance or container are vast, and the AWS community comes up with new ideas on how to use this service almost every day. Here are some of the more common examples that will help you better utilize Lambda:

- **File Processing**: Before the advent of FaaS, customers had one or more dedicated EC2 instances that would be used as the backend processors to process and analyze files before placing them in their next location. With the Lambda service, the processing can be run on demand without the need to manage any servers.

- **Security Alerts**: Using a library such as the boto3 library, you can trigger a Lambda function to send out either a **Simple Notification Service** (**SNS**) or **Simple Email Service** (**SES**) if a violation has been found based on events monitored either in CloudWatch logs or CloudTrail logs.

- **Serverless Websites**: Combining static content stored in S3, along with backend logic on AWS lambda with HTTP(S) endpoints served by API Gateway, allows customers to create more advanced websites without the need to spin up EC2 instances and autoscaling groups since the Lambda service can automatically scale out based on the number of requests.

- **Compliance Remediation**: Combining the power of Lambda functions with the power of the AWS Config service allows you to perform automatic remediations on resources in your account that fall out of compliance based on the rules you specify.

- **Document Conversion**: If you serve documents to your end users (especially those from dynamic websites), a Lambda function can convert those raw documents to PDF before delivery to the end user.

Security Considerations for AWS Lambda

Now that you have a general understanding of the AWS Lambda service, you can examine some of the security considerations to be aware of when using it:

- Set up one IAM role per Lambda and don't reuse roles across Lambda functions. This ensures that each Lambda function gets the least privileged access needed to perform its duties.

- Never expose your Lambda function directly; instead, use API Gateway to front the function if it needs exposure to outside users or services.

- Never store passwords or secrets unencrypted as environment variables or in the Lambda function. Instead, use AWS Secrets Manager or Systems Manager Parameter Store to store and manage the secrets securely and to be able to audit who and what has been accessing the secrets.

With a look at AWS Lambda, this section wrapped up the overview of AWS compute services. Next, you will look at the networking service of Route 53.

Route 53

The global DNS service that AWS provides is Route 53. This is one of the few services in AWS that is not tied to any specific region. The Route 53 service also has one of the most substantial commitments, stating that it will use commercially reasonable efforts to make Amazon Route 53 100% available.

The following three components of Route 53 are of foundational importance:

- Registration (and management) of domain names

- The DNS service

- Health checks (and subsequentially traffic routing) for your web application based on the fact that it's functional, available, and reachable

This section will cover some of the basic information about the Route 53 service and especially any topics that would be relevant to know for the Security Specialty exam.

> ### Knowing the Difference between a Domain and a Hosted Zone
>
> One of the first differences to understand between a domain and a hosted zone is that a domain is an internet construct of domain name servers that associates a person's or organization's unique name with a numerically addressed internet resource. Domains have zone files that are a text-mapping of the different resources and their associated names, addresses, and the type of record in which the asset is currently mapped.
>
> A basic understanding of the Route 53 service is needed for the Security Specialty exam; however, mastery of the difference between a domain and a hosted zone is not something that will be tested.

Route 53 Health Checks

The Route 53 service allows you to check the health of your applications and then reroute their traffic to other servers (or serverless services with an endpoint) based on the rules you provide. You can even see the recent status of your health checks in the web console.

Checking the Health of a Specific Endpoint

In this case, you would create a check from Route 53 that conducts checks at regular intervals specified by you. Your health checks monitor an endpoint that is either an IP address or a domain name. Route 53 then checks at specified intervals if the server, application, or other resource is operational and/or available. The request can be made to a URL that requires data from other services (such as cached data from Elasticache or static data served from S3 or CloudFront) that would mirror most of the actions your users would perform, or it could be a simple health check page that returns a 200 code showing that the server is up and running.

Calculated health checks (health checks that monitor other health checks) act as a root health check, where descendant checks can fail before the origin is considered unhealthy. This type of health check is designed to fail if any of the alarms are set off.

Security Considerations for Route 53

The following are some of the security considerations we should keep in mind when using the service:

- Use Route 53 health checks with the AWS CloudWatch service to monitor your AWS resources.
- For any domain names registered with the Route 53 service, make sure that you have the Auto Renew option selected. This prevents domain squatters from buying your name if there is a lapse in payment and then selling it back to you at a substantial markup.
- Ensure you have DNS query logging enabled for all of your Route 53 hosted zones.

Having gained a basic understanding of the Route 53 service and the best security practices, you can now go through a brief overview of the cloud databases available in AWS that can be used to store your data.

Cloud Databases

Looking at the following model (*Figure 2.5*), you may wonder why there are so many databases. This comes from the evolution of application architecture over the past few decades, where specialization, speed, and scale have become keys to success in the cloud computing industry.

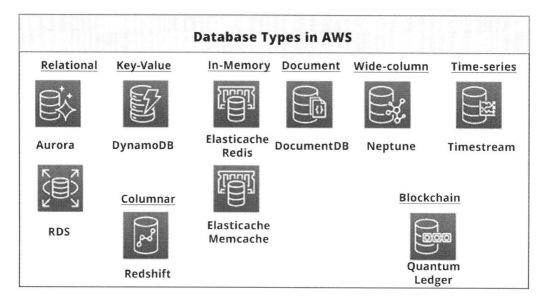

Figure 2.5: Database types and services in AWS

Going through each and every type of database that AWS offers is beyond the scope of this chapter. However, this section will cover some of the databases and their basic features, including security, as part of the foundational overview.

> **Note on Data Security**
> Data security will be covered in depth in *Chapter 17, Protecting Data in Flight and at Rest.*

Relational Databases

The word "database" usually brings to mind relational databases and star schemas with rows and columns. Schemas, rows, and columns are associated with relational databases or RDBMS systems. Relational databases in AWS give you the ability to choose from a variety of RDMBS engines, and they are easy to set up and provision, allowing you both to use the databases that you are familiar with and try ones you are not familiar with to see how they perform.

Relational databases in AWS come in three primary flavors. The underlying engines of these flavors can then be classified as community, commercial, or cloud-native. Cloud-native engines are used in the Aurora service since they are built based on community engines and replication capabilities.

As you go to provision a relational database in AWS, you will use Relational Database Service; take a look at that next.

Relational Database Service

Relational Database Service (**RDS**) aims to remove the tasks previously performed by a database administrator who had to be on staff but gave little to no actual value to the end product or project. These tasks include provisioning a new database, creating backups, scaling out to read replicas, patching and upgrading instances, as well as switching over to a high-availability instance when a fault occurs.

RDS streamlines the setup and installation of software and database provisioning. Using the managed RDS also allows an organization to achieve a standard set of consistency when creating and deploying a database. No custom scripts are needed to deploy, set up, or patch the database, as this is all handled in the background.

After deployment, developers and applications obtain a database endpoint that can be accessed readily and connections can be made with a client or authentication application and then queries can be sent to the database.

RDS comes in several different engine formats, including two commercial engines and three popular open-source engines. The two commercial engines supported are Oracle and Microsoft SQL Server. Both commercial engines are used in enterprises, and RDS supports access to Oracle schemas via **Oracle SQL**. Native tools for Microsoft SQL Server, such as **SQL Server Management Studio**, are also supported. In the community editions, RDS offers the ability to spin up databases using **MySQL**, **PostgreSQL**, and **MariaDB**. **MySQL** is one of the most popular community relational databases. AWS runs the community edition, defaulting to InnoDB tables, with the documentation stating that MyISAM storage does not support reliable crash recovery.

PostgreSQL is another extremely popular database with developers for its rich feature set. Postgres on RDS supports standard tools such as pgAdmin or connections via JDBC/ODBC drivers to connect to the database.

After deciding on your engine of choice, you can choose an instance type that will give you varying computing and memory power levels. There are burstable instances (**T family**) that, mostly, are only used for testing environments. A general (**M family**) and memory-optimized (**R family**) instance is preferred over taking your database workloads to a more productized environment.

A significant difference between RDS and the same types of engines that you would run yourself is how replicas work. Read replicas are extremely easy to provision with the click of a button, either in the same or a different Availability Zone. However, these nodes are read-only and do not enable writes. In the same context, you can make your instance highly available, replicating your data asynchronously to the copy of the primary node in another Availability Zone or region. Even if an incident occurs, your application will remain seamless for end users as the domain name used by both the master and replica node does not change. This replicated primary, however, cannot take any load off your main primary server as it cannot serve any other function (such as being a read replica) except for being a failover node. Read replicas can be promoted to a standalone database, and at that point, they can take writes but would no longer stay in sync with the previous master that they were replicating.

Security Considerations for RDS

Having gone through the RDS service and its capabilities, you can now examine some of the security considerations and best practices for RDS:

- Never use a root AWS user to create and manage RDS resources. Instead, create an individual user or group that manages the RDS resources.

- Control which IP addresses and AWS services can connect to your RDS instance, such as EC2 instances, using security groups.

- Utilize the encryption capabilities of RDS to protect your working data and snapshots.

- Use the principle of least privilege when granting permissions to users and service roles to perform their duties on the database.

- Take advantage of the AWS Backup service to create secure copies of your backup data via cross-account backups.

Amazon Aurora

Amazon Aurora was built in response to customers wanting the performance of commercial-grade database engines such as Oracle or Microsoft SQL Server without dealing with all the hassle of the licensing restrictions that come with those products.

Another important fact about Amazon Aurora is that, unlike other RDS engines backed by EBS storage, Aurora built its storage solution from the ground up after considering multiple customer requests over the years.

Amazon Aurora comes in either MySQL-compatible or PostgreSQL versions. You can run Aurora as a cluster or as a serverless version of the Aurora database.

Key-Value Databases

DynamoDB is the first of the NoSQL databases that will be discussed in this section. Although some users believe that NoSQL means Not SQL, most have come to the consensus that it stands for Not Only SQL.

Key-value databases store data in key-value pairs and are designed for high performance and scalability. They are often used for applications that require quick read-and-write operations. Each key is a unique identifier that can be used to retrieve the corresponding value from the database.

In-depth examples of using DynamoDB will be presented in *Chapter 17, Protecting Data in Flight and at Rest*.

In-Memory Databases

In-memory databases are databases where all the memory is stored in RAM and specialized hardware. The upside of this type of database is that it provides extremely fast performance and offers very low latency. The downside for in-memory databases is that because they use RAM as the backing hardware, they can be more expensive than other databases.

Items accessed by your users and applications frequently need a quick response to provide the best customer experience. The time it can take to perform the database query and render the results, especially if several queries are waiting to be performed simultaneously, can become a factor, and this is where adding an in-memory database as a caching layer can help reduce latency. AWS' managed in-memory database option is **Elasticache** and comes with two different engines: Redis and Memcached. Elasticache nodes and clusters are composed of SSDs, which allows encryption at rest, in contrast with other in-memory databases that are created purely out of RAM.

Document Databases

A document database is a non-relational (or NoSQL) database that allows you to store documents and data in the JSON-type format and query that data. One of the truly unique features of document databases is that there is no fixed schema and that they can have documents nested inside of each other.

AWS provides Amazon DocumentDB (with MongoDB compatibility) as a managed database service for users who have either used MongoDB in the past or are looking for the capabilities of a document database.

Document databases are particularly good for teams that don't want to deal with the administrative aspects of a database, want to simplify the way to use initial schema values with JSON, and want to start pushing data to the database, which will allow both simple and advanced querying later.

Message and Queueing Systems

As you start to build out cloud-scale applications, you need ways to decouple different tiers of the application so that it can scale independently. This is for several reasons, including making your application more resilient and allowing each available tier to scale independently of the other tiers. You might only need to have a single EC2 instance running at any point in time. Encapsulating this instance in an autoscaling group and connecting it to a managed queue allows the queue to take the requests and ensure that they get processed by the EC2 instance, even if it happens to stop and terminate for some reason. In another scenario, if there is a burst of traffic for any amount of time and it is too much for the single instance to handle, then having the request flow first in a queue allows an auto-scaling group to scale up more instances based on the number of requests coming in at a certain point in time. This is easy to think of in an order processing system, where, with a normal load of traffic, a single EC2 instance can handle the job. However, when there is a lot of traffic, for instance, if there has been a promotion by the marketing department and a flood of new orders have come through the system, then the number of orders, if they were going through the queue, would signal that more than one instance would be needed to complete the job in a timely manner.

The following sections will take you through the message and queueing systems provided by AWS, how they can benefit you, and some of their security considerations.

Simple Notification Service (SNS)

The ability to allow either your applications or even other AWS services to send messages and notifications without extra programming or complex configuration is provided by **Simple Notification Service (SNS)**.

SNS is a publisher and consumer system where publishers are able to push a message out to a topic, and then any consumer who has subscribed to that topic can consume that message.

The SNS topic acts as the channel where a single message can be broadcast to one or more subscribers. The publisher (in this case, the application shown in *Figure 2.6*) only sends the message out once to the topic, and each consumer (or subscriber) can receive the message to be processed in the way that works for them.

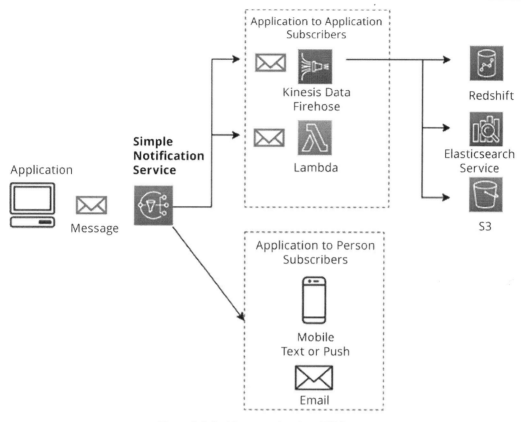

Figure 2.6: Architecture showing SNS fanout

Security Considerations for SNS

The following points present some of the security considerations and best practices when using SNS:

- Apply only the permissions needed to fulfill the duty of the job (the principle of **least privilege**):

  - An application sending and receiving messages from one or more topics doesn't need administrative permissions for those topics, such as the ability to create additional topics or modify or delete the topic. Leave those privileges to another specialized role rather than granting full access to all users and roles.

- Enforce encryption for data in transit for messages:

  - Use the secure HTTPS rather than the insecure HTTP when sending messages from an SNS topic to avoid becoming vulnerable to man-in-the-middle attacks.

- Use VPC endpoints to access Amazon SNS:

  - Route your requests from hosts in your VPC through VPC endpoints rather than the public internet; this limits topic access to only the hosts within a particular VPC.

Simple Queue Service (SQS)

The managed queue example at the beginning of this section referenced a queueing system wherein requests could be held until they were ready to be processed. This type of queue enables you to break apart or decouple your application in a cloud-native manner.

The simplicity of the SQS setup and use makes it appealing to many developers and organizations. SQS comes in two flavors: standard queues and **First In First Out** (**FIFO**) queues. Standard queues allow at least one-time delivery, whereas FIFO queues are capable of exactly one-time delivery of messages placed in the queue. Messages get processed exactly once but delivery can happen multiple times due to technical issues or high loads. The other significant difference between the two types of queues is that with FIFO queues, the messages are processed in the exact order in which they are received. A standard queue makes its best effort to try and preserve the ordering of the messages received. However, if a message is received out of order, it will not shuffle or re-order the messages to retain the original message order.

SQS is a distributed queue system spread out across different regional nodes. This is one of the design features that provides SQS its benefits, such as high scalability, availability, reliability, and durability. SQS also allows **Server-Side Encryption** (**SSE**), either through the service key provided by AWS via KMS or a custom key provided by you. You can also control access to the SWS via access policies that have access to the messages that are either produced or consumed.

Messages are placed in the SQS queue by producers. They are then distributed across the queue components for redundancy as shown in *Figure 2.7*. The graphic depicts two different application components inside three different containers. The first is a disparate application (the producer) that produces the messages and sends them to the queue. The second and third components are the two consumers that read the messages from the queue. The SQS service is distributed throughout different Availability Zones in a region, and each message is stored at least twice on different nodes for redundancy purposes.

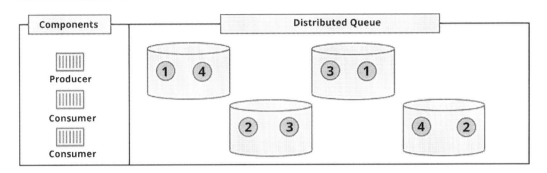

Figure 2.7: SQS distributed queue

When the consumer is ready to process a message, it uses either a long or short polling technique to see if there are any messages in the queue for processing. If the consumer detects one or more messages it can process, it pulls down (or processes) the messages. The messages are only flagged, and the visibility timeout begins. Once the consumer has successfully processed the messages and deleted them, they are removed from all nodes of the distributed queue.

Messages must be deleted by the consumer once they have been processed successfully. Because of the nature of the distributed system that SQS runs on, once a consumer has pulled down a message for processing, it is marked so that no other consumers can pull it down. There is a timeout period in which the consumer must acknowledge that the message was processed. If the SQS service never receives this acknowledgment, the flag is removed from the message, and it becomes available for another consumer to process.

> **Note**
>
> There are other queueing services offered by AWS, such as open-source message brokers or Amazon MQ, which is a managed service. This chapter will not go into great detail regarding these services since the basic concepts of queueing tasks are the same. Still, this service offers more advanced features, such as high availability and durability of messages across regions.

Security Considerations for SQS

Having gone over the functions of the SQS service along with how it differs from the SNS service, you can now examine some of the security best practices for SQS:

- Apply the principle of least privilege when granting access to SQS queues:

  Create a specific role for the administration of the queues that do not have access to consume or publish messages. This administrative role would only be able to create, delete, and modify queues. In the same context, create a role that's only to be used by consumers who can read and write to the queues but have no administrative privileges. You can break this role down further into producer and consumer roles.

- Implement server-side encryption:

  SQS can store its data at rest encrypted using keys from the KMS service.

- Use VPC endpoints to access Amazon SQS:

  Routing your requests from hosts in your VPC through VPC endpoints rather than the public internet limits topic access to only the hosts within a particular VPC.

- Tighten access policies so that SQS queues are not publicly available:

  Name specific resources for the principal instead of using the wildcard * in access policies.

Where Would You Use SNS or SQS?

When deciding which messaging service to use, there is a rule you can use to help determine which one will serve you best. Ask yourself the following set of questions:

- Are my messages going to be consumed only by my application?

  If the answer is yes, then SQS is going to be the best choice.

- Are my messages going to be consumed by multiple sources?

  If the answer is yes, then SNS is going to be the best choice.

Using these two questions, you can determine whether you are dealing with a closed loop of gathering the messages and then processing them for use in the application (SQS) or you are creating the message to be consumed outside the application (SNS).

Simple Email Service (SES)

SES allows you to set up and send emails without most of the complexities of running an SMTP server.

Although emails can originate anywhere globally, SES only receives emails from three regional endpoints: us-east-1 (N. Virginia), us-west-2 (Oregon), and eu-west-1 (Ireland). The service has (at the time of writing) over 18 regions for sending emails via the SMTP protocol.

Amazon helps you and others verify where your sent mail is coming from and provides trust in the emails you send your customers by adding a series of DKIM records to the email headers, which can be verified by the recipient's mail server.

Security Considerations for SES

- Use SES in conjunction with VPC endpoints. This will keep any emails (especially those going from services residing in AWS to your internal users) from traversing the public internet.

- Ensure that CloudTrail has been turned on in the region where your SES has been set up. This makes sure that any API activity is captured.

- Use IAM policies to restrict where the SES service can take requests from when sending emails. This helps to prevent a rogue spambot from using your SES service and sending emails with faux addresses. Refer to the following example policy:

```
{
  "Version":"2012-10-17",
  "Statement":[
    {
      "Effect":"Allow",
      "Action":[
        "ses:SendEmail",
        "ses:SendRawEmail"
      ],
      "Resource":"*",
      "Condition":{
        "StringEquals":{
          "ses:FromAddress":"sales@test.com"
        }
      }
    }
  ]
}
```

As you have now reviewed different types of messaging systems and delivery available in AWS, you can dive into the next section that discusses a very important access gateway, the API Gateway.

API Gateway

When trying to build RESTful and WebSocket APIs, AWS creates a fully managed service that is built around a simple interface. API Gateway can act as the entrance to other AWS services, such as data stored on RDS, or compute calls made by the EC2 or Lambda services, just as examples. API Gateway supports a number of protocols, including HTTP, HTTPS, and WebSocket.

One of the most compelling features of API Gateway is that since AWS manages all of the underlying infrastructure, you and your development team can concentrate on building the data being served by the API and hence reduce the cost of building and maintaining the API.

Security Considerations for API Gateway

With data and authorizations happening in the course of API events, understanding the security features that can and should be implemented when using the API Gateway service will help keep your data and applications fronted by API Gateway more secure:

- **Enable Logging**: When using API Gateway, make sure that logging has been turned on to capture the activity from the gateway and gather the logs in the CloudWatch Logs service.

- **Enable Integration with Web Application Firewall**: API Gateway can be monitored by the **Web Application Firewall** (**WAF**) service. This can help block a flood of attacks if they come into your API endpoint.

- **Add CloudWatch Alarms**: At a minimum, set alarms on pre-defined metrics in Amazon CloudWatch or go a step further and define some custom metrics based on your own custom API paths.

- **Add Authorization and Authentication**: Implement authentication mechanisms such as API keys, AWS IAM roles, or custom authorizers to verify the identity of users and customers accessing your APIs.

- **Implement API Rate Limiting and Throttling**: Rate limit and request throttling mechanisms can protect your APIs from abusive or malicious usage. Setting limits on the number of requests per second or minute prevents API abuse and ensures fair usage for all clients.

The next section dives into the final service to be discussed in this chapter—**AWS Trusted Advisor**.

Trusted Advisor

As the number of resources grows in your AWS account, it can sometimes take work to keep track of them all. Challenges start to arise in the account, such as security groups that have access to resource across the internet from a security perspective or unused Elastic IP addresses, which cost money despite being idle.

Every AWS customer and account can access the seven core security checks provided by the service. These are as follows:

- **Multifactor** (**MFA**) on the root account
- S3 bucket permissions
- EBS snapshots available for public access
- RDS snapshots available for public access
- Open access (0.0.0.0/0) on security groups

- That IAM users are being used (as opposed to the root user)

- Service limits (these are in the service limits section, not the security section)

If you are on the Basic support plan, then you can view these checks easily within the AWS Management Console by doing the following:

1. Select `Trusted Advisor` on the services list page from the `Management & Governance` category. (Or type `Trusted Advisor` in the search box).

2. Select either the `Security` or the `Service Limits` category and view the available services.

The following points summarize and define each of the five areas checked by Trusted Advisor:

- **Cost Optimization**: These checks help you identify resources not being optimally used and where you could save money by optimizing your infrastructure.

- **Performance**: Performance checks scan your resources and identify any that could make use of provisioned throughput and ones that are over-utilized.

- **Security**: Checks are performed to identify any weaknesses that could lead to vulnerabilities within your account.

- **Fault Tolerance**: The checks within this category determine whether you have adequate resiliency and fault tolerance built into your environment—for example, by using multi-Availability Zone features and autoscaling.

- **Service Limits**: This category checks whether any of your services have reached 80% or more against the allotted service limit. For example, you are only allowed five VPCs per region; once you reach four VPCs in a single region (80%), you will trigger the check and be notified if you have enabled notifications.

Now that you have a basic understanding of Trusted Advisor, you can explore the interface and findings when the set criteria have been breached.

Reviewing Deviations Using Trusted Advisor

As you use Trusted Advisor, over time, you will see that the service begins to highlight potential issues within your account. This section will cover how to review these deviations and how to interpret the severity of the issues found.

From within the AWS Management Console, select `Trusted Advisor` from the `Management & Governance` category list. This will then present you with the following summary:

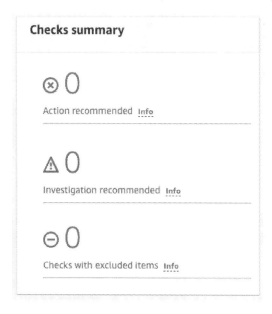

Figure 2.8: Trusted Advisor Checks summary

Even if the checks summary shows zero actions recommended, you can manually refresh the checks to see if your items are compliant. Do this by following the steps below:

1. Starting from the Trusted Advisor home page, in the top-left menu under the `Trusted Advisor` heading, click on the submenu labeled `Security`.

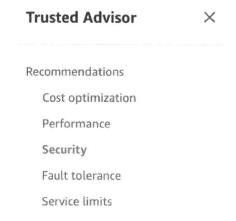

Figure 2.9: Security menu item highlighted in Trusted Advisor

2. Now, on the security checks page, see if you can find one of the basic checks that still need to be completed. This is signified by an icon that looks like a circle with a line in the middle of it. (An example is shown in the following screenshot of the Security Groups – Specific Ports Unrestricted window.)

Security Groups - Specific Ports Unrestricted

Checks security groups for rules that allow unrestricted access (0.0.0.0/0) to specific ports.

Figure 2.10: Incomplete security groups check with a gray circle

3. On the right side of the check, click on the circular arrow icon to refresh the check. If the check passes on your account, the gray circle with the arrow will be replaced with a green circle with a check inside it. If the check fails, however, the gray circle will be replaced by a red circle with an x in the middle, signifying that a critical check has failed, or a yellow triangle with an exclamation point if any other port besides the critical ports has been left unrestricted.

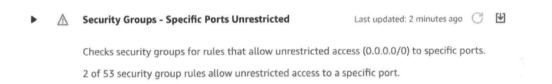

Security Groups - Specific Ports Unrestricted   Last updated: 2 minutes ago

Checks security groups for rules that allow unrestricted access (0.0.0.0/0) to specific ports.

2 of 53 security group rules allow unrestricted access to a specific port.

Figure 2.11: Security check that has a non-critical finding

Dig deeper into this deviation with the following steps to see what else Trusted Advisor can tell you.

4. Click the triangle to the left of the yellow arrow to expose more information regarding the finding. You can see that 6 out of 55 security groups currently allow unrestricted access to non-critical ports without revealing additional information.

Scroll down to see a list of the six security groups in question. The details provided by Trusted Advisor include `Region`, `Security Group Name`, `Security Group ID`, `Protocol`, and `Port Range`. And now that you know which security groups are in violation, you have two options: create an exception right here so that it will no longer cause a Trusted Advisor alert or remediate the anomalies using the information provided by Trusted Advisor.

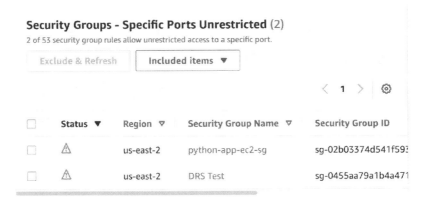

Figure 2.12: Trusted Advisor details of security group violations

With the conclusion of this topic, you should now understand the Trusted Advisor service, how to use it to check for security vulnerabilities, and how to use the details of those checks to help you remediate those vulnerabilities. Next is a quick recap of what you have learned in this chapter.

Summary

In this chapter, you reviewed many of the main services used in AWS architecture. These make up the majority of the services that will be part of your day-to-day responsibilities as AWS cloud security engineers and the services that will be referenced in the questions in the exam.

Having a baseline knowledge of these services will allow us to dive deep into the most relevant exam material rather than revisiting the basics.

Chapter 3, Understanding Attacks on Cloud Environments, will wrap up *Section I* by examining the different types of attacks that you need to look for in your AWS environments as a security engineer. It will discuss the relevant mitigation strategies to keep these attacks at bay as you examine each attack type, and you will also explore one of the most prevalent types of attacks, **Distributed Denial of Service** (**DDoS**) attacks, in detail.

Further Reading

For additional information on the AWS shared responsibility model and to gain a more comprehensive understanding of AWS security, please look at the following resources:

- AWS Control Tower Controls Reference Guide: `https://packt.link/XHYWT`

- AWS EC2 Frequently Asked Questions: `https://packt.link/q8OxD`

- Amazon RDS FAQs: `https://packt.link/VgKnY`

- Amazon DynamoDB FAQs: `https://packt.link/gUa6j`

- Amazon Route 53 FAQs: `https://packt.link/LmMKz`

- AWS SQS FAQs: `https://packt.link/zTe0n`

- Security overview of AWS Lambda: `https://packt.link/gz2Tr`

Exam Readiness Drill – Chapter Review Questions

Apart from a solid understanding of key concepts, being able to think quickly under time pressure is a skill that will help you ace your certification exam. That is why working on these skills early on in your learning journey is key.

Chapter review questions are designed to improve your test-taking skills progressively with each chapter you learn and review your understanding of key concepts in the chapter at the same time. You'll find these at the end of each chapter.

> **How To Access These Resources**
>
> To learn how to access these resources, head over to the chapter titled *Chapter 21, Accessing the Online Practice Resources*.

To open the Chapter Review Questions for this chapter, perform the following steps:

1. Click the link – `https://packt.link/SCSC02E2_CH02`.

    Alternatively, you can scan the following QR code (*Figure 2.13*):

Figure 2.13: QR code that opens Chapter Review Questions for logged-in users

2.   Once you log in, you'll see a page similar to the one shown in *Figure 2.14*:

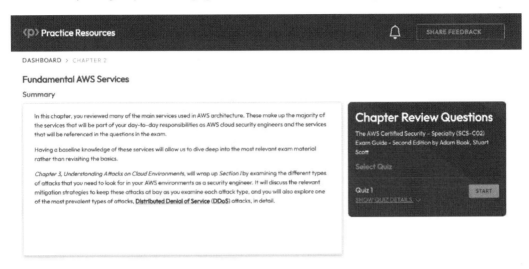

Figure 2.14: Chapter Review Questions for Chapter 2

3.   Once ready, start the following practice drills, re-attempting the quiz multiple times.

Exam Readiness Drill

For the first three attempts, don't worry about the time limit.

ATTEMPT 1

The first time, aim for at least **40%**. Look at the answers you got wrong and read the relevant sections in the chapter again to fix your learning gaps.

ATTEMPT 2

The second time, aim for at least **60%**. Look at the answers you got wrong and read the relevant sections in the chapter again to fix any remaining learning gaps.

ATTEMPT 3

The third time, aim for at least **75%**. Once you score **75%** or more, you start working on your timing.

> **Tip**
>
> You may take more than three attempts to reach 75%. That's okay. Just review the relevant sections in the chapter till you get there.

Working On Timing

Target: Your aim is to keep the score the same while trying to answer these questions as quickly as possible. Here's an example of how your next attempts should look like:

Attempt	Score	Time Taken
Attempt 5	77%	21 mins 30 seconds
Attempt 6	78%	18 mins 34 seconds
Attempt 7	76%	14 mins 44 seconds

Table 2.1: Sample timing practice drills on the online platform

> **Note**
>
> The time limits shown in the above table are just examples. Set your own time limits with each attempt based on the time limit of the quiz on the website.

With each new attempt, your score should stay above 75% while your time taken to complete should **decrease**. Repeat as many attempts as you want till you feel confident dealing with the time pressure.

3

Understanding Attacks on Cloud Environments

With an outline of what you are responsible for from an AWS customer perspective and a refresher of the baseline services that will be discussed throughout the different scenarios in your journey, this first section will conclude with an examination of some of the top risks that your cloud environment can be exposed to.

Even though this is not explicitly considered as one of the domains tested for on the Certified Security Specialty exam, these scenarios may be presented to you in the form of questions that are part of the exam itself.

Furthermore, understanding the different techniques that bad actors can use to evade the basic security measures placed on your account, as well as the mitigation techniques used to stop and prevent them, is helpful in your day-to-day responsibilities as a cloud security engineer.

The following topics will be covered in this chapter:

- Understanding the top cloud-native attacks on infrastructure
- Understanding the top cloud-native attacks on software
- **Distributed Denial of Service (DDoS)** protection
- Strengthening your cloud security posture
- AWS services that can be used to combat attacks

Technical Requirements

Successful completion of this chapter will require a basic understanding of AWS services and networking concepts.

Understanding the Top Cloud-Native Attacks on Infrastructure

The more customizable your service or platform, the more responsibilities you hold as the customer and, therefore, the more time and effort you need to both plan your security strategy and assess the attacks to which you are susceptible. These attacks can come from different angles and different points of entry. Having an understanding of the guidelines of best security practices helps, but as you will see in this chapter, grasping the mitigation techniques for some specific known attacks can ensure more comprehensive protection for your cloud environment.

If you do succumb to an attack, then it might take your business or a line of business down for any period of time. Having the means to restore your systems in a timely fashion is the subject of the first vulnerability that you will learn about.

Business Continuity and Resilience

Business continuity and resilience refers to the ability of a business to continue operations when a disruptive event such as a natural disaster, a technical outage, or an attack such as a ransomware attack occurs. Having a plan in place to mitigate these risks is imperative. When your business is inoperable, then it is not generating any revenue, and any business that is not generating revenue and only has expenses, such as vendors (think AWS, software vendors, and the like), staff, and others, will at some point run out of funds.

In the next section, *Mitigation for Business Continuity and Resilience*, you will see how you can put a plan in place to continue operations if there are natural disasters, technical outages, or attacks.

Mitigation for Business Continuity and Resilience

A business can often determine how to recover and protect a particular application much more easily than it can determine how quickly each application needs to be recovered. This can be resolved by setting a **Recovery Time Objective** (**RTO**) and a **Recovery Point Objective** (**RPO**) for each application.

How you mitigate your risk in this situation depends on the criticality of the workload being considered. For instance, in the case of a ransomware attack, highly critical workloads may need multi-site backups or air-gapped backups, based on network connectivity, that can't be corrupted. Non-critical workloads may be backed up to cold storage, such as AWS Glacier archives or S3 buckets with multi-region replication to be restored after more critical workloads have been attended to. You can refer to *Figure 3.1* for the type of backup and restoration system that would be needed, based on the amount of time that it would take to restore the system.

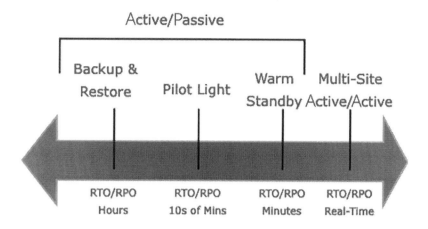

Figure 3.1: Disaster recovery options

Before any event, you want to have your workloads categorized for what RTO/RPO attention level they need. With AWS, you can use a tag for items such as EC2 instances or databases to designate criticality. The value of our criticality tag could have a value ranging from low, meaning that it would most likely be backed up once or twice a day, to very high, meaning that it would have to have a corresponding real-time backup and extra monitoring attached to the workload.

You just learned how to protect and restore your systems and data if there are outages. Next, you will learn about a type of attack that happens when someone (or something) gains access to your system and prefers not to be discovered – detection evasion.

Detection Evasion

When you enable CloudTrail on your AWS account or organization, you capture every API call from the AWS Management Console, the **Command-Line Interface (CLI)**, or some other programmatic method, such as a **Software Development Kit (SDK)**. A bad actor who has gained unauthorized access to your account may try to first disable the logs of CloudTrail so that their actions will not be captured, making it more difficult to determine what events took place when you finally realize that a breach has occurred.

Not only are the CloudTrail logs essential for the reconnaissance work afterward in uncovering the who, what, and when of an event, CloudWatch logs can also be a crucial part of a proactive strategy of alerting when combined with other services, such as Amazon EventBridge and **Simple Notification Service (SNS)**.

Mitigation for Detection Evasion

One of the most effective ways to control the manipulation of log files is using a **Service Control Policy** (**SCP**). If you have multiple accounts, this policy can be pushed down from the top of the AWS organization through the different accounts and organizational units so that it is implemented on all accounts:

```
{
    "Version": "2012-10-17",
    "Statement": [
        {
            "Action": [
                "cloudtrail:StopLogging",
                "cloudtrail:DeleteTrail"
            ],
            "Resource": "*",
            "Effect": "Deny"
        }
    ]
}
```

> **Note**
>
> *Chapter 14, Working with Access Policies*, deals with SCPs in depth.

A second mitigation technique, besides just stopping the ability to turn off the CloudTrail service, is enabling CloudTrail log file integrity.

This can be accomplished from the console by choosing YES for the `Enable log file validation` option when you create a CloudTrail or update an existing trail.

You can also enable log file integrity validation using the AWS CLI, with the following command:

```
aws cloudtrail update-trail --name cloudtrail-trail-name --enable-log-
file-validation
```

AWS Infrastructure Scanning

If you spin up an EC2 instance on a public URL and then check the logs, you will see that they are populated with scans that determine whether any standard software has been installed with the default settings.

Even though AWS itself does not publish the list of public URLs used for their instances, some sites have collected this information and made it available. Using this information, an individual (or organization) can perform reconnaissance to capture and map out the inventory for an account, along with points of weakness that could be subject to attack. This is known as a scanning attack.

Mitigation for Infrastructure Scanning

A preventive correction to make to your systems is changing the default settings (username/password) when installing software onto your cloud systems. Bad actors scan networks and systems for easy targets that have been installed and left at the default settings. No changes to the default passwords and usernames that are easily found in the installation guides of software manuals pose a risk.

You can take further action by adding a **web application firewall** and using **managed rules** to protect against common attacks. One of the features of this is the anonymous IP list managed rule group, which contains rules to block requests from proxies, Tor nodes, and VPNs trying to mask who they are.

Top Cloud-Native Attacks on Software and Data

Knowing what top cloud attacks are and how they can be prevented and mitigated is critical to keeping your organization as safe as possible from risks. These refer to a class of cyberattacks that target cloud computing environments such as public, private, or hybrid cloud infrastructure.

The following subsections describe the common vulnerabilities relevant to the authentication of users, software, and data systems running on the cloud.

User Identity Federation

One of the biggest threats to AWS accounts is the reuse of passwords by users with multiple accounts. This problem is solved with the use of identity federation. Users tend to find remembering various complicated passwords difficult. As a result, many users reuse the same passwords across multiple accounts. If one account gets compromised, even if it wasn't the cloud service provider's account, it allows the attacker to gain entry to another one of your accounts if the username and password are the same as the account that was compromised.

Often, users have multiple accounts that aren't managed by a federation server or service; such users use the same password across those accounts. This is illustrated in *Figure 3.2*, where the user on the left has multiple accounts but uses the same password for each one.

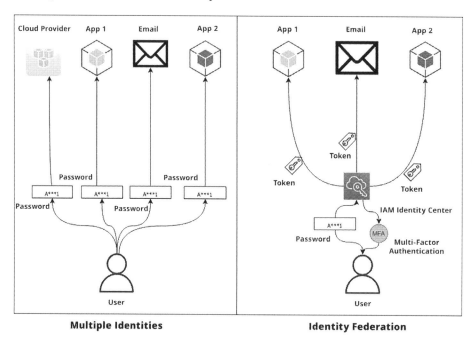

Multiple Identities   **Identity Federation**

Figure 3.2: Multiple identities versus identity federation

If this password were to be compromised, anyone with the username would have access to that user's data and permissions on all four accounts until the user's account was locked or a password change was performed.

> **Note**
>
> Subsequent chapters dive much deeper into AWS user account management, both from a user account management perspective and a federation perspective.

Mitigation for a Lack of Identity Federation

Implementing a modern identity service or platform helps mitigate the risk of password compromise with multiple identities. AWS's native IAM Identity Center allows you to connect with your existing SAML identity provider or create and manage your users and groups directly from the IAM service itself.

This helps prevent password reuse. This is especially important in the case of an account compromise in which a single account has been compromised and the username and password combination is used to access multiple accounts if the password is the same across those accounts.

Vulnerable IAM Policies

There are many examples of documentation wherein IAM policies have been scoped with wide-open permissions. This is done by design, for as you are learning about a new service or a new feature of a service in AWS, it can be frustrating to not have it work due to a permission issue. Having these wide-open roles in systems that will be used to communicate with production-level services and data can leave things in a vulnerable state.

As AWS users assume roles, the permissions passed on to them are taken on by the entity that uses that role. A `Principal` element is a necessary element in an IAM policy that specifies who is allowed (or denied) access to the resource. A wildcard, a character or symbol, used as a placeholder to match or represent one or more other characters in a string or filename, is often used when crafting the policy, especially when modeling IAM policies after example policies. This wildcard – designated by an asterisk (*) – allows everyone to assume the role.

A vulnerable policy, with the `Principal` of the policy having a wildcard, (*) is shown in the following example:

```
{
 "Version": "2012-10-17",
 "Statement": [
         {
                 "Effect": "Allow",
                 "Principal": { "AWS": "*" },
                 "Action": "sts: AssumeRole"
         }
     ]
}
```

The same can be said for IAM policies that use a wildcard with the `Resource` element of an IAM policy. The `Resource` element in the policy defines the specific object or objects that the preceding statement covers. Leaving the resource as a wildcard allows access to all items spun up in your account.

Mitigation of Vulnerable IAM Policies

Helping prevent vulnerable IAM policies comes back down to the principle of least privilege and taking the time to craft the permissions in the policies for the people and groups who are going to be assigned to those policies, along with the resources that they will be expected to manage with those policies.

Using only wildcards can leave your IAM policies vulnerable. However, this does not mean that a wildcard cannot be a valuable tool when crafting a policy to provide your users with the exact privilege that they will need. Another powerful tool when crafting policies is the use of policy variables.

The JSON policy variables are a way to identify a specific resource, but that resource does not have to be hardcoded into the JSON policy document itself.

The following example shows that a user with the previous policy attached can access any CloudWatch log group in US East 2 (Ohio) that matches the current user's name:

```
{
"Version": "2012-10-17",
"Statement": [
        {
                "Effect": "Allow",
                "Action": "cloudwatch:*",
                "Resource": "arn:aws:cloudwatch:us-east-2:log-
group:${aws:username}"
        }
    ]
}
```

The previous sections demonstrated how making some minor adjustments to your policies can help stave off attacks on your AWS account. You can also *shift left* your security practices by ensuring proper credential rotation and scanning for credentials and secrets in your code base before they ever make it to public or private repositories. This is discussed in the next section.

Vulnerable AWS Credentials

Another significant vulnerability for identity and access management is access credentials (specifically, an access key and secret access key) that are not rotated in a programmatic manner. These credentials are tied to a specific user and any capabilities or access that that user has been granted.

Mitigation of Vulnerable AWS Credentials

Create a policy and/or process to rotate access keys every 90 days. Since AWS allows you to have two sets of keys per user, the best practice is to make the active set inactive for a short period after creating the new set of access credentials. Then, if any systems are tagged *high* or *critical* and have stopped working, you can reactivate the original credential pair while you switch to the updated set of credentials on those systems.

Along with rotation, incorporating a check such as *git-secrets* in your **Continuous Integration (CI)** process as part of the **Static Application Security Testing (SAST)** testing can ensure that neither you nor any of your users' hard-coded keys in the source code will be vulnerable to theft or exploitation. The git-secrets tool scans commits and commit messages to prevent secret access keys and passwords from being added to your code repository. If a developer has added a key or secret to the code, then it will be flagged before being pushed to the repository, either public or private, and that secret can be removed and safely stored in a credential manager such as AWS Secrets Manager.

A preferred alternative, especially with larger enterprises in regulated industries, is to prevent users from using the long-term credentials of an access key and secret key. Instead, you would only provide access to AWS Security Token Service, which can set the credentials to automatically expire anywhere between 900 seconds (15 minutes) and 129,600 seconds (35 hours).

DDoS Protection

Distributed Denial of Service (DDoS) attacks are widespread and, if successful, can have a detrimental impact on an organization's service operation. Depending on the scale of the DDoS attack, it can render an entire website unavailable, and this could cause retail e-commerce businesses significant losses in sales.

Understanding DDoS and Its Attack Patterns

Initially, the initiator of a DDoS attack will focus on a specific target, such as a single host, network, or service, to compromise. This target will likely be a vital component of an organization's infrastructure. During the attack, an attempt will be made to severely disrupt the performance of the target, using a massive number of inbound requests from several different distributed sources within the same period.

This creates the following two problems:

- The additional traffic load floods the target and prevents authentic and legitimate inbound requests from reaching that target and being processed as genuine requests.

- The performance of the target is hindered, affecting the usability of the infrastructure and its associated resources. For example, if a DDoS attack is launched against a web server running a website, the site would appear unavailable or down to anyone using the site.

So far, you've only gotten a basic understanding of a DDoS attack. At a higher level, these attacks can be carried out using different patterns, as discussed in the next section.

DDoS Attack Patterns

There are many different DDoS attacks that can be used to achieve the end goal of disruption. The following subsections explain a couple of these at a high level to help you understand the principles of DDoS attacks.

> **Note**
>
> The exam will not test you on the different types of attacks and how they are initiated. This section was included as a foundation for the topic. More information on these topics is provided in the *Further Reading* section at the end of the chapter.

SYN Floods

This type of attack takes advantage of the three-way handshake that is used to establish a connection between two hosts, as shown in the following diagram:

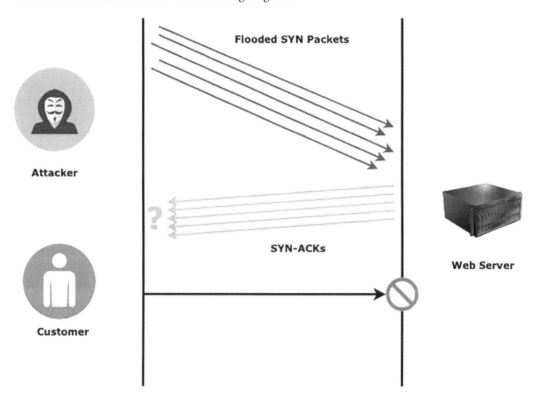

Figure 3.3: A SYN flood attack

This attack is named a SYN flood because a massive number of connections are made simultaneously to the attacked host (these being the SYN packets shown in the diagram). In the host's attempt to establish these incoming connections, it responds with a SYN/ACK packet. Typically, to complete the handshake, the sender would then respond with a further ACK packet. However, the sender does not send this final response. As a result, this leaves many open connections on the host, which results in the host unnecessarily using many resources. This, in turn, leaves minimal resources available to process legitimate requests.

HTTP floods

Similar to a SYN flood, the target in this type of attack is subjected to a substantial number of HTTP requests (for example, GET or POST requests), which, in turn, consume valuable resources on the host. This results in a lack of available resources to process and serve legitimate requests on the server, rendering the host unusable.

Ping of death (PoD)

As the name suggests, this type of attack isn't something that will help your environment. A PoD attack is initiated by a malicious user sending many oversized IP packets to a host through a series of pings. The attack works by exploiting a vulnerability in the way the target system handles fragmented IP packets. The maximum size of an IP packet is 65,535 bytes. However, due to the packets' fragmentation, they are larger than the allowed size when reassembled into a single packet on the host. Consequently, because the ping packet is deliberately malformed and oversized, the reassembly process can fail or cause the system to become overwhelmed. This manipulation causes the host to suffer from memory overflow, which is detrimental to its performance.

A Reflection Attack

In this type of attack, many requests are sent to the server by the attacker using the victim's IP address as the source address. Then, the server responds to the request, sending the responses back to the victim. With many requests returning to the victim's system, their network connection becomes overloaded, and access to the network is disrupted. This is by design by the attacker.

One of the challenges with defending against reflection attacks is that the traffic seems to be coming from legitimate sources, rather than an attacker's address. This makes the attack hard to distinguish from legitimate traffic.

Using AWS Web Application Firewall as a Response to Attacks

One of the primary purposes of a denial-of-service attack is to make the system being attacked unresponsive. Assets will be protected if you place your applications and web services, along with corresponding load balancers and **Content Delivery Networks** (**CDNs**), such as CloudFront, behind a **Web Application Firewall** (**WAF**).

AWS WAF helps protect traffic by configuring custom and managed rules to allow, block, or monitor (count) web requests, based on the conditions you define.

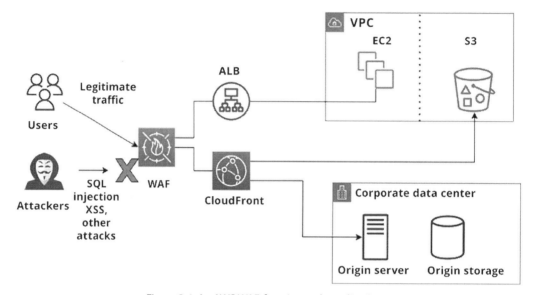

Figure 3.4: An AWS WAF-fronting web application

The primary function of the AWS WAF service is to protect your web applications from malicious attacks from a wide variety of attack patterns, many of which correspond to the OWASP Top 10. AWS WAF is used in conjunction with Amazon CloudFront and its distributions, an application load balancer or API gateway, to analyze requests over HTTP or HTTPS to help distinguish between harmful and legitimate requests sent to your applications and site. AWS WAF then blocks and restricts any access that is detected as forbidden.

The previous paragraph mentioned OWASP; for those unfamiliar with what or who that is, the following presents a brief explanation.

As you know, many security vulnerabilities are embedded in all applications. It is crucial to identify and assess the risks of potential exposure and resolve these weak points immediately. The **Open Web Applications Security Project** (**OWASP**) (https://www.owasp.org/) is a not-for-profit organization that helps the information security industry improve software security to benefit everyone.

OWASP provides a Top-10 list, which is often updated, of the most critical security risks relating to application architecture that enterprises face worldwide. At the time of writing, this list includes the following:

- Broken access control

- Cryptographic failures

- Injection

- Insecure design

- Security misconfiguration

- Vulnerable and outdated components

- Identification and authentication failures

- Software and data integrity failure

Going back to AWS WAF, to understand how it offers protection against these security risks, you need to look at the three primary components involved in its design:

- **Web ACL**: This is used to protect your AWS resources. They contain rules and rule groups that define what should be inspected within your requests.

- **Rules**: The rules themselves essentially comprise `if/then` statements and help define specific criteria for what the web ACL should inspect and what action (that is, allow, block, or count) to take upon the inspection result.

- **Rule groups**: Rule groups allow you to group a set of rules together.

Security Automations for AWS WAF helps deploy sets of preconfigured AWS WAF rules to filter common web-based attacks, such as the following:

- SQL injection

- Cross-site scripting

- HTTP floods

- Scanners and probes

- Known attacker origins (IP reputation lists)

- Bots and scrapers

Adding Layers of Defense with AWS Shield

While AWS WAF can provide several protections to your CloudFront origins and application load balancers, AWS Shield protects against more complex DDoS attacks, such as volumetric attacks. The following table compares AWS Shield and AWS WAF.

	AWS WAF	AWS Shield
	HTTP Floods	State-Exhaustion Attacks
	DNS Query Floods	Volumetric Attacks
Protection from	SQL Injection	
	Cross-Site Scripting	
	Remote File Injection	

Table 3.1: AWS WAF versus AWS Shield

With the preceding comparison between the two services covered, we will dive deeper into the details of the AWS Shield service in the following subsections.

The Two Tiers of AWS Shield

Your environment and how much protection you require at which level will determine the AWS Shield tier that you implement. Currently, there are two tiers available:

- **AWS Shield Standard**: This first tier is freely available to anyone with an AWS account. AWS Shield Standard provides basic protection against DDoS attacks.

- **AWS Shield Advanced**: This second tier is a premium tier with additional features and protection. These additional features come with additional costs.

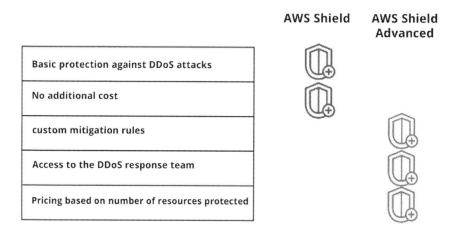

AWS Shield   **AWS Shield Advanced**

Basic protection against DDoS attacks
No additional cost
custom mitigation rules
Access to the DDoS response team
Pricing based on number of resources protected

Figure 3.5: AWS Shield versus Shield Advanced features

In summary, AWS Shield is a basic DDoS protection service, while AWS Shield Advanced provides enhanced protection and additional features for more complex and sophisticated DDoS attacks.

Strengthening the Security Posture of Your AWS Account

Having explored the different types of attacks you may be subject to, you might be wondering how you can effectively protect your organization against all the threats it will face. This section deals with the steps you can take for the same.

When running a **Cloud Security Posture Assessment** (**CPSA**) against your account(s), you will need to create a role that will give read-only permissions to the service or tool performing the assessment. The assessment thoroughly reviews an organization's cloud security policies, processes, and controls. It can also include an examination of the technical infrastructure that supports the organization's cloud environment. The assessor can uncover potential weaknesses that an attacker would exploit by reviewing the account's access controls, conducting vulnerability assessments, and analyzing security logs.

The following is a list of some of the vulnerabilities that are commonly found during a CSPA and reported back to the customer:

- **RDS**: Backups are not enabled and data is vulnerable

- **EC2**: An EC2 instance exposed directly to the internet increases the attack surface

- **CloudTrail**: Log file validation is not enabled, preventing additional integrity checks

- **IAM**: The root user has **multifactor authentication** (**MFA**) attached, which leaves the root account at risk of password hijacking

There are hundreds more checks that encompass a CPSA. These checks range from critical, high, medium, and low to informational. These checks are not there to simply show you where there are vulnerabilities in your account. Instead, the main goal of CPSA checks is to help your organization find areas that contain risks and weaknesses and develop an actionable plan to correct these items, improving your account's overall security posture. AWS provides a service that helps with organizing your CPSA as you continually work to plug vulnerabilities found in your account. This service is AWS Security Hub, and we will provide a full overview of it in *Chapter 6, Event Management with Security Hub and GuardDuty*.

Summary

In this chapter, you learned about some of the most prevalent attacks that security engineers face. This knowledge of common attacks puts the need for security services into perspective. It also gives you an understanding of the various services you will need as you go through the rest of this book with a crucial purpose. That purpose is to not only protect your cloud assets and data but to also gain knowledge about the very common, specific types of attacks that they may face.

You also explored one of the most prevalent attacks, DDoS, in depth, including how these attacks occur and which AWS services (namely, AWS WAF and AWS Shield/Shield Advanced, among others) help mitigate them.

The next chapter will detail sections dedicated to the AWS Certified Security Specialty domains, specifically *Domain 1: Incident Response*. It will begin with a focus on incident response and how it is handled in the context of an AWS account (or multiple accounts).

Further Reading

For additional information on the AWS shared responsibility model and for a better understanding of AWS security, refer to the following resources:

- **AWS Startup Security Baseline** (**AWS SSB**): `https://packt.link/TEj5U`

- AWS **Foundational Security Best Practices** (**FSBP**) standard: `https://packt.link/PUdKl`

- AWS Managed Rules group list for AWS WAF: `https://packt.link/3v6om`

- Security Automations for AWS WAF: `https://packt.link/g8xlD`

- OWASP Cloud-Native Application Security Top 10: `https://packt.link/2Hz5K`

- What is a DDoS Attack? `https://packt.link/2Hz5K`

- Disaster Recovery of Workloads on AWS: Recovery in the Cloud (whitepaper): `https://packt.link/V5tJO`

Exam Readiness Drill – Chapter Review Questions

Apart from a solid understanding of key concepts, being able to think quickly under time pressure is a skill that will help you ace your certification exam. That is why working on these skills early on in your learning journey is key.

Chapter review questions are designed to improve your test-taking skills progressively with each chapter you learn and review your understanding of key concepts in the chapter at the same time. You'll find these at the end of each chapter.

> **How To Access These Resources**
>
> To learn how to access these resources, head over to the chapter titled *Chapter 21, Accessing the Online Practice Resources*.

To open the Chapter Review Questions for this chapter, perform the following steps:

1. Click the link – `https://packt.link/SCSC02E2_CH03`.

    Alternatively, you can scan the following QR code (*Figure 3.6*):

Figure 3.6: QR code that opens Chapter Review Questions for logged-in users

2. Once you log in, you'll see a page similar to the one shown in *Figure 3.7*:

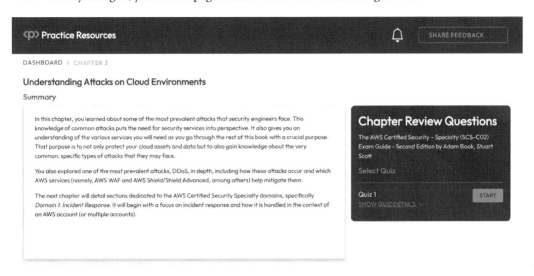

Figure 3.7: Chapter Review Questions for Chapter 3

3. Once ready, start the following practice drills, re-attempting the quiz multiple times.

Exam Readiness Drill

For the first three attempts, don't worry about the time limit.

ATTEMPT 1

The first time, aim for at least **40%**. Look at the answers you got wrong and read the relevant sections in the chapter again to fix your learning gaps.

ATTEMPT 2

The second time, aim for at least **60%**. Look at the answers you got wrong and read the relevant sections in the chapter again to fix any remaining learning gaps.

ATTEMPT 3

The third time, aim for at least **75%**. Once you score **75%** or more, you start working on your timing.

> **Tip**
>
> You may take more than three attempts to reach 75%. That's okay. Just review the relevant sections in the chapter till you get there.

Working On Timing

Target: Your aim is to keep the score the same while trying to answer these questions as quickly as possible. Here's an example of how your next attempts should look like:

Attempt	Score	Time Taken
Attempt 5	77%	21 mins 30 seconds
Attempt 6	78%	18 mins 34 seconds
Attempt 7	76%	14 mins 44 seconds

Table 3.2: Sample timing practice drills on the online platform

> **Note**
>
> The time limits shown in the above table are just examples. Set your own time limits with each attempt based on the time limit of the quiz on the website.

With each new attempt, your score should stay above 75% while your time taken to complete should **decrease**. Repeat as many attempts as you want till you feel confident dealing with the time pressure.

Section 2:
Incident Response

With the AWS fundamentals under your belt, you can now start to tackle the main domains of the *AWS Certified Security Certification Exam*. This begins with incident response. With this section, you will gain an understanding of how to handle incidents manually as well as how to automate responses.

Techniques for capturing events, preparing for an incident, and responding to the actual incident are covered in this section. You will also go through walk-throughs of various services, with a focus on the specifics of the **Systems Manager Incident Response**, **AWS Config Service**, **Security Hub**, and **GuardDuty** services.

This section comprises the following chapters:

- *Chapter 4, Incident Response*
- *Chapter 5, Managing Your Environment with AWS Config*
- *Chapter 6, Event Management with Security Hub and GuardDuty*

4

Incident Response

With a grasp on what you are responsible for from an AWS customer perspective, you can now turn to the pillars that will be tested in the exam. The first pillar is **incident response** (**IR**). Knowing how to prepare and then react, in both a manual and an automated fashion, when something occurs in one of your AWS accounts is necessary—not only from the exam perspective but also in real life.

As you will see in this chapter, preparation is crucial to IR. This includes gathering the correct team members responsible for participating in any IR activities. Preparation also includes creating (and testing) runbooks and playbooks that can help team members know the exact set of instructions to follow and cut down on the response time in the event of an incident. Further, enabling the correct set of logs and visibility services so that you and your team can construct monitoring mechanisms and alerts for abnormal activity are all part of the pre-incident process.

Unfortunately, it is not possible to stop all security events from arising. As technology changes, new vulnerabilities, threats, and risks are introduced. Combine that with human error, and incidents will undoubtedly occur. Because of these factors, there is a need to implement an IR policy and various associated processes.

The following main topics will be covered in this chapter:

- The goals of IR
- Using AWS Cloud Native services in IR
- Responding to an incident
- Adding automation for IR

Technical Requirements

There is a requirement to understand AWS and networking concepts, and you will need access to the AWS Management Console and an active AWS account to follow along with any of the step-by-step guides presented in this chapter.

The Goals of Incident Response

The goals of IR can be broken down into short-term and long-term goals. Ultimately, you want to be in a position where you no longer have to engage in IR. A short-term goal for an organization may be to ensure that all the logging is in place and notification systems are enabled in case of an incident. Long-term goals may take the form of compiling scripted playbooks with detailed steps so that new team members can quickly and efficiently respond to an incident or, better yet, prepare automated responses. For instance, services such as Systems Manager documents and Lambda functions that trigger automatically based on items found in logs mean no person needs to respond. The response happens before anyone can even turn on their computer.

It all begins with having a plan. A playbook with scripted steps that you or other team members can follow can relieve the stress of an event. An automated runbook or predefined templates (such as CloudFormation templates) can help you recover. Having such items already developed and tested can help shorten the event's time.

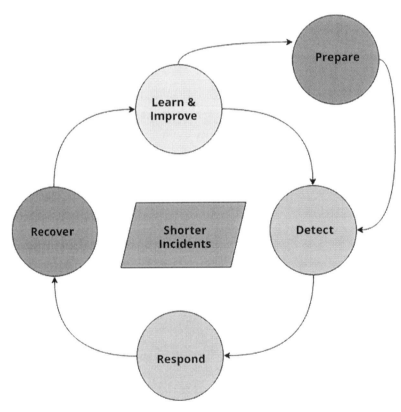

Figure 4.1: The Incident response process continual loop

In *Figure 4.1*, you see the IR cycle and how it can lead to shorter incidents, which is the goal of any IR. As you begin detection, you can respond to the abnormality detected. After the incident has been contained, you can recover and bring your account back to a steady running state. Once things are running normally, you can take time to learn and improve from the previous incident, noting any deficiencies that might have been encountered or steps performed that could be automated in the future. You also may notice that the information you are gathering needs to be more efficient and may need to turn on additional logging or that one or more of the instructions in the runbook must be corrected.

All of this can be corrected in the *Prepare* stage so that the IR team and systems are running as optimally as possible, and the cycle of the following incident becomes shorter.

As you will see later in this chapter, the AWS System Manager service has several tools that can help you from a technology perspective regarding the operational side of IR.

Now that you understand the goals of IR, take a look at some of the best practices that AWS has come up with in the area of **the AWS Well-Architected Framework (WAF)**.

The AWS WAF Security Pillars

For constructing or reviewing AWS accounts that are secure, highly available, and efficient, AWS has developed a framework that incorporates foundational best practices with regard to six pillars—the WAF. The pillars of the WAF consist of the following items:

- Operational excellence

- Security

- Reliability

- Performance efficiency

- Cost optimization

- Sustainability

This framework helps you transition and migrate solutions into the AWS cloud based on best practices and recommendations.

If you are not yet familiar with the AWS WAF, it is suggested that you review its contents.

This chapter will highlight some of the areas of the security pillar whitepaper written for the WAF (`https://packt.link/pg1da`) that are of specific relevance to IR, both on how you set up your accounts from a preparation standpoint and the stated goals of IR in the whitepaper.

WAF Security – *Security Foundations*

The first part of the WAF security pillar discusses the security foundations that should be part of every account. These are baseline best practices to help an account's security posture and mitigate the chances of a security incident. If an incident were to occur and these foundations were already put in place, then the essential tools would be there for items such as detection and isolation, which will be discussed later in this chapter.

The seven security foundation principles are as follows:

- **Implement a strong identity foundation**: Use the principle of least privilege when crafting IAM policies. Also, segregate user and group roles by the permissions needed to perform their job functions.

- **Enable traceability**: You can observe when changes are happening on your account with the appropriate level of logging turned on, monitoring available, and alerts sent out when something out of the ordinary happens.

- **Apply security at all layers**: A layered defense approach means that you have security controls starting at the boundary (edge nodes and moving on to the **virtual private cloud** (**VPC**)) and then moving inwards, protecting your load balancers, instances, and ultimately, your data.

- **Automate security best practices**: Have your architecture implemented as **infrastructure as code** (**IaC**) to rapidly recover any changes in your environment. Also, put in place automated processes to respond to security events.

- **Protect data in transit and at rest**: Any data previously classified as sensitive needs the appropriate level of protection, including encryption and access control.

- **Keep people away from data**: Use tools that minimize the need for people to access the data directly; you can control who and what gets access, decreasing the opportunities for data loss and corruption.

- **Prepare for security events**: Having security policies and processes in place before a security event occurs is necessary in today's world as any systems that are initiated are instantly subject to attack from sources worldwide.

Not all of these foundational principles apply to the concept of IR. However, they do apply to the concepts of securing your AWS account and looking and parsing through the questions of the *Security Specialty Certification*. Knowing these foundational guidelines and when they are or are not being applied in the exam questions can help you decipher some of the answers on the exam.

Out of the seven security foundations we defined, the following three are the most important for IR: enable traceability, automate security best practices, and prepare for security events.

Now that you have examined the security foundations of the WAF, you can dive deeper into how you can prepare for security events by creating a forensic AWS account.

Forensic AWS Account

A separate AWS account for forensic investigations is ideal to help you diagnose and isolate the affected resources. By utilizing a separate account, you can architect the environment to be more securely appropriate to its forensic use. You could even use AWS Control Tower to provision the account quickly, using the account vending machine. Once the account has been provisioned, you could use an additional CloudFormation template to set up all the correct S3 buckets and provision any other resources you would need from a configuration standpoint. A process such as this allows you to build the account and environment using a known configuration without relying on manual processes that could be susceptible to errors, which would be undesirable in the early stages of a forensic investigation. This setup can also allow you to spin up the account and take it back down when not in use for extended periods.

While investigating, you should ensure your steps and actions are auditable; this can be done by using logging mechanisms such as CloudTrail and CloudWatch logs. Having your logs all go to a centralized logging account for storage is the best practice. A centralized logging account is a security recommendation listed in the WAF security pillar.

The following section will examine prescriptive IR guidance based on the *AWS Security Incident Response Guide*.

Incident Response Guidance from AWS

AWS has taken lessons learned from a number of customer incidents and along with a few other industry-leading resources, such as the *NIST SP 800-61 Computer Security Incident Handling Guide*, compiled a guide to help with IR. This guide is composed of three major sections:

- **Preparation**: This involves detecting and responding to incidents when they occur in your accounts. This includes the preparation of playbooks and runbooks, which can be manual, automated, or a combination of the two. These allow quick and consistent responses to incidents.

- **Operations**: This is when the incident has occurred and you are following the NIST phases of IR: **detect**, **analyze**, **contain**, **eradicate**, and **recover**.

- **Post-incident activity**: Once the incident is over, the team needs to take time to understand and record how the events transpired. This is an excellent time to take away any lessons learned and action items to make the response go smoother the next time it is needed.

One of the main aspects addressed in the AWS security pillar whitepaper is containment. When an event requires an IR, you (and your team) must be able to contain the damage. According to the AWS security pillar whitepaper, you should have a containment strategy for any or all of the following reasons:

- To stop or prevent potential damage to and theft of your resources and data

- To preserve evidence

- If the response will take time to implement
- If you are unsure of the effectiveness of the response
- If you are unsure how long the response would be effective

There are multiple ways to enforce containment in an AWS account, which you will go through now.

Containment can be refined down to three main concepts:

- **Source containment** is the use and implementation of filtering access to all or specific resources from a specific IP or range of IP addresses. You can execute this type of containment using items such as security groups that can explicitly allow or deny traffic to EC2 instances or other AWS resources. S3 bucket policies or **access control lists** (**ACLs**) can also be used as a source containment method, and you could use the web application firewall service for more fine-grained control.

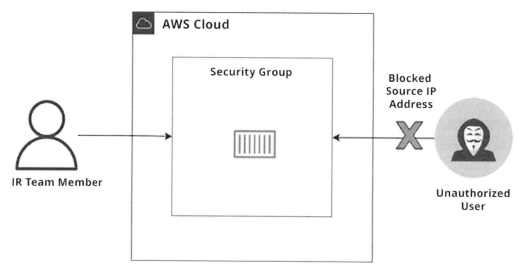

Figure 4.2: Source containment example

- **Destination containment** is the use and implementation of filtering access to a specific resource. This can be accomplished by shutting down the resource. You can also contain the resource by removing it or detaching it from any autoscaling groups or load balancers so that the EC2 instance can no longer receive traffic. Another method of destination containment is adding a **Network Access Control List** (**NACL**) and denying rules to prevent access to a particular resource. The rule could be created with a single deny rule for both inbound and outbound access to the targeted resource.

- **Technique and access containment** prevent the use of resources by limiting the actions that IAM principals and functions have concerning those resources. This can include actions taken, such as removing previously granted privileges or rescinding a combination of access keys or temporary access keys and security credentials.

Although containment is only one part of the IR process, the steps needed to perform containment for various scenarios should be preconceived before any exploit. This way, each scenario can be mapped to either a manual or an automated containment response.

The following section presents an overview of these areas from the security pillar whitepaper, as questions on the exam can come from knowing how to handle incidents in the manner that AWS prescribes.

A Common Approach to an Infrastructure Security Incident

The following quickly highlights a common response approach to an infrastructure-related security incident involving an EC2 instance:

1. **Capture**: You should try and capture any metadata from the instance before you proceed and make any further changes related to your environment.

2. **Protect**: To prevent the EC2 instance from being accidentally terminated, enable termination protection while you continue to investigate

3. **Isolate**: You should then isolate the instance by modifying the security group or updating the NACL to deny all traffic destined for the IP address of the instance.

4. **Detach**: Remove the affected instance from any autoscaling groups.

5. **Deregister**: If the instance is associated with any **Elastic Load Balancers** (**ELBs**), you must remove it from those load balancers.

6. **Snapshot**: Take a copy of any EBS volumes via a snapshot to investigate further without affecting the original volumes.

7. **Tag**: Using tags, you should highlight the instance that has been prepared for forensic investigation.

You will not be expected to know the commands to carry out the preceding steps via the AWS CLI, but should you wish to do this, please review the steps provided in the *AWS Security Incident Response Guide* located in the resource section of this chapter.

Using this set of steps as a guideline, you can map out steps and create runbooks to help you and your team members respond to incidents methodically. You will see these steps in action a bit later in this chapter.

With an understanding of the steps needed to take part in the operations side of IR, now examine some of the tools that AWS offers to aid in responding to incidents.

Technology Tools to Guide Us in the Operations Aspect

Across the many different AWS services, there are a handful of tools you should concentrate on when it comes to IR. Some of them come in the detection phase so that you can be alerted that an incident is either in the process of occurring or has recently occurred. The other tools fall into the response or operation phase, where you take actions to mitigate the incident and return to a normal running state.

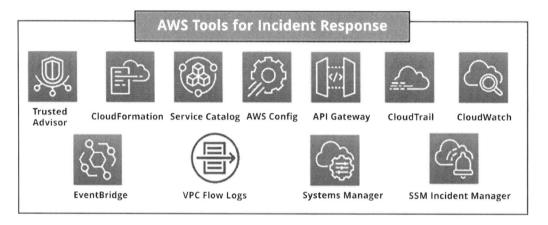

Figure 4.3: AWS Tools for IR

Having had a look at the majority of the native tools that would be used in IR, you can move on to the detection process next.

Detection

Detection can come in several different forms. There are a variety of different steps you can take: obtaining the logs for the data, visibility into your environments, and then parsing that data for relevant information to send an alert if something is out of the ordinary.

These processes are distinct but they often work together. The collected logs are shown on the services that provide visibility to you as the security or system administrator. These logs also contain the events and metrics, which trigger the alerting so that action can be taken on the account.

Logging

AWS has numerous services that offer logging capabilities to capture vital information when analyzing the source of a threat and how to prevent it. When using your chosen services, you should enable logging. This is often overlooked, which can be a massive regret for organizations should the worst happen. With active logging, you will have a much higher chance of rectifying an incident quickly and efficiently or even preventing it from occurring by spotting patterns and trends.

Logging allows you to baseline your infrastructure of what's *normal* and what can be considered *abnormal* operations. This helps identify and isolate anomalies quickly, especially when combined with third-party logging and analysis tools.

Again, having logs running continuously and automatically by the supported AWS services allows you to view the state of your environment before, during, and after an incident. This helps you gather intelligence and insight into where the incident occurred in your infrastructure and how to prevent it from happening again.

Some examples of services that offer logging in AWS include Amazon CloudWatch Logs, AWS CloudTrail logs, S3 access logs, VPC Flow Logs, AWS Config configuration recorder, CloudFront Logs, and Application Load Balancer logs. There are more logs available from AWS for other niche services; however, from this list alone, you can see that logging is an excellent method of helping you resolve a security incident as quickly as possible. These logs should be readily and easily available to the security and audit team in the event you are responding to an incident as part of your IR policy.

> **Note**
>
> Logging and monitoring will be covered in depth in *Section 3* of the book because the ability to understand logging and monitoring, especially regarding the security of your AWS environment, is one of the pillars of the AWS Certified Security – Speciality certification.

Alerting

When an event in your AWS account has occurred, you want to ensure you are notified. Base services such as Amazon **Simple Notification Service** (**SNS**) can send messages to those who are subscribed to the topics used in IR. However, a method must be in place to trigger the sending of the messages.

Amazon **EventBridge** is a service that allows rule creation to trigger actions on other services, such as Lambda functions, AWS Step Functions, and SNS topics. Understanding what services would necessitate either a notification being sent out or another service being started is one of the skills that an AWS security engineer needs to have a firm grasp of.

Visibility

Other services offered by AWS provide different visibility and insights into your accounts to help you understand where malicious activity or an incident could occur.

Amazon Detective is a security service that helps simplify the investigative process for security teams by using machine learning and statistical analysis to show the interactions between users and resources over time in an empirical view. Amazon Detective collects log data from several sources, such as VPC Flow Logs, CloudTrail, and **Amazon GuardDuty**, and then creates a unified interactive view of your resources and users over time.

Amazon GuardDuty is a region-based managed service powered by machine learning, specifically designed to be an intelligent threat detection service. It monitors logs from other services and features, including VPC Flow Logs, DNS Logs, and AWS CloudTrail event logs. AWS GuardDuty looks at these logs to detect unexpected and unusual behavior and cross-reference these analytics with many threat detection and security feeds that can help identify potentially malicious activity and anomalies.

Amazon Macie is the machine-learning-powered service that discovers and helps classify sensitive data stored in your account, such as **personally identifiable information** (**PII**), so you can assign a business value and keep both a closer track of this data and tighten the security policies as your organization sees fit.

AWS Security Hub integrates with other services, such as Amazon GuardDuty, Amazon Inspector, and Amazon Macie. This is in addition to various AWS Partner products and toolsets.

This scope of integration allows AWS Security Hub to act as a single-pane-of-glass view across your infrastructure, thus bringing all your security statistical data into a single place and presenting it in a series of tables and graphs. For those that manage multiple AWS accounts, Security Hub can operate across all of them using a primary-subordinate relationship. The service operates as an always-on service, continuously running and processing data in the background, automatically allowing the service to identify any discrepancies against best practices. The analysis of the data received by the different integrated services is checked against industry standards, such as the **Center for Internet Security** (**CIS**) benchmarks, thus enabling the service to spot and identify potential vulnerabilities and weak spots across multiple accounts against specific resources. Early detection of weaknesses and non-compliance is valuable in safeguarding your data.

> **Note**
>
> You will take a deeper look into AWS Security Hub and GuardDuty, along with a sample walkthrough, in *Chapter 6*, *Event Management with Security Hub and GuardDuty*.

These services are in conjunction with, not in competition with, the logging, monitoring, and alerting services discussed earlier. Running compute, network, and data environments is a complex operation and needs a defense-in-depth strategy to maintain the environment's safety.

With a solid grasp of how logging ties into your IR strategy, you are now ready to move on to see how to handle the actual response to the incident. This will be covered in the next section.

Response/Operation

After the incident has been detected, you need to be able to respond to the alert. Often, this will be a manual operation involving disabling any access gained in an unauthorized manner or removing any resources or instances created without prior consent.

Unauthorized Activity in Your Account

If you receive a notice from AWS support that there has been abuse in your account or if you suspect that there has been unauthorized activity in your account, the following steps can help you confirm that it was an actual unauthorized activity:

- Validate if any resources have been created illegitimately.

- Validate any unauthorized access or changes to your account.

- Validate any unauthorized actions that have been performed in the IAM service, including adding or modifying managed policies, users, or roles.

- Run the credential report for your AWS account to see when the last time each password and access key/secret key was used for each IAM user.

- Run the Trusted Advisor Reports to see if new violations have appeared since the last time you ran your report.

- Go to the AWS Cost Explorer and verify that extra resources have not been spun up (and possibly spun down) since the time you suspect the abuse.

What to Do if You Do Find Traces of Abuse

If performing the preceding steps shows signs of abuse in your account or illegitimate activity in your account, then you should take the following steps:

1. **Rotate and delete any exposed access keys / secret access keys**:

    I.   Create a new AWS access key and secret access key in AWS IAM.

    II.   Alter any applications using the previous access key to use the new access key.

    III. Deactivate the original access key only. Do not delete the original access key that is compromised yet.

    IV. After verifying that your applications are fully operational with the new access key, you can go back and delete the original access key.

    V.   Delete any root account access keys you do not use or did not create.

2. **Remove and rotate credentials for potentially compromised IAM users**:

    I.   Navigate to the IAM console.

    II.   Choose users from the left-hand navigation pane so that a list of users from your account appears.

    III. Delete any users that you (or your team) did not create. Running the IAM access analyzer tool will allow you to see any recently created users and show any usernames that do not conform to your corporate policy.

IV.   Moving back to the list of IAM users, select the name of the first IAM user on the list so that the IAM user's summary appears.

V.   In the `Permissions` tab, under the `Permissions policies` section, search for the policy named `AWSExposedCredentialPolicy_DO_NOT_REMOVE`. If the user already has this policy attached, you can go ahead and rotate the access keys for the user.

VI.   Replicate *Step III and Step IV* for all the users listed in your account.

VII. Change all passwords for all users in your account.

3. **Verify your account information**: Go to your account contact information and verify that the following is still correct:

- Your account name and email address

- Your contact information, including your phone number

- Any alternative contacts that you have put on your AWS account

Now that you know how to deal with an incident regarding unauthorized access into our AWS account, you can learn how to isolate an EC2 instance that you suspected of suspicious behavior to examine it further.

EC2 Resource Isolation

Assume you have an EC2 instance initiating unexpected API behavior. This has been identified as an anomaly and is considered to be an abnormal operation. As a result, this instance is showing signs of being a potentially compromised resource. Until you have identified the cause, you must isolate the resource to minimize the effect, impact, and potential damage that could occur to other resources within your AWS account. This action should be undertaken immediately. By isolating the instance, you prevent any further connectivity to and from it, minimizing the chances of data being removed. After creating a copy of the EC2 instance using an **Amazon Machine Image** (**AMI**), you should then terminate the initial instance which you have quarantined to stop any further misuse of it.

The quickest and most effective way to isolate an instance would be to change its associated security group with one that would prevent any access to or from the instance. As an additional precaution, you should remove any roles associated with the instance.

To perform a forensic investigation of the affected resources, you will want to move the EC2 instance to your forensic account (discussed previously). However, moving the same instance to a different AWS account is impossible. Instead, you will need to perform the following high-level steps:

1. First, create an AMI from the affected EC2 instance.

2. Share the newly created AMI image with your forensic account by modifying the AMI permissions.

3. From within your forensic account, locate the AMI from within the EC2 console or AWS CLI.

4. Finally, create a new instance from the shared AMI.

> **Note**
>
> For detailed instructions on how to carry out each of these steps, please visit the following AWS documentation: `https://packt.link/nMVwx`.

Copying Data

Again, following the previous example of a compromised EC2 instance, assume that the instance was backed by EBS storage. You may want to isolate and analyze the storage from this instance from within your forensic account, which can be achieved through EBS snapshots. These snapshots are essential incremental backups of your EBS volumes.

Creating a snapshot for your EBS volumes is a simple process:

1. Select the EC2 service from the Compute category within the AWS Management Console.

2. Select `Volumes` from under the `Elastic Block Store` menu heading on the left:

Figure 4.4: Elastic block store menu

3. Select your volume from the list of volumes displayed:

Figure 4.5: Volumes list

4. Select the `Actions` menu and select `Create snapshot`:

Figure 4.6: The Actions menu

5. Add a description and any tags that are required:

Create snapshot Info

Create a point-in-time snapshot to back up the data on an Amazon EBS volume to Amazon S3.

Details

Volume ID
🗗 vol-00280722717a00146 (MY_EBS_VOLUME)

Description
Add a description for your snapshot

| IR Snapshot |

255 characters maximum.

Encryption   Info
Not encrypted

Figure 4.7: Create snapshot

6. Select `Create snapshot`. At this point, you will get a message at the top of the console stating that the requested snapshot has succeeded:

Figure 4.8: Success message for snapshot creation

7. Click on Close.

8. You can now ensure that your snapshot has been created by selecting Snapshot from under the Elastic Block Store menu on the left:

▼ **Elastic Block Store**

Volumes

Snapshots

Lifecycle Manager

Figure 4.9: Elastic block store menu—Snapshots

9. From here, you will see your newly created snapshot:

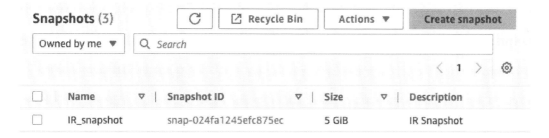

Figure 4.10: Snapshots list

As you can see, creating an EBS snapshot of your volumes is a straightforward process.

Similarly, for AMI images, you must modify the permissions of your EBS snapshots to share them from within another account. For more information on how to do this, please visit the following link: https://docs.aws.amazon.com/AWSEC2/latest/UserGuide/ebs-modifying-snapshot-permissions.html.

Once the snapshot has been shared with the forensic account, IR engineers will be able to recreate the EBS volume from the snapshot.

Systems Manager Incident Manager

AWS has a native tool that allows you to track, respond to incidents, and even alert those responsible for responding to the incidents, all from a single service: **Systems Manager Incident Manager**.

Before an incident ever happens, you need to prepare for it. This involves the formulation and analysis of escalation and response plans, the creation of System Manager Automation runbooks, and coordination with contacts at the three levels, all of which can be seen in the flow chart in *Figure 4.11*:

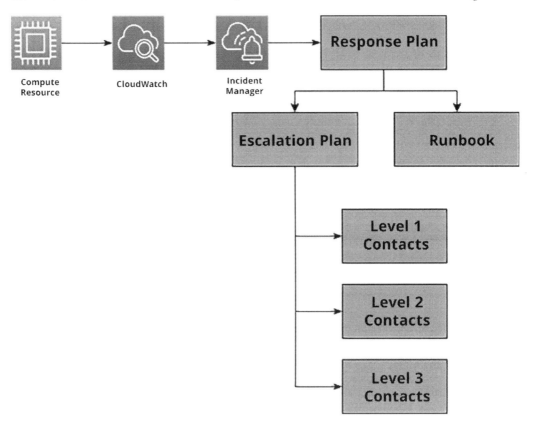

Figure 4.11: Systems Manager Incident Manager flow

One of the critical things to know about Incident Manager is how the runbooks are created. This is done from System Manager documents. There is a template that can be used as a response runbook in Incident Manager available for customization that includes four predefined steps: **triage**, **diagnosis**, **mitigation**, and **recovery**.

When creating your runbook, you need to clone and customize this template for your IR scenario.

You need to set up a System Manager Incident Manager to be able to respond to an incident. Before going through the Incident Manager service, you must create an IAM role for the service. If you do not complete this step and don't have a role that the Incident Manager can use, you will have to go back and create the role as you are trying to develop your response plan. To complete this process, perform the following steps:

1. Open up the AWS Console in the `IAM Service` from `https://console.aws.amazon.com/iam/`.

2. Choose `Roles` from the left-hand navigation and then choose `Create role`.

3. On the `Select trusted entity` screen, choose `AWS service` as the `Trusted entity type`.

Select trusted entity Info

Trusted entity type

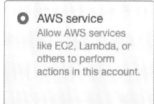

Figure 4.12: Trusted entity types

4. From the Use cases for other AWS services: dropdown, select Incident Manager.

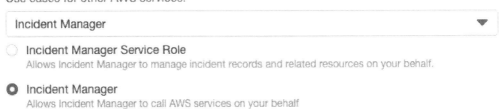

Figure 4.13: AWS services use cases dropdown

5. Click on the Next button at the bottom of the page to advance.

6. Choose Create policy, and then choose the JSON tab.

7. Use the following base policy but remember to replace the account number with your own account number. Once that is all in the JSON editor, click the Next: Tags button:

```
{
    "Version": "2012-10-17",
    "Statement": [
        {
            "Effect": "Allow",
            "Resource": "arn:aws:ssm:*:1234567890:automation-definition/*",
            "Action": "ssm:StartAutomationExecution"
        },
        {
            "Effect": "Allow",
            "Resource": "arn:aws:iam::*:role/AWS-SystemsManager-
AutomationExecutionRole",
            "Action": "sts:AssumeRole"
        },
        {
            "Effect": "Allow",
            "Resource": "arn:aws:ssm-incidents:*:*:*",
            "Action": "ssm-incidents:*"
        },
```

```
  {
    "Effect": "Allow",
    "Resource": "arn:aws:ssm-contacts:*:*:*",
    "Action": "ssm-contacts:*"
  }
  ]
}
```

8. Click on the `Next:Review` button to move to the screen where you can name your policy. Name your policy `Incident-Manager-Policy` and add a description if you wish. Click on the `Create policy` button at the bottom of the page.

Your IAM role is now ready, and you can go forward with setting up Incident Manager:

1. If you haven't already, open the AWS Console in the `System Manager Service`.

2. In the left-hand menu, under `Operations Management`, click on `Incident Manager`.

3. If you have never used the Incident Manager service, click the `Get prepared` button on the main screen.

    This will take you to a screen where you can start with the general settings. Put in the contact details of whoever you want to be contacted in case of an incident, then define your escalation plans and your response plan.

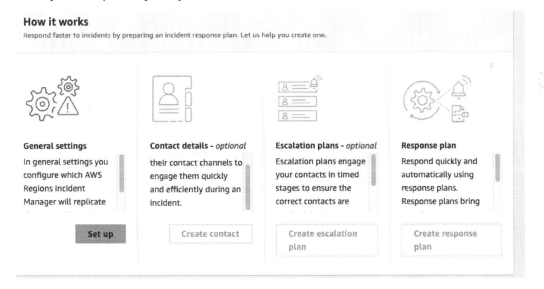

Figure 4.14: Incident Manager—How it works

4. To start the process of entering your general settings, click the Set up button under General Settings. You must agree to the terms and conditions by clicking the checkbox and then the Next button.

    At this point, you will be taken to a screen to select the regions where you want the Incident Manager to be active. The default region will be the AWS region that you are currently in. In this example, this region is US EAST (Ohio), and this is the only region that will be set up now.

Figure 4.15: Incident Manager—Regions

5. Located at the bottom of the same page are the KMS encryption settings and optional tags settings. For this demonstration, select Use AWS owned key.

Figure 4.16: The Incident Manager KMS key selection

When you have finished setting this up, click on the orange Create button at the bottom of the screen.

6. You will be brought back to the How it works screen, where it should take about a minute to configure the General Settings. Once these settings have been configured, you can define a contact to respond to an incident by clicking the Create contact button directly to the right.

7. In the Contact details box, enter the name of your first contact. You will also need to add an alias for each contact.

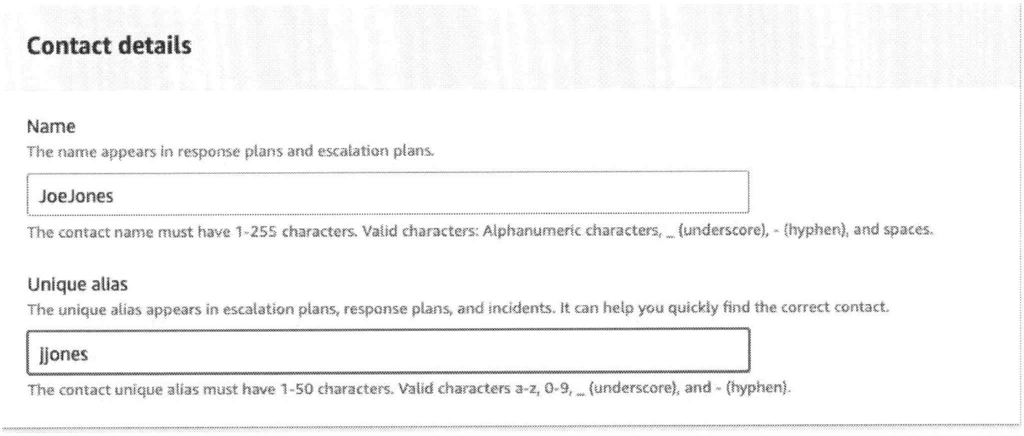

Contact details
Name
The name appears in response plans and escalation plans.
JoeJones
The contact name must have 1-255 characters. Valid characters: Alphanumeric characters, _ (underscore), - (hyphen), and spaces.
Unique alias
The unique alias appears in escalation plans, response plans, and incidents. It can help you quickly find the correct contact.
jjones
The contact unique alias must have 1-50 characters. Valid characters a-z, 0-9, _ (underscore), and - (hyphen).

Figure 4.17: Contact details screen

8. Then, under `Contact Channel`, choose from `Email`, `SMS`, or `Voice`. For this example, name the channel called `Tier1` and select `SMS`.

Contact channel
Contact channels are the methods Incident Manager can use to engage a contact. Use contact channels to define an engagement plan and engage the contact.
Type
Channel name
Detail
SMS
Tier1
+1234567890
Remove
Add contact channel

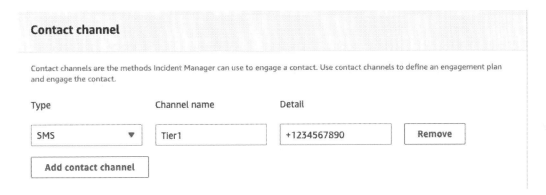

Figure 4.18: The Contact channel screen for Incident Manager

9. Under the `Engagement Plan`, choose when this set of contacts gets notified. Since this is the first tier of support, have them notified in 1 minute. Set the `Engagement time` to `1 Minutes after stage start`.
10. With all the details set for your initial contact, press the orange `Create` button at the bottom of the page.
11. After creating your contact, you will return to the `How it works` screen. At this point, move to the right side of the graphic for the column named `Response plan` and click the orange button called `Create response plan`.

12. Now, on the `Create response plan` page, in the `Response plan details` box, enter your response plan's name. For your particular response plan that you are creating, you will be shutting down an EC2 instance when you receive an alert as part of a containment strategy.

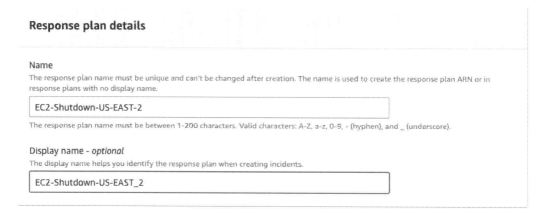

Figure 4.19: Response plan details for Incident Manager

13. Now, fill out the `Incident defaults`. This will tell anyone running your response plan what will happen and what steps to take.

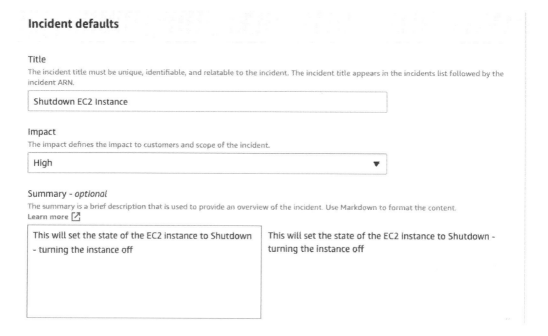

Figure 4.20: Incident defaults for Incident Manager

14. Next, scroll down on the page until you reach the box labeled `Engagements`. Here, click on the dropdown and select the contact you added before, `Joe Jones`, so he can be a part of this IR.

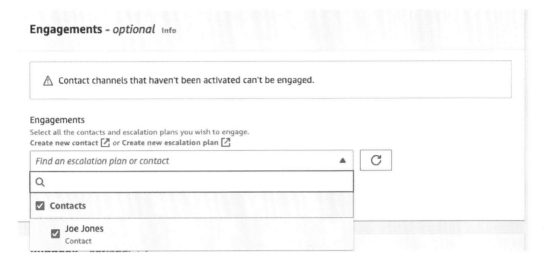

Figure 4.21: Engagements for Incident Manager

15. Finally, choose `Clone runbook from template` in the Runbook section. Keep the same runbook name as the one you have been using for your response plan, `EC2-Shutdown-US-EAST-2`. Since you previously created your role, you should be able to choose it from the dropdown.

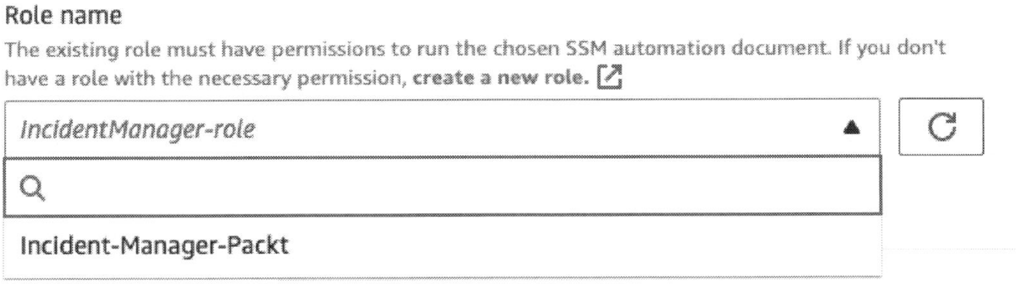

Role name

The existing role must have permissions to run the chosen SSM automation document. If you don't have a role with the necessary permission, **create a new role.**

IncidentManager-role ▲   C

Q

Incident-Manager-Packt

Figure 4.22: Role selection for Incident Manager

16. For `Execution Target`, choose `Response plan owner's account`.

17. At this point, you can scroll to the bottom of the page and click the orange button labeled `Create response plan`.

You have just gone through how to set up AWS System Manager Incident Manager to prepare it to respond to incidents in your AWS Account. Next, we will examine other ways to automate your responses to incidents in your AWS accounts.

Using Automation as a Response to Incident Response

AWS has several tools that allow you to automate security responses with human intervention and without it.

As you saw in the previous example, using Systems Manager Incident Manager and predefined runbooks allows a team member on the contact list to execute predetermined steps and procedures.

Other options can be executed without the engagement of any team members. These include AWS Lambda and AWS Step Functions.

A Real-Life Example of Automated Incident Response

To put what you have just learned about automated IR into context using a real-life example, you will now automate something discussed earlier in this chapter—a case when AWS access keys get exposed publicly. Using a combination of the Personal Health Dashboard, AWS EventBridge, Lambda Functions, and AWS Step Functions, you can see how an automated response can be created if this happens.

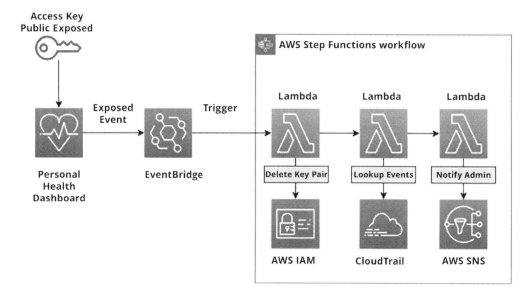

Figure 4.23: Security Incident Response Automation using AWS Step Functions

The following will walk you through the sequence of events referenced in the architectural diagram in *Figure 4.23*:

1. The event in this scenario is any access key that is publicly exposed. This can happen if a developer accidentally uploads their credentials to one of the popular code repositories monitored by AWS, such as GitHub.

2. When this happens, the AWS Health API discovers the key and generates an AWS_RISK_CREDENTIALS_EXPOSED CloudWatch event. At the same time, AWS will also limit the API calls that the exposed key can temporarily make.

3. Your AWS EventBridge has already been configured to be on the watch for this event, and the rule is set to start AWS Step Functions if the rule is triggered.

4. The initial Lambda in the Step Function will access the IAM service and delete the exposed key pair, mitigating any future damage.

5. The Step Function then moves on to the second Lambda function that will gather up the API activity for that key for a specified period of time (it could be 24 hours, or it could be all the records in the current CloudTrail log file). Those records are then made into a summarization digest to pass onto the last Lambda function.

6. The final Lambda function takes the output from the previous function in the Step Function and then adds that as the message to a specified topic using the AWS SNS service. Any administrator subscribed to that service can quickly look at the message to see what activity has happened with the key and know they will have to create a new key pair for the previously deleted set.

You just saw how alerts and automation can be used to quickly respond to an incident without the need for human intervention. You should now feel more confident in your understanding and skills of IR to security incidents within AWS environments.

Summary

This chapter examined the first domain of the AWS Certified Security – Specialty certification: IR. You were given a brief overview of two significant articles published on this topic: *Security Pillar - Well-Architected Framework* and *AWS Incident Response* whitepaper.

You learned how to detect events that may need to be addressed by your IR team, both from a logging and an alerting perspective.

You also looked at how using native tools such as AWS System Manager can help automate the response when an incident has been detected and can contact pre-defined personnel and track the progress of the incident. Finally, you saw how different IR operation procedures could be implemented from either a human intervention standpoint or using automation.

In the next chapter, you will look at another tool used in IR, AWS Config. It can help you become more proactive and show what changes are made to a specific resource.

Further Reading

For additional information on and a more comprehensive foundation to AWS security, please look at the following resources:

- AWS Security Incident Response Guide: `https://packt.link/eEh5p`

- AWS Well-Architected | Security Pillar | Incident response: `https://packt.link/LidxI`

- What do you do if you receive an abuse report from AWS about your resources? `https://packt.link/KF5j3`

- SANS Institute Information Security: Digital Forensic Analysis of Amazon Linux EC2 Instances: `https://packt.link/ik2iS`

Exam Readiness Drill – Chapter Review Questions

Apart from a solid understanding of key concepts, being able to think quickly under time pressure is a skill that will help you ace your certification exam. That is why working on these skills early on in your learning journey is key.

Chapter review questions are designed to improve your test-taking skills progressively with each chapter you learn and review your understanding of key concepts in the chapter at the same time. You'll find these at the end of each chapter.

> **How To Access These Resources**
>
> To learn how to access these resources, head over to the chapter titled *Chapter 21, Accessing the Online Practice Resources*.

To open the Chapter Review Questions for this chapter, perform the following steps:

1. Click the link – `https://packt.link/SCSC02E2_CH04`.

   Alternatively, you can scan the following QR code (*Figure 4.24*):

Figure 4.24: QR code that opens Chapter Review Questions for logged-in users

2. Once you log in, you'll see a page similar to the one shown in *Figure 4.25*:

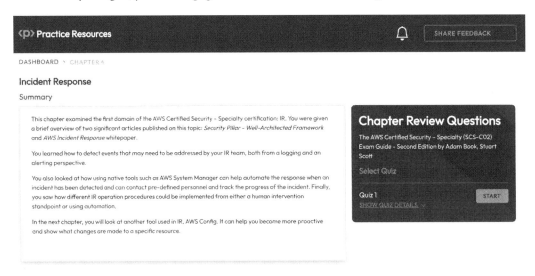

Figure 4.25: Chapter Review Questions for Chapter 4

3. Once ready, start the following practice drills, re-attempting the quiz multiple times.

Exam Readiness Drill

For the first three attempts, don't worry about the time limit.

ATTEMPT 1

The first time, aim for at least **40%**. Look at the answers you got wrong and read the relevant sections in the chapter again to fix your learning gaps.

ATTEMPT 2

The second time, aim for at least **60%**. Look at the answers you got wrong and read the relevant sections in the chapter again to fix any remaining learning gaps.

ATTEMPT 3

The third time, aim for at least **75%**. Once you score **75%** or more, you start working on your timing.

> **Tip**
>
> You may take more than three attempts to reach 75%. That's okay. Just review the relevant sections in the chapter till you get there.

Working On Timing

Target: Your aim is to keep the score the same while trying to answer these questions as quickly as possible. Here's an example of how your next attempts should look like:

Attempt	Score	Time Taken
Attempt 5	77%	21 mins 30 seconds
Attempt 6	78%	18 mins 34 seconds
Attempt 7	76%	14 mins 44 seconds

Table 4.1: Sample timing practice drills on the online platform

> **Note**
>
> The time limits shown in the above table are just examples. Set your own time limits with each attempt based on the time limit of the quiz on the website.

With each new attempt, your score should stay above 75% while your time taken to complete should **decrease**. Repeat as many attempts as you want till you feel confident dealing with the time pressure.

5

Managing Your Environment with AWS Config

Moving through the incident response domain, you have now come to the next critical service that you need to know about, one that helps to show you what has changed after an incident has occurred—**AWS Config**.

AWS Config and its configuration recorder can help you take a real-time inventory of most of the resources in a single account running in a single Region or can be configured to collate data across multiple Regions and even multiple accounts.

The service provides an even greater functionality when it comes to security. For organizations that need to maintain a compliance security standard, AWS Config can evaluate your resources instantly or on a fixed schedule and, with the help of Config rules, determine whether they are in or out of compliance. If they are found to be out of compliance, you can use a combination of Lambda and System Manager to automate remediations to either destroy items that do not meet the compliance standards or auto-remediate them to keep them compliant.

The following main topics will be covered in this chapter:

- Understanding the use and components of AWS Config
- Using Config rules to enforce business and compliance standards
- Using Config to help with audits
- Using Lambda functions to remediate violated Config rules automatically
- Aggregating multi-Region and multi-account data into AWS Config

Technical Requirements

You will require access to the AWS Management Console with an active account along with AWS CLI access. It is also helpful to have an understanding of coding concepts when you go through the remediation code presented in this chapter.

The Task of Internal Compliance and Audit Teams

Traditionally, security and compliance teams have spent a great deal of time manually managing systems compliance information and taking steps to improve compliance. As a security architect or engineering team member, a part of your responsibility is to prepare the working environment (in this case, the AWS cloud) so that, when an audit takes place, the necessary information is available. These tasks fall upon a small number of highly specialized individuals. This makes managing compliance manually a burdensome and time-consuming task that is much better automated with the use of specialized tools. After all, a manual process is not scalable in the cloud, especially as the number of accounts grows to tens or hundreds and the number of resources you need to keep track of scales exponentially with each account.

Preparing items for compliance and auditing is an annual event in a traditional IT account. This usually becomes the priority of an organization and takes resources away from other duties.

AWS Config introduces the concept of continuous compliance. By maintaining constant recordings of the state of resources, AWS Config ensures that any time a change occurs to one of the compatible resources on your system, it is captured along with which entity made the change. You no longer need to wonder whether your resources are meeting the compliance requirements. With continuous compliance, you can apply complete transparency to everything running in your AWS environments. You can also audit and report compliance levels at any time, on demand.

Understanding Your AWS Environment through AWS Config

With the number of services rising each year in AWS, it can be difficult to understand what resources might be running within your environment. How can you keep up with what instances you have running and where, what they are running, and whether the resources are still needed? You might be running some infrastructure that is no longer required but got overlooked among thousands of other virtual devices in production.

With a vast network of resources running within your account, do you have a clear understanding as to which resource is connected to which? What ENI is connected to which instance? Which subnet is that instance running in? Which subnets are connected to which VPCs? Do you have a logical mapping of infrastructure that quickly and easily allows you to identify a blast radius should an incident occur or visibility into resource dependencies should you change your configuration?

On top of that, do you know the current state of configuration? Are you certain the latest patches are implemented, or is there a chance that some of your infrastructure is exposed and has been left vulnerable to potential security threats?

If someone makes a change to your infrastructure and environment, do you have an accurate record of that change, what changed, and when it changed?

Returning to compliance, how can you be assured that the resources you are deploying and maintaining meet the compliance needs dictated by your internal and external control processes?

Answers to all the preceding questions are generally required when performing audits. However, gaining this information can be very cumbersome in traditional IT deployments, let alone cloud environments, which are far more dynamic and are subject to a far higher rate of change. However, AWS is aware of these audit and compliance requirements and has an AWS service called AWS Config to help you address many of these questions in an automated, auditable, and compliant way.

AWS Config is available in all Regions and continuously monitors your configurations. It permits you to automate the configurations of your current resources against your desired configuration settings.

Now that you have a basic understanding of the AWS Config service, you can go through a brief overview of its capabilities before further exploring the different components.

Capabilities of AWS Config

Within the AWS Config service, the following capabilities are presented to you:

- You can assess the AWS resource configurations to see whether they conform to the desired settings of the account.
- You can save the current configuration settings as a snapshot for supported resources.
- You can retrieve the historical configuration(s) for one or multiple supported resources.
- You gain a view of the relationships that exist between resources.
- You can use AWS Config to detect and catalog resources being initialized in an AWS account quickly and easily.
- You can reduce diagnostic time when trying to fix issues by comparing the last known good state to the current state and seeing what has changed.

Having understood the basic capabilities of AWS Config, you can now proceed to the following section, which discusses the various components of AWS Config.

Understanding the Various Components of AWS Config

In a standard AWS account, the resources that make up that account constantly change in one form or another. Instances are started, stopped, created, or destroyed as part of an autoscaling event. An admin or developer might add or remove a port to or from a security group for access or testing purposes to ensure that the correct protocols are communicating with various software and services.

Once you start the service, AWS Config scans your account for supported services/resources by default. As it finds these resources, it crafts a configuration item for each one.

The configuration recorder generates and records a new configuration item as the resource changes take place.

Figure 5.1 shows the process flow of the components of the Config service. These include the overall service itself, which depends on the configuration recorder to capture the events. Config then uses various sources, such as CloudTrail Logs for monitoring. These events are sent to a delivery channel and saved as configuration snapshots over time.

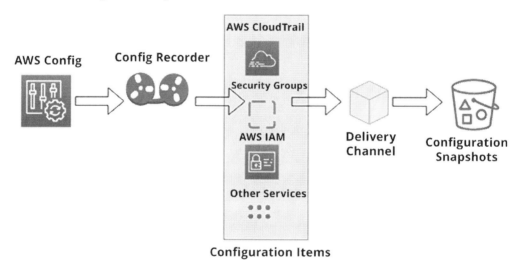

Figure 5.1: Process flow of the AWS Config service

Some other items in the Config service do not appear in *Figure 5.1*. These include the following:

- Configuration history
- The Config role
- Configuration streams
- Conformance packs

These will be discussed in greater detail in the following section to give you an understanding of all aspects of the AWS Config components.

AWS Config versus AWS CloudTrail and Their Responsibilities

When it comes to taking the AWS Certified Specialty exam, the ability to distinguish between two services with similar yet distinct functions is crucial to your success.

The two AWS services, Config and CloudTrail, have many similar traits. They are both services that monitor your AWS resources and provide a recorded history of what happens in your AWS account. Furthermore, they both provide information that can be used for compliance and auditing purposes.

The main concept to remember with *AWS Config* is that it captures **WHAT** has changed in the resource at a certain point in time.

This is in contrast to *AWS CloudTrail,* which captures **WHO** changed **WHICH** resource from **WHERE**, as well as the **RESPONSE**.

Consider *Table 5.1* for an example of when you would use which tool to find the correct information:

	AWS Config	**AWS CloudTrail**
Detect the creation of the security group	✓	✓
Who created the security group?		✓
What IP did they use to create the security group?		✓
Port change on the security group	✓	
Who made the port change?		✓
Was the change successful?		✓
When did the change occur?	✓	✓
Ports opened now versus before	✓	

Table 5.1: Comparison of data captured by CloudTrail versus Config

You can now clearly differentiate between AWS Config and AWS CloudTrail and can take a closer look at the components that make up the Config service, the first component being configuration Items.

Configuration items

As your resources change over time, there needs to be a way to capture those changes so they can be evaluated against both the rules set out in Config and the differences between the unchanged and changed resources themselves. A configuration item is a point-in-time snapshot stored in JSON format that holds that resource's characteristics at that instant. The JSON file contains an array of information about the resource including metadata, attributes, relationships, current configuration, and related events. Most but not all resources are supported by AWS Config, and the complete list of supported resources can be found at `http://packt.link/5LRkV`.

A new configuration item is updated every time a change is made on a particular resource. This includes actions such as creating the resource or calling the `update` or `delete` API against the resource.

The following presents a quick overview of the components of configuration items:

- The **Metadata** section contains information about the configuration item itself.
- The **Attributes** section focuses on the resource data the configuration item relates to.
- The **Relationship** section holds data related to any connected resource. For example, if the configuration item is related to a subnet, the relationship could contain data related to the associated VPC that the subnet was part of.
- **Current Configuration** shows the same information generated as that displayed if you were to perform a `describe` or `list` API call made by the AWS CLI.

Now that you know how Config stores its information about resources into configuration items, you are ready to examine the essential element that captures the configuration items—the configuration recorder.

The Configuration Recorder

Within the AWS Config service, the **configuration recorder** is used to discover any changes in new or existing resources and then capture these changes as configuration items. It's important to note that you must create a configuration recorder before AWS Config can monitor your resource configurations or enable you to remediate any configurations that do not meet your compliance standards using Config rules. This will be explained later in the section labeled AWS Config Rules.

There are multiple ways to set up the configuration recorder, including the AWS Management Console, the **Command-Line Interface (CLI)**, or via **Infrastructure as Code (IaC)** using a system such as **CloudFormation** or **Terraform**. Setting up the configuration recorder using the AWS Management Console will create configuration items for all resources in your account by default. If you use another means to create your configuration recorder, such as the CLI or via IaC, you can specify exactly which resources you want Config to monitor.

> **Note**
>
> In the *Exercises* available with this book, there is a walk-through of setting up AWS Config, the configuration recorder, and a conformance pack.

As you go through the *Basic Setup of Configuration Recorder* example that shows you the method of setting up the configuration recorder, it is suggested you type the JSON policy files by hand. They are simple enough, and the more practice you get in reading and knowing these types of policy files, the more prepared you will be for the exam. There might be a few question-and-answer sets that require you to parse out JSON or pieces of IAM code in your head, and the best way to do this expediently is to have hands-on experience.

The Config Role

During the setup of the configuration recorder, you will create and specify the IAM role that the recorder will need to gain read-only access to the resources to record the configuration items. The role also needs read and write permissions for the designated S3 bucket in order to publish the configuration snapshots. Permissions are also required for any KMS keys used to encrypt the snapshot along with publishing notifications to the SNS topics.

As you create the IAM role in the steps of the *Basic Setup of Configuration Recorder* example, you will see all the permissions in a policy file.

Configuration Streams

When a change against a resource occurs in your environment, the result is that a new configuration item is created. When that new configuration item is created, it is automatically added to a configuration stream, which is essentially an **SNS topic**. As you will see, when you set up your configuration recorder to capture the resources and changes in your AWS environment, you can specify the SNS topic for your stream.

When you declare the SNS topic for your configuration stream, especially for a topic you are actively monitoring, it helps you identify potential unexpected issues or security incidents.

Basic Setup of the Configuration Recorder

For a hands-on example of the Config service, you will now set up the service using the CLI:

1. Open your terminal and start by making a new S3 bucket to save your Config data and snapshots. You will need to use a unique name for your S3 bucket since no S3 bucket can be named the same across AWS:

```
aws s3 mb s3://packt-config --Region us-east-2
```

2. With your bucket created, make an SNS topic for the Config service. Do this with the following command line:

```
aws sns create-topic --name packt-config
```

If it was successful, you should get a response like the one that follows. You will need to save the ARN for when you later create your delivery channel:

```
-----------------------------------------------------------------
|                          CreateTopic                          |
+----------+----------------------------------------------------+
| TopicArn|  arn:aws:sns:us-east-1:1234567890:packt-config     |
+----------+----------------------------------------------------+
```

3. Next, create an IAM role for the Config service. Customize the baseline policy below, enter the bucket values and SNS topic, and then craft your policy in a text editor. Open a text editor in the terminal, such as vim, or use Notepad or your IDE to create a file named `iam_config.json`. When you are done, it should look like the following file. Note that `AWS:SourceAccount` needs to be changed to your AWS account ID once again:

```
{
    "Version": "2012-10-17",
    "Statement": [
      {
        "Sid": "AssumeRole",
        "Effect": "Allow",
        "Principal": {
          "Service": "config.amazonaws.com"
        },
        "Action": "sts:AssumeRole",
        "Condition": {
        "StringEquals": {
          "AWS:SourceAccount": "1234567890"
        }
        }
      }
    ]
}
```

4. After you have created the `iam_config.json` file, create the IAM role using the following command:

```
aws iam create-role --role-name Packt-Config --assume-role-
policy-document file://iam_config.json
```

5. If this is successful, it should come back with `role-arn` as part of the output, as shown in the following. Save your ARN for when you start up your configuration recorder:

```
arn:aws:iam::1234567890:role/Packt-Config
```

6. Having created the role, you now need to create the policy that the role can use. Do this in the same manner by which you created the role, using a text editor:

```
{
    "Version": "2012-10-17",
    "Statement": [
     {
       "Sid": "ConfigS3PutPolicy",
       "Effect": "Allow",
       "Action":[
         "s3:PutObject",
         "s3:PutObjectAcl"
       ],
       "Resource":[
         "arn:aws:s3:::packt-config/*"
       ],
       "Condition":{
         "StringLike":{
           "s3:x-amz-acl":"bucket-owner-full-control"
         }
       }
     },
     {
       "Sid": "ConfigS3GetPolicy",
       "Effect": "Allow",
       "Action":[ "s3:GetBucketAcl" ],
       "Resource": "arn:aws:s3:::packt-config"
     },
     {
       "Sid": "ConfigSNSPolicy",
       "Effect": "Allow",
       "Action": "sns:Publish",
       "Resource": "arn:aws:sns:us-east-1:182968331794:packt-
config"
     },
     {
       "Sid": "DescribeResources",
       "Effect": "Allow",
       "Action":[
```

```
        "ec2:Describe*"
    ],
    "Resource": "*"
    }


  ]
}
```

> **Note**
>
> Did you notice the `StringLike` and `StringEquals` operators in the policies contained in the condition statements? Knowing how to parse these out will be essential for deciphering the policies on the test. This will be covered in more detail in *Chapter 14, Working with Access Policies*.

7. Now create the IAM policy so you can attach it to the role. Name the policy `cr-policy` (where `cr` stands for configuration recorder):

```
aws iam create-policy --policy-name cr-policy --policy-document
file://iam_config_policy.json
```

8. Now attach the policy to the role using the `attach-role-policy` command. You need the full ARN you used when you created the `cr-policy` policy to run this command:

```
aws iam attach-role-policy --role-name Packt-Config --policy-arn
arn:aws:iam::182968331794:policy/cr-policy
```

9. Next, create a JSON file of the types of resources you want to capture. Only record the configurations of security groups and EBS volumes for this exercise. Open your text editor or IDE again to create a file named `resources.json`. It should look like the following file when you are done:

```
{
        "allSupported": false,
        "includeGlobalResourceTypes": false,
        "resourceTypes": [
                "AWS::EC2::SecurityGroup",
                "AWS::EC2::Volume"
        ]
}
```

10. With the file of resources that you want, you can now create your configuration recorder. Use the following command to start the configuration recorder in your account. If you saved the `resources.json` file to a different path from where you currently are, be sure to provide the full path so the CLI can find the file. Use the IAM Config service role but be sure to switch out your account number in the part of the command that says `{1234567890}`:

```
aws configservice put-configuration-recorder --configuration-
recorder name=packt,roleARN=arn:aws:iam::182968331794:role/
Packt-Config --recording-group file://resources.json
```

11. Assuming the preceding command is successful, you can now create a delivery channel file. This is where you will tell Config about the S3 bucket and the SNS topic set earlier. Open your text editor again and create a new file called `delivery.json`. Ensure it matches the following file but make sure that you enter the values for your account. This includes changing the account number and the S3 bucket name, and checking the SNS topic:

```
{
        "name": "default",
        "s3BucketName": "packt-config",
        "snsTopicARN": "arn:aws:sns:us-east-
1:1234567890:packt-config",
        "configSnapshotDeliveryProperties": {
            "deliveryFrequency": "Twelve_Hours"
        }
}
```

12. Once your `delivery.json` file has been created and saved, move on to creating the delivery channel with the following command:

```
aws configservice put-delivery-channel --delivery-channel
file://delivery.json
```

13. Now, with the delivery channel up and running, you can start the recording by running the following command:

```
aws configservice start-configuration-recorder --configuration-
recorder-name packt
```

It will take a few minutes to capture the configuration items; however, you are finished setting up the configuration recorder.

With the setup of the configuration recorder complete, give the AWS Config service a little time to discover the items in the two services that we stood up previously.

AWS Config Dashboard

After you have the configuration recorder up and running, you can go to the AWS Management Console to see the **AWS Config dashboard**. You can jump there directly using the following URL: `https://packt.link/U0bU9`.

When you open the dashboard, you will be able to see the number of configuration items recorded:

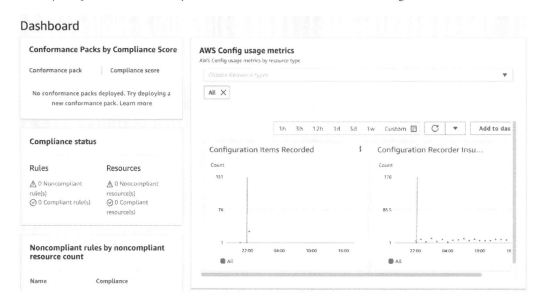

Figure 5.2: AWS Config dashboard after the initial recorder run

Resource Relationship

AWS Config allows you to find, for any of your resources, what other AWS resources they are connected to or associated with. You can obtain this information from either the AWS Management Console or via commands from the CLI. Since you are already in the Management Console looking at the dashboard, try viewing one of your resources and its relationships, as follows:

1. On the left-hand menu at the top, choose `Resources`.

2. To quickly find the resource you are looking for, filter via `Resource type`. In the `Resource type` dropdown, select `AWS EC2 Volume`. This should instantly show your current available volumes in the `Resource identifier` section near the bottom of the screen.

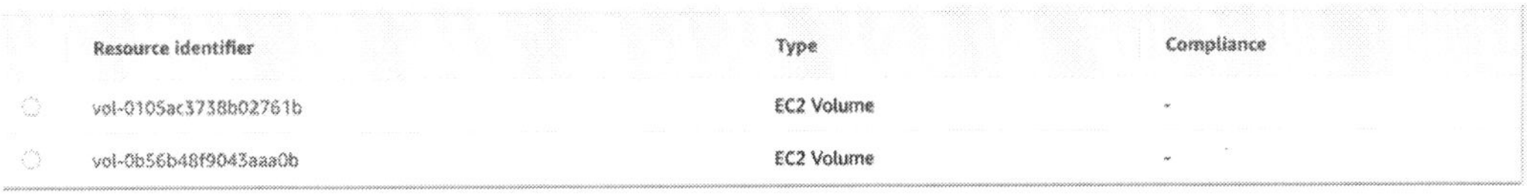

Resource identifier	Type	Compliance
○ vol-0105ac3738b02761b	EC2 Volume	-
○ vol-0b56b48f9043aaa0b	EC2 Volume	-

Figure 5.3: Resource identifier screen

3.   Choose one of your volumes and click on the volume ID to be taken to the details page.

4.   Now click on the box that says `View Configuration Item (JSON)` to expand it and see the full configuration item that holds the relationship data.

The following is an example snippet of the relationship data for an EC2 volume:

```
"relationships": [
  {
    "resourceType": "AWS::EC2::Instance",
    "resourceId": "i-069fe8fba4d4c9254",
    "relationshipName": "Is attached to Instance"
  }
],
```

You have seen how AWS Config can produce and show you the relationships between resources. The next section describes how you can use rules to enforce compliance with the service in your organization.

AWS Config Rules

AWS Config rules are the definitions you set by which to evaluate the current configuration settings of your AWS resources. The rules need to be triggered in order to run, which is done in two ways:

*   Detecting a change in a resource

*   On a periodic schedule (i.e., once every 24 hours)

With Config rules, you can enforce a consistent deployment approach, ensuring all resource types follow a set criterion, regardless of who deployed the resource or when.

Along with choosing what type of trigger you would like your rules to apply, one of the following items must be applied for the rules to run successfully:

*   A single ID or a set of resource IDs specified by both the resource type and the resource ID.

*   The resource types: You can have all types of a resource (i.e., EBS volumes) monitored by AWS Config.

*   A tag key with an optional value: AWS Config can be set up so that any resource with a certain AWS tag runs a rule or a key:value tag for a more specific option.

If none of the preceding values have been specified, then the rules will not be triggered.

From a compliance perspective, AWS Config rules are a great feature and should be implemented whenever you use AWS Config. Backed by AWS Lambda functions performing simple logic, Config rules automatically monitor your resources to ensure they meet specific compliance controls you might need to introduce within your AWS environment. If a resource is not compliant, you will be notified via SNS and the configuration stream, which will allow you to take corrective action.

AWS Config Managed Rules

AWS provides lists of *AWS managed rules*. These are predefined yet customizable rules that the Config service can use to evaluate your resources and determine whether they comply with the standard best practices that that rule set has laid out.

You do not need to write a corresponding Lambda function to perform a remediation action; the action would become a custom rule instead. At the time of writing, there were over 150 managed rules available for use that can be filtered according to the following four categories:

- List of managed rules by evaluation mode
- List of managed rules by trigger type
- List of managed rules by Region available
- Service-linked rules

> **Note**
>
> To see the complete list of rules, please visit the following URL: `https://packt.link/HrWsk`.

AWS Config Custom Rules

If you cannot find a rule that meets your needs, then you can create a custom rule in the AWS Config service. There are two methods of creation available to do this. The first is to use an AWS Lambda function, and the second is with Guard, which involves using the Guard policy as a code language.

> **Note**
>
> The ability to create a custom rule is not tested in the exam, nor is the syntax of Guard; hence, these topics will not be covered in detail. If you want to know more about Guard, visit its GitHub repository at `https://packt.link/ic0RW`.

The difference between an AWS Config custom rule and a managed rule is that you create a custom rule from scratch.

The following describes the process of setting up a managed rule for your AWS Config instance in the AWS Management Console. You must start the configuration recorder as in the previous exercise or manually via the AWS Management Console to successfully complete this exercise:

1. Log in to the AWS Config service on the Management Console using the following URL: `https://packt.link/s2AqI`.

   (Make sure that you are in the Region where your resources are being recorded.)

2. On the left-hand menu, click on the item named `Rules`.

Figure 5.4: Menu on the AWS Config service screen

3. In the main window, click the orange `Add rule` button.

4. Add an AWS managed rule. To do this, under the heading that says `Select rule type`, ensure that `Add AWS Managed Rule` is selected.

5. In the section labeled `AWS Managed Rules`, type `restricted-ssh` into the search box. Once the `restricted-ssh` rule appears, select it and click the orange `Next` button.

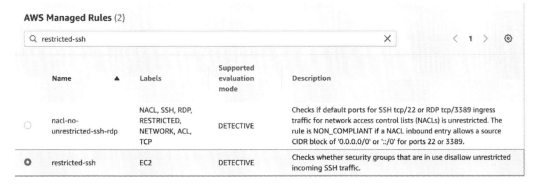

Figure 5.5: AWS Managed Rules screen

6. On the following page (labeled `Configure Rule`), scroll down to the bottom and click the orange `Next` button.

7. On the `Review and create` page, scroll down and click the orange `Add rule` button to create the rule in your AWS Config instance.

After completing all these steps, you should be back at the main `Rules` page with your new rule listed. Now that you have a rule in your account, you can look at the process of evaluating rules.

Evaluating Config Rules

Once the rules have been configured in the account and the specified triggers have been set, the AWS Config service will flag the resources that do not comply with those rules. As you initially set your rules, especially in the case of custom rules, you may have to review the items that have been flagged and make modifications to the rule to ensure that the rule is acting in the way you envisioned. This could include only running the rule against specific resources with a specified tag.

The rules from the AWS Config service are evaluated in two modes: **proactive mode** and **detective mode**. With the proactive mode, resources are evaluated as soon as they are deployed or provisioned. This means that, once a resource has been provisioned, the AWS Config service runs the rule and determines whether that new resource is compliant. On the other hand, with detective mode, AWS Config is running rules against resources that have already been deployed.

AWS Config Conformance Packs

Collections of AWS Config rules come in what are known as **conformance packs**. You can apply conformance packs either in the particular Region in which you are using AWS Config or, if you are using an aggregator (which will be discussed in just a bit), to combine the information from multiple Regions or multiple accounts. You can apply those same sets of rules across everything with a one-click setup.

Conformance packs make it simple to implement operational best practices for a number of AWS services, industries, and security controls, all with minimal effort. Sample packs for items ranging from Criminal Justice Information Services to HIPAA Security Rule are available.

> **Note**
>
> Although the different conformance packs will not be questioned directly in the exam, it is suggested that you explore the various titles available so that you know what resources are available in your day-to-day duties. To do so, have a look at the following URL: `https://packt.link/PbCDa`.

Configuration History

The configuration history is useful for audits and provides a complete record of all the changes made to a resource. By collating the configuration items for a resource, AWS Config can assemble a history of the modifications made to that resource. The history of your resource can be accessed via the AWS CLI or the AWS Management Console. Also, as part of the process, AWS Config will store a configuration history file of each resource type in the S3 bucket selected during the configuration of AWS Config.

You can select any changes using the AWS Management Console and dive deeper to understand what elements changed. Suppose there was a security incident or outage. In that case, this history would be beneficial to determine the timeline of events that led to the incident to help you resolve it quickly and efficiently.

Remediating Non-Compliant Resources with Config

AWS provides you the ability to take an automated approach to fix out-of-compliance resources as evaluated by Config rules. **System Manager Automation runbooks** carry out these actions.

There are several predefined automated remediations that you can choose from, or you can create custom remediations to suit your organization's needs.

Real-Life Example of Using Automated Remediations

Suppose you are part of a company that has developed an organization-wide policy that no EBS volume can be created without encryption. This would be the perfect opportunity for automatic remediation. First, you would create a rule to check whether a volume was encrypted and would be triggered when the resource was created. If the resource failed to meet these standards, you could create a custom System Manager Automation runbook that would instantly destroy that EBS volume before it even had the chance to be attached to an instance and have any data placed on it.

If you didn't want to delete the volume, you could choose the predefined automation rule of **AWS EBS DetachVolume**. Whenever someone tried to attach that volume, it would instantly be detached from the instance and thus become unavailable. In the latter case, the volume would still be an active resource and incur charges for the account.

Having reviewed how to remediate non-compliant resources in your account with AWS Config, you can now learn how to use Config across multiple Regions and multiple accounts.

Multi-Account and Multi-Region Data Aggregation with AWS Config

Many companies and organizations have moved past a single account structure and have multiple accounts and organizational units powered by AWS Organizations. You can collect all the compliance data and account configurations using an **aggregator**.

An aggregator in AWS Config is a type of resource that allows you to collect compliance data and configurations in any of the following scenarios:

- If you have only a single account but need a multi-Region setup, then you need to use an aggregator to collect the data in all Regions and present a unified view.

- If you have multiple accounts and multiple Regions and you want to present the findings in a unified view, then an aggregator can collect the information from all the accounts and store it in a single location.

- If you are running your accounts via AWS Organizations and you want to assemble all the data, then using the aggregator makes finding trends across accounts a much more simplified task.

You can see from *Figure 5.6* how the data would flow from either a separate Region or a separate account and then be presented in the aggregated view.

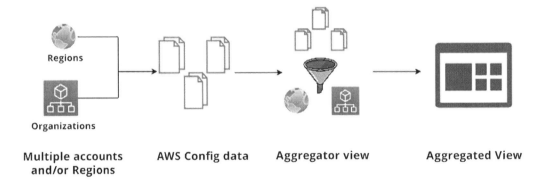

Figure 5.6: Flow of AWS Config data into the aggregator

Once the aggregator has collected the data, a dashboard on the Aggregators page displays all the configuration data, an overview of your rules, and your compliance packs, along with their compliance status.

The Aggregators dashboard also provides a combined count of all the resources and source accounts, which are then ranked by the highest number of resources.

Takeaways for the Certification Exam

As you have now reviewed all the functionality of the AWS Config service, having a vital understanding of the following concepts will be relevant when you take your AWS Certified Security Specialty exam:

- AWS Config records **WHAT** changes have taken place and **WHEN**.

- Once the configuration recorder has been turned on, it will discover all the supported resources in an account and then create a configuration file for each one in that Region, unless the aggregator has been used. This is essentially a service that provides a real-time running inventory for you or an auditor.

- AWS Config keeps a running count of resources that are both in and out of compliance.

- AWS Config can remediate items found to be out of compliance with the help of other services such as AWS Lambda and Systems Manager.

Summary

In this chapter, you examined the AWS Config service in detail. You saw how to start the configuration recorder to begin inventorying the resources in our AWS account, and reviewed the different types of rules available for AWS Config and how the rules get triggered inside an account.

You also learned how to use AWS Config in a multi-account or multi-Region setup and the differences between using a single-account setup. The chapter concluded with a list of the key points on the AWS Config service you will need to know for the AWS exam.

Chapter 6, Event Management with Security Hub and GuardDuty, will discuss the Incident Response pillar, diving deep into the services of AWS Security Hub and AWS GuardDuty. You will see how these two services can work hand in hand and provide visibility into your accounts while simultaneously detecting abnormalities that need to be remediated.

> **Note**
>
> If you have spun up the configuration recorder as part of the exercise given in this chapter, make sure to spin it down once you are through. It will incur charges as long as it is running in your account. The commands below can help you with this task.

To stop the configuration recorder, use the following command:

```
aws config service stop-configuration-recorder –configuration-
recorder-name packt
```

To delete the configuration recorder, use the following command:

```
aws configservice delete-configuration-recorder --configuration-
recorder-name packt
```

Further Reading

For additional information on the AWS shared responsibility model and the underlying foundation of AWS security, please look at the following resources:

- AWS Config FAQs: `https://packt.link/YEZft`

- AWS Config | Checking for Compliance with New Managed Rule Options: `https://packt.link/gsZMZ`

- AWS Config rules now support proactive compliance: `https://packt.link/ZK10E`

Exam Readiness Drill – Chapter Review Questions

Apart from a solid understanding of key concepts, being able to think quickly under time pressure is a skill that will help you ace your certification exam. That is why working on these skills early on in your learning journey is key.

Chapter review questions are designed to improve your test-taking skills progressively with each chapter you learn and review your understanding of key concepts in the chapter at the same time. You'll find these at the end of each chapter.

> **How To Access These Resources**
>
> To learn how to access these resources, head over to the chapter titled *Chapter 21, Accessing the Online Practice Resources*.

To open the Chapter Review Questions for this chapter, perform the following steps:

1. Click the link – `https://packt.link/SCSC02E2_CH05`.

   Alternatively, you can scan the following QR code (*Figure 5.7*):

Figure 5.7: QR code that opens Chapter Review Questions for logged-in users

2.   Once you log in, you'll see a page similar to the one shown in *Figure 5.8*:

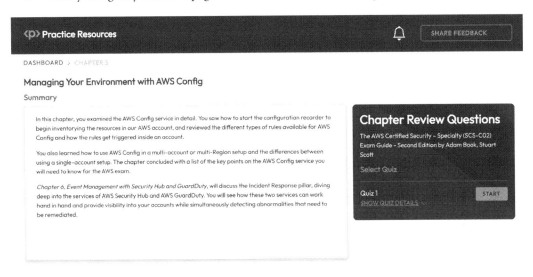

Figure 5.8: Chapter Review Questions for Chapter 5

3.   Once ready, start the following practice drills, re-attempting the quiz multiple times.

Exam Readiness Drill

For the first three attempts, don't worry about the time limit.

ATTEMPT 1

The first time, aim for at least **40%**. Look at the answers you got wrong and read the relevant sections in the chapter again to fix your learning gaps.

ATTEMPT 2

The second time, aim for at least **60%**. Look at the answers you got wrong and read the relevant sections in the chapter again to fix any remaining learning gaps.

ATTEMPT 3

The third time, aim for at least **75%**. Once you score **75%** or more, you start working on your timing.

> **Tip**
>
> You may take more than three attempts to reach 75%. That's okay. Just review the relevant sections in the chapter till you get there.

Working On Timing

Target: Your aim is to keep the score the same while trying to answer these questions as quickly as possible. Here's an example of how your next attempts should look like:

Attempt	Score	Time Taken
Attempt 5	77%	21 mins 30 seconds
Attempt 6	78%	18 mins 34 seconds
Attempt 7	76%	14 mins 44 seconds

Table 5.2: Sample timing practice drills on the online platform

> **Note**
>
> The time limits shown in the above table are just examples. Set your own time limits with each attempt based on the time limit of the quiz on the website.

With each new attempt, your score should stay above 75% while your time taken to complete should **decrease**. Repeat as many attempts as you want till you feel confident dealing with the time pressure.

6

Event Management with Security Hub and GuardDuty

In the process of creating your infrastructure and granting user access to your account, you need to be on the lookout for the security of your environment. There's a good possibility that your environment will be changing constantly. This means that the security status of your environment could change as well, potentially leading to new vulnerabilities.

One of the challenges of being a security professional is trying to stay on top of all these different changes. Simply being in charge of one account that is full of users is challenging on its own. In an enterprise-type environment in which you are responsible for a whole **AWS organization**, comprised of numerous accounts under different organizational units, it can be almost impossible to keep track of changes without help.

The **AWS Security Hub** tool was designed with the aforementioned problems in mind. It allows you to track multiple accounts from inside an account in the **Security OU** if launched in a **Control Tower** setup. It also has the flexibility to work for smaller accounts and organizations that still only work within the confines of a single account. Security Hub is complemented by the **GuardDuty** service. This is one of the native AWS tools that can report the threats it detects back to Security Hub.

After completing this chapter, you will have learned the following major aspects related to AWS Security Hub and GuardDuty:

- How AWS Security Hub can reduce the complexity and effort of managing security across your accounts

- How to meet compliance with Security Hub conformance packs

- How Amazon GuardDuty can intelligently detect threats

- The types of data sources that GuardDuty analyses

- How GuardDuty can help protect your account against malware

Technical Requirements

You will require access to the AWS Management Console with an active account and AWS CLI access for this chapter. You will also need minimal Git skills to clone a repository with example code. Finally, knowing how to find your IP address will help in one of the exercises.

Managing Threat Detection with Amazon GuardDuty

For those unfamiliar with **Amazon GuardDuty**, it is a fully managed, intelligent threat-detection service, powered by machine learning, that continually provides insights into unusual and/or unexpected behavioral patterns within your account that could be considered malicious. Amazon GuardDuty can process and analyze millions of events captured through your **AWS CloudTrail**, **DNS**, and **VPC Flow Logs** from a single account or multiple accounts. These events are then referenced against numerous threat detection feeds, many of which contain known sources of malicious activity, including specific URLs and IP addresses.

Amazon GuardDuty is continually learning, based on the day-to-day operations within your account, to differentiate between normal behavior and what could be considered abnormal behavior, allowing it to effectively indicate a threat within your infrastructure. This behavioral-based analysis allows GuardDuty to detect potential interactions and connectivity with unknown or unusual sources.

Being an *always-on* service, GuardDuty provides a very effective method of automatically identifying security issues without impacting performance. The service runs entirely on the AWS infrastructure without needing local agents. Any findings by Amazon GuardDuty are presented to you in the form of a list of priorities based on the results.

There are no upfront costs to enable GuardDuty. It can intelligently detect security threats without hindering the performance of your infrastructure, regardless of size, and provide centralized management by aggregating data from multiple AWS accounts. These factors make GuardDuty a very effective tool to protect your AWS resources and any stored data.

GuardDuty installs in your account in a *one-click* manner. This means there are no extra applications to install or agents to deploy on the network. It simply starts monitoring your environment once you enable the service.

Key Features of GuardDuty

As a managed threat detection service, GuardDuty provides the following key features:

- One-click activation with no impact on either architecture or performance
- Constant monitoring of your AWS resources and accounts, including users and roles
- Global coverage with results categorized regionally

- The ability to detect intel-based known threats

- The ability to detect behavior-based unknown threats through machine learning

- The ability to manage security across accounts, using a single security account through linking so that the security team can see all threats in a single place

Now that you have an idea of the key features that GuardDuty offers, the next sections will help you dive deeper into those features.

Data Sources for GuardDuty

The Amazon GuardDuty service derives most of its information from three primary sources of data – VPC Flow Logs, DNS logs, and AWS CloudTrail events. All these sources are logging files that GuardDuty correlates with, and then it parses that information to look for events.

VPC Flow Logs

VPC Flow Logs provide details about network communications, especially regarding behavioral detections and unknown threats. When GuardDuty analyses the flow logs, it gets information similar to NetFlow data that captures the IP you are communicating with, along with the origin IP address, the amount of data transferred, and the direction the traffic was flowing. Using this information, the GuardDuty service can detect whether the instance or service communicates with the IP address of a known bad actor on the threat intelligence list. This data is also used to feed the data models that detect unknown threat intelligence behavior. An example of this would be an EC2 instance that suddenly starts transferring an unusually large amount of data for a particular workload.

While VPC flow logs need to be turned on for you as a user to look at and parse to view the data, this is not the case with the GuardDuty service. GuardDuty uses an independent duplicate VPC flow log stream to gather and collect information. Thus, the flow logs you are charged for can be turned off at any point, which will not affect the GuardDuty findings.

AWS CloudTrail Events

Similar to CloudTrail logs, all API calls used to access the AWS Management Console, any SDK usage, and any usage of the AWS command line are recorded and stored for future reference. This allows user and account activity identification, including source IP addresses, to be captured and analyzed by GuardDuty. The data from the CloudTrail logs helps build a profile for your account to assist GuardDuty in understanding what normal activity is. As the model evolves, it understands the usage patterns and can more readily pick up on abnormal activity.

DNS logs

When an Amazon EC2 instance requests the **fully qualified domain name** (**FQDN**) of known and unknown instances, those instances generate a DNS log entry. DNS logs are obtained through a query resolver in your VPC, which is one of the reserved addresses in your VPC residing at the .2 address.

> **Note**
>
> You will learn more about the different address spaces that are reserved when creating a VPC in *Chapter 10, Configuring Infrastructure Security*.

Using the DNS logs, GuardDuty can analyze all the domains that your instances query and then compare them against the threat intelligence lists that AWS has compiled.

You are not required to enable the Amazon Route 53 service or stand up any hosted zones to generate DNS logs. The Amazon GuardDuty service can generate DNS-based findings with or without Route 53 enabled.

How GuardDuty Works

After enabling the GuardDuty service, data is collected from the aforementioned three sources and begins to be analyzed. The service can analyze tens of billions of events from multiple data sources, which are vetted for threat intelligence; it looks for abnormal activity on your account in this manner.

If GuardDuty notices anomalous or malicious activity, it will give a ranking to the item as high, medium, or low. This ranking helps you, as the security professional, decide which events you should follow up on and in which order. The findings that GuardDuty produces are delivered to Security Hub, your designated S3 bucket, and CloudWatch Events/Eventbridge simultaneously. This setup of delivering findings assumes that you have the Security Hub service up and running.

Connecting GuardDuty to Security Hub allows you to view and manage all the events from the GuardDuty service and the other security services with which Amazon Security Hub can connect. Adding a connection to Amazon EventBridge can allow near-real-time notifications using the SNS service, especially when a high-ranking event has been discovered.

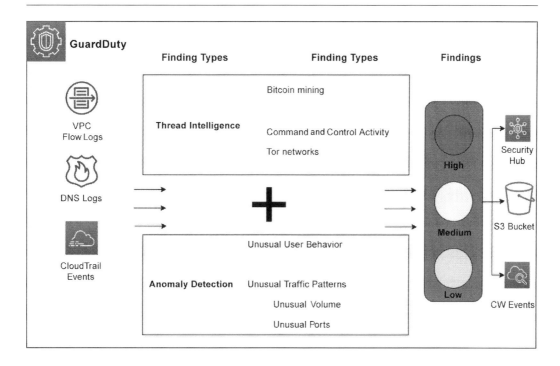

Figure 6.1: The process flow of Amazon GuardDuty

With a deeper understanding of how the GuardDuty service works, you can now move on to the different types of detections that the GuardDuty service can carry out. This is what you will explore in the next section.

What GuardDuty Can Detect

From the moment you enable it, Amazon GuardDuty harnesses threat intelligence from various sources. These sources include the following:

- AWS security intelligence
- AWS partners CrowdStrike and Proofpoint
- Customer-provided threat intelligence

Using a combination of this intelligence from the preceding sources allows the GuardDuty service to identify the following types of threats:

- Known malware-infected hosts

- Anonymizing proxies or Tor gateways

- Cryptocurrency mining pools and wallets

- Sites hosting malware and hacker tools

Now that you know what types of detections GuardDuty can help you find, examine the differences between the two GuardDuty and Amazon Macie services to prevent confusion, especially as they relate to questions on the *AWS Certified Security Specialty* exam.

Understanding the Differences between GuardDuty and Amazon Macie

Amazon Macie is a fully managed security service that helps organizations enhance data protection and compliance in their AWS environment. Leveraging machine learning, Macie automatically identifies and classifies sensitive data stored in Amazon S3, enabling users to gain insights into their data security posture, detect potential threats, and implement access controls and data protection measures. With customizable policies, compliance reporting, and integration with AWS CloudTrail, Macie empowers organizations to proactively safeguard sensitive information, respond to security incidents, and adhere to data privacy regulations.

> **Note**
>
> You will learn a lot more about Amazon Macie in *Chapter 17, Protecting Data in Flight and at Rest*.

Although there are a few similarities between the GuardDuty and Macie services, they each perform different security functions. Both services use machine learning, but apart from that, their functions differ. Amazon Macie concentrates on finding **Personally Identifiable Information** (**PII**) in your account so that you do not leave PII exposed or unprotected across different services in AWS.

GuardDuty is an intelligent threat detection platform that continuously aggregates and deciphers data from log files in your account, seeing whether there are any risks that need to be addressed imminently.

See *Table 6.1* for a graphical illustration of Amazon GuardDuty and Macie's differences.

	Amazon GuardDuty	**Amazon Macie**
Uses machine learning	✓	✓
Reads your S3 bucket		✓
Identifies data containing PII		✓
Aggregates CloudTrail log events	✓	
Aggregates VPC flow logs	✓	
Aggregates DNS logs	✓	
Identifies known and unknown threats	✓	
Regional service	✓	✓

Table 6.1: A comparison of GuardDuty versus Macie

Having understood the role of GuardDuty in your AWS account, you can now work through the process of enabling it step by step in the next section so that you can see it in action.

Enabling Amazon GuardDuty

Amazon GuardDuty is a regional service. You must first select the region where you will enable the service; once that is done, it is effortless to enable it. Just complete the following steps:

1. From the Amazon Management Console, find the GuardDuty service by going to `Services > Security, Identity, & Compliance > GuardDuty`, or search for GuardDuty in the top search bar.

2. Once on the GuardDuty page, click the orange `Get Started` button to enable the GuardDuty service.

3. This will bring you to the `Enable GuardDuty` page. GuardDuty needs to create a service role to monitor and protect your account. Since data is involved, click on the orange `Enable GuardDuty` button at the bottom of the page to allow GuardDuty to be enabled.

    After enabling GuardDuty, you will be brought to the main GuardDuty page (that is, the `Findings` page) by default. Since you have just enabled the service, three zeros in the page's top right-hand corner should indicate no high-, medium-, or low-severity alerts.

Figure 6.2: The severity alert count for GuardDuty

Customizing GuardDuty

With GuardDuty enabled, you can customize the service to meet your organization's needs.

Combining GuardDuty with the CloudWatch Events service allows you to match specific severity levels with either automated remediations and/or alerts sent out to a particular SNS topic. GuardDuty rates the items that it finds on a numerical scale, broken down into the following three categories:

- High-severity items are valued between *7.0–8.9*
- Medium-severity items are valued between *4.0–6.9*
- Low-severity items are valued between *1.0–3.9*

If the severity is not at a high level (say, for instance, if it is a 4 or 5), then you may only want to have the security team notified via the messaging channel (e.g., MS Teams or Slack) that they are constantly monitoring. Conversely, if the severity level is high (such as 7 or 8), you may want the security team and an executive stakeholder notified so that a response plan can be prepared, just in case it is needed.

Triggering GuardDuty

You can try modifying something in your account to see how a finding would look in the GuardDuty service.

AWS has created a lab to simulate malware in a contained environment and generate findings in the GuardDuty service. You can find the files for this exercise at `https://github.com/awslabs/amazon-guardduty-tester`:

1. Download the repo by going to your computer and running the following command:

   ```
   git clone https://github.com/awslabs/amazon-guardduty-
   tester.git
   ```

2. Now that you have the CloudFormation templates and testing scripts available locally, go to your AWS Management Console and run the template from the CloudFormation service. You can get there quickly by going to the following URL: `https://console.aws.amazon.com/cloudformation/`.

3. Once in the CloudFormation service, under Stacks (if you have not already been taken there by default), click the Create Stack button so that additional menu items appear. Choose the option labeled With new resources (standard) to create a new CloudFormation stack.

Figure 6.3: The screen to create a CloudFormation stack

4. On the Create Stack page, move to the section labeled Specify template. Choose the option labeled Upload a template file. Click the Upload File button and find the folder on your local drive named amazon-guardduty-tester. Inside that folder will be a file named guardduty-tester.template.

Figure 6.4: Upload a template file screen for GuardDuty

5. Once you have selected the guardduty-tester.template file, press the orange Next button at the bottom of the page.

6. You should now be on the Specify stack details page. Enter guardduty-tester as the name of the stack.

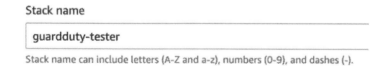

Figure 6.5: The stack name screen for GuardDuty

7. In the Parameters section, under Availability Zones, as the prompt says, just select the first AZ to keep things simple.

Figure 6.6: The Availability Zones selection screen for GuardDuty

8. The next item you should customize is Allowed Bastion External Access CIDR. Instead of keeping this open globally, enter your IP address followed by /32. This means that only your singular IP address will be allowed to access the bastion host.

Figure 6.7: The Bastion CIDR details screen for GuardDuty

9. The final item that needs customization in the template is the key pair name. Use the dropdown to select one of your current EC2 key pairs.

10. After customizing the template, move to the bottom of the screen and press the orange Next button.

11. This brings you to the Configure stack options screen; scroll down to the bottom of the page and click the orange Next button.

12. You should now be on the Review guardduty-test page. Once again, scroll down to the bottom of the page. Acknowledge that this template may create IAM resources by clicking in the blue box. Once done, press the orange Submit button to bring up the template's resources.

    After around 10 minutes, the template should have completed creating all the resources. You can now click on the Outputs tab and obtain the IP address of the Bastion host.

Figure 6.8: The GuardDuty Outputs screen

13. Next, open up a terminal window so that you can ssh into the Bastion IP address shown in the previous step. Use the IP provided with the username `ec2-user` to log in to the instance. You will also need the ssh key you designated when creating the template:

```
ssh -i ~/.ssh/key-name ec2-user@3.141.240.161
```

14. You will be greeted with a terminal window once you have entered the Bastion host. With the terminal window open, go to the EC2 service in the AWS Management Console and look for an instance named `RedTeam`. Click on this instance and copy (or write) its private IP address (you will need it in a moment).

15. You must place your SSH key on the Bastion host inside the `ssh` folder. On your local machine, print the key out, and then copy and paste it into the new file.

16. Returning to your terminal, create a file on your Bastion host at the path of `~/.ssh/{your-ssh-key}`. You can do this via the command line with the `vim` command:

```
vim ~/.ssh/{your-ssh-key.pem}
```

17. Once the Vim editor is opened, paste the value from your private key file.

18. Close and save the file by pressing the *esc* button at the top of the keyboard, and then type `:wq`. This is the write/quit sequence in the Vim editor. To make sure that the file has been saved correctly, run the following command:

```
cat ~/.ssh/{your-ssh-key}
```

19. After you have created the key file, change the permissions of the file using the following command:

```
chmod 0600 ~/.ssh/{your-ssh-key.pem}
```

20. With the key in the ~/.ssh folder located on the Bastion host, you can now log in to a tester instance simply with the command:

```
ssh -i ~/.ssh/{your-ssh-key.pem} ec2-user@{RedTeam EC2 IP}
```

21. At this point in the exercise, you should be on the Red Team EC2 instance. Here, you can run the guardduty_tester.sh script. Run the following command to generate the findings:

```
./guardduty_tester.sh
```

22. Once you have generated the findings, you should be able to clean up all instances and resources quickly and easily by terminating the CloudFormation template.

After learning how to enable Amazon GuardDuty and trigger it using a few scripts, the next step is to review the findings and see how the GuardDuty service detects unusual activity.

Reviewing the Findings in GuardDuty

If you went through the exercise in the previous section, you will see the findings appear inside the GuardDuty console after about 8 to 10 minutes. At the top of the screen, the colored ovals that previously contained all zeros will now have one in the medium-severity category and two in the high-severity category.

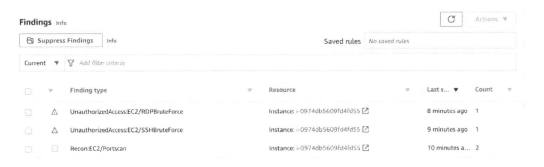

Figure 6.9: Findings from the GuardDuty Test exercise

From the dashboard setting in GuardDuty, you can sort the findings by different values, including severity, finding type, resource (in this case, it would be an instance ID to allow grouping of all the EC2 instances), the time when the incident last occurred, and finally, the numerical count of the type of attack.

If you click on the instance, it opens up in the EC2 service page. It also shows more information on the screen, with details of the finding and some remediation recommendations.

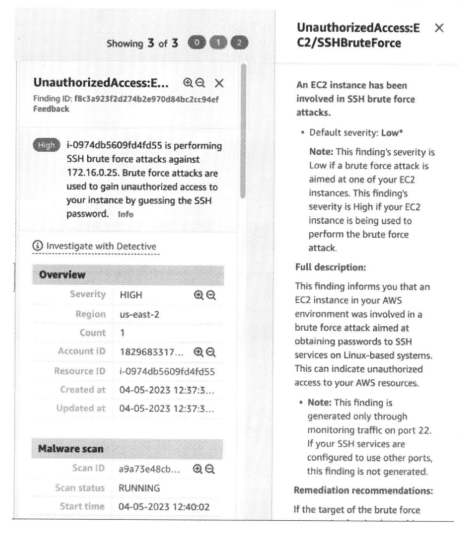

Figure 6.10: More details revealed about the GuardDuty findings

The next step after learning how to retrieve findings in the GuardDuty console manually is to examine how you can use CloudWatch Events and become a bit more proactive with the events that GuardDuty finds.

Reviewing Findings in CloudWatch Events

One of the significant advantages of using CloudWatch Events is that it allows you to get events in a push context (where the events come proactively to you) rather than a pull context (where you need to retrieve the events).

GuardDuty will also aggregate multiple similar events so that you are not bombarded with *noise* from the similar events it found. An excellent example of this would be when there are exposed access keys and one or more bad actors, to whom your resources are generally inaccessible, try to use these keys to gain access from various IP addresses. Once the key has been determined to be exposed, this type of access attempt may happen quite often in an hour or shorter period, and receiving multiple alerts of the same kind can become frustrating for you or other security team members. GuardDuty instead sends out an initial alert and then will wait to send out the next one, based on your pre-determined interval schedule. The default setting for this is that you would not get another alert for six hours after the initial alert was sent.

Performing Automatic Remediation

Amazon GuardDuty can also perform remediation on findings through automation, and again, this uses Amazon CloudWatch Events to do so. From the *Detect* phase, which Amazon GuardDuty is a part of, and by pushing the findings through to the Amazon CloudWatch service, you can then perform automatic remediations using CloudWatch Events (or EventBridge) to then remediate the specific service in question.

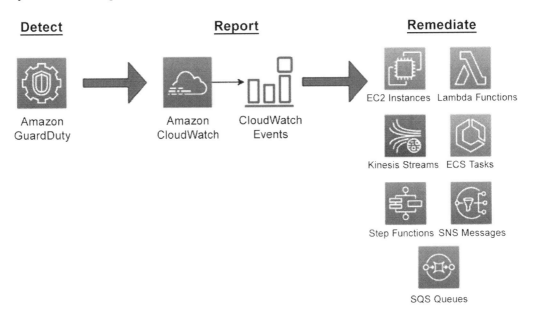

Figure 6.11: Automatic remediation using CloudWatch Events

Performing Manual Remediations

Although automated remediations are what professionals strive for in any instance, there are some occurrences where you have to automate all the steps, or the steps are complicated and manual intervention is required.

You can perform the following manual remediations on a finding, using the steps in the remediating security issues discovered by the *GuardDuty guide*, as mentioned in the *Further Reading* section of this chapter:

- A compromised EC2 Instance
- A compromised S3 bucket
- A compromised ECS cluster
- Compromised AWS credentials
- **Elastic Kubernetes Service (EKS)** Runtime Monitoring Findings
- A compromised database

With each of the preceding scenarios, a detailed set of instructions for step-by-step remediation has been provided to help you return your resource and account to a normal running state.

After remediating security issues with automated responses and manual steps using the Amazon GuardDuty service, the next step is to examine the Security Hub service to learn how you can gather all your security findings into a single view.

Security Alerting with AWS Security Hub

With so many security tools available in both AWS and from third-party providers, those that are responsible for managing the alerts need a single pane of glass to centralize all the alerts and notifications coming in. AWS Security Hub helps you consolidate many of your security findings, alerts, and compliance reports from AWS services, including the following:

- AWS **Identity and Access Management (IAM)**
- Amazon Macie
- Amazon GuardDuty
- Amazon Inspector
- AWS Firewall Manager

In addition to these native AWS services, AWS Security Hub can be incorporated into any third-party partner solutions, such as Sumo Logic, Splunk, and other vendors you might use in your organization. A complete list of these partners can be found at https://aws.amazon.com/security-hub/partners/.

The Security Hub service allows you to categorize and prioritize all the events coming in from various sources. This single-pane-of-glass view gives you a more comprehensive picture and a deeper understanding of any threats and vulnerabilities forewarning your account.

Security Hub, by default, is a regional service, but as with Amazon GuardDuty, it can be configured as an administration/member configuration from within a security account. Along with AWS Organizations, the organization management account specifies the Security Hub administrator account using the following configuration:

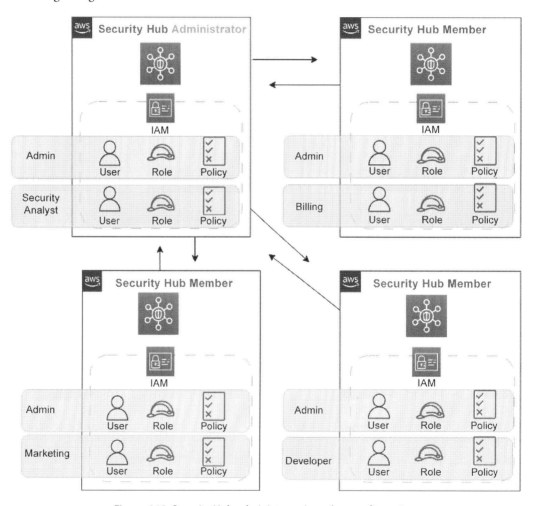

Figure 6.12: Security Hub administrator/member configuration

Suppose you have already configured your accounts, as shown in *Figure 6.12*, for the GuardDuty service to consume all the account data in a segmented security account. In that case, the Security Hub service can utilize this same setup without additional configuration.

One of the most compelling use cases for Security Hub is automated compliance and configuration checks. Keeping every account compliant becomes burdensome and time-consuming as your organization grows and expands to multiple accounts. Trying to understand whether a developer has configured something in one of the child accounts that goes against the compliance standards of the whole organization can be automatically displayed and reported on, via the Security Hub service, so that you can take appropriate action.

AWS Security Hub, out of the box, performs 43 fully automated, nearly continuous checks against your accounts based on the *CIS Foundations benchmark*. It then takes the findings from the checks and displays them on the main dashboard of Security Hub, allowing your security and audit team to have quick access to these findings. Security Hub mainly looks at configuration choices and usage patterns at the account level. This is in contrast to AWS Config, which reviews items at instance and resource levels. By focusing on CIS checks, AWS Security Hub helps ensure that your AWS infrastructure adheres to the recommended security best practices set forth by CIS.

Having AWS Config enabled is a prerequisite to ensure that compliance standards are met while using Security Hub. This is because Security Hub uses the information from Config to determine when there is a change in an account. This allows the Security Hub service to be refreshed in near real time.

Having covered how Security Hub works with multiple accounts and how it differs in its findings from the preceding AWS Config service, the following section will help you understand how Security Hub groups its findings to make things easier for security professionals.

Enabling AWS Security Hub

AWS Security Hub can be enabled from the AWS Management Console. However, because Security Hub needs to have the AWS Config service enabled (and prefers to have it fully enabled, watching all resources), you will follow the following steps via CloudFormation in this walk-through as well – all via the Management Console:

1. Go to `https://console.aws.amazon.com/securityhub/` to access the `AWS Security Hub` main page.

2. Click on the orange button labeled `Go to Security Hub` to start the process of enabling Security Hub.

3. You should be brought to a page labeled `Enable AWS Security Hub`. In the first section labeled `Enable AWS Config`, click on the `Download` button to download the CloudFormation script to quickly set up a full version of the AWS Config service for Security Hub. The file should be named `EnableAWSConfig.yml`.

4. In a new tab, go to `https://console.aws.amazon.com/cloudformation/` to open the CloudFormation main page. Make sure that, at the top of the screen, you can see you are in the same region where you want to initiate your Security Hub instance. Click on the orange `Create stack` button.

5. On the `Create stack` page, move to the second section, `Specify template`, and select the radio button labeled `Upload a file`. Then, click on the button marked `Choose a file`. Find the `EnableAWSConfig.yml` file you just downloaded, and then click `Open`.

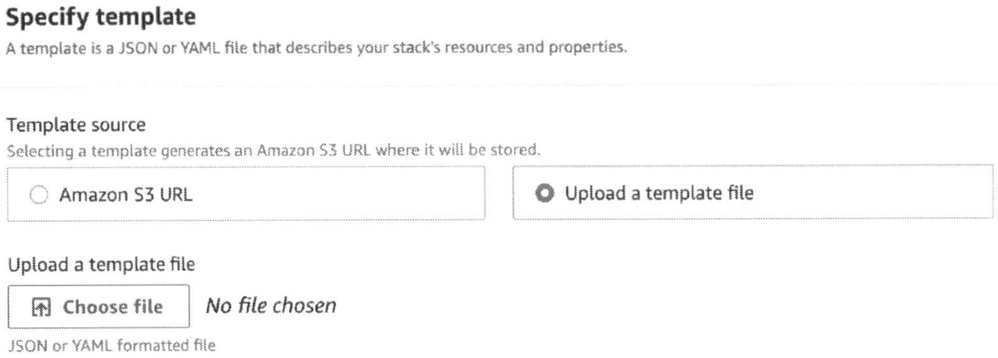

Specify template
A template is a JSON or YAML file that describes your stack's resources and properties.

Template source
Selecting a template generates an Amazon S3 URL where it will be stored.

○ Amazon S3 URL   ◉ Upload a template file

Upload a template file

⬆ Choose file   *No file chosen*

JSON or YAML formatted file

Figure 6.13: The template selection screen for Security Hub

6. Click the orange `Next` button at the bottom of the page.

7. You should now be on the `Specify stack details` page. Enter `enable-config1` as the stack name (note that you cannot have a space in a CloudFormation stack name). Leave all other items as default, since the main interest is the Security Hub service with this exercise. Scroll down to the bottom of the page and click on the orange `Next` button.

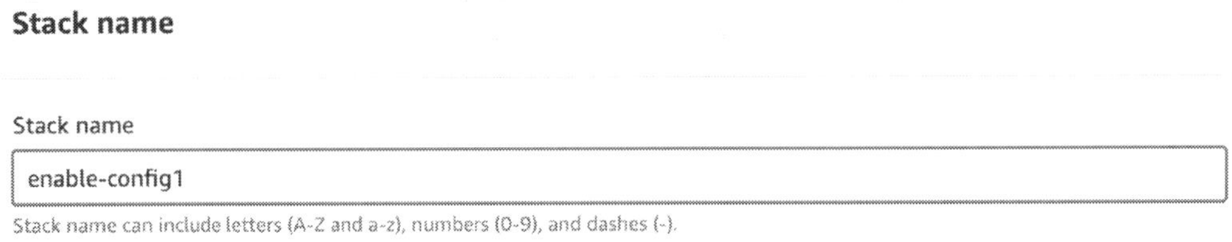

Stack name

Stack name

enable-config1

Stack name can include letters (A-Z and a-z), numbers (0-9), and dashes (-).

Figure 6.14: The stack name for Security Hub

8. On the `Configure stack options` page, scroll down to the bottom and click the orange `Next` button.

9. On `Review Enable-Config`, scroll down to the bottom of the page. Click on the blue checkbox acknowledging that this template might create IAM resources, and then click the final orange `Submit` button to create the stack.

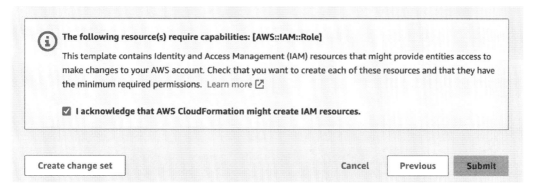

Figure 6.15: The acknowledgement screen for Security Hub

10. Once the AWS Config Recorder is up and running, return to the tab where you set up the Security Hub service.

11. Now back on the Security Hub service, you can focus on the box labeled `Security standards`. These are the checks that you want the service to review and give notifications on where security posture is lacking. For this example, select to enable the following standards:

    *   AWS Foundational Security Best Practices v1.0.0

    *   CIS AWS Foundations Benchmark v1.4.0

    *   NIST Special Publication 800-53 Revision 5

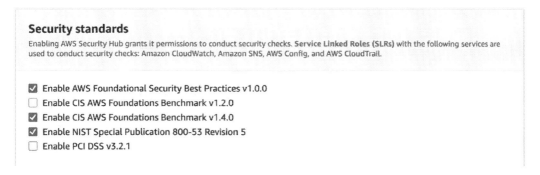

Figure 6.16: The Security standards screen for Security Hub

12. At this point, click the `Enable Security Hub` button.

When you initially enable Security Hub, you may see a warning message, stating that it could take up to two hours to see results from the newly enabled security checks.

After having set up the Security Hub, you are ready to take a closer look at the security standards and security checks it presents.

Security Standards versus Security Controls versus Security Checks

When enabling the Security Hub service, you were presented with several security standards that could be used to run checks against your environment. At the time of publishing, the security standards built into the Security Hub service are as follows:

- *AWS Foundational Security Best Practices v 1.0.0*

- *CIS AWS Foundations Benchmark v 1.2.0*

- *CIS AWS Foundations Benchmark v 1.4.0*

- *NIST Special Publication 800-53 Revision 5*

- *PCI-DSS v3.2.1*

Security standards allow you to focus on a specific compliance framework when viewing the results in AWS Security Hub. For example, the **Payment Card Industry Data Security Standard** (**PCI-DSS**) delivers a collection of AWS security best practices for handling cardholder data. The *NIST Special Publication, 800-53 Revision 5* set of best practices helps your organization protect the availability, confidentiality, and integrity of its information systems and critical resources. The National Institute of Standards and Technology developed it.

Each of the security standards has a corresponding set of security controls. The number of controls varies widely by security standard, as you can see in *Table 6.2*:

	Control count
AWS Foundational Security Best Practices	197
CIS AWS Foundations Benchmark v1.2.0	43
CIS AWS Foundations Benchmark v1.4.0	39
NIST Special Publication 800-53 Rev 5	216
PCI-DSS v3.2.1	45

Table 6.2: The number of security controls in each security standard

Once you have a control enabled, AWS will run security checks to confirm whether your resources comply with the rules included in the particular control.

AWS Security Hub uses the AWS Config service to run the security checks. Therefore, the security checks can be run on a periodic schedule or when there is a change made to a particular resource or service.

As the security checks are run, Security Hub generates findings and uses them to calculate a score across all the enabled controls for a specific standard.

Insights in Security Hub

As Security Hub gathers findings about your accounts, it aggregates and groups them. When it has a collection of related findings that it feels warrants attention and remediation, it presents those to you as an insight, and insights help you identify the actual root cause.

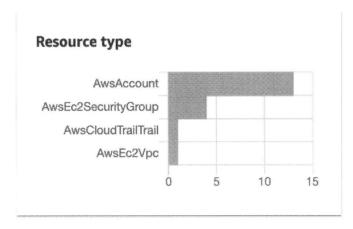

Figure 6.17: An AWS-generated graph of insights

Inside the insights feature of Security Hub, interactive graphs are built on the fly for you that allow you to drill down and gain more insightful information.

Security Hub features two types of insights:

- **Built-in and pre-defined managed insights**
- **Custom insights**

> **Note**
> You cannot modify or delete the managed insights provided by the AWS Security Hub service.

Managed Insights

Managed insights in Security Hub only return results if you have enabled the corresponding product integration or security standard that can produce matching findings.

Some examples of managed insights are as follows:

- AWS resources with the most findings
- S3 buckets with public read or write permissions
- AMIs that generate the most findings

Custom insights

If you want to create your own custom insight, you can do so with the help of the **Security Hub API**, the **AWS CLI**, or **PowerShell**.

You need to choose a grouping attribute, such as the product name, and then include any additional filters to display on your insight.

Having understood the basics of the insights provided by Security Hub, let's now take a look at how a real-world example would be shown in AWS Security Hub.

A Real-World Example of Using AWS Security Hub

If, in your accounts, you have deployed a custom-built AMI and that has now been found to have a vulnerability, Security Hub insights can aggregate the information and then show you that the AMI itself has an issue. This contrasts with presenting you with a list of a hundred instances created from the AMI and finding the same vulnerability that needs to be patched.

While that information would be relevant and somewhat helpful, it would also be noisy and not get to the root of the issue. With Security Hub presenting the root cause to you (the AMI in this case), you can then go and patch or fix the problem in the underlying AMI and then redeploy or patch those instances, ensuring that the particular issue is not shown again.

With an understanding of how Security Hub can be of assistance in aggregating the same security issue, when found multiple times, into a succinct piece of information, you can now review some other features of Security Hub.

Findings

A finding is a security issue or failed security check detected by the integrated AWS service and third-party solutions.

Integrations

The Security Hub service integrates natively with most AWS services through a button that allows you to turn findings on or off from the Management Console Service page.

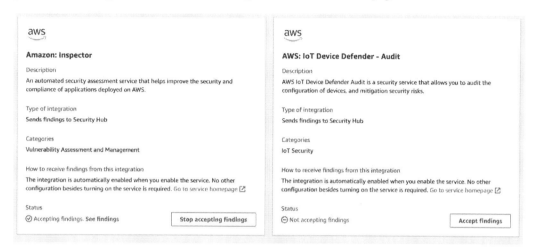

Figure 6.18: Services inside of the Integrations section of Security Hub

As you have seen in the previous sections, it is very easy to integrate both native AWS and third-party services so that Security Hub can report on their issues. You can now explore how using AWS Config conformance packs enhance the Security Hub service.

Automated Remediation and Responses from Security Hub

Automated responses from AWS Security Hub findings and system events can be activated so that you do not need to manually react to the notifications that appear on your Security Hub dashboard.

Examples of the responses that you can automatically trigger with Amazon EventBridge from Security Hub include the following:

- Having an AWS Lambda function invoked
- Having an EC2 run command invoked via Systems Manager
- Starting an AWS Step Functions state machine
- Sending a notification to an Amazon SNS topic
- Placing a message in an Amazon SQS queue
- Sending one of the findings to a third-party service, such as a chat window, SIEM, or ticketing system

For each individual response, you need to configure the rule and the severity separately in Amazon EventBridge.

> **Note**
> You will explore Amazon EventBridge in more detail in *Chapter 8, CloudWatch and CloudWatch Metrics*, as Amazon EventBridge has replaced Amazon CloudWatch Events.

Summary

This chapter concludes *Section 2* on incident response, with a review of the AWS services Security Hub and GuardDuty. You explored how the GuardDuty service works and how it presents its findings. You also walked through setting up the GuardDuty service from the Amazon Management Console.

You then took a look at the Amazon Security Hub service and examined how it can present security findings from AWS security services, such as GuardDuty, Amazon Macie, Amazon Inspector, AWS Firewall Manager, and third-party services in a unified view, thereby making tracking your security posture much easier on yourself as a security professional.

Chapter 7, Logs Generated by AWS Services, will begin the next domain in the AWS Security Specialty exam, *logging and monitoring*. This domain concerns the different types of logs you can capture, how to do so, and what they tell you.

Further Reading

For additional information on the AWS shared responsibility model and to gain more comprehensive understanding of AWS security, refer to the following resources:

- Amazon GuardDuty FAQs: `https://packt.link/6ZWIM`

- Remediating security issues discovered by GuardDuty: `https://packt.link/ghtre`

- Journey to Adopt Cloud-Native Architecture – Enhancing Threat Detection, Data Protection, and Incident Response: `https://packt.link/HU5cX`

- Building a Self-Service, Secure, and Continually Compliant Environment on AWS: `https://packt.link/hIZCS`

- Amazon Security Hub FAQs: `https://packt.link/CaHMF`

Exam Readiness Drill – Chapter Review Questions

Apart from a solid understanding of key concepts, being able to think quickly under time pressure is a skill that will help you ace your certification exam. That is why working on these skills early on in your learning journey is key.

Chapter review questions are designed to improve your test-taking skills progressively with each chapter you learn and review your understanding of key concepts in the chapter at the same time. You'll find these at the end of each chapter.

> **How To Access These Resources**
>
> To learn how to access these resources, head over to the chapter titled *Chapter 21, Accessing the Online Practice Resources.*

To open the Chapter Review Questions for this chapter, perform the following steps:

1. Click the link – `https://packt.link/SCSC02E2_CH06`.

    Alternatively, you can scan the following QR code (*Figure 6.19*):

Figure 6.19: QR code that opens Chapter Review Questions for logged-in users

2.   Once you log in, you'll see a page similar to the one shown in *Figure 6.20*:

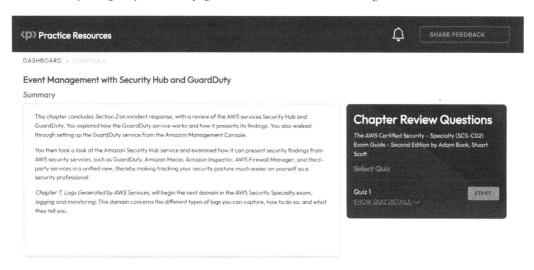

Figure 6.20: Chapter Review Questions for Chapter 6

3.   Once ready, start the following practice drills, re-attempting the quiz multiple times.

Exam Readiness Drill

For the first three attempts, don't worry about the time limit.

ATTEMPT 1

The first time, aim for at least **40%**. Look at the answers you got wrong and read the relevant sections in the chapter again to fix your learning gaps.

ATTEMPT 2

The second time, aim for at least **60%**. Look at the answers you got wrong and read the relevant sections in the chapter again to fix any remaining learning gaps.

ATTEMPT 3

The third time, aim for at least **75%**. Once you score **75%** or more, you start working on your timing.

> **Tip**
>
> You may take more than three attempts to reach 75%. That's okay. Just review the relevant sections in the chapter till you get there.

Working On Timing

Target: Your aim is to keep the score the same while trying to answer these questions as quickly as possible. Here's an example of how your next attempts should look like:

Attempt	Score	Time Taken
Attempt 5	77%	21 mins 30 seconds
Attempt 6	78%	18 mins 34 seconds
Attempt 7	76%	14 mins 44 seconds

Table 6.3: Sample timing practice drills on the online platform

> **Note**
>
> The time limits shown in the above table are just examples. Set your own time limits with each attempt based on the time limit of the quiz on the website.

With each new attempt, your score should stay above 75% while your time taken to complete should **decrease**. Repeat as many attempts as you want till you feel confident dealing with the time pressure.

Section 3:
Logging and Monitoring

Anything that happens in your accounts from an infrastructure standpoint is captured in some type of log. To pass the security specialty exam and set up a secure AWS environment, it is necessary to grasp which logs contain what type of values. This section takes you through logging and monitoring in AWS and the invaluable insights and clarity these processes offer regarding your infrastructure and applications.

The section comprises the following chapters:

- *Chapter 7, Logs Generated by AWS Services*

- *Chapter 8, CloudWatch and CloudWatch Metrics*

- *Chapter 9, Parsing Logs and Events with AWS Native Tools*

As your workloads run in AWS from day to day, they will generate different types of logs. These various types of logs are what you will learn about in *Chapter 7*. These logs range from networking logs generated by VPC flow logs and load balancers to access logs generated by the S3 service, along with CloudTrail, which records each API call. You will even learn about the different services that publish logs to the AWS native log service—**CloudWatch Logs**.

When it comes to logging and monitoring in AWS, it is crucial that organizations know how to take the values from the log files and build metrics and alerts so they know both when everything is at a baseline, calm state as well as when they need to be more alert. This concept is addressed in *Chapter 8*. Utilizing the CloudWatch service, you can not only capture logs from other AWS services but also capture metrics and then use those metrics to power automation. This helps you act faster and with fewer errors than you could manually.

In *Chapter 9*, you will learn how to parse all the information that has been gathered from logs so that you can determine the relevant pieces using tools and services native to AWS. You will review some sample architectures that allow you to capture streaming events and examine the logs you have already stored and need to find specific values from.

Logging and monitoring are important aspects of security, and they will be discussed in detail in upcoming chapters.

7

Logs Generated by AWS Services

As you, your users, and your customers perform your day-to-day functions in AWS, you can capture and store those actions in various logging formats from the different services.

Configuring and enforcing logging across your services helps significantly when identifying potential issues, not just from a security perspective but also from a performance and availability perspective.

This chapter will cover the various types of logs the AWS services produce. You will also examine where they are stored and review their different formats. Knowing how to toggle test logs on and off and how to read the various log files is essential when you need to investigate a particular event or respond to a security incident.

The following main topics will be covered in this chapter:

- S3 access logs
- VPC Flow Logs and traffic monitoring
- Enabling load balancer logs
- Setting up CloudTrail
- Services that publish to CloudWatch Logs

Technical Requirements

Access to the AWS Management Console with an active account and the AWS CLI are required. You also need to have access to a terminal console and a text editor.

S3 Access Logs

Whenever you or your users store or access different objects in Amazon S3, you, as the security professional, may need to know who is accessing the different files, when and where they are accessed, and from what location.

You can capture all the access logs and records of who accessed the various objects in a particular bucket via a simple setting in S3. One caveat is that the access logs for an S3 bucket cannot be stored in the same bucket as the items they are tracking. This means that you need to create a new bucket for storing those logs. You can use a single bucket to track multiple S3 buckets' access logs. Changing the access policy so that no users besides the security and audit teams or the service role that retrieves the logs may access this bucket is considered best practice.

The access logs are usually pushed to the secondary storage bucket on a best-effort basis, and this can result in a delay of a few hours before delivering the logs to the specified bucket. Sometimes logs are delivered faster, but don't expect to find your S3 access logs in real time.

Turning on Access Logs

Perform the following steps to turn on the access logs for one of your S3 buckets:

1. Open your terminal so that you can execute the commands using the AWS CLI.

2. First, create an S3 bucket to put objects and then access the objects. Now the name of the bucket will need to be unique to you, so replace `packt-test-object` with something that is unique to your account:

    ```
    aws s3 mb s3://packt-test-object
    ```

3. Next, create a bucket where the logs can go:

    ```
    aws s3 mb s3://packt-security-logs
    ```

4. Now create a JSON file describing your logging preferences. Open up a text editor and create the following file, but be sure to substitute the value of YOURBUCKET with what you have named your bucket in step 2. Open your text editor and create a file named `s3_access.json` with the following contents:

```
{
"LoggingEnabled": {
"TargetBucket": "packt-security-logs",
"TargetPrefix": "S3Logs/"
}
}
```

5. With your two buckets created, you can now enable access logging using the put-bucket-logging command, as shown:

```
aws s3api put-bucket-logging \
--bucket packt-test-object \
--bucket-logging-status file://s3_access.json
```

You should now have access logging enabled on the S3 bucket that you created on the object-test bucket for this exercise, with the logs going to the second logs bucket. Next, you will go through the practice of generating log files and viewing their contents.

Creating Some Log Files

Now that you have logging turned on, you need to perform some actions to generate a few logs. After completing the necessary steps, you will view the logs. You should already have your terminal open so that you can continue the command line with the AWS CLI. Further, rather than creating a whole new file to test with, use the JSON file created in the previous exercise:

1. First, place the JSON file you created into the bucket; remember to substitute YOURBUCKET with your bucket name:

```
aws s3 cp s3_access.json s3://YOURBUCKET/
```

2. Next, remove that same object:

```
aws s3 rm s3://YOURBUCKET/s3_access.json
```

3. Now, upload the file again using the s3-sync method (be careful if you have created the file in a directory that has many other files and large files in it as the s3-sync command will copy all files from that directory to your S3 bucket):

```
aws s3 sync . s3://YOURBUCKET/
```

4. Finally, download the file with a different name to your local hard drive:

```
aws s3 cp s3://YOURBUCKET/s3_access.json new.json
```

After running through that array of test commands, you can dissect the logs to see what information they provide.

Viewing the Access Logs

S3 access logs can be downloaded from the AWS Management Console or the AWS CLI. S3 access logs are not written in real time; they are created in batches that take a few hours to appear in your S3 logging bucket.

After a few hours, you can check your logging bucket to see whether the folder you had designated in your configuration file has appeared. *Figure 7.1* shows that the folder was created after a short time, and AWS batched up the initial set of requests.

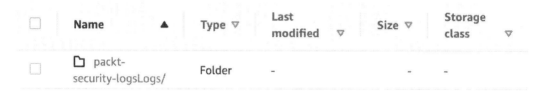

Figure 7.1: The logging folder for S3 access logs inside of our logging bucket

As you enter the folder that contains the S3 access logs, you will notice that unlike other batch groupings of logs that AWS gathers, these logs are not grouped in separate subfolders by month, day, and year. Instead, each log file's name begins with a time-date stamp and ends with a semi-random value.

The logs themselves are in text format but have no extension added to them.

Consider the following example log:

```
30cd0fc55a0a1b1164bfd69733c5b1bedd043dd0ce88e77cb1b2cb9e6418a3e5
packt-test-object [11/Apr/2023:01:59:50 +0000] 123.456.78.90
arn:aws:iam::123456789101:user/packt 5GP5E0KH8855K76Y REST.GET.
ACL - "GET /?acl HTTP/1.1" 200 - 556 - 14 - "-" "S3Console/0.4, aws-
internal/3 aws-sdk-java/1.11.1030 Linux/5.4.238-155.347.amzn2int.
x86_64 OpenJDK_64-Bit_Server_VM/25.362-b10 java/1.8.0_362 vendor/
Oracle_Corporation cfg/retry-mode/standard" - uhbLAOkdZMQTHAfP/
ixHjJtznBNWzDc4JcrOa0YTnqtBDJzmvUz2fViv2eL4IOZoadKJQet8rm0= SigV4
ECDHE-RSA-AES128-GCM-SHA256 AuthHeader packt-test-object.s3.us-east-1.
amazonaws.com TLSv1.2 - -
```

The following are the fields in the order in which they appear in the preceding example:

- **Bucket Owner**: Although this is a long alphanumerical value, this is the canonical user ID for the source bucket owner.

> **Note**
>
> If you would like to know how to find the canonical user ID for your own AWS account, then you can find out more with the following URL: `https://packt.link/Z0HUO`.

The value in the example is as follows: `30cd0fc55a0a1b1164bfd69733c5b1bedd043dd0ce8 8e77cb1b2cb9e6418a3e5`

- **Bucket**: This is the name of the S3 bucket where the action or request was processed. This field will be blank if this was a malformed request and AWS cannot determine the actual bucket.

  The value in the example is as follows: `packt-test-object`

- **Time**: This is the time the request was received in UTC (which stands for Universal Time Code).

  The value in the example is as follows: `[11/Apr/2023:01:59:50 +0000]`

- **Remote IP**: This refers to the apparent IP address of the requester; however, this is not always the correct IP due to proxies and firewalls.

  The value in the example is as follows: `123.456.78.90`

- **Requester**: This is the IAM of the user if the user is an IAM user or the canonical ID of the request. If this value is unknown or the user is unauthenticated, then the field has – for those types of requests.

  The value in the example is as follows: `arn:aws:iam::123456789101:user/packt`

- **Request ID**: This is a unique string to identify each request.

  The value in the example is as follows: `5GP5E0KH8855K76Y`

- **Operation**: This is the type of operation performed, such as `SOAP`, `REST`, `WEBSITE`, or `BATCH. DELETE.OBJECT`.

  The value in the example is as follows: `REST.GET.ACL`

- **Key**: This will be the object name, URL, or – if the operation does not have an object parameter.

  The value in the example is as follows: `-`

- **Request-URI**: This is the `Request-URI` part of the HTTP request message.

  The value in the example is as follows: `"GET /?acl HTTP/1.1"`

- **HTTP Status**: This is the status code of the HTTP response.

  The value in the example is as follows: `200`

- **Error Code**: This is the error code that S3 returned, or - if no error was returned.

  The value in the example is as follows: `-`

- **Bytes Sent**: This is the number of response bytes sent minus the protocol overhead. If this number is zero, it will be represented by -.

  The value in the example is as follows: `556`

- **Object Size**: This is the total size of the object.

  The value in the example is as follows: `-`

- **Total Time**: This shows the time in milliseconds that the request was in flight.

  The value in the example is as follows: `14`

- **Turn-Around Time**: This is the time in milliseconds that the S3 service spends processing the request.

  The value in the example is as follows: `-`

- **Referrer**: This is the value of the HTTP `Referrer` header.

  The value in the example is as follows: `"-"`

- **User-Agent**: This is the value of the HTTP `User-Agent` header.

  The value in the example is as follows: `"S3Console/0.4, aws-internal/3 aws-sdk-java/1.11.1030 Linux/5.4.238-155.347.amzn2int.x86_64 OpenJDK_64-Bit_Server_VM/25.362-b10 java/1.8.0_362 vendor/Oracle_Corporation cfg/retry-mode/standard"`

- **Version Id**: This is the version ID of the request.

  The value in the example is as follows: `-`

- **Host Id**: This is the x-amz-id-2 or Amazon S3 extended request ID.

  The value in the example is as follows: `uhbLAOkdZMQTHAfP/ixHjJtznBNWzDc4JcrOa0YTnqtBDJzmvUz2fViv2eL4IOZoadKJQet8rm0=`

- **Signature Version**: This is the SigV2 or SigV4 used to authenticate the request.

  The value in the example is as follows: `SigV4`

- **Cipher Suite**: This is the **Secure Sockets Layer** (**SSL**) cipher used in the HTTPS request.

  The value in the example is as follows: `ECDHE-RSA-AES128-GCM-SHA256`

- **Authentication Type**: This will be either `AuthHeader` for authentication headers or `QueryString` for pre-signed URLs or – for a request that was not authenticated.

  The value in the example is as follows: `AuthHeader`

- **Host Header**: This is the endpoint used to connect to the S3 service.

  The value in the example is as follows: `packt-test-object.s3.us-east-1.amazonaws.com`

- **TLS version**: This is the version of **Transport Layer Security** (**TLS**) negotiated by the client.

  The value in the example is as follows: `TLSv1.2`

- **Access Point ARN**: This is the ARN of the access point of the request.

  The value in the example is as follows: -

- **aclRequired**: This will be a Boolean if the requests require an **access control list** (**ACL**) for authorization.

  The value in the example is as follows: -

Now that you have seen what the S3 access logs look like, how to parse them manually, and where to retrieve them, take a look at another type of logging available from S3 object-level logging, discussed in the next section.

S3 Object-Level Logging

S3 object-level logging integrates with AWS CloudTrail data events. AWS CloudTrail is a service that records and tracks all API requests that are made. These can be programmatic requests made using an SDK, using the AWS CLI, from within the AWS Management Console, or with another AWS service.

When S3 object-level logging is enabled, you must associate it with a CloudTrail trail. This trail will then record both write and read API activity (depending on configuration) for objects within the configured bucket. Although Amazon S3 is being discussed here, S3 object-level logging relies heavily on CloudTrail. CloudTrail events will be discussed later in this chapter as you dive deeper into AWS CloudTrail and the logging capabilities that it contains.

Now that you have examined the logging capabilities of S3 you can explore how to capture and monitor the traffic coming through your virtual network or **Virtual Private Cloud** (**VPC**) in the case of AWS.

VPC Flow Logs and Traffic Monitoring

You likely have several different public and private subnets within your AWS account allowing external connectivity. You may even have multiple VPCs connected via VPC peering connections or AWS Transit Gateway. Either way, you will have a lot of network traffic traversing your AWS infrastructure from numerous sources, internally and externally, across thousands of interfaces. Flow logs allow you to capture this IP traffic across the network interfaces attached to your resources, which could number in the tens of thousands in a corporate environment.

Flow logs can be configured for the following resources:

- Your VPC

- A subnet within your VPC

- A network interface from your EC2 instances or interfaces created by **Elastic Load Balancing (ELB)**, **Amazon RDS**, **Amazon ElastiCache**, **Amazon Redshift**, **Amazon WorkSpaces**, **NAT gateways**, and **Transit Gateway**

As flow logs can capture information at these levels, they are a tool to help troubleshoot network issues and identify security threats. The latter could be placed if network traffic is reaching or trying to reach a resource or subnet that it shouldn't. This might be partly due to overly permissive security groups, lack of rules in **network access control lists (NACLs)**, or other controls. Either way, it identifies weaknesses, allowing you to build a greater defense and remediate potential resource vulnerabilities.

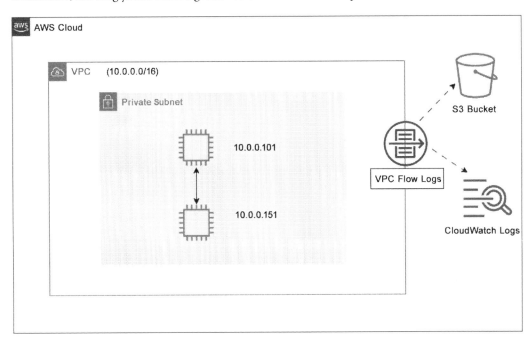

Figure 7.2: VPC Flow Logs architecture

Flow log data can be published to an S3 bucket or Amazon CloudWatch Logs. Upon enabling the log stream, you will choose the destination where the flow logs will go.

When you create a flow log, you specify three main items:

- The resource for which you want to create the item (for example, an endpoint or a NAT gateway)

- The type of traffic you want to capture (rejected traffic, accepted traffic, or all traffic)

- Where you want to publish the flow log data (which S3 bucket or **CloudWatch log stream**)

Now that you know the basics of VPC Flow Logs, you are ready to learn why it is beneficial to choose S3 versus CloudWatch Logs when deciding on log storage.

Why Choose an S3 Bucket over CloudWatch Logs?

When enabling your VPC Flow Logs to capture the traffic, you have an immediate choice of where to store the logs. The industry that your organization is in, along with the types of compliance regulations you need to follow, should play a part in this decision.

There are pros and cons to each storage system. This section will first cover storing logs in S3 from the view of a security professional. As a security professional, you are often tasked directly or indirectly with gathering system logs and ensuring that they are ready for an audit. These audits may happen on a regular basis, such as an annual security audit, or they may occur randomly. You may be subject to data retention regulations based on the industry you work in for storing that log data for 1, 2, 6, or even 10 or more years. This exact scenario is where storing the log files on the S3 service comes into play. Some characteristics have made S3 a popular service for over a decade, such as the 11 9s of reliability, low-cost storage, and the ability to create life cycle policies that move files seamlessly from one storage class to another so that cost savings can be maximized. Because of these characteristics, S3 works well for large files and large quantities of files, such as in the case of the log files that you collect.

The alternate option is to use CloudWatch Logs. This is often a much easier option, as this can be a one-click setup with numerous AWS services and will automatically group logs by day, week, month, and year. However, the ease of CloudWatch Logs does come with a set of limitations, including the fact that using CloudWatch Logs for extended storage can become a cost burden on your organization.

Further, while CloudWatch Logs does have native search functionality built in, when performing more sophisticated queries, CloudWatch starts to reach its threshold in usefulness.

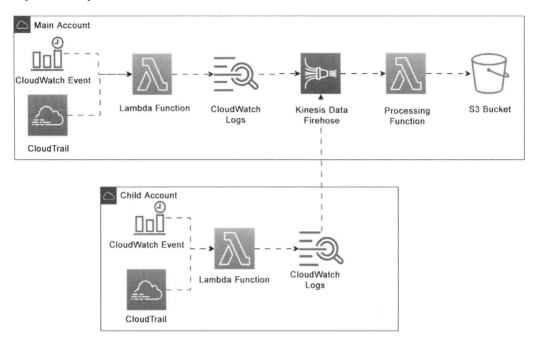

Figure 7.3: Exporting CloudWatch Logs to an S3 bucket via Kinesis Data Firehose

The following section teaches you how to enable VPC Flow Logs on your account so that you can start to examine them.

Enabling VPC Flow Logs

Before you can parse or read any VPC Flow Logs, you must enable them on one of your VPCs. You could use the AWS Management Console or a **software development kit** (**SDK**), but for this example, use the Amazon CLI:

1. Open your terminal window to access your CLI.

2. Start by making a bucket for your logs to be saved into. Remember, your bucket name needs to be unique across all of AWS, and the bucket name shown in the following example (`packt-security-logs`) must be replaced with your bucket name. (NOTE: If you made a bucket for logging your access logs in the previous exercise, you can skip this step and use the same bucket.)

```
aws s3 mb s3://packt-security-logs
```

3. With a place to store your logs, you now need to find the ID of your default VPC. Do this with the following command:

```
aws ec2 describe-vpcs --region us-east-2 --output text
```

This will give you the output you are looking for in a compact form, `vpc-x00x000`, with some other information, such as the statement that defaults to `True`. With these two pieces of information, you can turn on the VPC Flow Logs.

4. But first, check to make sure that they are not already on with the following command:

```
aws ec2 describe-flow-logs --region us-east-2
```

5. You are ready to turn on the flow logs without output from your query. Do that with this command:

```
aws ec2 create-flow-logs \
--resource-type VPC \
--resource-ids vpc-f80e0490 \
--traffic-type ALL \
--log-destination-type s3 \
--log-destination arn:aws:s3:::packt-security-logs/vpc-flow-logs/ \
--max-aggregation-interval 60 \
--region us-east-2
```

And with that, your VPC Flow Logs have been turned on. You will have received a `FlowLogId` value and a `CreateFlowLogs` ClientToken back on the command line signaling that the command was successful.

One thing of significance to point out in the command is the `--traffic-type ALL` flag. When you are capturing VPC Flow Logs, you have three choices for the traffic you are capturing:

- The `ALL` option captures both accepted and rejected traffic in the logs.
- The `REJECT` option captures only traffic that was rejected from the VPC (i.e., people and bots trying for ports that aren't open or users trying to access a page that isn't available).
- The `ACCEPT` option captures only the traffic accepted on the network and passed on from source to destination.

Now that your logs are turned on, you can learn where to retrieve them and examine the values contained in the log files.

Accessing VPC Flow Logs for Reading

After you have enabled VPC Flow Logs, the next step is to figure out how you will access them to take advantage of the data that has been collected.

You can access your logs via the AWS Management Console. Since the logs will be stored in S3, you can access them if an appropriate period of time has passed:

1. Start by logging in to the S3 console. You can quickly use the following URL to visit the S3 service: `https://packt.link/jlula`.

2. After you are logged in to S3, navigate to the bucket you created in step 3 of the previous exercise. In this case, the bucket was named `packt-security-logs`.

3. Click on the bucket name to be taken to the folders inside the bucket. You should see a folder named `bucketnameLogs` (see the following figure). Click on this folder.

Name ▲	Type ▽
📁 packt-security-logsLogs/	Folder

Figure 7.4: S3 bucket selection for VPC Flow Logs

4. Once inside the folder, you will see the logs generated by date. Choose any of the files and click on it. Once on the file page, click on `Download` to download the file locally and open up the file in a text editor.

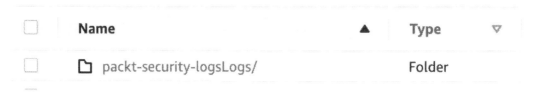

Figure 7.5: VPC Flow Logs file download screen

The next important step after accessing your VPC Flow Logs (as stored in the previously created S3 bucket) is to is to look at the contents of one of the log files. This is covered in the next section.

Parsing the Content of VPC Flow Logs

AWS VPC Flow Logs contain information about the traffic through the network interfaces in your VPC, including the source and destination IP addresses, protocol, port numbers, packet and byte counts, and timestamps. The following is an example of the information contained in a VPC Flow Logs record:

```
2 123456789010 eni-01234567890123456 10.0.0.101 10.0.0.201 443 1234 6
10 500 1617087245 1617087301 ACCEPT OK
```

The following dissects the fields in this example so you know what they mean:

- 2: This is the version of the VPC Flow Logs format.

- 1234567890: This is the AWS account ID for the owner of the network interface.

- eni-01234567890123456: This is the ID of the **elastic network interface** (**ENI**) that captured the traffic.

- 10.0.0.101: This is the source IP of the traffic or where the request originated from.

- 10.0.0.201: This is the destination address of the traffic.

- 6: This is the IP protocol number (TCP in this case).

- 10: This is the number of packets in the flow.

- 500: This is the number of bytes in the flow.

- 1617087245: This is the start time of the flow, in Unix time.

- 161708301: This is the end time of the flow, in Unix time.

- ACCEPT: This is the action taken on the traffic (in this case, it was allowed).

- OK: This is the reason for the action (in this case, there were no errors).

Understanding Flow Log Limitations

Before turning on VPC Flow Logs on every VPC in your accounts and across your infrastructure, be aware that their use has a few limitations. Some key points to note are as follows:

- You can't enable a flow log for a VPC that is peered but not in your account.

- Once enabled, you cannot change a flow log configuration or record format. You would need to delete the current flow log and recreate a flow log to enable any changes.

- Delivery of logs to the designated S3 bucket happens in 5-minute intervals.

- When the packet's destination is the secondary private IPv4 address, then the primary IPv4 of the instance will appear in the dstaddr field of VPC Flow Logs.

> **Note**
> For a complete list of the limitations, you can visit the following URL: `https://packt.link/XGTBI`

With a fuller understanding of VPC Flow Logs and how to read them, you can now move on to a different network logging capability, VPC Traffic Mirroring.

VPC Traffic Mirroring

VPC Traffic Mirroring, as the name implies, allows you to duplicate network traffic from ENIs attached to instances so that the duplicated traffic can then be sent to third-party tools and services for traffic analysis and inspection.

When configured, the duplicated traffic is sent to a target; this could be a Network Load Balancer, using UDP as a listener, that sits in front of a fleet of appliances dedicated to network analysis. Alternatively, you could use another EC2 instance as a target, pointing it to the ENI of the instance. These targets could also be in a different VPC for additional management if required.

With a grasp of VPC traffic monitoring, you can move to the logs you can obtain from the ELB service.

Elastic Load Balancer Access Logs

The **ELB service** allows you to turn on **optional logging**, which captures and monitors the requests flowing through your load balancers. These logs can also help you analyze traffic patterns and troubleshoot issues with the targets to which the load balancers are sending requests.

The access logs, once enabled, are delivered to an S3 bucket that you specify during the setup and the log files are compressed. You need to decompress the files before accessing the raw log files.

AWS ELB log files can be used for several purposes, including the following:

- **Troubleshooting**: The ELB log files contain detailed information about the requests that were served by the load balancer, including the source address, the request URL, the HTTP status code, and the response time. This information can be used to troubleshoot issues with your application, such as slow response times, errors, or connectivity problems.

- **Performance analysis**: ELB log files can provide insight into the performance of your application by you or another team member analyzing the response time and latency of requests served by the load balancer. This can help you identify areas of your application that may require optimization, such as slow database queries or inefficient code.

- **Security analysis**: ELB log files can be used to analyze traffic patterns and detect potential security threats, such as **distributed denial of service (DDoS)** attacks, bot traffic, or suspicious behavior.

- **Compliance and auditing**: ELB log files can be used to comply with regulatory requirements and auditing standards by providing detailed information about the traffic served by the load balancer.

- **Capacity planning**: ELB log files can be used to analyze traffic patterns and forecast future capacity requirements for your application, allowing you to plan for future growth and scale your infrastructure accordingly.

The following section presents an example log file and teaches you how to read and understand its contents.

Load Balancer Access Log Files

Even if a request never reaches the intended target, it is captured in an **access log**. This includes **malformed requests** and is especially helpful in the context of security since malformed requests can sometimes be attempts at things such as directory transversal attacks.

A sample of what is contained in the load balancer log files is shown here:

```
https 2018-07-02T22:23:00.186641Z app/packt-
loadbalancer/50dc6c495c0c9188
192.168.131.39:2817 10.0.0.1:80 0.086 0.048 0.037 200 200 0 57
"GET https://www.example.com:443/ HTTP/1.1" "curl/7.46.0" ECDHE-
RSA-AES128-GCM-SHA256 TLSv1.2
arn:aws:elasticloadbalancing:us-east-2:123456789012:targetgroup/sec-
targets/73e2d6bc24d8a067
"Root=1-58337281-1d84f3d73c47ec4e58577259" "packt.example.
com" "arn:aws:acm:us-east-2:123456789012:certifica
te/12345678-1234-1234-1234-123456789012"
1 2018-07-02T22:22:48.364000Z "authenticate,forward" "-" "-"
"10.0.0.1:80" "200" "-" "-"
```

The following points discuss the first few fields of the log files and describe what they contain:

- **Type**: This shows the type of connection or request. It can be one of several types of values to start the log entry: http, https, ht (for HTTP/2 over TLS), grpcs (for gRPC over TLS), ws (for WebSockets), or wss (for WebSockets over TLS).

- **Time**: This is the time when the load balancer generated a response to the client. For WebSockets clients, it is the time when the connection was closed. Times are in *ISO 8601* format.

- **Elb**: This field identifies the resource ID of the load balancer that took the response.

- **Client:port**: This is the requesting client's IP address and port.

- **Target:port**: This is the target's IP address and port that processed the request. If the request were a Lambda function, you would see - instead of an IP address.

- **Request_processing_time**: This is the total time in sections that it took the target to process the request. This is shown in millisecond precision.

- **Elb_status_code**: This is the load balancer's response status code.

- **Target_status_code**: This is the target's response status code.

> **Note**
> You can find the complete list of all the fields and their descriptions on the *Elastic Load Balancing Documentation* pages: `https://packt.link/f5Sfs`

ELBs are one entry point to your applications and workloads. **Web Application Firewalls (WAFs)** can be a primary entry point that filters requests before they hit the ELB, especially Application Load Balancers. You are now ready to explore the types of logs that they produce.

Web Application Firewall Visibility and Analytics

When requests come to your WAF, they are logged via the CloudWatch service. Using CloudWatch gives you real-time metrics on how many requests hit your AWS WAF and how many match a particular rule. Metrics are published for every rule you set in the WAF. This includes both managed rules from AWS and custom rules that you write yourself. Even if you put your WAF on a blocked or count mode, the metrics still pass on to the CloudWatch service.

Using the CloudWatch service and its ingestion of the metrics produced by AWS WAF, you can set specific alarms for the different metrics, such as if the number of blocked requests is too high for a particular period. Along with tracking the metrics in the CloudWatch service, you can also get sampled web requests.

The following subsections will take you through the different types of logs that can be collected with the WAF service from AWS.

AWS WAF Full Logs

AWS WAF also allows you to get detailed logs for every request that comes through. Compared to the sampled web requests, which provide information about several requests, it includes every request that passes through the WAF and which rule or set of rules matches that particular request. With Full Logs enabled, you have all the details about what kind of request came in and what type of operations the WAF performed rather than just a simple set of metrics, and you can use these detailed logs for tasks such as security analytics, automation, auditing, and compliance.

WAF Full Logs Features and Benefits

The following is the feature set of Full Logs with WAF:

- The logs are available in JSON format.

- You can redact sensitive fields from the logs, such as cookies or the **Auth header**.

- You can stream the logs to another source using Amazon Kinesis Data Firehose.

- WAF Full Logs log every request and contain all request headers along with the rule IDs that match that request.

AWS WAF Full Logs provide comprehensive insights into the traffic that your web applications receive, enhancing your ability to monitor, analyze, and respond to potential security threats. These logs provide a detailed record of requests and responses, including HTTP headers, IP addresses, and query strings. By detailing incoming and outgoing traffic, these logs allow users to identify suspicious patterns, unusual behaviors, or potentially malicious activities. This helps you and your organization stay ahead of attackers by enabling proactive response measures and timely adjustments to your security rules.

Although sampled requests (which you can return with the `GetSampledRequest` query) do produce some information, it will only return a maximum of 500 log files from the first 5,000 requests your WAF has received. This can be insufficient for a firewall with a lot of active traffic constantly traveling across it. As a security professional, you most likely need to examine all the traffic to verify when an event has happened and not just a traffic sample.

Keeping in mind the preceding comparison between WAF Full Logs to WAF sampled requests, you can now look at the various services that send their logs to the CloudWatch service.

Services that Publish Logs to CloudWatch Logs

Most services send their logs to the **CloudWatch Logs** service. This section deals with the different services that generate logs and then send those logs to CloudWatch.

> **Note**
> *Chapter 8, CloudWatch and CloudWatch Metrics*, will discuss in detail how to utilize the capabilities of CloudWatch as a whole, including log retention, log querying, metrics, and events (including Amazon EventBridge).

Although you will not be made to memorize the list of services that can push their logs out to CloudWatch Logs for the exam, it is recommended that you have a robust understanding of which services *do not* have the ability to send logs to CloudWatch Logs without an intermediary step. Further, knowing the services that send their logs out to CloudWatch Logs (think Lambda functions) still helps you when it comes to reading and understanding the test questions.

One of the best ways to retain this information is not to study these lists but rather to perform hands-on exercises with the services. *Table 7.1* shows a comparison of AWS services and how their logs can be delivered using Amazon S3, CloudWatch Logs, and Kinesis Data Firehose as the three primary sources for log ingestion:

Log Type	Amazon S3	CloudWatch Logs	Kinesis Data Firehose
Amazon API Gateway access logs		✓	
Amazon Chime media quality metrics logs and SIP logs		✓	
CloudFront access logs	✓		
CloudWatch Evidently evaluation event logs	✓	✓	
Amazon ElastiCache for Redis logs		✓	✓
AWS Global Accelerator flow logs	✓		
Amazon MSK broker logs	✓	✓	✓
Amazon MSK Connect logs	✓	✓	✓
AWS Network Firewall logs	✓	✓	✓
Network Load Balancer access logs	✓	✓	
Amazon Route 53 resolver query logs	✓	✓	
Amazon SageMaker events		✓	
EC2 Spot Instance data feeds	✓		
AWS Step Functions Express workflow logs		✓	
AWS Step Functions Standard workflow logs		✓	
Storage gateway audit logs		✓	
Storage gateway health logs		✓	
Amazon VPC Flow Logs	✓		✓
AWS WAF logs	✓	✓	✓

Table 7.1: Log types and methods of storage

As you can see from the preceding table, most services allow you to send logs to the CloudWatch service. Some of the services allow more than one location to send their log files. Finally, a select number of services, such as CloudFront access logs, only allow their logs to be delivered to an S3 bucket.

In addition to the pros and cons of storing logs in S3 versus CloudWatch Logs earlier in the chapter, you also need to grasp how to use native tools to sift through the mountain of log files to find the information you are seeking quickly. That said, if you are going to use any of the three aforementioned options, logging to an S3 bucket, using CloudWatch Logs, or having logs streamed via Kinesis Data Firehose, the correct IAM permissions need to be in place so that the corresponding service can place the logs in the desired storage. The following section discusses those permissions.

IAM Permissions for Publishing Logs to CloudWatch Logs

There is a specific set of permissions that must be enabled for a user or service to send logs to the CloudWatch Logs service:

- `logs:CreateLogDelivery`
- `logs:PutResourcePolicy`
- `logs:DescribeResourcePolicies`
- `logs:DescribeLogGroups`

If you have CloudWatch Logs being sent to a log group in CloudWatch Logs, you also need the `logs:CreateLogDelivery` permission.

IAM Permissions for Publishing Logs to S3 Buckets

If you want to send logs to an S3 bucket, then you must enable the following permissions:

- `logs:CreateLogDelivery`
- `s3:GetBucketPolicy`
- `s3:PutBucketPolicy`

IAM Permissions for Publishing Logs to Kinesis Data Firehose

There is a specific set of permissions that must be enabled for a user or service to send logs to the Kinesis Data Firehose service:

- `logs:CreateLogDelivery`
- `firehose:TagDeliveryStream`
- `iam:CreateServiceLinkedRole`

If you are setting up the service for the first time, you also need to add the permissions of `logs:CreateLogDelivery` and `firehose:TagDeliveryStream`.

You just looked at a triad of options available for different AWS services that help you build your account. There is a separate set of logs generated when users (and services) gain authentication and authorization to the AWS platform and when they carry out additions, subtractions, or modifications to the underlying infrastructure. The service capturing all of this is called CloudTrail. In the next section, you will learn how CloudTrail captures activity at the API level.

Logging API Activity with CloudTrail

The service in AWS that enables governance, compliance, risk auditing, and operational auditing is CloudTrail. It does all this by recording the API calls performed either through the AWS Management Console, the AWS CLI, any of the AWS SDKs, or any third-party tool that uses the AWS API. CloudTrail can work in a single account within a single Region, or it can be used to monitor all Regions within that same single account. You can also configure the service to collect events from multiple accounts and then aggregate them in a single bucket for storage. When a company utilizes AWS Organizations often, they oftentimes utilize a specialized account for logging or auditing. Here, the logs from all other accounts in the organization flow into the auditing account, where access is limited except for a select group of individuals.

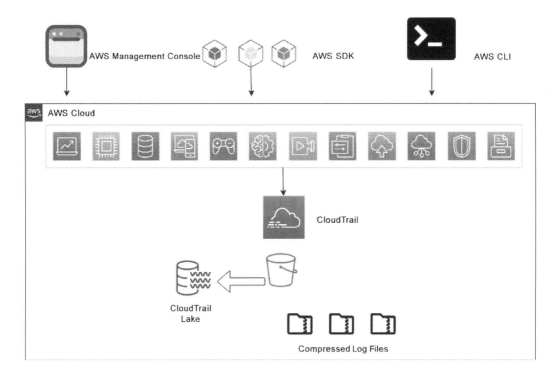

Figure 7.6: CloudTrail API log flow

To understand how CloudTrail logging works and the information that it captures, review the following components of the service first:

- **Trails**: These are the fundamental building blocks of CloudTrail itself, and they contain the configurable options you want to monitor and track. For example, you can create a trail that monitors single or multiple Regions.

- **Events**: Each time an API call is made, AWS CloudTrail intercepts and captures that API request and stores it as an **event**. These events record vital data relating to the API request, which is then stored within a log file. A new event is created for every API request made.

- **Log files**: Log files are created approximately every 5 minutes and are delivered to and stored in a target S3 bucket as defined within the associated trail.

- **API activity filters**: These provide a search and filter functionality when looking at your API activity history from within the AWS Management Console.

When looking at the different components of the CloudTrail service, one of the main ones to be sure you understand is events.

Types of CloudTrail Events

As discussed previously, an event is captured every time a call to the AWS API is made. This could be from the AWS Management Console, the AWS CLI, or one of the AWS SDKs. There are several types of events in CloudTrail. As a security professional and someone looking to take the *AWS Certified Security Specialty Certification* exam, you need to be able to distinguish between the different types of events:

- **Management events**: These are the events logged by default by the service and capture the management operations occurring in your account. AWS describes these as the **control plane operations**. The following are some examples of what would be captured as a management event:

    - Items associated with configuring security, for example, creating a role or deleting a role (e.g., `DeleteRole` API operations)

    - Items associated with registering devices, for example, creating or destroying an EC2 instance (e.g., `RunInstances` API operations)

    - Items associated with routing data, for example, adding, removing, or modifying rules on a security group (e.g., `CreateSecurityGroup` API operations)

    - Items associated with logging operations, for example, creating or modifying a CloudTrail trail (e.g., `CreateTrail` API operations)

    When any activity occurs in your account, CloudTrail will capture and record that activity as a CloudTrail event. The event will contain the following details:

    - Who performed the request

- The date and the time that the request was performed

- The source IP of the request

- How the request was made

- What action was being performed

- The Region the action was conducted in

- The response to the request itself

- **Data events**: These events are not logged by default but can be turned on for a specific trail. Data events tend to come in at a high-volume rate; for this reason, you specify the exact type of event or events that you would like to be captured in your trail. There is an additional cost associated with capturing data events. Therefore, you need a strategy for what you want to capture and possibly for what amount of time. Look at these examples of what can be captured as a data event:

  - Data activity on a DynamoDB table such as `PutItem`, `UpdateItem`, and `DeleteItem` API operations

  - The `Invoke` API operation on an AWS Lambda function

  - Amazon Cognito data events, including calls to the `GetCredentialsForIdentity`, `GetId`, `GetOpenIdToken`, `GetOpenTokenForDeveloperIdentity`, and `UnlinkIdentity` API calls

  If you would like to see the complete list of data event types, you can find them at the following URL: `https://packt.link/wkQOX`

- **Insight events**: These events are not logged by default and can be optionally turned on. Once turned on, they capture unusual API call rate or error rate activity in your AWS account by analyzing management events. There are no specific insight events, as the insight events judge "normal" activity on your account versus the unusual activity it detects. Some examples of insight events could be the following:

  - Unusual AWS Management Console sign-in events

  - Access to AWS resources from new or unusual locations

  - A sudden increase in API calls to a specific resource

  - Suspicious API call patterns that could be indicative of an attack

  - An unusual amount of resource creation or deletion activity

  - An unusual volume of data transfer from an S3 bucket or other storage resource

- Unusual activities by the AWS account user

- Significant or unexpected changes to **Identity and Access Management (IAM)** policies that suggest a security compromise

These examples are for demonstration purposes only; each account's insight events are based on usage patterns and activity.

With an understanding of the different types of events available to be logged by the AWS CloudTrail service, you will now learn how CloudTrail is set up by default.

Default Settings for CloudTrail

Before diving deeper into the features and functionality of the CloudTrail service, you first need to understand its default settings. Knowing this can be helpful when deciphering questions and answers regarding the CloudTrail service on the Security Specialty Certification exam. Be sure that you understand the following base concepts for the exam:

- CloudTrail is enabled on your AWS account when you create it.

- CloudTrail logs are encrypted using Amazon S3 **server-side encryption (SSE)**. This can be changed to create logs encrypted with a KMS key.

- CloudTrail publishes logs on average about every 5 minutes, multiple times per hour.

- Trails are only viewable in the AWS Regions where they log events.

Now that you understand the default settings with the CloudTrail service, the next section will take you through the process of setting up a new trail.

Creating a New Trail in AWS CloudTrail

Even though CloudTrail is enabled by default in accounts, there are cases where turning on an additional trail makes sense. As part of the security team, you must ensure that all Regions and events are captured and stored with integrity. With all the valuable data in the trail, this can be a handy tool for developers working on items such as infrastructure as code or IAM features. Creating an additional trail in a particular Region for developers mitigates the risk of anything happening to the data contained in the original trail. It also allows the developers to toggle the features of the secondary trail on and off as they see fit.

The following steps will take you through the process of turning on an additional CloudTrail trail in a single Region:

1. First, go to the CloudTrail service on the AWS Management Console using the following URL: `https://packt.link/kB07A`

    You should now be on the dashboard page of CloudTrail.

2. Click on the button labeled `Create Trail` on the right side of the page.

    You should now be on a page named `Choose trail attributes`.

3. For the name of the trail, enter `security-cert`. Leave the box blank to enable all the accounts in your organization, as this is just a single trail for a single Region.

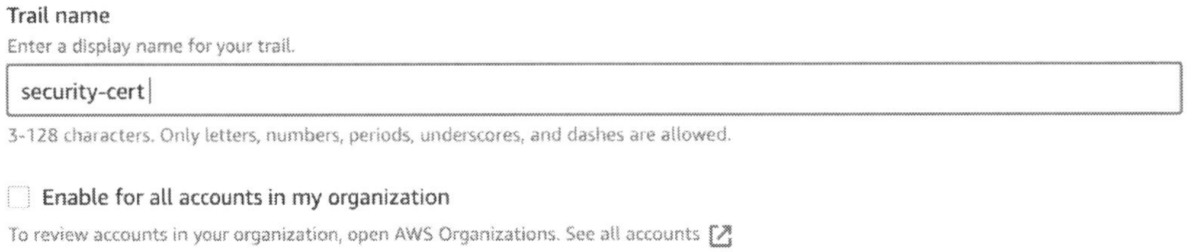

Trail name
Enter a display name for your trail.

| security-cert | |

3-128 characters. Only letters, numbers, periods, underscores, and dashes are allowed.

☐ **Enable for all accounts in my organization**

To review accounts in your organization, open AWS Organizations. See all accounts [↗]

Figure 7.7: CloudTrail setup screen

With this trail, you examined a scenario where developers needed access to the trail data. Therefore, you need to create a brand-new bucket to provide the correct access control to the development team to view the CloudTrail logs.

4. Keep the default name given here or name it something more relevant for you.

Trail log bucket and folder
Enter a new S3 bucket name and folder (prefix) to store your logs. Bucket names must be globally unique.

| packt-security-cert-ctrail-logs | |

Logs will be stored in packt-security-cert-ctrail-logs/AWSLogs/182968331794

Figure 7.8: S3 bucket and folder selection for CloudTrail

5. With the sensitive nature of CloudTrail data, such as usernames and account numbers, enable `Log file SSE-KMS encryption` and, with that, create a new key. It is recommended that you name your key for this exercise `packt-cloudtrail` (this way, you know it will be safe to delete once you are done studying).

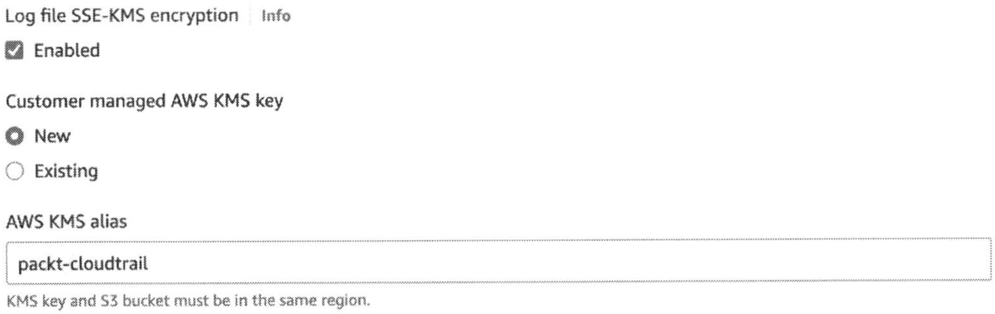

Log file SSE-KMS encryption   Info

☑ Enabled

Customer managed AWS KMS key

◉ New

○ Existing

AWS KMS alias

| packt-cloudtrail |

KMS key and S3 bucket must be in the same region.

Figure 7.9: CloudTrail encryption key creation

6. For this example, turn off `Log file validation` since you are only making a single trail for a set of developers. Uncheck this box under `Additional settings`.

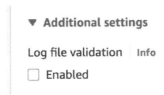

▼ **Additional settings**

Log file validation   Info

☐ Enabled

Figure 7.10: Additional settings dropdown

7. After completing the previous steps 1-6, you can scroll down to the bottom of the page and click on the orange `Next` button.

Once you press that `Next` button, you will be brought to the page to select which types of events you would like CloudTrail to log to this trail.

8. Management events is selected by default but enable Data events for this particular trail. Just remember that there is an additional charge for each additional dataset you choose for CloudTrail to record.

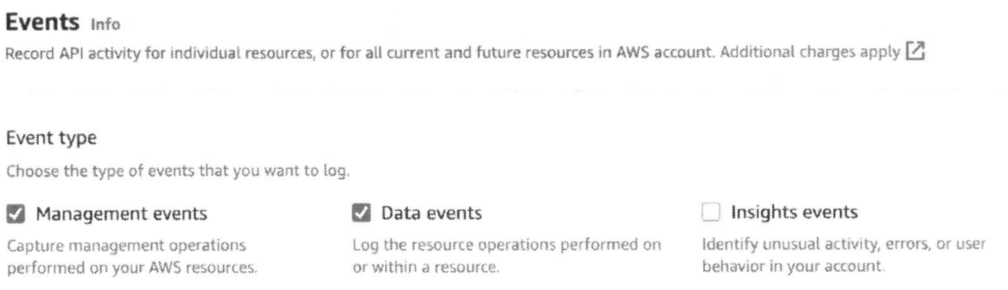

Events Info

Record API activity for individual resources, or for all current and future resources in AWS account. Additional charges apply ↗

Event type

Choose the type of events that you want to log.

☑ **Management events**

Capture management operations performed on your AWS resources.

☑ **Data events**

Log the resource operations performed on or within a resource.

☐ **Insights events**

Identify unusual activity, errors, or user behavior in your account.

Figure 7.11: Event type selection for CloudTrail

9. Now scroll down to Management events and make sure that both the Read and Write API activities are checked.

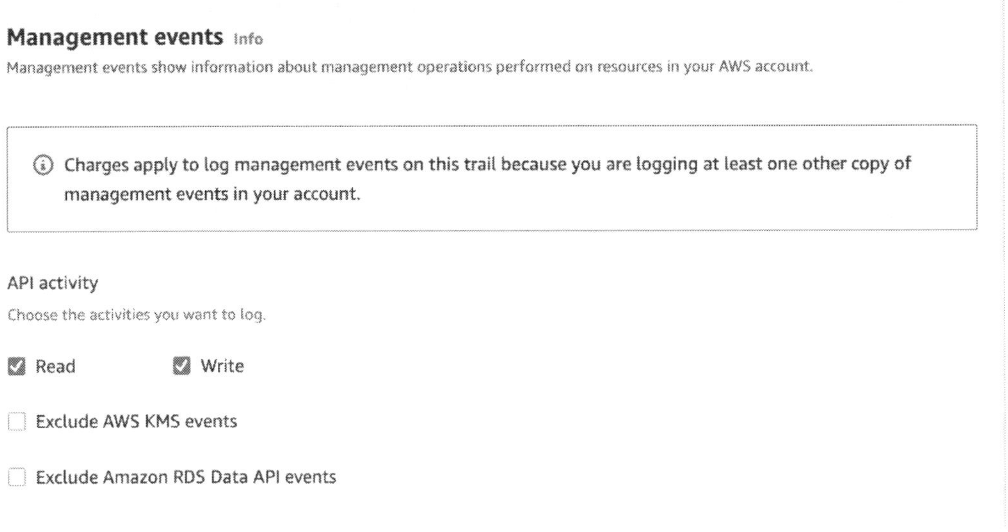

Management events Info

Management events show information about management operations performed on resources in your AWS account.

> ⓘ Charges apply to log management events on this trail because you are logging at least one other copy of management events in your account.

API activity

Choose the activities you want to log.

☑ Read   ☑ Write

☐ Exclude AWS KMS events

☐ Exclude Amazon RDS Data API events

Figure 7.12: Management events activity selection for CloudTrail

For data events, there are many options that you could choose to have recorded.

10. To keep things simple, select all S3 data events by choosing the S3 data event type and keep the Log all events option.

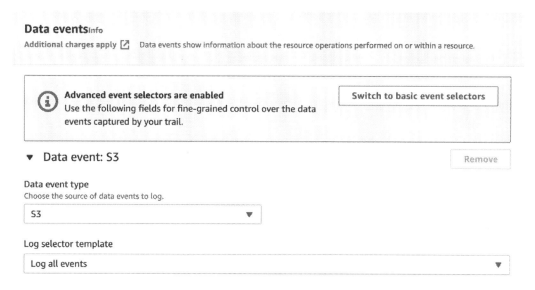

Figure 7.13: Data event type selection for CloudTrail

11. Now scroll to the bottom of the page and click on the Next button.

12. This will bring you to the Review and create page for your new trail. Check the details to ensure that you have entered everything correctly, and if everything seems in order, scroll down to the bottom of the page and click the Create trail button.

You can now look at the data events for the S3 buckets enabled in your new CloudTrail trail.

Data Events for S3 Buckets

When you created your new trail, you enabled the data events for S3 objects. These logs closely resemble the S3 access logs but are stored in the CloudTrail logging system rather than a specified S3 bucket (in the case of S3 access logs). One of the most obvious reasons to do this would be having a multi-account setup with a specified logging account where all the CloudTrail logs flow to a separate logging account that cannot be accessed by anyone but the audit or security team. This would then keep a record of any S3 object activity for each account where the data events have been enabled separately from the actual account in which the activity is happening.

It is often possible to view the properties of an S3 bucket and see that S3 access logging has been enabled. If someone has access to that bucket, they might have permission to turn off that logging and delete those logs. In the case of data events for S3, as the events are being recorded, this only appears in the settings of the CloudTrail service itself and not in the bucket settings. If you have placed the correct amount of access control on the CloudTrail service via an organizational/account service control policy, finely scoped permissions for roles, or both, then you have a better protective barrier on your log generation service.

With your new trail created, you need to perform some activity in your account and/or your S3 buckets so that the trail can record your actions. Go ahead and browse through your AWS Management Console so that some management events are recorded. The following section will show you how to search through these events.

Querying the Event History in CloudTrail

In the AWS Console, you have the ability to search through events that have occurred in the past 90 days. If you need to search for a period prior to this, then you would have to either import your logs into a third-party tool, extract compressed logs to an S3 bucket and attach Amazon Athena, or download the logs to a local system to create your own search index.

The following steps will show you how you can use the CloudTrail service to perform a few simple queries and see what you can discover:

1. First, log directly in to the CloudTrail service using the following URL: `https://packt.link/eq3Yi`.

2. Once on the `CloudTrail` service, from the left-hand menu, click on `Event history`.

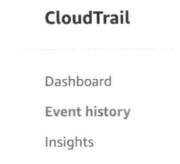

CloudTrail

Dashboard

Event history

Insights

Figure 7.14: CloudTrail service menu

You will be brought to the main event history page. This should be all the API calls performed for the Region that you are currently in.

3. Next, turn your attention to where the page says `Lookup attributes`. Filter by `Event source`.

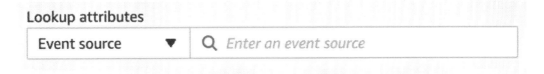

Figure 7.15: Event source selection for a CloudTrail query

4. Next to the search box where you can enter the event source, enter `s3.amazon.aws`.

Figure 7.16: Event source selection for a CloudTrail query

You should now have a filtered list of only S3 events on the page in front of you.

If you click on the X by `s3.amazon.aws.com`, you can test different event sources.

Having learned how to look up and query events in CloudTrail, the next step is to explore how CloudTrail can be expanded with CloudTrail Lake.

CloudTrail Lake

AWS CloudTrail Lake is a solution that helps you store and analyze AWS CloudTrail data at a much larger scale instead of dealing with a single trail at a time. It uses Amazon S3, Amazon Athena, and AWS Glue to create a data lake that can store CloudTrail logs for an extended period of time.

By leveraging AWS CloudTrail Lake, you can gain deeper insights into your AWS environment, such as identifying potential security threats, troubleshooting issues, and auditing compliance. It provides a central location to store, manage, and analyze CloudTrail data, making it easier to perform ad hoc queries, build custom reports, and gain insight into user activity across multiple AWS accounts.

Rather than storing the events in the JSON format, CloudTrail Lake converts existing events into a row-based Apache ORC format. This is a columnar storage format that is highly efficient for retrieving stored data.

Summary

This chapter covered the different types of logs produced by various AWS services and how they can be stored for later use and consumption or, if needed, for an audit.

You saw how S3 can record access to its objects and folders using S3 access logging. You also explored how to troubleshoot and record network activity using VPC Flow Logs. In reviewing another way to capture network traffic, you saw the capabilities of both ELB logging and WAF logs.

You also learned about the service that records all API calls, CloudTrail. You examined how to turn on a new trail for a specific purpose and how to look up events in that trail. In case using the legacy trail becomes limiting, you looked at how to expand the capabilities of CloudTrail using CloudTrail Lake.

Chapter 8, CloudWatch and CloudWatch Metrics, will discuss the CloudWatch service and how it consumes logs. You will also see how CloudWatch can gather and publish predefined and custom metrics from our services.

Further Reading

For additional information on the AWS Shared Responsibility Model and an underlying foundation of AWS security, please check out the following resources:

- Logging options for Amazon S3: `https://packt.link/7pTi5`

- Analyze Network Traffic of Amazon Virtual Private Cloud (VPC) by CIDR blocks: `https://packt.link/yiNeO`

- Well-Architected Framework – Security Pillar, Detection: `https://packt.link/ZLCA7`

Exam Readiness Drill – Chapter Review Questions

Apart from a solid understanding of key concepts, being able to think quickly under time pressure is a skill that will help you ace your certification exam. That is why working on these skills early on in your learning journey is key.

Chapter review questions are designed to improve your test-taking skills progressively with each chapter you learn and review your understanding of key concepts in the chapter at the same time. You'll find these at the end of each chapter.

> **How To Access These Resources**
>
> To learn how to access these resources, head over to the chapter titled *Chapter 21, Accessing the Online Practice Resources.*

To open the Chapter Review Questions for this chapter, perform the following steps:

1. Click the link – `https://packt.link/SCSC02E2_CH07`

   Alternatively, you can scan the following QR code (*Figure 7.17*):

Figure 7.17: QR code that opens Chapter Review Questions for logged-in users

2.   Once you log in, you'll see a page similar to the one shown in *Figure 7.18*:

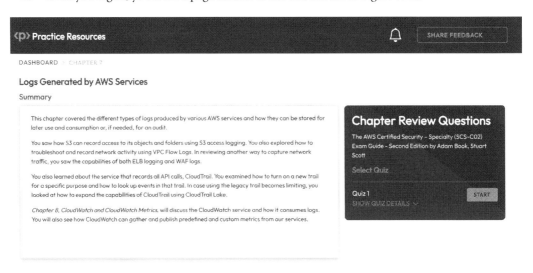

Figure 7.18: Chapter Review Questions for Chapter 7

3.   Once ready, start the following practice drills, re-attempting the quiz multiple times.

Exam Readiness Drill

For the first three attempts, don't worry about the time limit.

ATTEMPT 1

The first time, aim for at least **40%**. Look at the answers you got wrong and read the relevant sections in the chapter again to fix your learning gaps.

ATTEMPT 2

The second time, aim for at least **60%**. Look at the answers you got wrong and read the relevant sections in the chapter again to fix any remaining learning gaps.

ATTEMPT 3

The third time, aim for at least **75%**. Once you score **75%** or more, you start working on your timing.

> **Tip**
> You may take more than three attempts to reach 75%. That's okay. Just review the relevant sections in the chapter till you get there.

Working On Timing

Target: Your aim is to keep the score the same while trying to answer these questions as quickly as possible. Here's an example of how your next attempts should look like:

Attempt	Score	Time Taken
Attempt 5	77%	21 mins 30 seconds
Attempt 6	78%	18 mins 34 seconds
Attempt 7	76%	14 mins 44 seconds

Table 7.2: Sample timing practice drills on the online platform

> **Note**
> The time limits shown in the above table are just examples. Set your own time limits with each attempt based on the time limit of the quiz on the website.

With each new attempt, your score should stay above 75% while your time taken to complete should **decrease**. Repeat as many attempts as you want till you feel confident dealing with the time pressure.

8

CloudWatch and CloudWatch Metrics

In the previous chapter, you looked at the different types of log files AWS can generate. This chapter will focus on the **CloudWatch** service. Amazon CloudWatch is the leading monitoring service used in AWS and cloud data and metrics from all supported AWS services. It allows you to gain a better understanding of the performance of your environment. CloudWatch lets you collect valuable logging information from many different services, such as EC2 instances and Route 53, and even has the capability to collect and store CloudTrail logs.

In addition, CloudWatch has built-in metric monitoring and reporting capabilities with **CloudWatch Metrics**. Metrics can be gathered and used in multiple formats, such as creating alarms to help notify your security team when certain thresholds are breached (such as too many log-in attempts during a specific time period) or alarms for other groups depending on their needs. Dashboards can also be created to graphically present the metrics, which further helps easily visualize what happens with a particular service or metric over a short or extended period.

Finally, the chapter will wrap things up with a review of Amazon EventBridge, the processor of **CloudWatch Events**. Having an understanding of the aforementioned **event-driven architectures (EDAs)**, especially in the context of security, can help you automate your responses to various events detected by CloudWatch alarms and other AWS services. This leads to faster response times and allows manual intervention in other tasks.

The following main topics will be covered in this chapter:

- Using and searching CloudWatch Logs
- The CloudWatch Logs agent
- Basic metrics provided by the services and creating custom metrics
- Amazon EventBridge overview
- EventBridge rules and templates

Technical Requirements

You will need to have access to the AWS Management Console with an active account and AWS CLI access for this chapter.

CloudWatch Overview

Amazon CloudWatch is the de facto AWS native service used to help you monitor your services and resources. While other services may help with monitoring specific tasks such as networking or security, CloudWatch considers the services holistically. The primary function of CloudWatch is to help you monitor and track the performance of your AWS workloads, services, and applications.

When working with your systems, especially during peak periods of traffic, you never know what to expect. You need to have visibility into your overall system along with individual components in case the response times start to become sluggish or unresponsive. Applications, and correspondingly their requirements, including security requirements, are becoming more complex. The number of different platforms being used is constantly evolving, and logs are constantly being generated from different sources. Through all of this, you need a way to keep an eye on your systems. The preceding aspects represent a tiny sliver of the issues, such as performance or security-related issues, that the CloudWatch service tackles as it helps you monitor your applications and environment.

For example, consider a company that runs an e-commerce application that also stores sensitive data. As the security engineer, your top priority is to ensure the security of the data stored on the AWS platform and prevent unauthorized access. If you notice an unusual number of failed login attempts from the main site's login page, your company might be undergoing a brute-force attack. You can use the features of CloudWatch to help monitor and proactively solve this issue using the following features it offers:

- **Monitoring log data**: CloudWatch Logs can be set up to capture and centralize log files from your application servers, including login-related events.

- **Log metrics and filters**: You can use the AWS CloudWatch service to filter the log files by failed login attempts and then create customized metrics based on the number of these events. You would define the filter pattern that captures entries with the *failed login* keywords.

- **Threshold alarms**: After setting up your filters and metrics, you can configure a CloudWatch alarm if the number of failed login attempts exceeds a certain threshold within a specific time period, for example, 45 failed logins in 5 minutes.

- **Notifications**: Although notifications themselves are part of **Simple Notification Service (SNS)**, CloudWatch alarms can couple with SNS to send out a notification if the threshold has been breached.

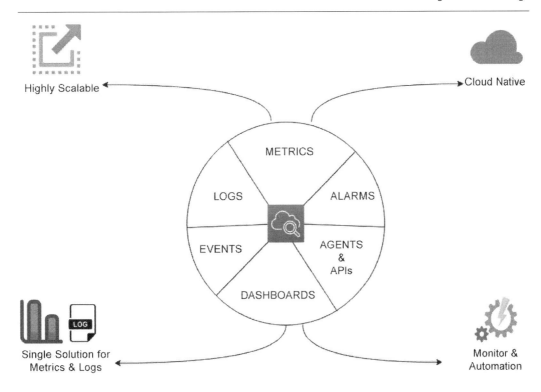

Figure 8.1: The features of AWS CloudWatch

When monitoring systems, the CloudWatch service either uses alarms to notify team members through SNS or uses the events to trigger automated responses to downstream targets, as you will see later in this chapter. The CloudWatch service consists of four main components: metrics, alarms, logs, and events.

Understanding CloudWatch Logs

CloudWatch Logs allows you to ingest logs from your AWS services. The CloudWatch Logs service helps you move logs off your host and onto durable storage. The S3 service backs this durable storage. Once they have moved there, they are retained until you change the retention period.

With logs stored in CloudWatch Logs, you can perform basic text searches across the data stored. You can also create custom metrics and alarms from the data parsed from the logs. CloudWatch Logs can be an essential tool in your security and compliance frameworks, as they allow you to create an audit trail, serve as evidence for forensic analysis, and provide critical information in case of an incident. From the rules, you can impose the usage, access to, and auditability of the logs.

Having gained a basic understanding of the CloudWatch Logs service, you will now learn about some of the key terms.

CloudWatch Logs Terminology

You should be familiar with some key terms that may appear when working with the CloudWatch service and on the *Certified Security Specialty* exam:

- **Filter pattern**: The filtering expressions restrict which logs get forwarded in the AWS destination resource.

- **Log events**: A record of some activity recorded in CloudWatch Logs is a log event. Event messages must be in the *UTF-8* format.

- **Log streams**: A log stream in CloudWatch is a sequence of log events that share the same source. It's essentially a log file continuously being written to, with each log event representing a line in the log file.

- **Log groups**: A group of log streams that share the same source are grouped in the CloudWatch Logs console as log groups. There is no limit on how many log streams can be a part of one log group.

- **Retention settings**: These settings determine how long you keep your logs in CloudWatch Logs. By default, logs are kept indefinitely and never expire, and this can lead to extra costs. If you do not need your logs after a specific period of time, you can choose a retention period between 1 day and 10 years for each log group. Once the retention period is met, the logs are automatically deleted.

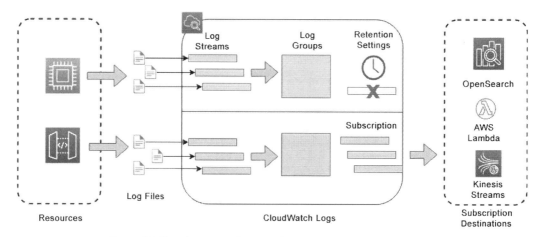

Figure 8.2: How logs move from AWS resources to CloudWatch Logs

Figure 8.2 shows how the different AWS resources generate the log files that turn into log streams. Those log streams then turn into log groups. The log groups can be part of a subscription that is consumed by other services to be stored in other long-term storage or used for analysis. CloudWatch Logs also has the ability to retain logs for the time period that you specify.

The next section will show you how to save log files indefinitely or for a specific period of time.

Retaining and Expiring CloudWatch Logs

As logs come into the CloudWatch service, they are stored in a log group and by default never expire. This can lead to extra charges for your account, especially for items such as developmental logs that don't need to be saved in the account for extended periods of time due to compliance requirements.

If you would like for the logs of a particular log group to expire automatically, you can customize this configuration. The setting is customizable from 1 day to 10 years (3,653 days).

Figure 8.3: CloudWatch log groups log retention options

You can change this setting from any CloudWatch log group by clicking on the current retention setting. This will bring up a dialog window like the one shown in *Figure 8.3* from which you can choose your new log retention setting. Any logs in the log group older than the setting would then be deleted.

Now that you know how to adjust the retention settings for the logs that come into the CloudWatch Logs service, you are ready to install the CloudWatch agent on an EC2 instance to capture both logs and metrics.

Installing and Using the CloudWatch Logging Agent

One of the best ways to understand how CloudWatch sends and collects logs, along with how the unified agent works, is to install the agent on an EC2 instance. The following tutorial will take you through the steps of standing up an EC2 instance and installing the agent onto the instance with the assistance of AWS Systems Manager. Once this has been completed, you can send some traffic to the instance and then look at the generated logs.

> **Note**
>
> A CloudWatch agent configuration file will be created and stored in the **Systems Manager** parameter store during the configuration. This part of the process is only required once. Once this configuration file has been created, the same file can be used on all your EC2 instances.

Creating the Necessary Roles

Start the process of configuring the CloudWatch logging agent by creating two new **IAM roles**. The first will be used to collect the log data and then pass that data on to the CloudWatch service. The second role will be communicating with the Systems Manager service to create and store your agent configuration file. This secondary role is especially crucial if you are trying to roll out a unified system with your EC2 instances and want to collect the same log files on each instance quickly. Another case where this is helpful is if you have a handful of different logging scenarios (e.g., where different flavors of Linux have logs stored in different paths). You need to have a separate configuration file for each operating system. All you need to maintain is the top-level configuration file and then have SSM do the actual installation on the instances.

Begin by creating the first IAM role. To make your role, open up the AWS Management Console. You can create the two roles that are needed through the following steps:

1.   To quickly get to the IAM service, use the URL `https://packt.link/2CFNv`.

2.   Once on the IAM dashboard, choose `Roles` from the left-hand-side menu.

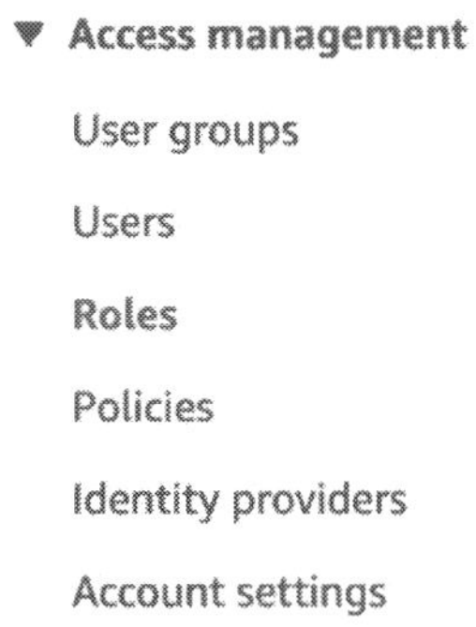

▼ **Access management**

User groups

Users

Roles

Policies

Identity providers

Account settings

Figure 8.4: IAM dashboard menu

3. In the top-right corner, click the `Create Role` button.

4. Now that you're on the `Select trusted entity` page, under `Trusted entity type`, ensure that `AWS service` is selected.

Trusted entity type

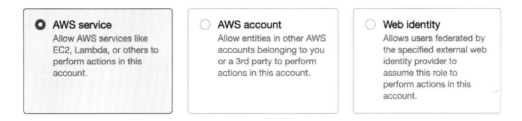

Figure 8.5: Trusted entity type screen

5. At the bottom of the page, select `EC2` as the use case. Once you have done that, you can click the `Next` button at the bottom of the page.

Figure 8.6: Use case screen for IAM

After pressing the Next button, you should be on the Add permissions page. You will need to add two AWS-managed policies to this role.

6.   Search for the policies by name and then select the box to the left side of the policy name. The policies are named CloudWatchAgentServerPolicy and AmazonSSMManagedInstanceCore. Once both policies are selected, press the Next button at the bottom of the page to proceed.

Figure 8.7: Policy name for roles

You now have the opportunity to enter the role details.

7.   For the role name, enter CloudWatchAgentServerRole. Once done, scroll down to the bottom of the page and ensure that both policies have been attached to the role. Then press the blue Create role button.

You have now created the first role needed. Now go through the process of creating the second role. It is very similar to the previous steps, so refer to the preceding steps or the screenshots if you need to.

If you have just finished creating the previous role, you should be back on the IAM page showing the roles in your account. On this page, perform the following steps:

1.   Click on the Create role button in the top-right corner of the page.

2.   Once on the Select trusted entity page, choose Trusted entity type for AWS service on the top half of the page. Scroll to the bottom of the page and choose EC2 for Use case. Once you have finished these selections, click on the blue Next button at the bottom of the page.

3.   Moving on to the Add permissions page, use the search box to add the policies named CloudWatchAgentAdminPolicy and AmazonSSMManagedInstanceCore to the role. Select the box at the side of each policy to add them. Once done, click on the blue Next button at the bottom of the page.

4.   For the role details, enter CloudWatchAgentAdminRole for the role name. Double-check that both policies have been added to the role before scrolling down the page; then click the blue Create role button.

You have now created the IAM roles needed for the CloudWatch logging agent. The next section will take you through the process of creating an instance and then installing the CloudWatch agent on that instance.

Installing the CloudWatch Agent on an EC2 Instance

In order to install the CloudWatch agent on an EC2 instance, you will need to have an EC2 instance that is running and with which the SSM can communicate successfully. One of the easiest ways to do this is to use an EC2 instance running Amazon Linux. If you are using a different variety of operating system, there are ways to get SSM Agent running on your system. Sometimes it has to be manually installed, as in the case of the Ubuntu operating system.

You will first launch an EC2 instance to carry out the exercise:

1. Direct your browser to the EC2 service using the following URL: `https://packt.link/aGtjo`.

2. You will be brought to the EC2 dashboard. Click on the orange button labeled `Launch instance` in the middle of the page. When it pops up, choose `Launch instance` again.

3. On the `Launch an instance` page, name your instance `CloudWatchAgentTest`.

4. For the AMI, choose the latest Amazon Linux AMI; this example has the Amazon Linux 2023 AMI selected. Select the following parameters:

   • `Instance size:` `t2.micro` is OK to keep.

   • `Key pair:` Keep this blank as we will use SSM to manage this instance.

   • `Network Settings:` Create a security group to SSH from your IP address.

Key pair name - *required*

Proceed without a key pair (Not recommended)	Default value ▼

Figure 8.8: Key pair selection screen for EC2 instance

5. Click `Advanced details` to expand the settings; under the IAM instance profile, click on the drop-down box and choose the `CloudWatchAgentServerRole` role you created in the previous step.

6. Once you have completed all this, click the `Launch instance` button on the bottom right-hand side of the page.

   Once you have an Amazon Linux EC2 instance up and running, you can move on to installing the CloudWatch agent.

7. Navigate to the Systems Manager service in the AWS Management Console either by searching for the service in the search bar at the top or by using the following URL: `https://packt.link/V1KKl`.

8. From the left-hand menu, under the Node Management menu heading, choose the Run Command menu item.

Figure 8.9: Node Management menu

9. Next, click the orange button in the main window labeled Run a Command.

10. On the Run a command screen, use the search box to search for the document named AWS-ConfigureAWSPackage. Select the radio button next to the document once it is found.

11. Scroll down to the Command Parameters section of the page. The name of the package to install is AmazonCloudWatchAgent. You should be able to keep the default action of Install and keep Installation Type as Uninstall and reinstall. You do not have to fill in any values for the Version or the Additional Arguments sections.

Command parameters

Action
(Required) Specify whether or not to install or uninstall the package.

Install

Installation Type
(Optional) Specify the type of installation. Uninstall and reinstall: The application is taken offline until the reinstallation process completes. In-place update: The application is available while new or updated files are added to the installation.

Uninstall and reinstall

Name
(Required) The package to install/uninstall.

AmazonCloudWatchAgent

Figure 8.10: Command parameters screen for running a command

12. After filling in the command parameters, scroll down on the page until you reach `Target selection`. This is where you will search for the EC2 instance you just launched, `CloudWatchAgentTest`. You can do this by manually selecting the radio button in the box at the center labeled `Choose instances manually` and then selecting your instance.

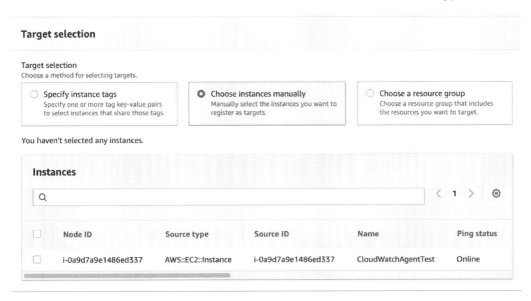

Figure 8.11: Instance selection screen for CloudWatch

> **Note**
>
> If you were trying to do this for a large number of instances in an automated fashion, then the best course of action would be to label those instances to get the CloudWatch agent with a particular tag and value – for example, `CloudWatchAgent` as the tag and the `date` as the value. This way, you could use the `Specify instance tags` option and look up the exact tag-value pair for the installation. If you only used the tag of `CloudWatchAgent` and didn't use the date as the value, or if you used a value such as `true`, then you could run into a case where any instances where the agent had previously been installed would require you to re-install the agent, which could lead to metric or log disruption during the process.

13. Your next step is to scroll down to the `Outputs options` section of the page. You want the output from the run command to go to CloudWatch Logs rather than an S3 bucket, so uncheck the box labeled `Enable an S3 bucket` and then check the box labeled `Enable CloudWatch Logs`. You do not need to create a custom log group name, as the CloudWatch service will use default naming.

14. Once you have enabled the output of the run command, scroll down to the bottom of the page and press the orange Run button.

After pressing the Run button, you will be taken to a screen showing your command's state. Initially, the command will be in the In Progress state. After a minute or two, you should see Success appear under Overall status.

Overall status	Detailed status	# targets	# completed	# error	# delivery timed out
⊘ Success	⊘ Success	1	1	0	0

Figure 8.12: CloudWatch command's state screen

You can now go to the CloudWatch service and look at the log groups or the metrics for this specific instance. With the agent installed, you can customize which logs on the server are being captured. If this were a Linux web server running Apache, you could tell request CloudWatch agent, under the logs configuration, to gather the HTTPD log files and then send them back to CloudWatch Logs for safekeeping and analysis.

There are alternative ways to set up the CloudWatch Logs agent without using the Systems Manager runbook. You could upload the agent via the *secure copy* command, which allows you to copy files from a local source folder and a remote directory over a secure protocol. This is fine if you are doing it on a single instance, but once the agent is on the remote machine, you still need to go into the machine and hand-configure the settings manually. You could place the agent files in an S3 bucket where the EC2 roles would have read access to that bucket and, therefore, can pull down the agent file as part of a cloud initialization script. One of the differences between using the cloud-init process and the SSM process is that if something faltered during the cloud-init process, you would need to access the instance and will then have to perform the commands again remotely. This is in contrast to the SSM document, wherein the command(s) could quickly be rerun from either the CLI or the SSM console without needing to access the instance itself.

You just saw how to install a CloudWatch agent on an EC2 instance running Systems Manager Agent to quickly and easily configure the agent. You also learned that there are multiple ways to install the CloudWatch agent on an instance and reviewed some of the pros and cons of using those ways. In the next section, you will learn how to search through some of the logs you collect with CloudWatch.

Querying and Searching CloudWatch Logs

CloudWatch Logs provides you with a few different search capacities to efficiently analyze your log data and search through your log files. These capacities include the following:

- **Text-based search**: Using simple search queries, you can search for specific text strings within your logs data.

- **Filter expressions**: You can use filter expressions to narrow down your search results based on specific log fields, values, or patterns.

- **Metric filters**: You can create metric filters to extract metric data from your log data, which can be used to create custom metrics and alarms.

- **Log Insights**: You can use CloudWatch Logs Insights to run ad hoc queries and visualize log data with graphs and tables.

The following section presents a simple scenario for searching through log files stored in CloudWatch Logs.

Performing a Search in CloudWatch Logs

Go through the following steps to search the log files stored in CloudWatch Logs:

1. If you still need to log in to the AWS Management Console and access the CloudWatch service, go ahead and do that. You can use the following URL to get there quickly: `http://console.aws.amazon.com/cloudwatch/`.

2. On the left-hand menu, click the `Logs` heading to expand the submenu items. Then, click on `Log groups`.

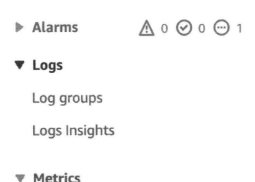

Figure 8.13: CloudWatch menu screen

3. Choose one of your GuardDuty log groups (or any other group if you still have not done the *Enabling Amazon GuardDuty* exercise in *Chapter 6* and created one). Click on the log group name to be taken inside the log group.

Figure 8.14: Log group selection screen

4. Click the `Search log group` button.

5. In the search box, if searching the GuardDuty logs, type `THREATS_FOUND` and press *Enter*.

You will see the log files that match the result.

You have just seen how to search through your CloudWatch log files. Next, you will take a look at metrics, both AWS-generated and custom-made.

CloudWatch Metrics

Metrics, which are quantitative measurements representing a specific aspect of a resource's performance, behavior, or utilization, are automatically collected in Amazon CloudWatch from AWS services such as DynamoDB database instances and Lambda functions. As metrics are collected over time, you can quickly graph their values and then choose the timeframe (e.g., 3 hours, 1 day, or 1 month) that you would like to see them.

You can also create a custom metric. These metrics are relevant to your organization and can be made based on the values in your log files. Custom metrics can track any essential data in your company, infrastructure, or application. Examples could be the number of requests your application receives or how many errors a particular application returns.

In the next section, you will see how to create metric filters in CloudWatch from predefined and custom metrics.

Metric Filters in CloudWatch

In AWS CloudWatch, a **metric filter** provides a way to extract the data from your log files and then transform it into custom metrics. These metric filters allow you to create custom metrics from log data and then use those custom-created metrics to monitor your environment, create alarms, and perform analytical analysis.

To create a metric filter, you must define a pattern that CloudWatch uses to pull data from log events. This pattern can be a complex regular expression looking for various terms that will match within its bounds, or it could be a very simple string that is a true or false match. Once you have determined what you are looking for in the log files, you can then specify which fields to search in the logs. The search could be narrowed down to the `DateTime` field or one of the values in the log entry.

After you have created the metric filter, the CloudWatch service will automatically apply it to any new log data that comes into the log group and extract the metric data based on the filter pattern. Results will then be shown on the CloudWatch console and can be used to make custom dashboards or create alarms for the values in the metric data.

An example would be a metric filter that automatically searches for `Access Denied` in log-in attempts from web application logs streaming to CloudWatch Logs. You could create the metric that monitors for this in the log files to create a count. A CloudWatch alarm could also be created if the count rises above a certain number in a specific period (such as 5 minutes) to notify the security team of a brute-force attack on the application.

You can effectively extract and transform log data into actionable metrics with metric filters. The next section dives deeper into CloudWatch alarms.

CloudWatch Alarms

With the metrics that CloudWatch provides, the service also allows you to monitor metrics and events that can automatically initiate actions (such as sending out an SNS notification) when certain conditions are met, in near real time. CloudWatch alarms can be used for a multitude of purposes, including detecting unusual behavior or performance issues with your AWS resources.

A metric alarm monitors a specific metric of CloudWatch. It has a threshold set for monitoring when initially created. These thresholds define the values of when the alarm will be triggered and are based on the metrics that you specify, such as CPU utilization, network traffic, or available disk space. Additionally, initial monitoring periods allow for a grace period after the alarm is created, during which nothing is triggered.

When you create a metric alarm, you select a CloudWatch metric, set a threshold value for the metric, and specify the actions to be taken when the threshold is breached. These actions can include sending a notification, initiating an automatic scaling process, or executing a specific AWS Lambda function. You can also use CloudWatch alarms to perform autoscaling actions such as adding more EC2 instances or removing extra EC2 instances from autoscaling groups. Alarm actions also enable you to perform Systems Manager actions such as running command documents.

For example, if you are monitoring the CPU utilization of an EC2 instance, you can create a metric alarm to trigger when the CPU utilization exceeds a certain percentage. This can help you identify potential performance issues or bottlenecks in your application.

Knowing a few facts about CloudWatch alarms can help you when taking the AWS Security Specialty exam. You probably will not be tested on these concepts directly in a question. However, the knowledge of these facts may be indirectly incorporated into a question on the exam. The following are a few key facts to remember about AWS CloudWatch alarms:

- Alarm names can only comprise ASCII characters.

- You can create up to 5,000 alarms per Region per account.

- You can add alarms to CloudWatch dashboards.

- You can test alarms by using the SetAlarmState setting (to either engage or disengage the alarm).

- The CloudWatch service saves alarm history for 14 days.

Next, you will go through the process of creating a CloudWatch alarm.

Creating a CloudWatch Alarm

If you completed the previous exercise, you already have an EC2 instance that is being monitored by the CloudWatch service. In the upcoming steps, you will use this instance to create the CloudWatch alarm:

1. Open up your terminal to execute the following commands using the AWS CLI.

2. First, create a topic with SNS, as follows:

```
aws sns create-topic --name alarm-test
```

If the topic has been created successfully, you should see a return on your screen as shown here:

```
----------------------------------------------------------------
|                          CreateTopic                          |
+----------+-----------------------------------------------------+
|  TopicArn|   arn:aws:sns:us-east-2:123456789012:alarm-test   |
+----------+-----------------------------------------------------+
```

3. After creating your topic, you need to subscribe to the topic using your email address. This way, when the alarm is triggered, you will be notified. Subscribe using the following command:

```
aws sns subscribe \
--topic-arn {ARN} \
--protocol email \
--notification-endpoint securitycert@packtpub.com
```

This should now give you feedback letting you know that the subscription is pending until you confirm it.

4. Now go to your email account and find the email the SNS service sent. There will be a link in the email that says Confirm Subscription. Click on it.

The prerequisites have been met for creating and subscribing to the topic.

5. Now, return to the AWS Management Console and proceed to the EC2 service. Once on the EC2 main dashboard, click the Instances link on the left-hand menu or in the main window. This will bring up the list of instances currently running in your selected Region. Find the instance you created in the previous exercise named CloudWatch and copy the InstanceID value.

6. In a new tab, navigate to the CloudWatch service in AWS. On the left-hand menu, find the Alarms heading and click to expand to see the submenu items. When the submenu has expanded, click on the All alarms option to be taken to the Alarms screen.

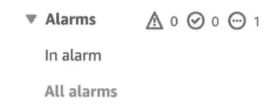

Figure 8.15: Alarms section under CloudWatch menu

7. Now that you are on the Alarms page, click the orange button labeled Create Alarm to create a new alarm. This will bring up the prompts for the alarm creation.

8. Click on the Select metric button. This will bring up a dialog to choose the metric. Click on EC2 to be brought into the EC2 metric.

Figure 8.16: Metrics selection screen

9. Once in the EC2 metric, paste the InstanceID value you copied in *step 5* in the search box. This will bring up a link to the Per-Instance metrics for this instance. Click on this link.

10. Scroll down and click on the box next to the metric named CPUUtilization. Once this is selected, press the Select metric button.

| ☑ | CloudWatchAgentTest | i-0a9d7a9e1486ed337 | CPUUtilization |

Figure 8.17: Metrics selection screen

You should now be on the Specify metric and conditions page. You will be shown a graph of the latest percentage of the CPU utilization being used for the instance.

11. Scroll down the page until you reach the heading labeled Conditions. Keep the threshold as Static. Keep the alarm condition as Greater. Set the value to 0.05. Once you have set these values, click the Next button.

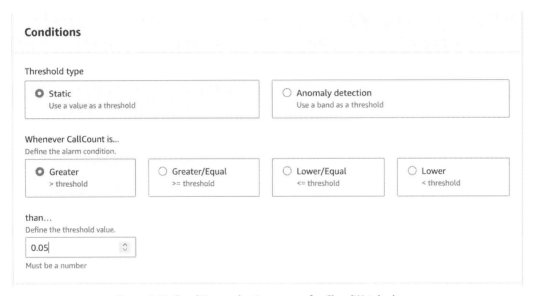

Figure 8.18: Conditions selection screen for CloudWatch alarms

12. On the Configure actions page, you can now add the SNS topic that you created at the beginning of this exercise. In the Notification box, keep the default settings of In alarm and then click on the search box under the Send a notification heading to reveal your SNS topics in the current Region. Once you have selected your SNS topic, scroll to the bottom of the page and click on the Next button.

13. The next page will be named `Add name and description`. Name your alarm something that is meaningful, such as `Chapter8-test`. Click on the `Next` button at the bottom of the page once you have entered the page.

14. Finally, you will be brought to the `Preview and create` page. Review the information as you scroll down the page. If all of the information seems correct, press the `Create alarm` button at the bottom of the page.

You just created an alarm based on the metrics being monitored by CloudWatch. The next section will detail how those metrics can be displayed graphically using CloudWatch dashboards.

CloudWatch Dashboards

While the collection of metrics generating lines and lines of information on disparate files serves a purpose for tracking particular indicators, tracking a number of these over time is much easier in a graphical format. **AWS CloudWatch dashboards** allow you to create customizable, real-time visualizations of your metrics, resources, and applications. You can then monitor and analyze your metrics, logs, and events across your entire infrastructure. The CloudWatch dashboard thereby gives you and your organization a single-pane-of-glass view of your AWS environment.

The CloudWatch service has many built-in dashboards for the native AWS services. One of the superb features of CloudWatch dashboards is the ability to share the dashboards that you create with people who don't have an AWS account. This can be done in a few ways, but one of the easiest ways is to either create a shareable link to the dashboard or show the dashboard on a screen in an office context. You can also share dashboards with particular IAM users with whom you provide the correct IAM permissions. At any point in time, you can see how many of your dashboards are being shared or have been made public, as well as revoke any public dashboards.

When you create a dashboard in CloudWatch, it becomes available globally. While most services are tied to a single Region, CloudWatch dashboards are not Region-specific. Using CloudWatch dashboards can help you quickly identify patterns and trends in your account, and this can assist you in the ability to act on and improve the performance of your account. Especially when coupled with CloudWatch alerts sent via SNS to team members, it becomes a valuable tool in helping to quickly diagnose and determine what issue is happening and where from a graphical perspective.

You just learned how CloudWatch dashboards can be a valuable tool for examining and optimizing your environment as well as for use in incident response. Next, you will see how to automatically respond to incidents with AWS EventBridge.

Event-Driven Applications with AWS EventBridge

You may have heard the term **loosely coupled** or **event-driven** if you have dealt with cloud architects over the past few years. The term loosely coupled refers to a design approach where the components of the modules of a system are designed to have minimal dependencies on each other.

In other words, loosely coupled systems are designed in such a way that changes or modifications to one component do not have a significant impact on other components. This allows for greater flexibility and scale in the system and easier maintenance and development.

Two critical components in building a loosely coupled system in AWS are either a queueing system that can receive messages and hold them until they are processed by a downstream process and/or an event bus that can take events from a variety of different sources and send out instructions to a set of corresponding targets.

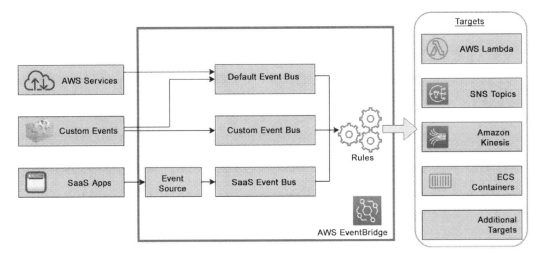

Figure 8.19: AWS EventBridge flow

Amazon EventBridge is a serverless service that allows you to connect AWS services and components with third-party and custom events using a set of rules you create inside your event bus. The rules match the **events** coming into the event bus and then push them along to one or more of the associated **targets** for processing.

Amazon EventBridge can help you create event-driven responses to events happening in your environment based on the contents of log files or CloudWatch metrics triggering alerts. Before you further learn about the inner workings of Amazon EventBridge, take a moment to explore EDA.

Understanding Event-Driven Architecture

EDA is a software design pattern in which the flow of the system is determined by events rather than a central control flow. In EDA, the system responds to events that occur asynchronously, such as messages received from AWS services, custom events, or even third-party **Software as a Service (SaaS)** applications.

An event-driven system consists of three main components:

- **Event producers**: These are the components or processes that generate events.

- **Event consumers**: These are the components that react to the events and can include things such as handlers and workflows. They are shown in *Figure 8.19* as `Targets`.

- **Event bus**: This communication channel allows event producers and consumers to exchange event data. It provides a loosely coupled mechanism for event-driven systems to interact with each other.

EDA has the following advantages:

- **Scalability**: Event-driven systems can easily scale horizontally by adding more producers or consumers as needed.

- **Flexibility**: Because events are loosely coupled, modifying or replacing individual components is easy without affecting the entire system.

- **Responsiveness**: Event-driven systems can respond quickly to events as they occur rather than waiting for a central control flow to process requests.

- **Resilience**: Event-driven systems can recover from failures quickly and easily by restarting failed components and resuming event processing.

With a basic understanding of how the EventBridge service works, you are now ready to examine how to use targets by combining the Lambda and SNS services and Amazon EventBridge.

Using EventBridge with AWS Lambda and SNS

In *Chapter 5, Managing Your Environment with AWS Config*, you looked at how AWS Config could be used to record and track changes to your infrastructure as soon as they happen and how these events can be written to logs and processed into other services, such as Amazon CloudWatch. Using this data, you can configure controls to look for specific events for further investigation. These could be events that might signify a security breach or a threat.

This is a simple method of implementing an automated level of remediation by monitoring and identifying events from different services to look for potential security breaches and implementing an automated response using AWS Lambda to rectify the problem. In addition to CloudWatch log groups, you can use Amazon EventBridge to trigger a service such as Lambda to provide the remediation or fix for the issue discovered in the CloudWatch log group.

To briefly recap, AWS Lambda is a serverless compute service that automatically provisions compute power, allowing you to run code for your applications either on-demand or in response to events without having to provision any compute resources yourself. Using this serverless technology removes a level of administrative responsibility of maintaining a compute instance; instead, that is all managed by AWS. This allows you to focus purely on the application and logic code.

Removing the need to provision and run an EC2 instance can provide significant cost savings as, when using AWS Lambda, it only charges you for the compute power per 100 ms of use when your code is running, in addition to the number of times your code is run.

EventBridge events can be used to react to specific events within your infrastructure, which can trigger an automated response.

Configuring a Custom Event Bus

When you want to receive events, you will need an **event bus**. This is the pipeline in the AWS system of resources that receives the events. The event bus comprises rules that are examined as the different events come into the event bus. You can have multiple event buses, and each rule is associated with a specific event bus.

There are some basic facts to know about EventBridge event buses:

- The default event bus in each of your AWS accounts is the one that receives events from the AWS services.

- You can create a custom event bus that receives events from another account than the one where the event bus is located.

- You would use a partner event bus to send or receive events from a SaaS partner.

- Each event bus can be configured for up to 300 rules. If you need more than 300 rules for a single event bus, you will need to create another custom event bus.

The next section will take you through creating a rule in the default event bus that would receive an event from one of the services from our AWS account.

Adding a Rule to the Event Bus

A simple exercise of adding a rule to the default event bus can help you gain a better understanding of how rules and events all work together in the EventBridge service. Follow these steps to enter a rule in your event bus:

1. Go to the EventBridge service at `http://console.aws.amazon.com/events/`.

2. On the left-hand navigation pane, choose `Rules` under the `Buses` main heading.

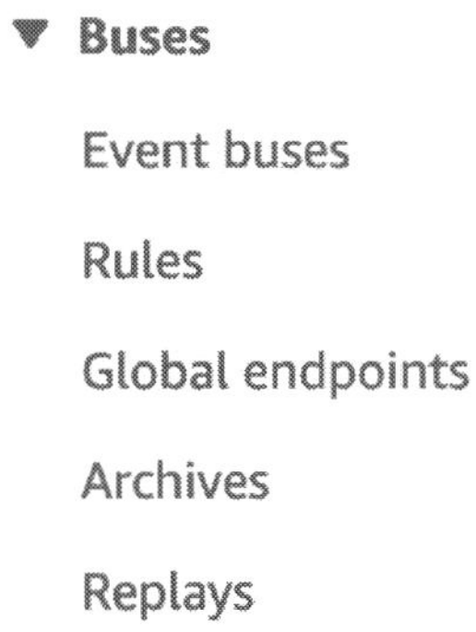

▼ **Buses**

    Event buses

    Rules

    Global endpoints

    Archives

    Replays

Figure 8.20: EventBridge menu screen

3. Now, on the `Rules` page, click on the orange button labeled `Create rule`.

4.   After clicking the `Create rule` button, you should be on the `Define rule detail` page. For Name, enter `EC2-termination`. You can leave the rest of the default settings as they are since this rule will be triggered with an event pattern and not by a schedule. After entering the rule name, scroll to the bottom of the page and click on the orange `Next` button.

5.   Clicking the `Next` button will bring you to the `Build event pattern` page. In `Event source`, you should be able to leave this selected as AWS events or EventBridge partner events.

6. Move down the page until you see the heading of Event pattern. On the left side, where the drop-down menus are, choose EC2 from the AWS service dropdown. Under Event type, select EC2 Instance State-change Notification, then choose terminated for Specific state(s). After you have done this, press the orange Next button at the bottom of the screen.

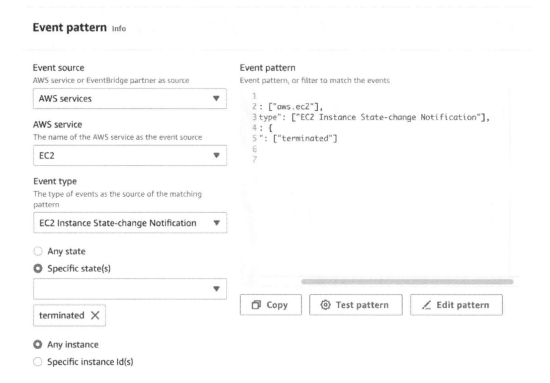

Event pattern Info

Event source
AWS service or EventBridge partner as source

| AWS services ▼ |

AWS service
The name of the AWS service as the event source

| EC2 ▼ |

Event type
The type of events as the source of the matching pattern

| EC2 Instance State-change Notification ▼ |

○ Any state
◉ Specific state(s)

| ▼ |

| terminated ✕ |

◉ Any instance
○ Specific instance Id(s)

Event pattern
Event pattern, or filter to match the events

```
1
2 : ["aws.ec2"],
3 type": ["EC2 Instance State-change Notification"],
4 : {
5 ": ["terminated"]
6
7
```

[⎘ Copy] [⚙ Test pattern] [✎ Edit pattern]

Figure 8.21: Event pattern screen for EventBridge

7. Now it's time to select your targets. Hopefully, you have an SNS topic from one of the earlier exercises in *Chapter 5* or *6*. Choose AWS service under Target type. Under Select a topic, click the drop-down menu and find SNS topic. Use the drop-down menu to select the topic name. After choosing these configuration settings, press the orange Next button at the bottom of the page.

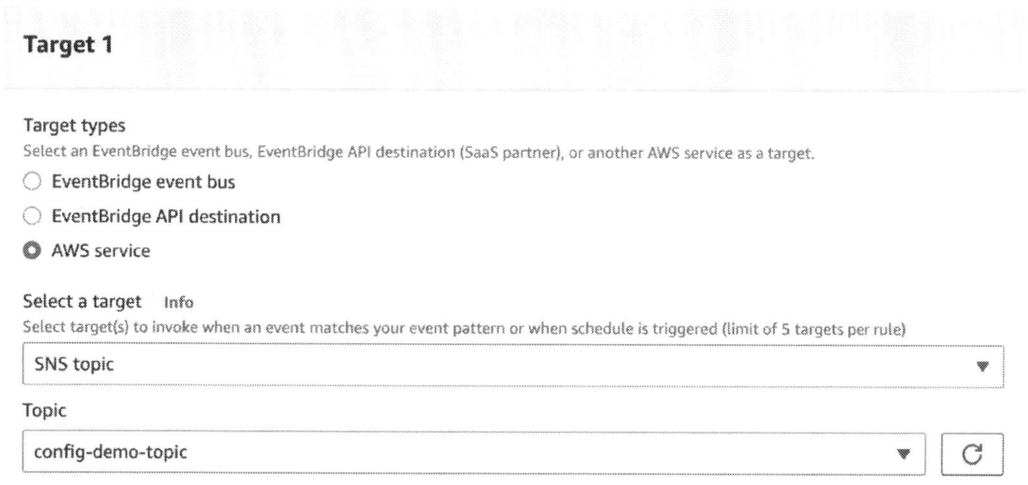

Target 1

Target types

Select an EventBridge event bus, EventBridge API destination (SaaS partner), or another AWS service as a target.

○ EventBridge event bus

○ EventBridge API destination

◉ AWS service

Select a target   Info

Select target(s) to invoke when an event matches your event pattern or when schedule is triggered (limit of 5 targets per rule)

SNS topic	▼

Topic

config-demo-topic	▼	C

Figure 8.22: Target selection screen for EventBridge

8. This should take you to the `Tags` page. Press the orange `Next` button to move on.

9. Finally, on the `Review and create` page, look over the settings you have entered and ensure everything seems correct. If it is, scroll to the bottom of the page and click the `Create rule` button.

To test your rule, you can terminate the instance you created as part of the CloudWatch agent exercise. Once the instance has reached a termination state, you should receive a notification via email if you are subscribed to the SNS topic.

You can also automate tasks using EventBridge by running them on a schedule. The next section discusses this.

Running Events on a Schedule

With the scheduling capabilities of EventBridge, you have the opportunity to create, run, and manage tasks that you schedule to run at a later date for a singular event or on a recurring basis.

These tasks can be as simple as sending out weekly notifications to your team to logging timesheets every Friday via SMS. In a different type of task, to optimize cost savings, you could scale down all of your non-essential instances on Friday afternoons and then have another scale-up event happen early on Monday mornings so that all necessary instances are up and ready to take traffic by the time it starts to come in.

Before the EventBridge scheduler, teams had to either create their own scheduling capabilities or use a third-party tool to perform their scheduling capabilities.

Summary

In this chapter, you looked at AWS's CloudWatch service and its multiple functionalities. You saw how it can gather logs for many of the other services running in AWS and store them for the specified period. You also saw how the CloudWatch service provides monitoring and metrics for the different services running in AWS. You looked at both predefined metrics and custom ones.

With the metric capabilities of CloudWatch, you can track your resources and create alarms and dashboards to monitor and keep track of services within your purview.

The chapter concluded with a discussion of Amazon EventBridge, the event bus service. You saw how EventBridge can take events from multiple sources, both internal to AWS and external, and use rules to process the events and then send the events to one or more specified targets for proper processing. You also learned how EventBridge can help you build a decoupled EDA in AWS.

In *Chapter 9, Parsing Logs and Events with AWS Native Tools*, you will look at using cloud-native services to sort through a mountain of log files when looking for a particular item. This can be done using services such as **Kinesis Data Firehose** and **Amazon Athena**.

Further Reading

For additional information on the AWS Shared Responsibility Model and the underlying principles of AWS security, please check out the following resources:

- AWS CloudWatch FAQs: `https://packt.link/qCEmt`
- Introducing Amazon EventBridge Scheduler: `https://packt.link/T4KbU`
- Amazon EventBridge FAQs: `https://packt.link/cdauX`

Exam Readiness Drill – Chapter Review Questions

Apart from a solid understanding of key concepts, being able to think quickly under time pressure is a skill that will help you ace your certification exam. That is why working on these skills early on in your learning journey is key.

Chapter review questions are designed to improve your test-taking skills progressively with each chapter you learn and review your understanding of key concepts in the chapter at the same time. You'll find these at the end of each chapter.

> **How To Access These Resources**
>
> To learn how to access these resources, head over to the chapter titled *Chapter 21, Accessing the Online Practice Resources*.

To open the Chapter Review Questions for this chapter, perform the following steps:

1. Click the link – `https://packt.link/SCSC02E2_CH08`

   Alternatively, you can scan the following QR code (*Figure 8.23*):

Figure 8.23: QR code that opens Chapter Review Questions for logged-in users

2. Once you log in, you'll see a page similar to the one shown in *Figure 8.24*:

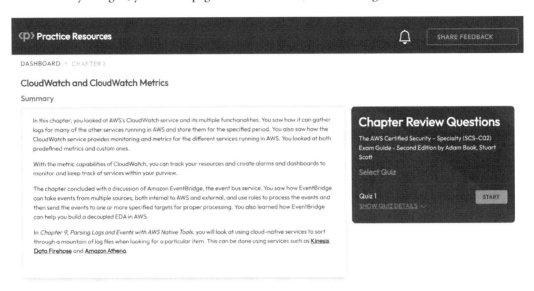

Figure 8.24: Chapter Review Questions for Chapter 8

3. Once ready, start the following practice drills, re-attempting the quiz multiple times.

Exam Readiness Drill

For the first three attempts, don't worry about the time limit.

ATTEMPT 1

The first time, aim for at least **40%**. Look at the answers you got wrong and read the relevant sections in the chapter again to fix your learning gaps.

ATTEMPT 2

The second time, aim for at least **60%**. Look at the answers you got wrong and read the relevant sections in the chapter again to fix any remaining learning gaps.

ATTEMPT 3

The third time, aim for at least **75%**. Once you score **75%** or more, you start working on your timing.

> **Tip**
>
> You may take more than three attempts to reach 75%. That's okay. Just review the relevant sections in the chapter till you get there.

Working On Timing

Target: Your aim is to keep the score the same while trying to answer these questions as quickly as possible. Here's an example of how your next attempts should look like:

Attempt	Score	Time Taken
Attempt 5	77%	21 mins 30 seconds
Attempt 6	78%	18 mins 34 seconds
Attempt 7	76%	14 mins 44 seconds

Table 8.1: Sample timing practice drills on the online platform

> **Note**
>
> The time limits shown in the above table are just examples. Set your own time limits with each attempt based on the time limit of the quiz on the website.

With each new attempt, your score should stay above 75% while your time taken to complete should **decrease**. Repeat as many attempts as you want till you feel confident dealing with the time pressure.

Parsing Logs and Events with AWS Native Tools

The previous chapter showed you how the CloudWatch service can help collect and store logs from a myriad of services in AWS. You are now ready to turn your attention to the most cost-effective ways to retain those log files for long-term storage, along with the methods to pull out the necessary data from them.

One of the critical duties of a security professional is to assimilate all the information coming in from different sources and distinguish the relevant bits of information from that which is just noise. Services and applications in any environment (not just the cloud) constantly produce logs. Knowing which services and techniques can gather, collect, and then help you quickly sift through and analyze these logs is an essential skill for real-life situations as well as for the AWS Security competency exam.

Several services can help you with this task. This chapter will cover such services, including storing logs on the S3 storage service, using Amazon Kinesis Data Firehose to move the logs to other storage options, and using Amazon Athena and OpenSearch to search through the log files.

The following main topics will be covered in this chapter:

- Log storage options and their cost implications
- AWS OpenSearch Service
- Using AWS Kinesis to ship logs
- Running queries with Amazon Athena

Technical Requirements

You will require access to an active AWS account, the AWS Management Console, the CLI, and a text editor for this chapter.

Log Storage Options and Their Cost Implications

As you think about storing all the logs generated in your account, there are a few different factors that you should consider as you come up with long-term solutions for log storage for your organization:

- **Building a storage solution that is both secure and resilient**: Your logs should be stored in a secure manner that includes, at a minimum, default encryption on that log storage. Furthermore, the space you create for the log storage should be able to store all of your logs in real time without delays in processing and storing.

- **Central storage for the log files**: You need a location to direct any internal or external auditors should they need access to the log files generated for your account. This is also true for any configuration changes that have occurred in the different accounts you manage, as the logs need to be stored in a centralized location both for auditors and in case of access for incident response.

- **Establishing log file integrity when storing log files**: You need to refer to your raw log files as the source of truth for what actions have occurred in the accounts for which you are accountable. Therefore, it is crucial to make sure that those log files have not been tampered with in any way such that their integrity is intact. Using tools such as IAM access controls to prevent the modification of the log files combined with generated checksum values for the logs can help establish log file integrity.

- **Understanding how long logs need to be retained according to organizational policy**: Working with the leaders of your organization to establish how long the logs should be retained based on both the company's needs as well as any regulatory guidelines will drive the retention process of log files. Once these timelines have been set, you can create automated (or manual) workflows to remove older log files that are no longer needed to save both storage space and costs. When log files must be retained strictly for compliance purposes, they can also be moved to lower-cost, infrequent-access storage for cost savings.

- **Defining a process for adding new logs to the log storage**: As new logs are generated in your system, either through new services being added, new accounts being added, or new applications being added to existing services, you and your organization should set some standards to ensure that all defined logs are captured and stored in your centralized log storage. Optimally, this would be an automated process so that no logs are lost accidentally.

- **Granting access to the log storage and files**: As you define your log storage and think about the need for ensuring the integrity, there will be some users (i.e., development team members) who will need access to some or all of the log files as they perform their day-to-day duties. The access should be provided on a role-by-role or user basis using the principle of least privilege, granting only read access to the logs necessary to perform their job capabilities. Going a step further, you could provide time-based access, which only allows read-only access when requested for a short period of time, such as 24 hours, limiting access only to those who request access for the files they need temporarily.

- **Monitoring the log storage**: If you are the responsible party for the log storage, then you need to ensure both the health of the log storage and the success of the files being delivered to the log storage system. Having a plan in place for automated alerts for errors such as low space warnings, failures on delivery, or deletions of log files can help you rectify any issues before it's too late, such as when you are trying to retrieve those log files when you need them most.

After looking at the foundational aspects of what goes into building the log storage solution for your organization, the next step is to examine the details of storing logs on the Amazon S3 service.

Storing Logs on S3

One of the optimal places to store log files—either initially or after placing them in another store—is the S3 storage service. This service provides both the resiliency and durability desired for long-term storage and objects such as log files. Where it can fall short is the ability to search the various files directly.

Different Storage Tiers of S3

Amazon S3 offers several storage classes or tiers with different performance, durability, and cost characteristics. These storage tiers are designed to help you and other customers optimize their storage costs based on the frequency of access to your data, the performance required, and your business needs.

The following subsections will take you through the different storage tiers in detail and see how they are both similar and different.

S3 Standard

When you set up an S3 bucket, objects and files will be stored in the S3 Standard tier if you don't choose any particular storage tier. This highly available, general access storage policy allows millisecond access to objects when requesting their retrieval. Although this is the most expensive of all the storage tiers, S3 Standard storage is a highly cost-effective solution compared to other types of storage services such as File (think of the Elastic File System or EFS service) and Block (think of the Elastic Block Store or EBS service).

Key Points to Remember about S3 Standard

- The Standard tier provides high throughput, low latency, and high performance for object uploads and downloads.

- If no other storage tier is indicated, then Standard is the default storage class.

- It is ideal for objects that need frequent access.

- It is constructed for 99.99% availability and 99.999999999% durability via multiple Availability Zones during a given year.

- It can support SSL for data in transit and encryption at rest.

S3 Intelligent-Tiering

When you don't know how often you need to access your data or objects stored in a particular S3 bucket, the best option may be S3 Intelligent-Tiering. AWS uses a proprietary algorithm to monitor the access of objects in the designated bucket to move them to the correct Frequent and Infrequent Access levels, along with pricing for the respective levels. Using this storage tier saves you from having to develop complex lifecycle policies for the objects in your bucket, allowing you to concentrate on your other tasks.

Key Points to Remember about S3 Intelligent-Tiering

- It is designed to optimize storage costs by automatically moving objects to the most cost-effective storage tier. Savings can be up to 40% of Standard tier pricing.

- It is designed for more extended storage of at least 30 days (minimum 30-day charge), and it takes 30 days to start figuring out access patterns.

- It stores objects in three access tiers and optimizes storage based on frequently, infrequently, and archived instant access objects.

- There is no performance impact or additional fees when Intelligent Tiering moves objects between tiers.

- It was constructed for 99.9% availability and 99.999999999% durability during a given year.

- It can support SSL for data in transit and encryption at rest.

S3 Standard Infrequent Access (S3 Standard-IA)

If you have data you don't access frequently but still need to retrieve in real time, the S3 Standard-IA storage tier provides an excellent option. If you decide to use this storage tier, consider the following: the files and objects you would store in your S3 bucket would need to be at least 128 KB in size, or they will be charged for being that size at a minimum. Also, you need to keep the files in this storage tier for at least 30 days, so volatile files constantly being created and deleted would not be a good choice for storing in the S3 Standard-IA storage tier.

Key Points to Remember about S3 Standard-IA

- It is designed for files over 128 KB (smaller files will be charged at 128 KB size).

- It is designed for more extended storage periods of at least 30 days (minimum 30-day charge).

- There is a higher **GET**, **PUT**, **COPY**, **POST**, **LIST**, and **SELECT** charge than S3 Standard storage but lower storage cost, so it is designed for infrequent access, as the name suggests.

- Objects are available to access in real time with no delays.

- It is constructed for 99.99% availability and 99.999999999% durability during a given year, with copies stored in multiple Availability Zones.

- It can support SSL for data in transit and encryption at rest.

S3 One Zone Infrequent Access (S3 One Zone-IA)

S3 One Zone-IA has many of the features of Standard-IA but at a lower cost point. This is because the data is being stored in only one Availability Zone instead of the minimum of three Zones, as in the case of Standard-IA. This storage class is not a good option for critical data but can present considerable cost savings for infrequently accessed files and can be recreated if necessary.

Key Points to Remember about S3 One Zone-IA

- It is ideal for data that can be recreated or object replicas when setting cross-Region replication.

- It is designed for a more extended storage period of at least 30 days (minimum 30-day charge).

- Objects are available for real-time access.

- It is constructed for 99.5% availability and 99.999999999% durability during a given year.

- Data is subject to loss stemming from data center outages due to disasters such as floods or earthquakes.

S3 Glacier Instant Retrieval

When you have files and records that need to be archived in order to save costs but might still need instant access, then the S3 Glacier Instant Retrieval storage class fits your needs from both cost and access standpoints. Data stored in S3 Glacier Instant Retrieval can be accessed in milliseconds, the same time it takes to access an object in S3 Standard storage. Yet this storage class offers up to 68% cost savings over S3 Standard access. Furthermore, because data is stored across multiple Availability Zones, you don't have to worry about durability or availability in order to achieve these cost savings.

Key points to remember about S3 Glacier Instant Retrieval:

- It allows for data retrieval with the same performance as S3 Standard, in milliseconds.

- It is designed for files over 128 KB (smaller files will be charged as if they were 128 KB in size).

- It is constructed for 99.9% availability and 99.999999999% durability during a given year.

- Any data stored in this tier is resilient to the destruction of up to one entire Availability Zone.

S3 Glacier Flexible Retrieval

The S3 Glacier Flexible Retrieval storage tier provides you with a low-cost, durable storage archive with low fees for data retrieval. There are three tiers of retrieval speeds to bring back your data for access to your S3 bucket. However, unlike the Glacier storage service available from AWS, you do not have to wait for days until your data is available. The first availability tier is an expedited one that can return your objects in one to five minutes. The second tier is the standard retrieval tier, which restores objects in three to five hours. The third and final tier is the bulk tier. Objects in this bulk tier take around 12 hours to be restored.

Key Points to Remember about S3 Glacier Flexible Retrieval

- It is designed for extended storage periods of at least 90 days (minimum charge of 90 days).
- It has a durability of 99.999999999% (11 9s).
- It is constructed for 99.9% availability during a given year.
- Objects can be locked via the VAULT LOCK feature.
- Glacier Flexible Retrieval times can be configured from minutes to hours.
- Appropriate for low-cost data archival on infrequently accessed objects, especially for compliance-type purposes.

S3 Glacier Deep Archive

Glacier Deep Archive can be a practical solution for your storage needs if you have items that you rarely access but are necessary to archive and retain. These can often be cases such as moving from tape backup to a digital tape backup system where you would only be retrieving the data once or twice per year and could withstand waiting 12 hours for data retrieval. These controls come with deep savings, as storage in Glacier Deep Archive only costs $1 per TB per month.

Key Points to Remember about S3 Glacier Deep Archive

- It is designed for long-term digital storage, which may be accessed once or twice during a given year.
- It has a durability of 99.9999999% (11 9s).
- It is constructed for 99.9% availability during a given year.
- It is designed for more extended storage of at least 180 days (minimum 180-day charge).
- It can be an alternative to on-premises tape libraries.

Now that you fully understand the different storage tiers that can be used in the S3 service and how the cost and access options differ, you will look at how to use lifecycle policies to move objects automatically between the tiers without user interaction.

Using S3 Lifecycle Policies to Manage Logs

S3 Lifecycle policies provide a tool that helps you manage storage costs for objects residing on the Amazon S3 storage service for lengths of time greater than 24 hours. When adding an S3 Lifecycle configuration, a set of rules defining actions for the underlying objects stored in a particular S3 bucket, you can move those objects between different classes of storage tiers (both up and down) and expire/delete the objects altogether.

Lifecycle policies in Amazon S3 can apply to all objects in the bucket, or they can be made to work on items with particular prefixes (think of files that are being placed in a `logs/` folder). They can also apply to files that have a specific set of tag values placed on them. If you have a bucket that is only being used for logs and nothing else, then you could craft the policy such that it moves all the objects with the same cadence. Suppose the bucket is multi-use, as in the case of a development team's bucket where they have both static assets (e.g., pictures or images) and code assets, and they are storing their log files back to this same bucket as they and their service role has both read and write access to this bucket. In this case, you may need to place the Lifecycle policy only in the `logs/` folder within the S3 bucket.

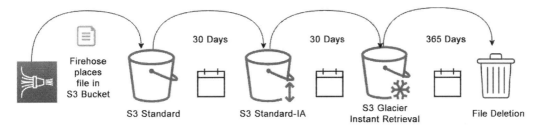

Figure 9.1: Object going through the S3 Lifecycle policy

If you look at the flow depicted in *Figure 9.1*, you will see that logs are initially ingested from a source to Kinesis Data Firehose. The logs go into the destination S3 bucket, where they are stored with the default tier of S3 Standard. This bucket has a Lifecycle policy on it, so in 30 days' time, those initial log files that have been placed in the bucket will move from the default Standard tier to Standard-IA. After 60 days in the bucket, the log files are then moved to the S3 Glacier Instant Retrieval tier, adding to further cost savings for the customer. Finally, 365 days after being placed in the bucket by Kinesis Data Firehose, the files will be deleted by the Lifecycle policy without manual intervention.

In the following exercise, you will create a new S3 bucket and then add a Lifecycle policy to that bucket that will mock the end of the lifecycle shown in *Figure 9.1* of deleting the file after 24 hours.

Creating a Lifecycle Policy for an S3 Bucket

This exercise uses the AWS Management Console. To create a Lifecycle policy on a new S3 bucket, perform the following steps:

1. Log in to the AWS Management Console and navigate to the S3 service page using the following URL: `https://packt.link/CgmUd`.

2. Once on the S3 page, in the middle of the main screen, click the `Create bucket` button.

3. Now, on the `Create Bucket` screen, under `General Configuration`, choose a name for your S3 bucket. This example bucket uses the name `packt-security-chapter9`. You will need to come up with a unique name for your bucket. Keep all other settings the default settings, scroll down to the bottom of the page and click on the `Create bucket` button to create the new bucket.

Figure 9.2: Configuration for S3 bucket screen

4. After creating your new bucket, you should be back at the S3 main page. Find the name of the new bucket you just created and click on its name to be taken to the bucket. This is where you will make the Lifecycle policy for the bucket.

5. Once on the bucket's main page, click on the `Management` tab on the main screen.

    This will bring up the `Lifecycle rules` section in the middle of the main screen. It should have a zero (0) right after `Lifecycle rules`, meaning no lifecycle rules are currently associated with this bucket.

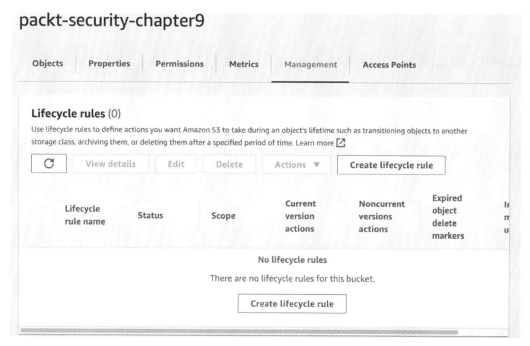

Figure 9.3: Management screen for S3 bucket

6. Now, click the button in the `Lifecycle rules` section labeled `Create lifecycle rule`. This will bring you to an area that allows you to create one or more lifecycle rules for the bucket.

    You will create a rule that deletes objects in your bucket after one day. You could create multiple rules using the same process, taking advantage of the storage tiers discussed in this chapter's *Different Storage Tiers of S3* section. However, to ensure that your costs stay low in your testing account, the most straightforward lifecycle rule is to have one that deletes objects after 24 hours of placement into the target bucket.

7. Use the rule name `security-cert-delete-24hours`.

8. Under the rule scope, select `This rule applies to all objects in the bucket.`

9. Click the checkbox that appears stating, I acknowledge this rule will apply to all objects in the bucket.

Lifecycle rule name

security-cert-delete-24hours

Up to 255 characters

Choose a rule scope
○ Limit the scope of this rule using one or more filters
◉ Apply to all objects in the bucket

⚠ **Apply to all objects in the bucket**
If you want the rule to apply to specific objects, you must use a filter to identify those objects. Choose "Limit the scope of this rule using one or more filters". Learn more ☑

☑ I acknowledge that this rule will apply to all objects in the bucket.

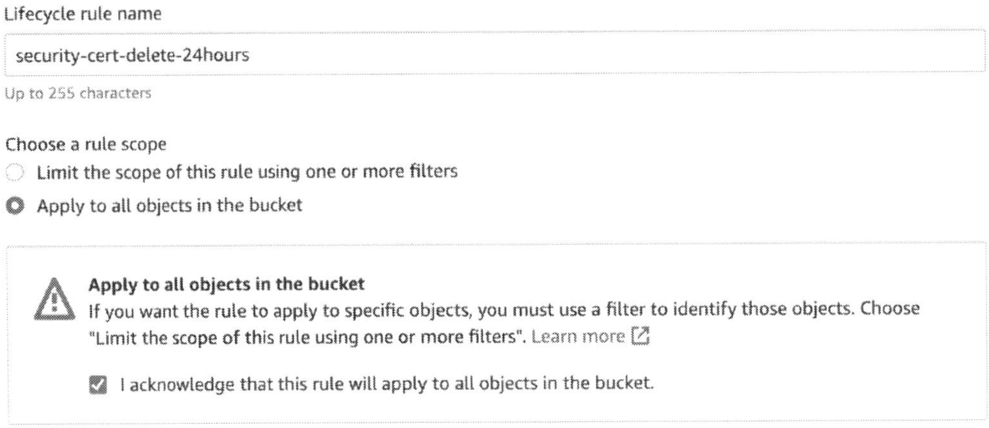

Figure 9.4: Rule configuration screen for S3

10. Under Lifecycle rule actions, select the box labeled Expire current versions of objects.

Lifecycle rule actions
Choose the actions you want this rule to perform. Per-request fees apply. Learn more ☑ or see Amazon S3 pricing ☑

☐ Move current versions of objects between storage classes
☐ Move noncurrent versions of objects between storage classes
☑ Expire current versions of objects
☐ Permanently delete noncurrent versions of objects
☐ Delete expired object delete markers or incomplete multipart uploads
    These actions are not supported when filtering by object tags or object size.

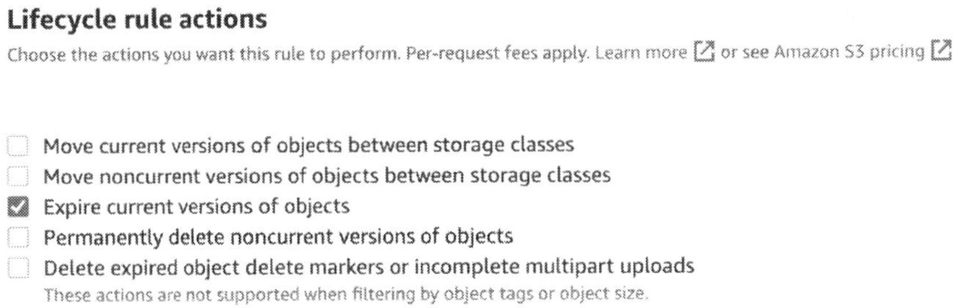

Figure 9.5: Lifecycle rule actions for S3 bucket

11. Scrolling down to the `Expire current versions of objects` box, enter 1 in the textbox under the heading `Days after object creation`.

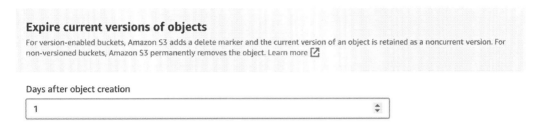

Expire current versions of objects

For version-enabled buckets, Amazon S3 adds a delete marker and the current version of an object is retained as a noncurrent version. For non-versioned buckets, Amazon S3 permanently removes the object. Learn more

Days after object creation

1

Figure 9.6: Lifecycle rule actions for S3 bucket

12. Scroll down to the bottom of the page and click the orange `Create Rule` button to enable the lifecycle rule on your bucket.

You can test this lifecycle rule by uploading any object or file to the bucket and then waiting a day. The next day, the object should be deleted automatically. When referring to this rule in context, this part of the lifecycle appears at the end of the diagram in *Figure 9.1*, after 365 days have passed from the initial placement of the object into the S3 folder.

Next, you will see how the costs compare between storing logs in the S3 service versus storing logs in CloudWatch Logs.

Comparing Costs of Storing Logs in S3 versus CloudWatch Logs

You may think that because you are studying for a test that emphasizes security, the pricing does not matter. However, this is not the case because keeping costs under control is everyone's responsibility in an organization. The ability to choose the proper storage for the logs in an organization is not only a real-world, sought-after skill but also helps you determine the most cost-effective solution for items that present themselves on the AWS certification exams. Remember that the most cost-effective solution is not always the least expensive, as some features and benefits must be considered with each service and solution.

> **Note**
>
> In the *Certified Security Specialty exam*, you will likely find a question or scenario that asks you not only about the most appropriate but also the most cost-effective solution. To be as prepared as possible, you do not need to memorize the pricing for the different storage solutions but, rather, understand which services have higher total price points compared to the features they deliver.

To help you with transitioning from one storage system to another, the next section discusses moving logs from CloudWatch Logs to other storage systems.

Moving Logs from CloudWatch Logs

Although CloudWatch Logs provides a sustainable logging solution right away, storage can be a little more costly than other solutions for logs that are not being utilized and just need to be kept for compliance purposes. Additionally, the service does not have the ability to search across multiple log groups at the same time. If you need to either cut costs for your log storage or search across multiple streams of logs for trends and anomalies, you will need to move those logs to another storage system.

It all begins with the use of CloudWatch subscription filters. As you will see in the following exercise, subscription filters allow you to push all or a subset of the logs that are coming into the CloudWatch Logs group to a Kinesis Data Firehose stream or a Lambda function, or even export the data to an S3 bucket.

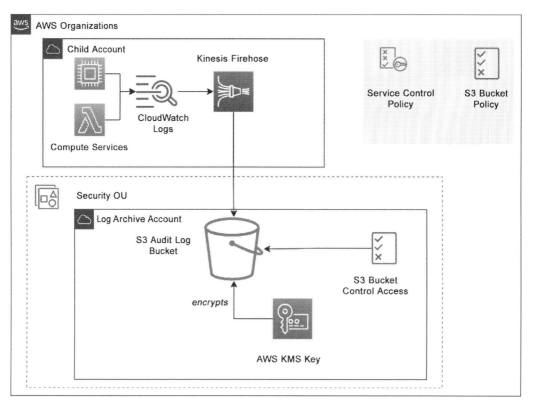

Figure 9.7: Moving log files from CloudWatch Logs to S3

The next section will dive deeper into subscription filters in CloudWatch logs.

Using CloudWatch Logs Subscription Filters

Subscription filters are a feature of Amazon CloudWatch Logs that allow users to create a real-time stream of log events from a CloudWatch Logs group to a destination such as Kinesis Data Firehose, an Amazon Lambda function, or an Amazon SNS topic.

If you didn't want to save all of your logs from a particular CloudWatch Logs group and only wanted to retain logs that were of importance to you and your team (say, for instance, logs that contained ERROR), then this would be a good use case for setting up a CloudWatch Logs subscription filter.

A subscription filter can match a particular pattern or specific keywords and send those log events to an Amazon Kinesis Data Firehose delivery stream. The Firehose delivery stream's destination would be an S3 bucket or Amazon OpenSearch Service cluster so that those logs could be stored more permanently.

Subscription filters can also be used in concert with other AWS services. In the next section, you will see how to ship logs to an S3 bucket using subscription filters and Amazon Kinesis.

Using Amazon Kinesis to Process Logs

Amazon Kinesis Firehose is a fully managed service that can scale automatically with the volume of the data throughput that you are sending to it. It can scale automatically if large quantities of data suddenly appear and then scale back down again. Data can be encrypted and sent to its final destination using the Firehose service.

The following are some key facts to understand about Amazon Kinesis Firehose:

- Kinesis Firehose is serverless.
- Kinesis Firehose is elastic and can scale automatically based on data volume.
- Kinesis Firehose can transform data with the help of AWS Lambda.
- Kinesis Firehose can deliver data to AWS OpenSearch Service, Amazon Redshift, Splunk, or Amazon S3.
- Kinesis Firehose can handle errors and the buffering of data but does not have the capability to replay data.

Kinesis Firehose can also transform the data that passes through it before it is delivered to its final destination. An example of this is a log received from a web server. As the Kinesis Data Firehose service ingests the log, it would get the raw data string as shown here:

```
199.72.81.55 - - [01/Jul/1995:00:00:01 -0400] "GET /history/apollo/
HTTP/1.0" 200 6245
```

It can then take that raw log file and transform it into a JSON file, such as the one shown here:

```
{
"verb": "GET",
"ident": "-",
"bytes": 6245,
"@timestamp": "1995-07-01T00:00:01",
"request": "GET /history/apollo/ HTTP/1.0",
"host": "199.72.81.55",
"authuser": "-",
"@timestamp_utc": "1995-07-01T04:00:01+00:00",
"timezone": "-0400",
"response": 200
}
```

This is especially useful when storing the logs on a service such as Amazon OpenSearch Service. Records in this format can be iterated over and counted for items such as the number of GET requests (versus the number of POST requests); response codes are much more easily tallied, and other metrics can be analyzed quicker and easier since the log has been broken into usable chunks.

One thing to note is that an additional service is available from Amazon Kinesis, which is Kinesis Data Streams. Kinesis Data Streams is used more for analytical processing and needs configuration for the shards. You do not need to know the details of Kinesis Streams for the AWS Security Specialty exam. If you want to learn more about the service, you can visit the following URL: https://packt.link/jz5FP.

With an overview of Kinesis Data Firehose under your belt, you are now ready to look at how you can use the Firehose service to move logs out of CloudWatch Logs to other storage options.

Moving Logs with Kinesis Data Firehose

If you have decided that storing your logs on CloudWatch Logs will be cost-prohibitive to your organization, then you need to determine a way to get the logs out of CloudWatch and into your S3 bucket. The Kinesis Data Firehose service can help you accomplish this task; you will see how in the next exercise.

As a prerequisite to this exercise, you should have already created one (or more) CloudWatch Logs groups in your account and have at least one Amazon S3 bucket available for the new Kinesis Data Firehose to deliver the logs:

1. In your Amazon Management Console, navigate to the Kinesis Data Firehose service. You can get there quickly by going to the following URL: https://packt.link/gR7Wj.

2. Once in the Kinesis Firehose service, click the Create delivery stream button on the right side of the main page.

3. This should take you to the page named `Create delivery stream`. Under the `Choose source and destination` heading, select `Direct PUT` for the source and `Amazon S3` for the destination.

Choose source and destination

Specify the source and the destination for your delivery stream. You cannot change the source and destination of your delivery stream once it has been created.

Source Info

| Direct PUT ▼ |

Destination Info

| Amazon S3 ▼ |

Figure 9.8: Source and Destination selection screen for Firehose

4. Moving down to the heading of `Delivery stream name`, use the delivery stream name of `packt-chapter9-firehose` in the textbox for the stream name.

5. Once you have filled in the delivery stream name, scroll down to the box labeled `Destination settings`. Under the `S3 bucket` heading, click the `Browse` button and select a previously created bucket.

Destination settings Info

Specify the destination settings for your Firehose stream.

S3 bucket

| s3://packt-security-chapter9 | Browse | Create ☑ |

Format: s3://bucket

Figure 9.9: Destination settings for Firehose

> **Note**
>
> If you choose the bucket you created earlier in this chapter, either remove the lifecycle policy that will delete any files created in the bucket after 24 hours or check the logs sent to that bucket before those log files are deleted.

6. After choosing your S3 bucket for delivery, scroll down to the bottom of the page and click the `Create delivery stream` button.

    Your Amazon Kinesis Data Firehose has been set up, but it still needs to deliver data. There are two additional steps to accomplish before Kinesis Data Firehose sends logs to the S3 bucket you have designated when setting up the firehose. To create the IAM role, use the terminal.

7. Open up your terminal console or file editor and create a file named `FirehoseTrustPolicy.json`.

8. In the file, add the following text:

```
{
        "Statement": {
                "Effect": "Allow",
                "Principal": { "Service": "logs.us-east-2.
amazonaws.com"},
                "Action": "sts:AssumeRole"
        }
}
```

After creating the file, you can use the AWS CLI to create the role using the following command:

```
aws iam create-role --role-name FireHoseTrustRole --assume-role-
policy-document file://FirehoseTrustPolicy.json
```

If the command succeeds, an ARN should be returned to you on the command line.

Next, you need to craft the access policy for the Kinesis, open up your text editor again, create a file named `FireHoseAccess.json`, and use the contents below to populate the file. Be sure to replace the account number in the statement (123456789012) with your own account number:

```
{
        "Statement":[
                {
                    "Effect":"Allow",
                    "Action":["firehose:*"],
                    "Resource":["arn:aws:firehose:us-east-
2:123456789012:deliverystream/packt-chapter9-firehose"]
                },
                {
                    "Effect":"Allow",
                    "Action":["iam:PassRole"],
```

```
                "Resource":["arn:aws:iam::    123456789012:role/
FireHoseTrustRole"]
                }
        ]
    }
```

Once you have the policy created, you can attach the policy to the role using the following AWS CLI command:

```
aws iam put-role-policy --role-name FireHoseTrustRole
--policy-name FirehoseAccessPolicy --policy-document file://
FirehoseAccess.json
```

After creating the IAM role, you will need to go back to the **CloudWatch Logs** service and configure it start sending the logs to the Firehose service. Follow the steps below:

1. Switch back to your AWS Management Console and navigate to the CloudWatch service. You can get there quickly by using the following URL: `http://console.aws.amazon.com/cloudwatch/`

2. Once you have reached the `CloudWatch` page, check the top-right corner of the page to confirm that you are in the Ohio region since you have used us-east-2 configuring other parts of this exercise. After confirming the region, use the left-side navigation to find the main header of `Logs` and choose the sub-menu item of `Log groups`.

Figure 9.10: CloudWatch Logs Menu

3. From the list of all your log groups on the page, click the name of a log group where there are active logs streaming or where you can have logs generated to that log group. (In the example, a simple Lambda function will be invoked to easily generate log files.) This will take you to the details of the log group.

4. Now on the details page of the log group, click on the `Actions` button, which is located directly beneath the name of the log group.

Clicking on the actions button will cause a drop-down menu to appear. Inside that drop-down menu, you will see a menu choice named `Subscription filters`, which is also a dropdown.

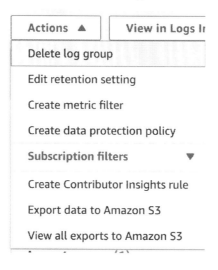

Figure 9.11: Action menu in Log group details

5. Click on the `Subscription Filters` dropdown to make another set of options appear, including `Create Kinesis Firehose subscription filter`. Use this choice to start the process of connecting your log group to your Kinesis Firehose.

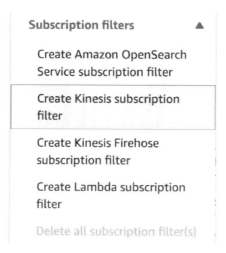

Figure 9.12: Subscription filters for log groups

You should now be on the `Create a Kinesis Firehose subscription filter` page.

6. In the first box labeled `Choose Destination`, keep the `Destination account` of `Current account` selected. Under the `Kinesis Firehose delivery stream` heading, click in the textbox, and select your `packt-chapter9-firehose` stream that you created earlier in this exercise.

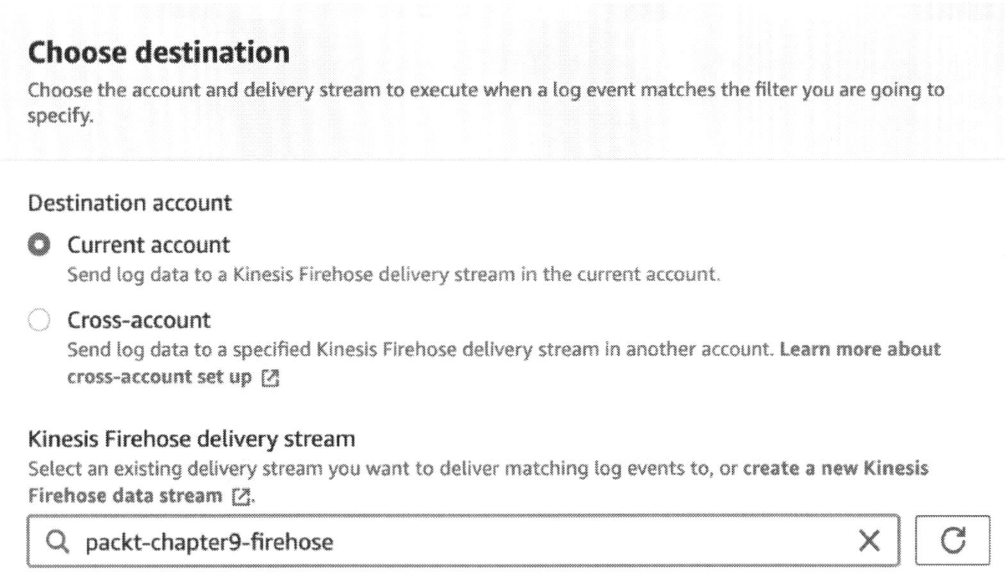

Choose destination

Choose the account and delivery stream to execute when a log event matches the filter you are going to specify.

Destination account

🔘 **Current account**
Send log data to a Kinesis Firehose delivery stream in the current account.

⭕ **Cross-account**
Send log data to a specified Kinesis Firehose delivery stream in another account. **Learn more about cross-account set up** ⬦

Kinesis Firehose delivery stream

Select an existing delivery stream you want to deliver matching log events to, or **create a new Kinesis Firehose data stream** ⬦.

🔍 packt-chapter9-firehose	✕	⟳

Figure 9.13: Destination selection for Firehose delivery stream

7. Scroll down on the page to the box labeled `Grant permission`. Under the heading `Select an existing role`, once again, click inside of the box, and you should be able to select the role you created earlier in this exercise named `FireHoseTrustRole`.

Grant permission

To grant CloudWatch Logs permission to put data into your delivery stream, select an existing role below or create a new role .

Select an existing role
If your newly created role is not showing up in the dropdown list, please try the refresh button to the right.

Figure 9.14: Grant permission screen for Firehose delivery

The next box on the page should be labeled `Configure log format and filters`. For these settings, you will need to add a subscription filter name.

8. Add the name `Chapter9-Firehose`.

Configure log format and filters
Choose your log format to get a recommended filter pattern for your log data, or select "Other" to enter a custom filter pattern. An empty filter pattern matches all log events.

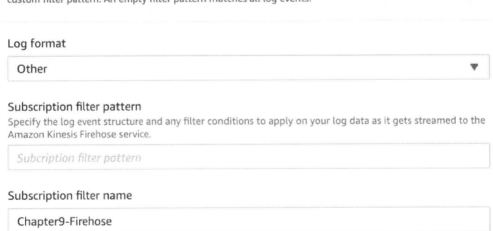

Figure 9.15: Log format configuration for Firehose filter

9.   After you have filled in these values, scroll down to the bottom of the page and click the Start streaming button.

Once you have the subscription filter set up, you only need to send some logs to the log group. Kinesis Firehose should pick up the logs via the subscription filter and place them in the S3 bucket you designated. You could even set your CloudWatch Logs group to expire in 3, 5, or 7 days since the logs are placed in long-term storage elsewhere.

After exploring so many different ways to move your log data from CloudWatch to other durable and more cost-effective storage such as S3, you now need a way to search through those stored files quickly should the need arise. The following section will examine just the tool needed to accomplish this: Amazon Athena.

Running Queries with Amazon Athena

With so much valuable data within CloudTrail and other logs, finding effective ways to query the data for specific entries is always a top priority. The Amazon Athena service makes running ad hoc queries on extensive datasets much more straightforward. When discussing storing logs on the S3 service earlier in the chapter, one of the feature's shortcomings was the ability to query the logs. This gap in capabilities is filled by using the Amazon Athena service.

Amazon Athena is a serverless service that allows you to quickly analyze data stored within Amazon S3, such as your CloudTrail logs. Athena does this by using an interactive query service and letting you write your queries using standard **Structured Query Language (SQL)**. As a result, it is an efficient service to help you scan massive datasets.

The following are some key facts to understand about Amazon Athena:

*   Athena separates storage from compute by utilizing Amazon S3 for storage.

*   The Amazon Athena service is serverless, meaning there is no infrastructure or resources to manage.

*   You only pay for the data you scan.

*   It supports the following open-storage file formats:

    *   Apache Web Logs

    *   CSV and TSV files

    *   JSON files

    *   Parquet

    *   ORC

- It is a secure solution, allowing for IAM authentication and encryption at rest and in transit.

Figure 9.16: Capturing logs from AWS WAF and searching with Amazon Athena

As shown in *Figure 9.16*, the logs are first enabled on the AWS WAF. Kinesis Data Firehose is configured to ingest the logs and place them in the desired S3 bucket. The AWS Glue Data Catalog then transforms the log data from JSON into a format that Amazon Athena understands. You can then use Amazon Athena to query the data using standard SQL to mine the detailed data that will be used in the visualizations in Amazon QuickSight. Finally, Amazon QuickSight uses the Athena data as the data source for the visualizations.

> **Note**
> QuickSight is not a necessary solution to search the logs. QuickSight allows for interactive visualization using both your queries and your data.

The next section will introduce a native solution that provides extremely fast searching and visual graphing capabilities—Amazon OpenSearch.

Storing and Searching Logs in Amazon OpenSearch Service

As logs and other pieces of data you are responsible for securing are generated in your environment, be sure to consider your security goals for the data itself and your organization as a whole. Ask yourself whether these goals include the following:

- Protecting confidential business data
- Maintaining business access controls
- Having the ability to audit user actions
- Possessing the ability to integrate with SAML identity providers
- Keeping your systems and data compliant with a myriad of compliance frameworks such as HIPAA, SOC, PCI, and others

If the answer is yes to one or more of these items, then provisioning an Amazon OpenSearch Service cluster could help meet your needs.

Amazon OpenSearch Service is a search and analytics engine developed to be compatible with Elasticsearch, a popular search engine based on Elasticsearch provided by the Elastic company. In addition to the ability to store and quickly search through the information stored in it, OpenSearch offers powerful visualization capabilities powered by OpenSearch Dashboards that let you and your team members graphically see results over time.

OpenSearch is designed to handle large amounts of data and provide rapid search results coupled with analytics capabilities. Some use cases for OpenSearch include log analytics, full-text search, and real-time application monitoring. A positive feature of Amazon OpenSearch Service is that it supports many different data types for ingestion and storage and easily integrates with other AWS services such as AWS Lambda and Kinesis.

Many security features are built into Amazon OpenSearch Service, but you should first and foremost understand how it handles data protection.

The key points and benefits to remember (especially for the exam) about OpenSearch Service are the following:

- **It's fully managed**: You can have it up and running in minutes without worrying about patching, backups, or keeping up with updates and versions.

- **You and your team have the ability to access all data**: Once the data has been placed into your OpenSearch cluster, it can be searched and analyzed across datasets. You're not limited to just the data in a particular bucket or log group.

- **It's secure**: After deploying in your VPC, you have a variety of ways to allow users to access securely, including IAM and SAML. You can even restrict access using security groups.

- **It can scale as your data grows**: It only takes a few clicks or a few commands from the API to resize your cluster instantly, giving you more space and/or speed.

- **It integrates seamlessly**: It ingests logs and data from AWS sources and provides auditing capabilities.

Summary

In this chapter, you learned how to review and analyze many log files using native tools found in AWS.

You also had a brief overview of how costs can affect your decisions when choosing the correct storage solution for your long-term log storage for your account and your organization. This overview was presented through the different tiers of storage available in the S3 service and their durability and reliability ratings.

Next, you explored how to move logs out of CloudWatch Logs using subscription filters. You learned that combining CloudWatch subscription filters with the Kinesis Data Firehose service allows you to take incoming logs to CloudWatch Logs and push them into an S3 bucket where they could be stored at lower costs and then be queried by the Amazon Athena service.

You also examined how you could use Kinesis Data Firehose to stream the logs to Amazon OpenSearch, the fast search engine with custom visualizations based on Elasticsearch.

The next chapter marks the beginning of the next section on *Infrastructure Security*. In *Chapter 10, Configuring Infrastructure Security*, you will start with configuring infrastructure security. This includes the steps to set up a **Virtual Private Cloud** (**VPC**), security groups, and **Network Access Control Lists** (**NACLs**).

Further Reading

For additional information on the AWS shared responsibility model and the underlying foundation of AWS security, please look at the following resources:

- AWS Pricing Calculator: `https://packt.link/o2kod`
- Managing your storage lifecycle (in S3): `https://packt.link/2TQrC`
- Stream Amazon CloudWatch Logs to a Centralized Account for Audit and Analysis: `https://packt.link/Ij7my`
- Amazon OpenSearch FAQs: `https://packt.link/Wz8Cb`
- Amazon Athena FAQs: `https://packt.link/CSKmD`

Exam Readiness Drill – Chapter Review Questions

Apart from a solid understanding of key concepts, being able to think quickly under time pressure is a skill that will help you ace your certification exam. That is why working on these skills early on in your learning journey is key.

Chapter review questions are designed to improve your test-taking skills progressively with each chapter you learn and review your understanding of key concepts in the chapter at the same time. You'll find these at the end of each chapter.

> **How To Access These Resources**
>
> To learn how to access these resources, head over to the chapter titled *Chapter 21, Accessing the Online Practice Resources*.

To open the Chapter Review Questions for this chapter, perform the following steps:

1. Click the link – `https://packt.link/SCSC02E2_CH09`

    Alternatively, you can scan the following QR code (*Figure 9.17*):

Figure 9.17: QR code that opens Chapter Review Questions for logged-in users

2.   Once you log in, you'll see a page similar to the one shown in *Figure 9.18*:

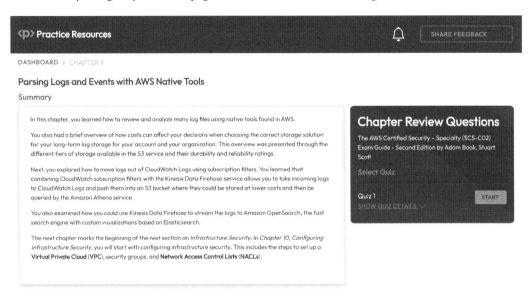

Figure 9.18: Chapter Review Questions for Chapter 9

3.   Once ready, start the following practice drills, re-attempting the quiz multiple times.

Exam Readiness Drill

For the first three attempts, don't worry about the time limit.

ATTEMPT 1

The first time, aim for at least **40%**. Look at the answers you got wrong and read the relevant sections in the chapter again to fix your learning gaps.

ATTEMPT 2

The second time, aim for at least **60%**. Look at the answers you got wrong and read the relevant sections in the chapter again to fix any remaining learning gaps.

ATTEMPT 3

The third time, aim for at least **75%**. Once you score **75%** or more, you start working on your timing.

> **Tip**
>
> You may take more than three attempts to reach 75%. That's okay. Just review the relevant sections in the chapter till you get there.

Working On Timing

Target: Your aim is to keep the score the same while trying to answer these questions as quickly as possible. Here's an example of how your next attempts should look like:

Attempt	Score	Time Taken
Attempt 5	77%	21 mins 30 seconds
Attempt 6	78%	18 mins 34 seconds
Attempt 7	76%	14 mins 44 seconds

Table 9.1: Sample timing practice drills on the online platform

> **Note**
>
> The time limits shown in the above table are just examples. Set your own time limits with each attempt based on the time limit of the quiz on the website.

With each new attempt, your score should stay above 75% while your time taken to complete should **decrease**. Repeat as many attempts as you want till you feel confident dealing with the time pressure.

Section 4: Infrastructure Security

Up until this point, you have looked at the different types of attacks that your accounts could be at risk of while managing your day-to-day security responsibilities, along with how to use the services provided by AWS to respond to those incidents. This included instructions on how to gather metrics and logs to keep track of the activity happening in your accounts contained within your **AWS Organization**.

Protecting the perimeter of your accounts, like placing a fence around your property, is both a deterrent and a barrier for keeping those who are unwanted out of your account. You can't rely on perimeter protection alone, so ensuring that the instances running your applications are using secure best practices is also necessary. Managing access to your data via a trackable system that leaves a trail of auditable logs is essential, not only for just those companies running with a need for compliance but for almost every enterprise.

This section comprises the following chapters:

- *Chapter 10, Configuring Infrastructure Security*
- *Chapter 11, Securing EC2 Instances*
- *Chapter 12, Managing Key Infrastructure*

In *Chapter 10*, you will look at how to secure the perimeter of your cloud infrastructure, starting with the constructs of the Virtual Private Cloud. Building security groups and network access controls to allow only the traffic that is authorized to your services will lead you directly to the components of *Chapter 11, Securing EC2 Instances. Chapter 11* looks at how to remove risks and vulnerabilities from the Elastic Compute Cloud service, both initially and on an ongoing basis. We finish off this section with *Chapter 12* with a look at how to use and manage the Key Management Service (KMS) so that the data stored on the various storage systems of AWS can be kept encrypted and see how to use a combination of key policies and IAM policies to allow access to only those who need permission to use the data.

10

Configuring Infrastructure Security

As you construct your cloud environment, understanding how to build the virtual walls that will protect the data and the resources you hold inside is crucial to becoming a well-rounded security professional. Knowing how to grant access to trusted entities and deny others all starts with the concept of the **Virtual Private Cloud** (**VPC**).

When considering your cloud architecture and infrastructure from an IaaS perspective, you, as the customer, are responsible for implementing, maintaining, and managing the security of that infrastructure. This includes your VPC and all the components that make up that VPC.

Knowing how to create a VPC in AWS, connecting multiple VPCs together securely, and then connecting the various services in AWS in the most secure manner are vital parts of being a security professional, regardless of whether the primary responsibility for these actions falls on you. In this chapter, you will look at several of the components used for networking in AWS along with their security implications.

The following main topics will be covered in this chapter:

- Understanding security groups, **network access control lists** (**NACLs**), and VPC security
- Using interfaces to connect to AWS services without the internet
- When peering, CloudHub, or a Transit Gateway makes sense
- Public subnets, private subnets, **internet gateways** (**IGWs**), and **network address translation** (**NAT**)
- Using load balancers and CloudFront to protect origins

Technical Requirements

Access to AWS CLI and the AWS Management Console with an active account are both required for this chapter. A basic understanding of network terms will also help as you work through this chapter.

If you need help understanding networking fundamentals and basic terms such as CIDR, route, and access control list, refresh your knowledge of these topics before going through this chapter and attempting the *AWS Certified Security – Specialty* exam. If you need a resource on CIDRs, the following link should help you understand the topic better: `https://packt.link/9JMFl`.

Understanding VPC Security

You can think of a VPC as your own private section of the AWS network. It allows you to create a virtual network infrastructure that you can segment into different networks. VPCs can be segmented for public-facing access, in which services have IP addresses that are reachable by the entire internet, and private access, in which the IP addresses are accessible only once you have entered the VPC network and a route has been provided.

Before you start reviewing the different aspects of VPC security, first look at some of the terms that will be used throughout this chapter in discussions on AWS networking:

- **Subnets**: A subnet defines a range of IP addresses in a VPC; there are both public and private subnets. Each subnet can only inhabit one **Availability Zone** (**AZ**) and cannot traverse multiple AZs or Regions.

- **Security groups**: Security groups act as virtual firewalls in Amazon VPC. You can have up to five security groups per EC2 instance, and security groups are enforced at the instance level (not at the subnet level).

- **NACLs**: NACLs work at the subnet level (unlike security groups which work at the instance level). NACLs are stateless compared to stateful security groups, and any traffic that needs to return through an NACL needs to have the port and IP range opened for both the ingress and egress ports. NACL rules are evaluated in order with the lowest rule being processed first.

- **NAT**: A NAT device forwards traffic from the instances in a private subnet to the internet or other AWS services. Since the advent of VPC endpoints, using NAT to talk to other AWS services in your account is considered a non-secure practice and should never be followed in production environments.

- **VPC endpoints**: An AWS VPC endpoint is a highly available and scalable resource that allows you to privately connect your Amazon VPC to AWS services without needing to traverse the public internet. It enables secure and efficient communication between your VPC and AWS services, such as Amazon S3 and DynamoDB, while keeping the traffic within the AWS network.

- **AWS Direct Connect**: Direct Connect provides the shortest path between your network and AWS resources. Using a Direct Connect connection means your data never travels over the public internet. Instead, you get a dedicated connection to an AWS Region. Direct Connect can help reduce data transfer costs, improve latency, and provide a more consistent network connection.

- **Elastic network interface (ENI)**: An ENI is a virtual network card that is a logical networking component in a VPC. You can create and configure ENIs in the same AZ that you would attach to your EC2 instances.

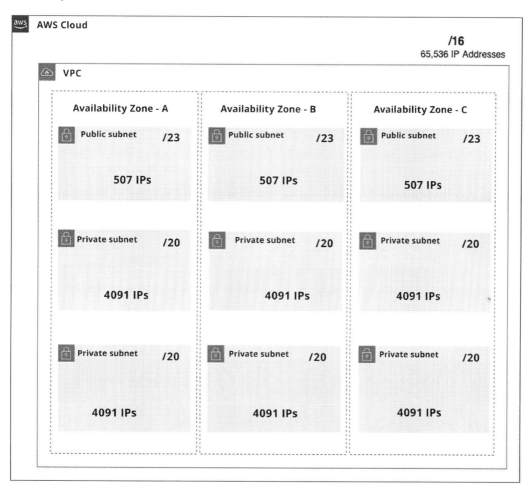

Figure 10.1: VPC with private and public subnets with CIDR notation (which is actually a range of IP addresses)

The VPC shown in *Figure 10.1* depicts one built with a full CIDR range of /16 that allows for a total of 65,536 IP addresses. The VPC has been spread out across three AZs in the Region, with one public and two private subnets placed in each AZ.

There are five IP addresses reserved for AWS's use to create a subnet CIDR block (the following example uses the `192.0.0.0/24` CIDR range):

- `192.0.0.0`: Network address.
- `192.0.0.1`: Reserved by AWS for the VPC router.
- `192.0.0.2`: Reserved by AWS.
- `192.0.0.3`: Reserved by AWS for future use.
- `192.0.0.255`: Network broadcast address. Since AWS does not support broadcast in a VPC, AWS reserves this address.

Think of these reserved IP addresses as specific roles or addresses that are automatically set up for your VPC to function correctly within the AWS environment. They help manage and direct traffic, keep track of devices, and ensure that data is routed to the right destinations efficiently.

So, if you have a VPC with a CIDR range of `192.0.0.0/24`, there are 251 IP addresses available for your resources within that VPC. The five reserved addresses are separate from this pool and do not reduce the number of usable addresses. You can use any of the remaining 251 addresses for your instances, databases, and other services as needed.

Those five reserved IP addresses in an AWS VPC are essential for the VPC's internal functioning but do not impact the total number of usable IP addresses for your resources in the VPC. The size of your VPC's IP range, as defined by the CIDR notation, determines the total number of addresses available to use.

With an understanding of the basic terms you will be using in this chapter and how VPCs are constructed, you are now ready to try creating a basic VPC in your AWS account, which you will do in the following exercise.

Adding a New VPC to Your AWS Account

Even though every account and Region has a default VPC, they may not present the security options you are looking for in your organization. Some organizations may have specialized networking teams whose only role is creating the account's networking components. These include creating the VPCs, adding the security group and NACL rules, establishing the Direct Connect connections, setting up the **virtual private networks** (**VPNs**), and similar capabilities.

As a security professional, it is imperative that you have a basic understanding of the foundational aspects of these items so that if you need to communicate with a networking team, you can do so with confidence. Furthermore, your organization may not have a networking team, and these responsibilities may fall on your shoulders. In a different scenario, the development teams may be able to create new VPCs. However, knowing the intricate details of the networking aspects is crucial so that you can inspect (either manually or via automation) these VPCs created by other team members for potential vulnerabilities.

As these VPCs are all virtual, they are straightforward to create, and there are a few different ways to do this within AWS. You can use the AWS Management Console, the AWS **Command Line Interface** (**CLI**), or an **infrastructure-as-code** (**IaC**) language, such as CloudFormation or Terraform, to spin up and revise a VPC quickly.

Creating a VPC with a CloudFormation Template

Throughout this book, you have used the AWS Management Console and the CLI in exercises. For the following activity, you will use a CloudFormation template to allow you to spin up your new VPC quickly.

You can see from the template that the new VPC has both a public and private subnet and an IGW, and it contains a NAT gateway and very basic routes along with route tables for traffic.

Open up an editor such as Vim, Notepad++, or Visual Studio Code to create a new file named demo-vpc.yml. CloudFormation templates can be composed in either JSON or YAML. Since this is a YAML file, spacing makes a difference, and if some spacing is off, it can cause errors.

> **Note**
>
> Suppose you want to validate your YAML file before uploading it to the CloudFormation service. In that case, you can use an online YAML validator or validate it on the command line by installing a library such as yamllint.

After creating your new demo-vpc.yml file, add the following content and save:

```
Resources:
  MyVPC:
    Type: AWS::EC2::VPC
    Properties:
      CidrBlock: "10.0.0.0/16"
      Tags:
        - Key: Name
          Value: MyVPC
  MyPublicSubnet:
    Type: AWS::EC2::Subnet
    Properties:
```

```
        VpcId: !Ref MyVPC
        CidrBlock: "10.0.1.0/24"
        MapPublicIpOnLaunch: true
        Tags:
          - Key: Name
            Value: MyPublicSubnet
  MyPrivateSubnet:
    Type: AWS::EC2::Subnet
    Properties:
      VpcId: !Ref MyVPC
      CidrBlock: "10.0.2.0/24"
      MapPublicIpOnLaunch: false
      Tags:
        - Key: Name
          Value: MyPrivateSubnet
  MyInternetGateway:
    Type: AWS::EC2::InternetGateway
    Properties:
      Tags:
        - Key: Name
          Value: MyInternetGateway
  MyGatewayAttachment:
    Type: AWS::EC2::VPCGatewayAttachment
    Properties:
      VpcId: !Ref MyVPC
      InternetGatewayId: !Ref MyInternetGateway
  MyPublicRouteTable:
    Type: AWS::EC2::RouteTable
    Properties:
      VpcId: !Ref MyVPC
      Tags:
        - Key: Name
          Value: MyPublicRouteTable
  MyPrivateRouteTable:
    Type: AWS::EC2::RouteTable
    Properties:
      VpcId: !Ref MyVPC
      Tags:
        - Key: Name
          Value: MyPrivateRouteTable
  MyPublicRoute:
    Type: AWS::EC2::Route
    DependsOn: MyGatewayAttachment
```

```
   Properties:
     RouteTableId: !Ref MyPublicRouteTable
     DestinationCidrBlock: "0.0.0.0/0"
     GatewayId: !Ref MyInternetGateway
 MyPrivateRoute:
   Type: AWS::EC2::Route
   Properties:
     RouteTableId: !Ref MyPrivateRouteTable
     DestinationCidrBlock: "0.0.0.0/0"
     NatGatewayId: !Ref MyNatGateway
 MyNatGateway:
   Type: AWS::EC2::NatGateway
   DependsOn: MyPublicSubnet
   Properties:
     AllocationId: !GetAtt MyEIP.AllocationId
     SubnetId: !Ref MyPublicSubnet
     Tags:
       - Key: Name
         Value: MyNatGateway
 MyEIP:
   Type: AWS::EC2::EIP
   DependsOn: MyGatewayAttachment
   Properties:
     Domain: vpc
```

After you create your CloudFormation template, return to your Management Console and quickly create your VPC:

1. Navigate to the CloudFormation service using the following URL: `https://packt.link/12NOB`.

2. Once on the CloudFormation page, ensure that you are on the `Stacks` page of the service. You can verify that `Stacks` is highlighted on the left-hand menu. If you are on another section of CloudFormation, click on the `Stacks` menu item on the left-hand side.

Stacks

StackSets

Exports

Figure 10.2: The Stacks menu

3. On the Stacks page, towards the right side of the screen, click the Create stack button. When the drop-down menu appears, select With new resources (standard).

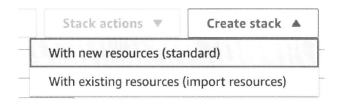

Figure 10.3: The create stack drop-down menu

4. You should now be on the Create Stack page. Keep the values set in the Prepare template section so that the template is ready. In the Specify template section, select the Upload a template file radio button under the Template source header.

Template source

Selecting a template generates an Amazon S3 URL where it will be stored.

○ Amazon S3 URL   ◉ Upload a template file

Figure 10.4: The Template source options

5. You will see a Choose file button appear. Click this button, then locate and upload the YAML template you created, which is called demo-vpc.yml. Once you have done this, click the Next button at the bottom of the page.

Upload a template file

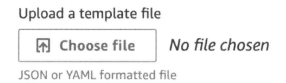

⤒ Choose file   *No file chosen*

JSON or YAML formatted file

Figure 10.5: The Choose file option

6. You will now be on the page where you can specify the stack's details. The only thing you will need to add to this page will be the stack name. Enter a name such as chapt10-vpc for the name of your stack, and then press the Next button at the bottom of the page.

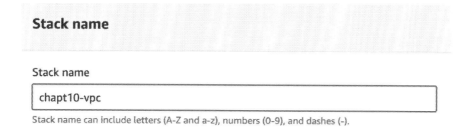

Stack name

Stack name

chapt10-vpc

Stack name can include letters (A-Z and a-z), numbers (0-9), and dashes (-).

Figure 10.6: Choosing the stack name

7. There is nothing to configure on the `Configure stack` options page; scroll down to the bottom of the page and press the `Next` button.

8. You should now be at the `Review` screen for your stack. Scroll down to the bottom of the page and press the `Submit` button. This will create your stack and ultimately create your new VPC.

9. After you click the `Submit` button, you should see the different events that take place on the CloudFormation page. When completed, you should see a green checkbox and a `CREATE_ COMPLETE` option. Once you see this, go to the `Resources` tab where you have been watching events.

Figure 10.7: The Resources tab

10. In `Resources`, you can scroll and find the VPC that you just created and then click on the link to view it in the VPC section of the Amazon Management Console.

Now that you have your VPC created, the next step will be to review the components in the AWS Management Console.

Examining the VPC You Created

If you have gone through the steps of creating the VPC in the previous section, you should have at least two VPCs running in the current Region of your AWS account: the one that you just created and the default VPC.

To look at the different components shown to you in this section, navigate to the VPC service in your Amazon Management Console. You can get there quickly by using the following URL: `https:// packt.link/hTMAh`.

Once in the VPC dashboard (which is the main area you are brought to when you go to the VPC service), at the top of the page, use the drop-down box to filter the components shown to you by selecting a particular VPC. In this case, you will select the VPC you just created, named MyVPC, as shown in *Figure 10.8*.

Figure 10.8: The Filter by VPC drop-down box

With one VPC selected, only those particular components will be shown in the main window without filtering since the filtering has already been accomplished at a service level. The first component to look at is the one listed on the left-hand menu, Subnets.

Subnets

Selecting Subnets from the left-hand menu will bring up all the subnets associated with a particular VPC. If you do not have VPC filtering on, then all subnets created for the Region will be displayed.

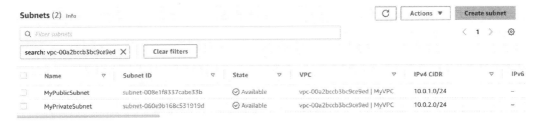

Figure 10.9: List of subnets

There is an excellent analogy that can help you understand the relationship between VPCs and subnets. Think of your house as your VPC. Within your house, you have many different rooms: the kitchen, the lounge, bedrooms, the study, and bathrooms. These rooms could be thought of as your subnets. Each room in your house performs a different function. The same can apply to your subnets. Each subnet should be configured to perform a specific task. Perhaps one subnet contains all your application servers and another all your database servers.

Later in this chapter, in the *Public and Private Subnets* section, you will learn more about subnets, how they are divided, and their role in public and private subnets.

Select a subnet from within the VPC dashboard within the AWS Management Console, and you will see that each subnet has several attributes and associations.

The Description Screen

The `Details` screen provides an overall summary description of how the subnet is configured.

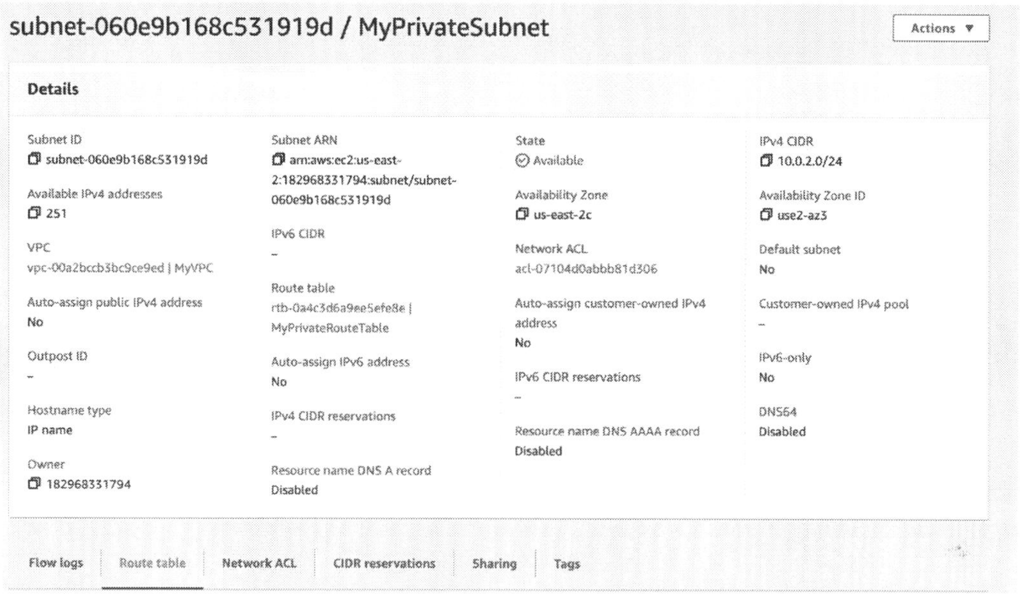

Figure 10.10: The VPC description screen

The main points to highlight at this stage are `VPC`, `Availability Zone`, `Network ACL`, `IPv4 CIDR`, and `Route table` as shown in *Figure 10.10* and discussed in the following points:

- **VPC**: When a subnet is created, it exists within a single VPC. In this example, you can see the associated VPC ID and its name, `MyVPC`.

- **Availability Zone**: A subnet can only reside in a single AZ. In this case, it is the `us-east2-2c` AZ. Note here is that the AZ is not the same as the AZ ID, nor does the AZ ID map on a one-to-one basis in alphabetical order depending on the Region you are in. The AZ ID comes into play as you get into more advanced networking tasks where traffic packets need to follow the same path with which they were initialized.

- **Network ACL**: A NACL will always be associated with a subnet. If you don't specify a particular NACL on creation, it will use the VPC default NACL. As shown, the NACL will also have a corresponding ID, `acl-07104d0abbb81d306`.

- **IPv4 CIDR**: The `IPv4 CIDR` value shows the current CIDR block for this subnet.

- **Route table**: Finally, `Route table` shows the associated route table that this subnet will use to route traffic. Again, a subnet will use the default VPC route table if no route table is defined. So, in essence, both the NACL and route table can be changed for each subnet.

To reiterate, network segmentation through subnets helps with security by maintaining network borders, whereby protective measures are put in place to filter network traffic, both inbound and outbound.

The Flow Logs Tab

The `Flow Logs` tab allows you to set up and configure flow logs. These logs enable you to capture IP traffic sent between the network interfaces of your subnet. Flow logs can also be configured at the VPC level for each network interface on your instances.

However, a tab will only configure flow logs for one particular subnet. The data captured in these logs can help you resolve network communication issues and traffic flow incidents. The logs are also helpful in identifying traffic that shouldn't be traversing the network. So, from a security stance, they are also handy for IP traffic.

Flow logs were covered in detail in *Chapter 7, Logs Generated by AWS Services*.

The Route Table and Network ACL Tabs

The `Route table` and `Network ACL` tabs allow you to view the associated route table and NACL with the subnet and make changes as necessary.

The following screenshot shows a default route (local) with another route pointing to the NAT gateway. The NAT gateway handles internet requests (`0.0.0.0/0`) for this private subnet.

Figure 10.11: The Route table screen for the subnet

In the following `Network ACL` tab, which is the tab after the previously shown `Route table` tab, you will see two rules, including a default rule denying *all* traffic to the subnet that doesn't meet any other rules in the access control list. NACLs are covered in more detail in a later section of this chapter titled *The Role of NACLs in VPC Security*.

It's worth pointing out that a subnet can only be associated with a single NACL and a single route table, but multiple subnets can share the same NACL and route table. The topics of route tables and NACLs will have more coverage as you go further through the chapter.

The CIDR Reservation and Sharing Tabs

The `CIDR Reservations` tab shows any blocks of IP addresses that you have set aside so that Amazon cannot assign them to your network interfaces. Any reservations that you have in place currently that fall into that subnet's CIDR range will be shown in the tab.

In the `Sharing` tab, you are shown which accounts you are currently sharing your subnet with. This tab also allows you to share the subnet you are on with another account in your organization using `Resource Access Manager`.

If you would like to read more on how Resource Access Manager can be used with microservices architectures and Network Load Balancers, AWS has published an article that you can read at the following address: `https://packt.link/b5XHV`.

The Tags Tab

The `Tags` tab allows you to use key-value pairs to categorize and organize your subnets. You can see from the screenshot provided in *Figure 10.12* that, in addition to the name of the subnet, some automated tags have been added to this subnet since it was created using CloudFormation.

Figure 10.12: The Tags screen for the subnet

You should have more than a basic understanding of the components that make up a VPC subnet and how to navigate those components on the AWS Management Console. The next section discusses the component of your VPC that helps move the packets to the correct locations: route tables.

Route Tables

Route tables provide a way of directing network traffic to the appropriate locations. When a route table packet leaves a subnet, it needs to determine how to reach its destination and uses the route table to find that route.

Whenever a new VPC is created, by default, a main route table is also created and will typically look as shown in the following screenshot if the VPC has been created from scratch:

Destination	▽	Target	▽	Status	▽	Propagated
10.0.0.0/16		local		⊘ Active		No

Figure 10.13: Main route table of a VPC

It is very basic and will contain a single route. This `local` route allows every subnet created within the VPC to route to each other. This main route table can't be deleted. However, you can modify it and add routes as and when needed.

You aren't just limited to this single route table for your VPCs, as you saw when creating the new VPC from the CloudFormation template. You can create additional route tables and associate those different route tables with different subnets. Every route table you create will *always* have this default local route.

The route table comprises several different tabs, just like the subnets, which are discussed in detail in the following subsections.

The Details Tab

The `Details` tab provides a high-level overview of data surrounding the route table, detailing which VPC it resides in, the account owner ID, the route table ID, and any explicit associations, as shown in the following screenshot.

Figure 10.14: The Details tab

These explicit associations relate to any subnets that have been configured to use this route table using the `Route Table` tab within the subnet configuration. Whenever you create a new subnet, it will automatically use the main route table created by your VPC. However, as mentioned earlier, you can create different route tables. If you configured your VPC to use one of these new route tables, it would be implicitly associated.

The Routes Tab

This tab shows the actual routes that are in place to direct traffic and contains several different fields, as shown here:

Figure 10.15: The Routes tab

The following points will take you through these fields one by one:

- **Destination**: This shows a CIDR block range for a network that your traffic needs to route to.

- **Target**: This is a gateway that allows you to reach the destination. In this example, you have a route with a destination of `0.0.0.0/0`. This destination is used to imply any destinations unknown by the route table (for example, an internet address). The `Target` value for this route is **igw-00cef31fb7078b315**, which is an ID for an IGW. This route means that, for any destination not listed within the route table that resides outside of your subnet, you use the IGW to get that address.

- **Status**: This shows the status of your routes within the table—for example, `Active`.

- **Propagated**: Route propagation is used when working with a **virtual private gateway** (**VPG**), which can automatically propagate routes if configured to do so; this implies that you don't need to enter VPN routes to your route tables manually.

When routes are added to the route table, you must ensure that the correct subnets use the right table. This is achieved by configuring the subnet associations. The next section discusses this.

The Subnets Associations Tab

This tab shows any explicit subnet associations with this route table that have taken place, along with any subnets within the VPC that are using the main route table.

Figure 10.16: The Subnet associations tab

You can have multiple subnets associated with a single route table, but only a single route table can be associated with a subnet.

The Route Propagation Tab

If you have a VPG configured, you can configure the route propagation setting on the Route propagation tab shown in the following figure.

Figure 10.17: The Route propagation tab

Route propagation allows the automatic population of detected routes across your VPN connection, which helps ensure that the correct routing is in place between your gateways.

> **Note**
>
> As with all AWS resources, you can also set up key-value pairs associated with your route table using the `Tags` tab.

Now that you have reviewed the route tables, the next thing to cover will be NACLs, which help restrict traffic at a subnet level.

NACLs

NACLs are a type of security control used in VPC environments that act as a firewall for inbound and outbound traffic at the subnet level. They are stateless, meaning that they apply to all traffic regardless of the connection state.

The primary role of NACLs in VPC security is to provide an additional layer of defense for the VPC by filtering traffic at the subnet level. This can help prevent unauthorized access to resources within the VPC and limit the impact of potential security breaches. NACLs can also be used to implement more granular access controls that are possible with security groups, which are another type of security control used in VPCs.

NACLs are associated with subnets and are evaluated in the order in which they are defined. Each NACL contains a set of rules that specifies the allowed or denied traffic based on criteria such as source IP address, destination IP address, port number, and protocol. NACL rules can be configured to allow or deny inbound and outbound traffic and can be modified as needed to reflect changes in the VPC environment.

Overall, NACLs are an essential component of VPC security and can help provide in-depth defense by complementing other security controls such as security groups and networking routing rules.

For each NACL, there are two fundamental components: inbound rules and outbound rules. These rules control what traffic flows in and out of your subnet at a network level. NACLs are stateless, meaning that they do not keep the state of network connections as security groups do. Instead, NACLs evaluate each packet independently based on the rules you have defined (either inbound or outbound) and make a decision to allow or deny the traffic accordingly.

The following subsections discuss the configuration of NACLs and will help you grasp how they work.

The Details Box

This provides an overview of the NACL itself, showing the VPC association and the number of subnets that the NACL is associated with. It also details the NACL ID, as shown in the following screenshot:

Figure 10.18: The NACL Details screen

To understand the configuration of the NACL itself, you need to look at the inbound and outbound rules.

The Inbound and Outbound Rules Tabs

These sets of rules are used to control what traffic flows into and out of your subnet. The Inbound rules and Outbound rules tabs are comprised of six fields:

Figure 10.19: The NACL Inbound rules tab

- **Rule number**: The rule numbers are used to ascertain the order in which the rules are read. When your NACL processes traffic, the rules are read in ascending order until a rule match is found. Considering this, it's best practice to leave some gaps in your rules to allow you to add more over time without having to move everything around.

- **Type**: Here, you can select several common protocol types, such as LDAP, HTTP, and DNS. You can alternatively specify custom TCP, UDP, or ICMP protocols as well.

- **Protocol**: Depending on your selection in the previous Type field, you might be able to select a specific protocol (number).

- **Port range**: Here, you can enter the port range for any custom protocol entries you selected.

- **Source**: Much like the **Source** entry with your route tables, this can be a network subnet CIDR range, a single IP address using a /32 mask, or exposure to traffic from anywhere using the 0.0.0.0/0 CIDR range.

- **Allow/Deny**: With every NACL rule, you must specify whether the traffic that matches this rule should ALLOW or DENY the traffic coming into the subnet.

The final rule in an NACL will always have an explicit deny rule, which will drop all traffic that does not match any rule within the NACL. This safeguard mechanism prevents traffic from getting through to your subnet that you haven't specified.

The Subnets Associations Tab

This section shows which subnets are associated with this NACL, and as mentioned when discussing subnets, you can have multiple subnets associated with a single NACL, but only a single NACL can be associated with a subnet:

Figure 10.20: The NACL Subnet associations screen

If you fail to associate your NACL with the correct subnets, then your subnet might not have the appropriate security safeguards in place and could allow unwanted network traffic to be processed. Additionally, your NACLs could be created and configured but not associated with any subnet, providing no security measures.

The Tags tab, as previously discussed, helps you create key-value pairs that can be associated with your NACL.

Now that you know how to control security at the subnet/network level, you are ready to move on to a layer that operates at the instance level: security groups.

The Role of Security Groups in VPC Security

Security groups are much like NACLs in that they provide a virtual firewall level of protection but at the instance level rather than the network level. Security groups are associated with instances rather than subnets and control the traffic to and from your instances within your VPC. Again, only a single security group can be applied to an instance, but the same security group can be associated with multiple instances.

Security groups allow for stateful traffic, meaning that if the traffic is allowed in via the rules, then it is returned, notwithstanding any rules in place. You can specify inbound traffic rules based on a combination of port, IP range, or another security group. There are also other subtle differences between NACLs and security groups within the rule base. The following subsections will take you through the security group tabs.

The Details Tab

The `Details` tab provides an overview of the security group, showing the security group ID, the name of the security group, its VPC association, and the rule counts—both inbound and outbound:

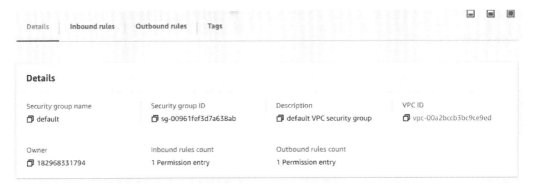

Figure 10.21: The security group Details screen

To review the security setup of a security group, examine the inbound and outbound rulesets.

The Inbound Rules and Outbound Rules Tabs

The following screenshot shows the inbound traffic rules associated with this security group:

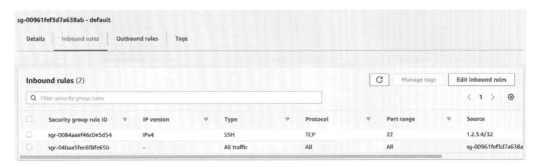

Figure 10.22: Security group inbound rules screen

Figure 10.21 contains six fields of pertinent information:

- **Security group rule ID**: This is the unique ID/identifier for the security group.

- **IP version**: This shows if the rule only works for a particular type of IP address, such as IPv4 or IPv6.

- **Type**: This represents the type of protocol that you would like to open up to network traffic (for example, HTTPS).

- **Protocol**: This shows the protocol associated with the type.

- **Port Range**: This shows the port range of the protocol. If using a customer **Type** and **Protocol**, you can manually enter the port range.

- **Source**: Much like the `Source` entry with your route tables/NACL, this can be a network subnet CIDR range, a single IP address using a `/32` mask, all exposure to traffic from anywhere using the `0.0.0.0/0` CIDR, or another security group ID. Security groups can give access to each other by providing another security group ID from the same VPC as the source.

Notice that there is no field for **Allow** or **Deny** as with NACLs. This is because security groups only provide `Allow` rules by default. Therefore, if a rule is in a security group, it is considered allowed. If a match for traffic is not found within the security group, then the traffic is simply dropped. Also, there is no **Rule number** field. This is because all rules are evaluated by the security group before a decision is made about whether access should or should not be allowed.

> **Note**
>
> The `Outbound rules` tab shows exactly the same fields as the `Inbound rules` tab. However, the rules affect the traffic going out of the resource rather than coming into the resource associated with the security group.

Table 10.1 presents a quick comparison between how NACLs and security groups operate:

Security Method	Operates At	Rule Types	State	Rule Processing
NACLs	Subnet level	Allow/Deny	Stateless	Rules are read in ascending order until a match is found
Security groups	Resource level	Allow	Stateful	All rules are evaluated before a decision is made

Table 10.1: Comparison of security groups versus NACLs

Now that you have a better understanding of security groups and how to navigate them in the VPC services section of the Management Console, you are ready to take a deeper look at subnets and when to use public versus private subnets.

Public and Private Subnets

Subnets are an essential tool for network administrators to manage large networks. **Subnetting** is achieved by dividing a network into smaller network segments, each with its unique network address and subnet mask. The subnet mask defines the network and host portions of the IP address, allowing the network to determine which devices are on the same network and which require routing.

Dividing a more extensive network into smaller subnets can also enhance network security. Subnets can help improve network security by isolating different parts of the network and allowing better control over access to network resources. This can help prevent unauthorized access to sensitive data or systems.

Subnet address	Range of addresses	Hosts	Join					
10.0.0.0/21	10.0.0.0 - 10.0.7.255	2046	/21	/20				
10.0.8.0/21	10.0.8.0 - 10.0.15.255	2046	/21		/19			
10.0.16.0/21	10.0.16.0 - 10.0.23.255	2046	/21	/20				
10.0.24.0/21	10.0.24.0 - 10.0.31.255	2046	/21			/18		
10.0.32.0/21	10.0.32.0 - 10.0.39.255	2046	/21	/20				
10.0.40.0/21	10.0.40.0 - 10.0.47.255	2046	/21		/19		/17	
10.0.48.0/21	10.0.48.0 - 10.0.55.255	2046	/21	/20				/16
10.0.56.0/21	10.0.56.0 - 10.0.63.255	2046	/21					
10.0.64.0/21	10.0.64.0 - 10.0.71.255	2046	/21	/20				
10.0.72.0/21	10.0.72.0 - 10.0.79.255	2046	/21		/19	/18		
10.0.80.0/20	10.0.80.0 - 10.0.95.255	4094		/20				
10.0.96.0/19	10.0.96.0 - 10.0.127.255	8190			/19			
10.0.128.0/17	10.0.128.0 - 10.0.255.255	32766					/17	

Figure 10.23: Subnets dividing a larger /16 CIDR range

A public subnet should be used for resources that the internet will access. A private subnet should be used for resources that will not be accessible from the public internet.

When to Use a Public Subnet

Sometimes, you need to allow those outside your AWS network access to a limited number of resources in your account. These could be situations such as customers accessing an e-commerce platform or a specific API call to gain access to data. The situation could even be as specific as a trusted team member trying to enter the network to perform a task. Yet, their originating source address is outside the AWS and corporate network.

The following are some use cases for public subnets in AWS:

- **Bastion hosts**: If you need to access instances in private subnets using **Secure Shell** (**SSH**) or Remote Desktop Protocol, you can use a bastion host placed in a public subnet. The bastion host is a gateway to secure access instances in the private subnet.

- **Public data storage**: If you need to store public data that users on the internet can access, then you can place the data storage servers in a public subnet. For example, if you are hosting public files that anyone could download on the internet, you can place the storage servers in a public subnet.

- **Public-facing applications**: If you are running a web application that needs to be accessed by users on the internet, you would typically place the frontend servers in a public subnet. These servers must be directly accessible from the internet to serve web pages and accept user requests.

Using Bastion Hosts to Connect to Your VPC

Bastion hosts are used to gain access to your instances that reside within your private subnets from the internet, and the bastion itself resides within the public subnet. The difference between a public subnet and a private subnet is that subnets only become classed as public when an IGW is attached to a VPC and a route exists within a route table associated with the subnet with a destination value of 0.0.0.0/0 via the target of the IGW, for example, as shown in the following figure:

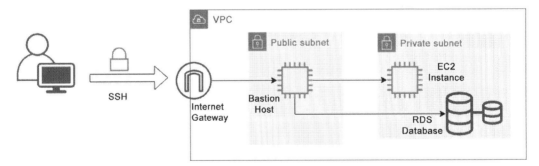

Figure 10.24: Connecting to your VPC via a bastion host

Any subnet associated with a route table pointing to an IGW with a destination address of 0.0.0.0/0 is considered a public subnet as it has direct access to the internet. Any subnet without this route is considered private, as there is no route out to the internet or vice versa.

So, to clarify, for a subnet to be public, the following must be the case:

- The VPC must have an IGW attached
- The subnet must have a route pointing to the internet (0.0.0.0/0) with a target of the IGW

When a subnet is public, instances within this subnet will have a publicly accessible IP address and can communicate with the outside world. This allows your engineers to SSH into your public-facing instances for support and maintenance if needed (providing NACLs and security groups have been configured to allow this access).

However, should you experience issues with your instances within your private instances, how can those same engineers SSH into them from the internet; perhaps as a remote fix? The answer is they can't, as they are private, and there is no route to the outside world. A bastion host must be installed within the public subnet to get around this.

The bastion host is a hardened EC2 instance with restrictive controls that acts as an ingress gateway between the internet and your private subnets without directly exchanging packets between the two environments. Hardening the host ensures that the chances of your systems being compromised are significantly reduced. As this is a gateway to your internal resources, you need to ensure that you follow best practices to harden your instance.

As part of the security group configuration associated with the bastion host, the sources allowed to access the bastion must be restricted as much as possible, such as restricting access to a small CIDR block or a single IP address. The security group for the private instances should allow SSH or RDP from the bastion host IP *only*.

When connecting to instances, you use a key pair for authentication. For Linux instances, this is stored as a * . pem file and is downloaded when the instance is created. However, once you connect to your bastion host (using the pem key file), you must use the * . pem file associated with the private instance to connect. This file will not be stored on the bastion host and should not be stored on the bastion host for security purposes.

> **Note**
>
> You will see bastion hosts in greater detail in *Chapter 11, Securing EC2 Instances*, including how to build and configure a bastion host for secure connectivity into your network, along with what are some alternatives that AWS presents to bastion hosts.

A bastion host is a secure standard known to many as a way to securely gain access from an outside network to the internal resources inside that network. The following section will discuss how you can build some of those networking components in the VPC service.

Networking in a VPC

Networking within an AWS VPC is the foundational infrastructure that enables the secure and efficient operation of cloud resources. It provides a controlled environment where users can create isolated networks (known as VPCs) and define the rules governing communication between these resources.

Within a VPC, subnets are established. Subnets are like distinct neighborhoods within your VPC, allowing resource organization and segregation. You can control if outside users are able to access your resources by using public and private subnets.

To enable communication between resources in the VPC and the internet, an IGW is attached to the VPC. It serves as the entry and exit point for data, facilitating the secure flow of traffic.

As with public subnets in AWS, the EC2 instances and other services that reside in your private subnets can still require limited connectivity to the internet. This topic is dealt with next.

Adding Internet Access to a Private Subnet

In AWS, a NAT gateway is a managed network service that provides outbound internet connectivity for resources in a private subnet within a VPC.

When you have instances in a private subnet, they cannot communicate with the internet by default. Even if you have set up an IGW, you want to separate your private instances from direct internet access. This is where a NAT instance or a NAT gateway comes into play.

The primary role of a NAT gateway is to enable instances within a private subnet to access the internet and receive traffic initiated from the internet while blocking incoming traffic not requested by the instances.

A NAT gateway is a stateful service. It keeps track of the connections initiated from the private subnet and ensures that the response traffic from the internet reaches the correct instance in the subnet. A NAT gateway also automatically provides better scalability and better performance than standalone NAT instances because the gateway is a managed service provided by AWS and can automatically scale based on the network traffic demand.

To use a NAT gateway, you must create the NAT gateway in a public subnet and configure the private subnet to route its traffic destined for the internet through the NAT gateway.

As you just learned, placing resources in a private subnet does not mean they are cut off from internet access. In the next section, you will see how to use different techniques to tie multiple VPCs together to form a more extensive network.

VPCs Together

As you and your team build your accounts, you will likely have more than one VPC for each account. If you operate in multiple Regions, there will need to be at least one VPC per account per Region. As you segment out your network for different purposes, different VPCs (both public and private) hold various resources, and the traffic routed to those VPCs follows a set of rules that can sometimes become complex. You need to have a way to connect these various VPCs, whether they be in the same account or across disparate accounts.

There are several different techniques that you can use to network VPCs together. Which method you use depends mainly on your requirements. The most common are shown in the following list:

- **VPC peering**: This lets you connect two VPCs via a direct, private network connection. VPC peering enables traffic flow between VPCs as if they were part of the same network. This approach suits scenarios that require a connection between VPCs in the same Region or across Regions within the same AWS account.

- **Transit Gateway**: This fully managed service allows you to connect multiple VPCs in a hub-and-spoke model, making it easier to manage network traffic between VPCs. Transit Gateway acts as a centralized hub to connect multiple VPCs, simplifying network routing and security configuration. This approach is suitable for scenarios that require connections between multiple VPCs within the same Region or across multiple Regions within the same AWS account.

- **VPN connections**: This allows you to establish a secure, encrypted connection between your VPC and an external network, such as your on-premises data center or another VPC. VPN connections can be used to connect VPCs utilizing the internet as a transport medium. This approach suits scenarios that require connections between VPCs in different AWS accounts or Regions or from your VPC to an on-premises network.

- **AWS Direct Connect**: This allows you to establish a dedicated, private network connection between your VPC and your on-premises data center or co-location facility. Direct Connect provides a more reliable and consistent network connection compared to a VPN connection. This approach suits scenarios that require connections between VPCs in different AWS accounts or Regions with high bandwidth and low latency.

Having gone through an overview of the techniques used to network VPCs together, you can proceed to take a deeper look at peering two or more VPCs together.

What Is Peering When It Comes to VPCs?

Suppose you need to create a direct, private network connection between one or two VPCs. In that case, you can use VPC peering. It is a networking solution that allows you to connect two Amazon VPCs together so that they can communicate using private IP addresses. VPC peering can span multiple VPCs within the same Region or multiple Regions and can even connect VPCs in different accounts.

The following are some scenarios where VPC peering may be helpful:

- Connecting VPCs within the same account or different accounts

- Connecting VPCs in different Regions

- Simplifying network management by avoiding the need for VPN connections or multiple VPC gateways

- Transferring data between VPCs without incurring data transfer costs

When you create a VPC peering connection, you establish a direct network connection between the VPCs. This connection is private and secure; traffic between the VPCs doesn't leave the AWS network. VPC peering supports communication between VPCs using IPv4 and IPv6 addresses with the same security and networking features that you use within a single VPC, such as security groups, NACLs, and routing tables.

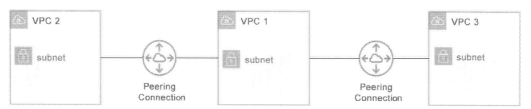

Figure 10.25: VPC peering across three VPCs

As you can see in *Figure 10.25*, VPC 1 is the primary network being peered by two other networks, VPC2 and VPC3. When requesting the peering connection, each VPC must accept the peering connection individually. Once the peering connection has been established, and as long as entries are placed in the routing tables to allow network traffic flow, the other VPCs can connect. As shown in *Figure 10.25*, any instance located in VPC 2 could not contact VPC 3 unless a separate peering connection was made between those VPCs. Even though VPC 1 seemingly acts as a bridge between VPC 2 and VPC 3, each connection is distinct on its own.

VPC peering is useful if you need to quickly connect one or two VPCs, even if they are not in the same account. There are limitations when using VPC peering; the next section will explain them.

Limitations of VPC Peering

Although VPC peering is relatively easy to understand and implement, there are some limitations that you must be aware of as well:

- You cannot create a VPC peering connection between VPCs with matching or overlapping IPv4 CIDR blocks. Similarly, you cannot create a VPC peering connection between VPCs with matching or overlapping IPv6 CIDR blocks.

- You cannot have more than one VPC peering connection between two VPCs at the same time.

- If VPC 1 has an IGW, neither VPC 2 nor VPC 3 could use that IGW to access the internet via the peering connection.

- If VPC 1 has a gateway endpoint for either S3 or DynamoDB, neither VPC 2 nor VPC 3 can use that gateway endpoint to access those services.

- Unlike in a regular VPC, you cannot create a security group rule referencing a peer VPC security group. Instead, you must reference the IPv4 ranges.

The preceding list was of the most prevalent rules. For a complete list of VPC peering limitations, visit the following URL: `https://packt.link/Jkkhv`.

Using Transit Gateway to Connect VPCs

Transit Gateway can be thought of as a router in the cloud that works on a per-Region basis. Transit Gateway can also centralize your AWS Direct Connect connection as well as a VPN connection coming into Transit Gateway.

It can scale with your organization as you grow since each Transit Gateway hub can support 5,000 attachments. From a network security perspective, Transit Gateway is able to segment traffic based on route tables to ensure that specific segments of traffic do not talk to each other.

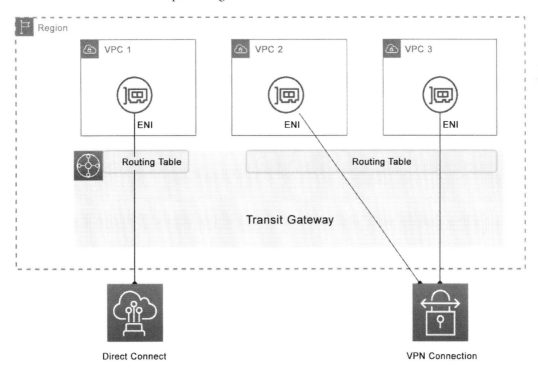

Figure 10.26: Transit Gateway connecting to multiple VPCs in a Region

Figure 10.26 shows how Transit Gateway can help you either connect multiple VPCs to each other or segment them from each other based on the values in the Routing Table. Based on the initial Routing Table, VPC 1 allows inbound and outbound connections associated with the Direct Connect IP range. It does not allow data to connect to VPCs 2 or 3. VPCs 2 and 3 enable data and connections between those VPCs, along with ingress and egress connections associated with the VPN connection.

After examining how to connect multiple VPCs using Transit Gateway so that various segmented VPCs can talk to each other, you will explore the various options for securely connecting your facilities and locations to your AWS cloud network.

Connecting Your On-Premises Network to Your VPC

Even as you look to build your footprint in the AWS cloud, there will often be cases in which you need to connect directly to the network that you have established for your on-premises locations. These might be locations where several employees are located or where you have data and compute resources that you have either not moved to the cloud yet or do not plan on moving. Whichever one of these cases that might be, this presents an opportunity for you to use some of the services provided by AWS to create a secure connection for data to be transported to and from the resources allocated there.

You are presented here with how to connect to a single VPC, and that VPC becomes the entry point to your AWS account, AWS organization, or both.

> **Note**
>
> This book concentrates on security and how to create secure network connections in AWS and presents the information on network connectivity needed for the *AWS Certified Security – Specialty* exam. Networking in AWS, the cloud, and as a practice is a much larger topic, and it is recommended you dive into it further. This short chapter is by no means a definitive guide.

Now, if you have multiple locations for your on-premises connectivity, you can look to **AWS VPN CloudHub** as an option for securing multiple locations to the same AWS VPC. Using a Hub and Spoke model, VPN CloudHub allows multiple office locations to connect to a VPG, making a secure connection. The primary condition that you must abide by when setting up CloudHub is that none of the sites can have overlapping IP ranges; this is to prevent IP collisions.

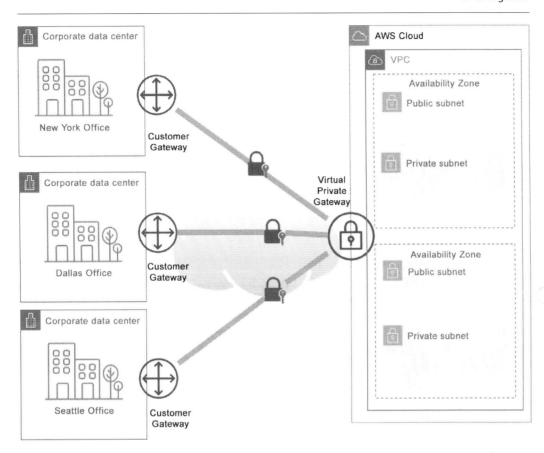

Figure 10.27: AWS CloudHub connecting multiple locations in the spoke-and-hub model

The network setup in *Figure 10.27* shows an established VPN on the right-hand side. There are three different corporate data centers that need to connect to the AWS resources located in different locations. None of these data centers have conflicting IPv4 CIDR ranges. Using a **customer gateway** (**CGW**) connection in each location, along with AWS CloudHub, allows all the data centers to connect to the resources in AWS and network with each other.

Using Direct Connect to Secure On-Premises Connectivity

Like an AWS VPN connection, Direct Connect extends your infrastructure and joins it to your AWS architecture as if it were a single network. However, with Direct Connect, you do not use a public network to initiate the connection. Instead, your connection runs across a private network via an AWS Direct Connect location.

These AWS Direct Connect locations are data centers where your network and the AWS network physically connect to each other via cross-connects using standard fiber-optic cables between your router and an AWS Direct Connect router. AWS Direct Connect manages these Direct Connect Delivery Partner data centers.

> **Note**
>
> For more information on these Delivery Partners, please visit `https://packt.link/8PX50`.

Direct Connect is one option for securing connectivity between your corporate infrastructure and AWS, and uses private infrastructure as the underlying backbone. The following section discusses VPC connections, which use the internet instead.

Connecting with a VPN Connection

As an alternative to a direct connection, you can use a VPN to connect your on-premises network to an AWS VPC. A VPN provides a secure and encrypted connection, which is useful when you need to extend your on-premises network to include resources in your VPC. To establish this VPN connection, your VPC must have at least one subnet and must enable communication between itself and the on-premises network by creating an AWS Site-to-Site VPN connection. VPNs are a secure option to establish a connection between your on-premises infrastructure and the AWS cloud.

Connecting to a VPC using a VPN involves the following steps:

1. **Set up a VPG**: A VPG is a logical representation of an Amazon VPC that enables VPN connections from on-premises data centers or remote networks.

2. **Configure a CGW**: A CGW is a physical or software appliance located in your on-premises data center or remote network. It acts as a secure endpoint for your VPN tunnel to terminate.

3. **Create a VPN connection**: Create a VPN between your VPC and your customer gateway using the VPG and CGW you set up in *steps 1* and *2*.

4. **Configure routing**: Configure routing for your VPC and on-premises network so traffic can flow through the VPN tunnel.

Once you have completed these steps, you can connect to your VPC using your VPN client software and network credentials.

> **Note**
>
> You will see more details on the security and routing of AWS Direct Connect and VPN connections in *Chapter 18, Securely Connecting to your AWS Environment*.

Securing your connections is vital so those listening on the wire don't eavesdrop and gather sensitive information. Some techniques can be used in AWS so that connecting to the services without using the public internet is possible. In the next section, you will examine such techniques.

Connecting to Your AWS Services without the Internet

In addition to using the internet to access the VPC via an IGW, you can also connect to a VPN from your data center. This enables you to create a link between your on-premises network and your VPC without using the public internet.

Although an IGW added to your VPC or even a NAT gateway can help you connect to both the internet and the public IP addresses of AWS services such as S3 buckets and EC3 instances, there are many times when connecting to the different services via an endpoint protects the security of the connection rather than going over the public internet.

A VPC endpoint in AWS is a virtual network interface that allows you to privately access AWS services without using a public IP address or going over the public internet.

Historically, when connections had to be made to services such as DynamoDB or S3 buckets, they would need to use a NAT gateway or public IP address. In this manner, the traffic would be routed over the public internet from the source until it reached its destination. This was even the case if the source was an EC2 instance inside the same VPC as the DynamoDB database.

The Different Types of Endpoints Available in VPCs

If you have an application running inside your VPC and that application needs to connect to AWS services that usually connect over the public internet, such as Amazon S3, Amazon SNS, Amazon SQS, and Amazon API Gateway, then you can use AWS endpoints as a more secure way of making connections inside of your VPC.

Traditionally, when you access AWS services such as S3 or DynamoDB from within a VPC, you would need to use a public IP address or a NAT gateway to route traffic through the internet. This can introduce security risks and increase latency.

With VPC endpoints, you can establish a private connection between your VPC and the AWS service without going over the internet. This allows you to access the service securely and with reduced latency.

The following two types of endpoints are available:

- **Interface endpoints**: These are powered by ENIs and allow you to connect to AWS services over PrivateLink. PrivateLink is a highly available and scalable technology that provides secure and private communication between VPCs and AWS services.

- **Gateway endpoints**: These are powered by **Gateway Load Balancer** (**GWLB**) and allow you to connect to S3 and DynamoDB over a VPC endpoint.

To reiterate, the only services supported by gateway endpoints are Amazon S3 and DynamoDB.

The following section will teach you the process of setting up an endpoint in your established VPC so that you have a better understanding of the concept of endpoints.

Creating a VPC Endpoint

Generally, traffic traveling to the Amazon S3 service would use the public internet to get to its destination. If this had originated from an EC2 instance from within your VPC, then this route could take an IGW if the instance was in a public subnet or a NAT gateway if it was in a private subnet.

If you want to keep your traffic more secure and don't want that traffic to traverse over the public internet, you must add a VPC endpoint:

1. Start by opening the Amazon Management Console to the VPC service at `https://packt.link/uCREd`.

2. On the left-hand side menu, click on `Endpoints`.

Managed prefix lists

Endpoints

Endpoint services

NAT gateways

Peering connections

Figure 10.28: The AWS VPC menu

3. Once the `Endpoints` screen appears on the main window, click on the `Create endpoint` button located at the top-right side.

4. Now, on the `Create endpoint` screen, scroll down to the box labeled `Endpoint settings`. For the `Name` tag, name your endpoint `chapt10-s3` and select `AWS services` in the `Service category` section if this is not already selected.

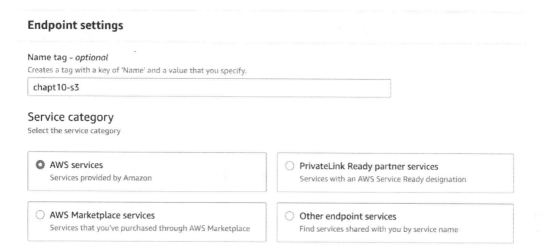

Figure 10.29: The Endpoint settings screen

5. Scroll down until you reach the `Services` section. Select the item labeled `com.amazonaws.s3-global.accesspoint`.

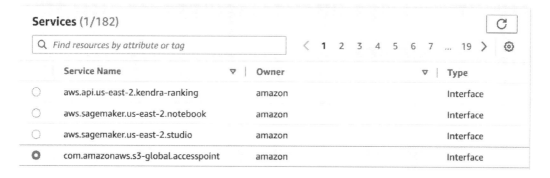

Figure 10.30: The Endpoint Services screen

6. Scroll down to the box labeled VPC. Choose the VPC you created earlier, named My VPC. If you didn't create the VPC earlier, you could choose your default VPC for this example, which does not have a name.

Figure 10.31: The VPC screen

7. Once you have your VPC selected, scroll down to the box labeled Subnets. Select any available subnets, and then in the drop-down box, choose the private subnets if available.

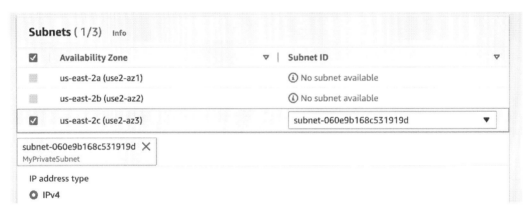

Figure 10.32: The Subnets selection screen

8. Scroll down to Security groups and select any security groups that will be attached to your instances, Lambda functions, or other resources that would need access to the S3 buckets from the endpoint.

Figure 10.33: The Security group selection screen

9. Scroll down to the `Policy` section. Keep the policy setting set as `Full access`.

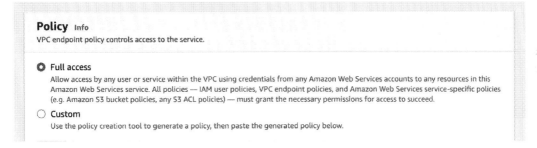

Figure 10.34: The Policy selection screen

10. Now, scroll down to the bottom of the page and click on the button labeled `Create endpoint`.

You now have an endpoint created for direct communication with your S3 buckets without having to traverse the public internet.

Summary

In this chapter, you reviewed the foundational networking component of the AWS cloud, the VPC. You learned how to create a VPC network using a CloudFormation template with both a public and private subnet and then attach an IGW for internet connectivity. After creation, you explored the different components of the VPC to become familiar with them.

You then reviewed the different network connectivity options available for the VPCs in the account you are working on as well as other accounts and then the network traffic back to data centers that need to connect to AWS resources. These included options for connecting over public networks, such as VPNs to keep your transmissions secure and encrypted, along with Direct Connect, peering, and endpoints to keep your transmissions off the public internet.

Chapter 11, Securing EC2 Instances, will discuss how to secure EC2 instances when you are inside the perimeter of your network.

Further Reading

For additional information on the AWS shared responsibility model and the underlying foundation of AWS security, please look at the following resources:

- Building a Scalable and Secure Multi-VPC AWS Network Infrastructure: `https://packt.link/nzWWg`

- AWS Direct Connect FAQs: `https://packt.link/yhBO1`

- Amazon Virtual Private Cloud Connectivity Options: `https://packt.link/Rq6Mr`

Exam Readiness Drill – Chapter Review Questions

Apart from a solid understanding of key concepts, being able to think quickly under time pressure is a skill that will help you ace your certification exam. That is why working on these skills early on in your learning journey is key.

Chapter review questions are designed to improve your test-taking skills progressively with each chapter you learn and review your understanding of key concepts in the chapter at the same time. You'll find these at the end of each chapter.

> **How To Access These Resources**
>
> To learn how to access these resources, head over to the chapter titled *Chapter 21, Accessing the Online Practice Resources.*

To open the Chapter Review Questions for this chapter, perform the following steps:

1. Click the link – `https://packt.link/SCSC02E2_CH10`

   Alternatively, you can scan the following QR code (*Figure 10.35*):

Figure 10.35: QR code that opens Chapter Review Questions for logged-in users

2.   Once you log in, you'll see a page similar to the one shown in *Figure 10.36*:

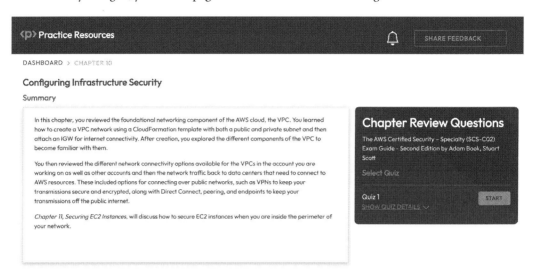

Figure 10.36: Chapter Review Questions for Chapter 10

3.   Once ready, start the following practice drills, re-attempting the quiz multiple times.

Exam Readiness Drill

For the first three attempts, don't worry about the time limit.

ATTEMPT 1

The first time, aim for at least **40%**. Look at the answers you got wrong and read the relevant sections in the chapter again to fix your learning gaps.

ATTEMPT 2

The second time, aim for at least **60%**. Look at the answers you got wrong and read the relevant sections in the chapter again to fix any remaining learning gaps.

ATTEMPT 3

The third time, aim for at least **75%**. Once you score **75%** or more, you start working on your timing.

> **Tip**
>
> You may take more than three attempts to reach 75%. That's okay. Just review the relevant sections in the chapter till you get there.

Working On Timing

Target: Your aim is to keep the score the same while trying to answer these questions as quickly as possible. Here's an example of how your next attempts should look like:

Attempt	Score	Time Taken
Attempt 5	77%	21 mins 30 seconds
Attempt 6	78%	18 mins 34 seconds
Attempt 7	76%	14 mins 44 seconds

Table 10.2: Sample timing practice drills on the online platform

> **Note**
>
> The time limits shown in the above table are just examples. Set your own time limits with each attempt based on the time limit of the quiz on the website.

With each new attempt, your score should stay above 75% while your time taken to complete should **decrease**. Repeat as many attempts as you want till you feel confident dealing with the time pressure.

11
Securing EC2 Instances

AWS **Elastic Compute Cloud** (**EC2**) is one of the most commonly used compute services in AWS. With a wide variety of operating systems and the flexibility of processing and memory options available, along with an array of performance variations to meet various workloads, the EC2 service makes it extremely easy to get up and running in the cloud. Furthermore, if you have long-running or predictable workloads, with the EC2 service, you can take advantage of cost savings in Reserved Instances or Savings Plans. Even for short-term instances, EC2 offers its extra capacity as Spot Instances at significant discounts.

Unfortunately, there will always be malicious actors with the sole aim of harming and hindering your infrastructure. As a result, you need to learn the techniques that not only keep your perimeter secure, as discussed in *Chapter 10*, but also maintain the security of the EC2 instances running your application code inside your AWS environment. These security techniques also explain how to securely access your EC2 instances to minimize the surface through which unauthorized users can gain entry.

In this chapter, you will look at several ways in which security relates to the actual EC2 service and how you can configure and implement the security measures.

The following main topics will be covered in this chapter:

- Securing key pairs
- How to isolate instances for forensic inspection
- Using Systems Manager to configure instances
- Patch and configuration management guidelines
- Performing an internal vulnerability scan using Amazon Inspector

Technical Requirements

To complete some of the exercises in this chapter, you will need an AWS account with an EC2 Linux instance running and permission to access the instance. You will also need permission to run and configure Amazon Inspector and AWS Systems Manager.

Securing Key Pairs for EC2 Instances

The more customizable your service or platform, the more responsibilities you hold as the customer. With the EC2 service, you can create a set of encryption keys that will allow secure access to your EC2 instances.

Creating and Securing EC2 Key Pairs

As part of the process for creating an EC2 instance, you are asked to create a new key pair or select an existing one. This section will discuss the importance of these key pairs and how you can manage them.

Key pairs allow you to connect to your instance, whether it's Linux-based or Windows-based. The methods for connecting to each of these operating systems with key pairs differ, and you will review the different techniques shortly.

Each key pair uses public key cryptography using *2,048-bit SSH-2 RSA keys* and is used to encrypt and decrypt administrative logs on credentials for that instance. It is worth noting, however, that key pairs, once created, are not tied down to a specific instance and can be used for multiple instances. Public key cryptography uses two separate keys to encrypt and decrypt data: the public key and the private key. The EC2 instance maintains the public key and the private key is kept secure by you, the customer. You must download and store this private key securely, as you cannot recover it if you lose it. The public key encrypts the credentials, and your private key decrypts them, allowing you to access the instance.

Key pairs created in AWS are created for use in a single region by default. However, suppose you want to use the same key in multiple regions. In that case, you can import the private key into the EC2 service either via the console or using the CLI after changing the region. Once imported for all regions or your chosen regions, that same key you initially generated will work on EC2 instances in multiple regions.

Creating Key Pairs

You will now learn to create a new key pair that can be used for an instance. Not creating these key pairs can hinder your ability to connect to your EC2 instances, especially if those instances are not running Systems Manager Agent, as you will see later in this chapter in the *Accessing an EC2 Instance Using Session Manager* section.

There are two methods for creating key pairs:

- Creating key pairs during EC2 deployment
- Creating key pairs within the EC2 service in the AWS Management Console

Both methods are shown in detail in the sections below.

Creating Key Pairs during EC2 Deployment

When you create a key during an EC2 instance creation, you will be able to create the new key pair in the `Key pair (login)` dialog box when configuring your new EC2 instance on the AWS Management Console (see the screenshot below).

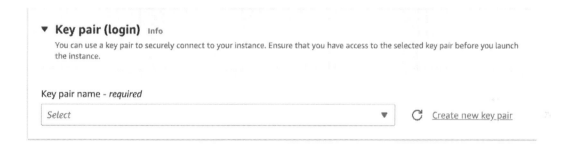

Figure 11.1: Key pair screen for EC2 deployment

The following steps will show you how to create a new key pair using the AWS Management Console:

1. Instead of selecting the key pair name, click on the link on the right-hand side labeled `Create new key pair`.

2. Once you have done this, a new dialog box will appear on the screen. Here, enter the key name, the key type, and the private key format.

3. Once you have filled out all the values, click the `Create key pair` button, and your new key pair will be created. You will then be prompted to download the private key for safekeeping.

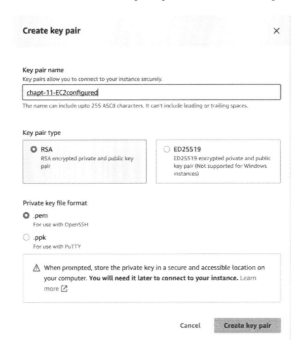

Figure 11.2: Key pair creation screen for EC2

Although creating a key pair when creating an EC2 instance seems convenient, you should also know how to plan out your key pairs beforehand. This is discussed next.

Creating Key Pairs within the EC2 Console

To create a new key pair from the EC2 dashboard, follow these steps:

1. From the EC2 console, select Key Pairs from the left-hand menu in the Network & Security sub-section.

▼ **Network & Security**

    Security Groups

    Elastic IPs

    Placement Groups

    Key Pairs

    Network Interfaces

Figure 11.3: Key pair in the EC2 console menu

2. At the top-right of the page, click the button labeled Create key pair.

3. You will be brought to the Create key pair page. Here, give your key pair a name, such as chapter11-RSA. You may also change the encryption algorithm (Key pair type) to ED25519 but note that the RSA algorithm is the one that works with both Linux and Windows instances.

Key pair

A key pair, consisting of a private key and a public key, is a set of security credentials that you use to prove your identity when connecting to an instance.

Name

chapter11-RSA|

The name can include up to 255 ASCII characters. It can't include leading or trailing spaces.

Key pair type   Info

◉ RSA

◯ ED25519

Figure 11.4: Key pair screen for EC2

4. If you are using a Windows machine and connecting to your instances via the PuTTY client, save your key format in the .ppk format. Otherwise, keep the default .pem setting for the private key file.

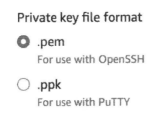

Private key file format

◉ .pem
   For use with OpenSSH

◯ .ppk
   For use with PuTTY

Figure 11.5: Key pair format selection

5. Finally, press the Create key pair button and you will be prompted to download your private key file.

Your key pair will now appear in the list of active key pairs and can be used when you create new EC2 instances.

With the preceding steps, you learned how to create a key pair. But what if you ever need to delete it? The following section will deal with this.

Deleting a Key

Over time, you may want to delete a key pair for several reasons. Reasons for this could be an employee who had created or been assigned a specific key pair leaving the company or your company setting a specific security policy to rotate the EC2 key pairs on a regular basis.

When you delete a key pair from the EC2 service in the Amazon Management Console, you can no longer use it for any new EC2 instances. However, this deletion simply deletes the copy of AWS's public key; it does not delete the public keys attached and associated with any EC2 instances already created with it. Therefore, as long as you have the private key to the same pair, you can still connect to that same EC2 instance.

Deleting a Key Using the AWS Management Console

To delete a key using the EC2 service on the AWS Management Console, follow these steps:

1. From the EC2 console, select `Key Pairs` from the menu on the left under the `Network & Security` sub-heading.

Figure 11.6: Key Pairs option in the EC2 console menu

2. Select the key pair that you want to delete, which is `chapter11-RSA` for this example.

Figure 11.7: Key pair selected

3. At the top of the main screen, click the `Actions` button on the right. This will bring up a sub-menu. Select `Delete` from the list of choices.

Figure 11.8: Key pair deletion menu

4. A dialog box will appear; type the word `Delete` as a confirmation before pressing the `Delete` button to confirm that you want to delete the specified key pair.

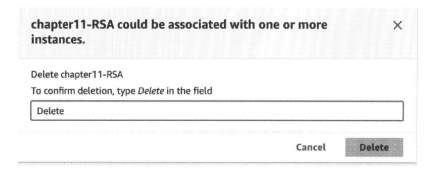

Figure 11.9: Key pair deletion confirmation screen

Now that you have created a set of secure keys for your EC2 instances and have seen how to delete unneeded key pairs, you need some instances to use those key pairs with. One of the secure ways to access your instances is via a bastion server.

Building a Hardened Bastion Server

In *Chapter 10, Configuring Infrastructure Security*, you were introduced to the concept of a **bastion server**. This server is installed in one of the public subnets and acts as a jump box to access the other systems on your AWS network, especially in cases where you need to get in from an external IP address.

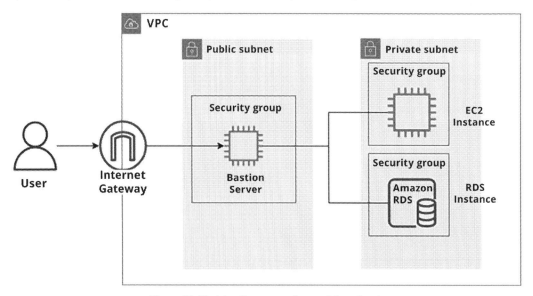

Figure 11.10: A bastion server in a public subnet

Figure 11.10 depicts a user outside the network where the AWS VPC resides entering the VPC from the internet gateway with access to the public subnet. Suppose the user's external IP address has been granted access to the bastion server in the bastion's security group. In that case, that user can authorize themselves and gain access to the bastion. Once on the bastion server, the user is on the network and can either directly go to the EC2 instance or create an SSH tunnel to one of the resources in the private subnet, such as the EC2 instance or the RDS instance.

As you create your bastion host, be aware that its job is only to provide a secure starting point from your outside environment to your AWS environment and no more. It should not be used for any compute functions, nor should it be used for any other tasks as it is exposed to the internet.

Here are some guidelines for creating a hardened bastion server:

- Choose an **Operating System (OS)** that is minimal. A minimal OS means that there are no extra packages or software installed besides the basic requirements. The bastion server's job is just to be a point of entry. However, if you and your team are more comfortable with a particular OS and how to secure it, that might be your best choice.

- Limit the active processes and services running on that OS. When you get your bastion up and running, look at the different processes running on the system using the `top` or `ps` commands. Stop any services that do not need to be running on the bastion. An excellent example of this would be the mail daemon. There is no need for a bastion to have the ability to send out mail.

- Harden default OpenSSH configurations. While SSH is the standard protocol you should use to access the bastion server, you can still make it more secure by adjusting the SSH daemon configuration file that can usually be found in `/etc/ssh/sshd_config`. Ensure you disable the root login and password authentication and set an idle timeout value.

- Make sure that all unnecessary ports are closed. Any security group attached to your bastion EC2 instance should not be open to the entire internet (`0.0.0.0/0`). Instead, it should accept connections from a few fine-tuned IP addresses or ranges. If you need to travel to a different location that is not currently on the allowlist, use your access to the AWS Management Console to add your temporary IP to the security group and then remove it once you no longer need that IP address.

You just learned how to make a bastion host much more secure than spinning up a new base instance you chose. Bastion servers still leave you with the responsibility of an instance to maintain, patch, and keep secure. There are alternative methods to connect to your EC2 instances, which you will look at next.

Alternate Ways to Connect to a Host

Having a bastion server on your network is useful if you need to access your account from an external entry point, and it does leave not only you but others a point of entry into the network as well. However, AWS also provides a way to access your instances without needing a bastion server.

AWS Session Manager and a bastion server serve similar purposes of enabling secure remote access to EC2 instances, but they differ in their architecture and implementation:

- **Architecture**: A bastion server is a standalone server deployed in a public subnet of your VPC. It acts as a single entry point to access your private EC2 instances by forwarding SSH/RDP traffic. On the other hand, AWS Session Manager does not require a bastion server. It utilizes the AWS Systems Manager service and communicates with EC2 instances directly through Systems Manager Agent, which is installed on them.

- **Access method**: With a bastion server, you typically establish a traditional SSH/RDP connection to the bastion server and then use it as a jump host to connect to your target EC2 instance (or instances). In contrast, AWS Session Manager provides a web-based shell directly within the AWS Management Console, eliminating the need for direct SSH/RDP access to the instances. It uses a clientless browser-based interface to establish a secure connection to your instances.

- **Security**: Bastion servers require careful management and maintenance to ensure their security. They must be hardened appropriately, regularly patched, and monitored for any security vulnerabilities. With AWS Session Manager, you can avoid the complexities of managing a bastion server since AWS services handle access and communications. The communication between the Session Manager client and the EC2 instances occurs over secure AWS infrastructure using encryption and IAM-based access controls.

- **Network configuration**: A bastion server requires inbound ports (such as SSH or RDP) to be open in the security group associated with the instance. This introduces a potential attack surface that needs to be properly secured. AWS Session Manager does not require opening inbound ports on your security groups. It relies on outbound connections from the EC2 instances to the Session Manager service in AWS, simplifying the network configuration and reducing exposure to the public internet.

Overall, AWS Session Manager provides a more streamlined and secure approach to accessing EC2 instances than a bastion server does. It eliminates the need for managing and securing a separate server, reduces the attack surface, and offers an intuitive web-based interface for remote access administration.

Now that you have grasped the differences between a bastion host and Systems Manager Session Manager, in the next section you will learn how to access one of your hosts using the Session Manager service and gain a more comprehensive understanding of its capabilities.

Accessing an EC2 Instance Using Session Manager

AWS Session Manager provides a secure and convenient way to access your EC2 instances without needing a public IP address or opening inbound SSH/RDP ports. You can see how easy it is to access your EC2 instances by following the steps below:

> **Note**
>
> If you already have an EC2 instance running with the Amazon Linux operating system that you can use in your account, you can skip to *step 8* of this exercise. You may need to create and attach the Systems Manager Role to your running instance to connect via Session Manager.

1. Log in to your AWS Management Console and navigate to the EC2 service. You can quickly get there by using the following URL: `https://packt.link/37VBj`

2. Find the `Launch Instance` button toward the bottom of the screen in the center. Click on the button, and when the sub-menu appears, choose `Launch Instance`.

3. You should now be on the page named `Launch an Instance`. Name your instance `chapt11-SessionManager` in the box labeled `Names and tags`.

Figure 11.11: Name and tags options for EC2

4. Next, scroll down to the box labeled `Application and OS Images (Amazon Machine Image)`. Make sure that you select the latest version on Amazon Linux. Amazon Linux comes with Systems Manager Agent already installed on the instance.

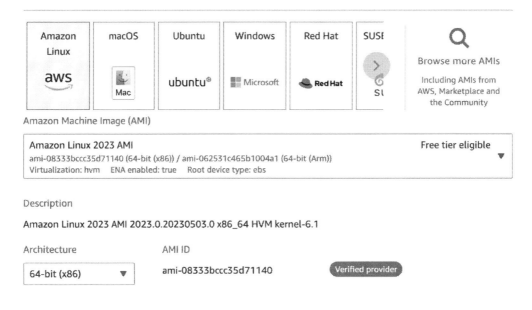

Figure 11.12: AMI selection screen for EC2

5. Scroll down to the box labeled `Key pair (login)`. Click on the drop-down menu and choose the item marked `Proceed without a key pair (Not recommended)`.

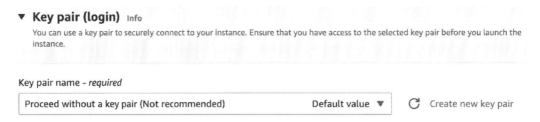

Figure 11.13: Key pair screen for the new instance

6. Now, scroll down to the box labeled Network settings. If you completed the exercise to create the VPC in *Chapter 10*, switch your VPC to the one labeled MyVPC and change the subnet to the private subnet.

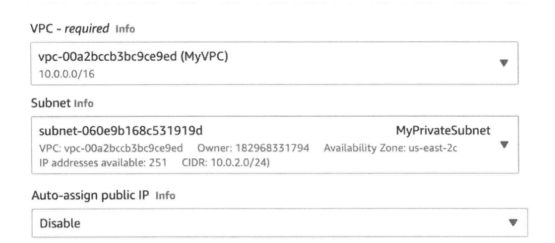

VPC - *required* Info

vpc-00a2bccb3bc9ce9ed (MyVPC)
10.0.0.0/16   ▼

Subnet Info

subnet-060e9b168c531919d   MyPrivateSubnet
VPC: vpc-00a2bccb3bc9ce9ed   Owner: 182968331794   Availability Zone: us-east-2c   ▼
IP addresses available: 251   CIDR: 10.0.2.0/24)

Auto-assign public IP Info

Disable   ▼

Figure 11.14: VPC and subnet selection screen for EC2

If you didn't create the MyVPC virtual private cloud in the exercise in *Chapter 10*, then create a new security group but uncheck the box labeled Allow SSH traffic from.

7. Click on the Advanced details bar to expand the options.

8. In the Advanced details section, find IAM instance profile. Click the Create new IAM profile link that appears on the right. Depending on your browser settings, this will open a new tab (or window).

9. The new tab/window should take you to the IAM > Roles page. Find the button labeled Create role in the top-right corner of the page and click on it to start the process of creating a new role.

10. You will now be brought to the page named Select trusted entity. Keep the default value of Trusted entity type as AWS service and then scroll down to the bottom of the page. Under Use case, choose the radio button next to the value EC2. After making these selections, click the Next button at the bottom of the page.

Figure 11.15: Trusted Entity selection for EC2

11. After you select EC2 as your trusted entity, you will be brought to a page labeled Add permissions. You will not have to craft a custom policy because an AWS managed policy exists for Systems Manager access. In the search box, use the term SSM to find the Systems Manager managed policies.

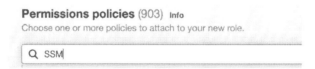

Figure 11.16: Permissions selection search bar

12. Once you have the SSM policies filtered, choose the policy labeled AmazonSSMManagedInstanceCore. When you have selected the checkbox next to this policy, scroll down to the bottom of the page and press the Next button to continue.

13. On the Name, review, and create page, give your role the name of chapt11-SSM so that you can find it easily when you return to the EC2 service. After giving the role a name, scroll down to the bottom of the page and click on the Create role button.

Figure 11.17: Role creation screen

14. With your Systems Manager role created, you can close the browser tab for the IAM service and continue configuring your EC2 instance.

15. You should be back on your EC2 instance screen and in the `Advanced details` section. Below the `IAM instance profile` heading, use the drop-down list to find the role you just created named `chapt11-SSM`. Make sure this is selected in the box before moving on.

IAM instance profile Info

chapt11-SSM
arn:aws:iam::182968331794:instance-profile/chapt11-SSM

Figure 11.18: IAM role selection screen for EC2

16. Finally, scroll down to the bottom of the page and click the `Launch instance` button to create your new EC2 instance.

    Your instance should launch successfully at this point.

17. You are now ready to go to the Systems Manager service. You can get there quickly using the URL: `https://packt.link/y7LlZ`.

18. From the Systems Manager menu on the left, under the `Node Management` heading, find `Session Manager` and click on that menu item.

▼ **Node Management**

    Fleet Manager

    Compliance

    Inventory

    Hybrid Activations

    Session Manager

    Run Command

    State Manager

Figure 11.19: Systems Manager console menu

19. Once on the Session Manager main screen, click on the `Start Session` button.

20. On the main screen, you should see a box labeled `Target instances`. If you have attached your role correctly, you will see your instance on the screen. Select the radio button next to the instance name and then press the `Start session` button, and you will be in the instance without needing a key.

Figure 11.20: Target instances screen

You just learned how to connect to your instances via AWS Session Manager. There are cases where either your bastion or another host can get compromised, and if this does happen, how would you isolate this for forensic analysis? This is the topic you will examine next.

Isolating EC2 Instances for Forensic Inspection

If you are going to perform forensic inspection or forensic analysis, you need to have created the required infrastructure beforehand. The optimal way to do this is with AWS Organizations and the creation of a specialized forensic account. Some companies skip creating the forensic account and instead use their security account inside the AWS organization structure. This practice can be dangerous. For example, if you have moved an instance or function over to the quarantine in the forensic account because it had malicious software that could spread to other parts of the account and perform destructive actions such as deleting files, you don't want the same happening in your specialized security account. *Figure 11.21* presents a graphical representation of the isolated placement of forensic accounts in an AWS Organizations structure.

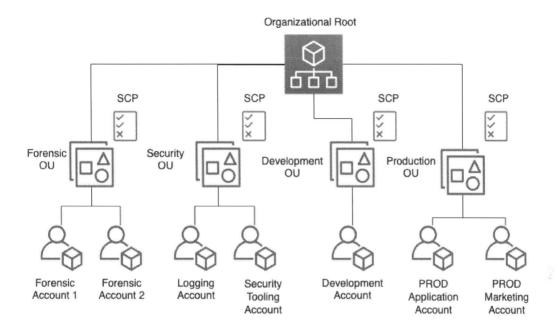

Figure 11.21: Forensic account placement in AWS organizational structure

Isolation

Once you have identified a compromised instance, you must isolate it from everything else and remove it from your production network. This will prevent anything else from gaining access to it. There are various ways to do this:

- You could create a snapshot of the EC2 instance. Once the snapshot has been created, you can share that snapshot with the forensic account and launch the instance there to perform further forensic analysis.

- If possible, take a memory dump of the instance.

- Create a separate forensic account purely for compromised instances.

- Enable logging, such as via VPC Flow Logs.

- Create specific IAM roles that allow read-only access to resources. This prevents you from changing any data in the instance, preserving the condition through forensic analysis.

Your primary goals are to remove the compromised instance from the production network as quickly as possible (usually achieved by changing the instance's security group) and to preserve the instance in its exact state as much as possible. The latter is to ensure you are not responsible for making any changes that could appear in logs during the investigation. These changes could slow the investigation down. By taking a snapshot of the instance, you can restore it in a different environment or a separate forensic account, allowing you to analyze it in safer and more restrictive circumstances.

In the next section, you will see how you can use Amazon Detective to help investigate security issues in your account.

Understanding the Role of Amazon Detective

Amazon Detective is a service that helps you to investigate and analyze security issues within an AWS environment. It can help you and your security team identify the root causes of potential security issues or suspicious activities, making it easier to understand the nature and scope of incidents.

Amazon Detective uses machine learning, statistical analysis, and graph theory techniques to automatically gather data from various AWS resources, including AWS CloudTrail logs, Amazon VPC Flow Logs, and AWS GuardDuty findings. It then aggregates this data to generate visualizations and interactive dashboards, enabling security analysts to investigate and analyze security-related events more effectively.

This service provides insights into activities such as unauthorized access attempts, data breaches, and privilege escalations. It uses algorithms to identify patterns and relationships between different data points, helping uncover hidden connections and potential security risks. Amazon Detective also provides contextual information and timelines for security events, thereby allowing analysts to understand the sequence of events and take appropriate action.

As a service, Amazon Detective provides insights into activities such as unauthorized access attempts, data breaches, and privilege escalations. It uses algorithms to identify patterns and relationships between different data points, helping to uncover hidden connections and potential security risks. Amazon Detective also provides contextual information and timelines for security events, allowing security team members to understand the sequence of events and take appropriate action.

By automating data collection and analysis, Amazon Detective aims to reduce the time and effort required to investigate security incidents, enabling security teams to respond quickly and effectively. It provides a centralized view of security-related information, making identifying and addressing potential threats within an AWS environment easier.

The ability to speed up the investigation of security issues is a real plus. However, it is preferable to prevent security issues altogether. In the next section, you will learn how to do this using the automatic configuration capabilities for EC2 instances of AWS Systems Manager.

Using Systems Manager to Configure Instances

Earlier in the chapter, you saw how one of the components of the Systems Manager service, Session Manager, could be used in lieu of a bastion server to connect to remote EC2 instances. Systems Manager has many other uses when it comes to managing your AWS environment, especially for a security engineer.

AWS Systems Manager is a powerful tool that allows you to easily and quickly administer and perform operational actions against your instances (both Windows- and Linux-based) at scale for both on-premises resources and within AWS without having to SSH or RDP to those instances. From a security standpoint, being able to remove these protocols from security groups reduces the attack surface of your instances even further. A single dashboard providing this administration also allows you greater infrastructure visibility. You will, for example, be able to see system configurations, the patching levels of your instances, and other software installations on the instance. Systems Manager also facilitates your compliance requirements by scanning instances against a set of patch baselines and anti-virus definitions.

Creating Inventory in Systems Manager

In this example, you will create a resource group of your EC2 instances tagged with the following information. You will need to go back to one of your running instances and add the following key/value pairs given in *Table 11.1*:

Key	Value
Project	AWS
Domain	Security

Table 11.1: Key value pairs

If you need assistance in adding the key/value pairs to your running instance, follow the steps below:

1. Log in to the AWS Management Console and navigate to the EC2 service. You can get there quickly by using the following URL: `https://packt.link/hhCIK`.

2. From the EC2 dashboard, at the center of the screen, click on the box labeled `Instances (running)` under the `Resources` heading.

3. You should now be on the page that shows your running instances. Select the checkbox next to the name of the instance that you want to tag and add to the resource group. At the bottom of the screen, the details of the instance will appear. Click on the menu tab named `Tags`.

Figure 11.22: Tags menu tab

4. Once the tags are displayed, click the `Manage tags` button. This will bring up a new screen that allows you to add a new tag. Add the two new tags and then click the `Save` button.

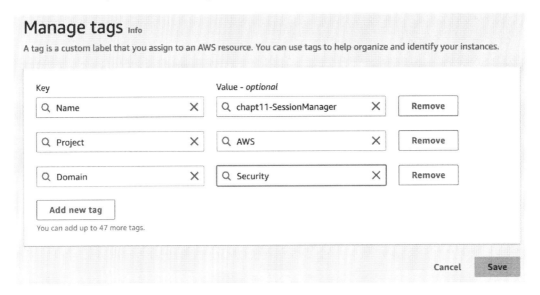

Figure 11.23: Manage tags screen

With the key/value pairs added to your EC2 instance(s), you can add the instance to an inventory for management in Systems Manager.

5. Log in to the AWS Management Console and navigate to the `Systems Manager Service`. You can get there quickly by using the following URL: `https://packt.link/xdTVK`.

6. From the left-hand side menu, under the `Node Management` heading, click on `Inventory`.

▼ Node Management

    Fleet Manager

    Compliance

    Inventory

    Hybrid Activations

    Session Manager

    Run Command

    State Manager

    Patch Manager

    Distributor

Figure 11.24: Systems Manager console menu

7.   Once on the `Inventory` page, click on the `Set up inventory` button.

8.   You should now be on the `Set up inventory` page. Go down to the first box named `Provide inventory details`. Here, you can name your inventory something like `Chapter-11`.

Figure 11.25: Inventory setup screen

Next, you need to set up your `Targets`. You can do this with the tag you specified on your instance.

9.   In the box labeled `Targets`, click the radio button next to `Specifying a tag`. Then when the form fields appear, enter `Domain` for the key and `Security` for the value.

10. Finally, scroll down to the bottom of the page and click the `Set up inventory` button.

After between 5 and 30 minutes, you should start seeing the graphs on the Inventory page populate.

Viewing your instance and inventory is a step in the right direction. In the next section, you will see how you can write a script using the `Run` command and *Systems Manager Documents*.

Using Systems Manager Run Command with Documents

Scripts created automatically (whether in PowerShell, Bash, or Python) to perform tasks on your resources can become powerful tools in your toolbox, especially if you are a security professional. If instances or other types of resources become tainted, you may not have time to log in one by one to shut down specific processes. Even simple tasks that you may save for junior engineers, such as installing antivirus software, can be quickly and easily automated once you have the scripting parameters set in place.

The following steps will show you how to run a script with a specific value using Systems Manager Documents and Run commands:

1. The first thing you need to do is create a document. From the main `Systems Manager` screen, from the left-hand side menu, under the `Shared Resources` heading, choose `Documents`.

2. Once on the `Documents` page, click on the `Create document` button. When the drop-down list appears, choose the option labeled `Command or Session`.

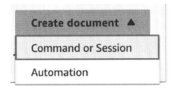

Figure 11.26: Create document dropdown

3. You should now be on the `Create document` page. First, fill in the `Document details` section. For the name of the document, use the name `install_and_run_clamscan`. For the target type, type EC2 in the search box and then find the value or type `/AWS::EC2:::Instance`. You can leave the `Document type` option set to the default `Command document` setting.

Figure 11.27: Document details screen for Systems Manager

4. Now move on to the `Content` section of the document. Change the content type from `JSON` to `YAML` and add the YAML script below the screenshot. Once you have entered the script, scroll down to the bottom of the page and press the `Create document` button.

Content

Figure 11.28: Document context selection

```yaml
---
schemaVersion: "2.2"
description: "Command Document Example YAML Template"
parameters:
  Message:
    type: "String"
    description: "Document Example"
    default: "Chapter Eleven"
mainSteps:
- action: "aws:runShellScript"
  name: "example"
  inputs:
    onFailure: exit
    runCommand:
    - |
      #!/bin/bash
      sudo yum install -y clamav clamav-update clamd
      sudo sed -i -e "s/Example/#Example/" /etc/freshclam.conf
      sudo sed -i -e "s:#DatabaseDirectory /var/lib/
clamav:DatabaseDirectory /var/lib/clamav:" /etc/freshclam.conf
      sudo sed -i -e "s:#UpdateLogFile /var/log/freshclam.
log:UpdateLogFile /tmp/log/freshclam.log:" /etc/freshclam.conf
      sudo sed -i -e "s/#DatabaseOwner clamupdate/DatabaseOwner
clamupdate/" /etc/freshclam.conf
      echo "FINSIHED INSTALLING....RUNNING FRESHCLAM"
      sudo systemctl stop clamav-freshclam.service
      sudo freshclam
```

You can run your document on your instance now that you have created it.

5.   On the main Systems Manager documents page, in the navigation bar at the top, click the Owned by me tab.

Figure 11.29: Systems Manager document navigation bar

6. Once you have filtered to the documents owned by you, you should see your `install_and_run_clamscan` document. Click on the document's name to go to its main page.

7. At the top of the page, there should be an orange button labeled `Run command`. Click this button to go to the `Run a command` section of Systems Manager and have this particular document selected to run.

8. On the `Run a command` page, scroll down until you find the section labeled `Target selection`. Make sure that the `Target selection` option is set to `Specify instance tags`. Then, in the `Specify instance tags` field, enter `Domain` as the key and `Security` as the value, just as you did when tagging your instance and setting up the inventory. Press the `Add` button to add the key-value pair as the target.

Figure 11.30: Target selection screen for Systems Manager

9. Scroll down until you find the `Output options` on the page. Uncheck the box next to `Enable an S3 bucket`, then check the box next to `Enable CloudWatch logs`.

Figure 11.31: Output options for Systems Manager

10. When you have configured the preceding options, scroll down to the bottom of the page and click the Run button.

As you just reviewed, it is quite easy to run a simple or complex script on one or any number of EC2 instances tagged with a specific value using Systems Manager Documents and run commands when trying to manage hundreds or thousands of instances and install or remove software.

Letting Systems Manager Patch Your Instances

One of the best-known types of vulnerabilities can be found in systems that become outdated in terms of patch management. When servers, either in AWS or on-premises, fall behind with patch management and are not regularly updated with the latest patches and security updates, the following negative consequences can arise:

- They can be subject to security vulnerabilities because of outdated software and missing patches.

- They have an increased risk of exploitation. After all, the longer a server goes unpatched, the more widely known that vulnerability becomes, and more and more hackers or nefarious actors will try to access these known exploits.

- The server can run the risk of stability issues since many patches are provided by vendors and software publishers to fix known bugs.

- Your servers can fall out of compliance if you don't keep your patches current.

To mitigate these risks, it is crucial to establish a robust patch management process that includes regular monitoring, testing, and timely deployment of patches across your EC2 and on-premises servers. The Patch Manager service included in AWS Systems Manager can help you accomplish this.

AWS Patch Manager helps users automate the process of managing patches for their AWS resources, especially EC2 instances. It simplifies the task of keeping software up to date and ensures the security and compliance of your AWS infrastructure. The following are some critical capabilities of AWS Patch Manager:

- **Patch management automation**: AWS Patch Manager enables you to automate the patching process for various AWS resources, such as Amazon EC2 instances, on-premises servers, and Amazon RDS databases. It allows you to define patching schedules, configure maintenance windows, and automate the deployment of patches across your resources.

- **OS patching**: AWS Patch Manager supports patching popular OSs, including Amazon Linux, Ubuntu Server, **Red Hat Enterprise Linux** (**RHEL**), CentOS, and Windows Server. It provides pre-built patch baselines for each supported OS, which include the recommended patches supplied by the respective OS vendors.

- **Patch baselines**: Patch baselines in AWS Patch Manager define the patches that should be applied to your resources. You can create custom baselines that specify specific patches or use predefined baselines provided by AWS. Baselines can be versioned, allowing you to manage different sets of patches over time.

- **Patch compliance reporting**: AWS Patch Manager provides detailed reporting on the patch compliance status of your resources. You can view the compliance status of individual resources or generate aggregated reports to assess the overall security posture of your infrastructure. The reporting feature helps you identify any missing patches or vulnerabilities that need to be addressed.

- **Maintenance windows**: With AWS Patch Manager, you can define maintenance windows during patching activities. This allows you to schedule patch deployments at convenient times to minimize the impact on your applications and users. You can configure maintenance windows based on a specific time or recurring schedule.

- **Patching for on-premises servers**: In addition to patching AWS resources, Patch Manager also supports patching for on-premises servers. You can install Systems Manager Agent on your on-premises servers and manage their patching using the same Patch Manager capabilities as your AWS servers.

With AWS Patch Manager, you can easily and automatically manage patches for your AWS resources, and this ensures the security and compliance of your infrastructure.

Having learned how to automatically keep your instances up to date with software and vendor patches, you are now ready to learn about how to scan your instances for vulnerabilities with Amazon Inspector.

Performing a Vulnerability Scan Using Amazon Inspector

Amazon Inspector is a security assessment service provided by AWS. It helps you identify potential vulnerabilities and security issues in your AWS resources and applications. Amazon Inspector is designed to automate the assessment of security vulnerabilities and deviations from security best practices, enabling you to analyze the security posture of your AWS environment quickly and efficiently.

The service uses a combination of network-based and host-based assessments to gather information about your resources. It analyzes this data to generate findings that highlight security issues such as common software vulnerabilities, insecure configurations, and inadequate access controls. These findings are presented in a comprehensive report with detailed information about the identified vulnerabilities and recommended remediation steps.

Amazon Inspector offers pre-built assessment templates based on best practices and industry standards, such as the **Center for Internet Security** (**CIS**) benchmarks and AWS security best practices. These templates can be customized to suit your specific requirements and can be scheduled to run regularly or triggered manually.

Amazon Inspector works on a variety of AWS services and resources. It primarily focuses on assessing the security of EC2 instances but can also analyze other resources in your AWS environment. Some of the services that Amazon Inspector supports are as follows:

- **Amazon EC2**: Inspector can assess the security of EC2 instances by analyzing their OS, applications, and network configurations.

- **Amazon Elastic Load Balancing (ELB)**: Inspector can evaluate the security of your load balancers and identify potential vulnerabilities or configuration issues.

- **Amazon RDS**: Inspector can assess the security of Amazon **Relational Database Service (RDS)** instances, including the database engines and their configurations.

- **Amazon S3**: Inspector can analyze the permissions and access controls of your S3 buckets to identify potential security alerts.

- **Amazon VPC**: Inspector can evaluate the security of your **Virtual Private Cloud (VPC)** configurations, including network settings, security groups, and access controls.

- **AWS IAM**: Inspector can assess the security of your **Identity and Access Management (IAM)** configurations, including user permissions, roles, and policies.

- **AWS Lambda**: Inspector can analyze your AWS Lambda functions' security configuration and code quality.

At the end of the vulnerability assessment, a report is generated detailing the findings based on the packages selected for the assessment.

There are two different modes in which Amazon Inspector can operate—**Classic inspection** and **Deep inspection/continual vulnerability management**. The Classic mode uses the Inspector agent to scan EC2 instances.

When used with EC2, the Amazon Inspector service uses an agent to help perform the assessment. This agent allows Amazon Inspector to monitor the instance's behavior during a scheduled assessment. It looks for activity across the entire EC2 instance, from network activity to processes being run at the time of the assessment. When the assessment ends, the data is collected, and this telemetry data is then sent back to Inspector for review and assessment. Utilizing an agent allows you to implement Inspector across your existing fleet of instances easily.

You can install this agent in the following ways:

- You can install the agent on each EC2 instance by logging into the resource and running one of the appropriate scripts.

- You can install the agent on a group of EC2 instances or a single instance using the Run command from within Systems Manager, as you saw in an earlier section in this chapter.

- When defining the targets that you want Amazon Inspector to assess, you have the option to install the agent as part of that initial assessment.

- Alternatively, you could use an **Amazon Machine Image** (**AMI**) that already has the agent installed. This implies that you do not have to perform any manual installation. This AMI is called **Amazon Linux 2 AMI with Amazon Inspector Agent**, as shown in the following screenshot, and can be found in the AMI Marketplace (`https://packt.link/W5jug`):

Figure 11.32: Amazon Linux AMI with Inspector Agent

Previously in this chapter, you explored using the `Run` command to perform administrative tasks on your EC2 instances. Next, you will learn to install the script manually so you can get hands-on experience for this alternative method.

Installing the Amazon Inspector Agent

You will need an EC2 instance to install the Amazon Inspector agent. This EC2 instance will need access to the internet so that it can download the agent and any other packages that it needs. If you created the EC2 instance for the Session Manager exercise earlier in this chapter, feel free to use that or quickly go through those steps to create a usable instance for this exercise:

1. Connect to your EC2 instance.

2. Make sure that you are in a writable directory. Use the `cd` command with a tilde (`~`)to switch to your home directory:

```
cd ~
```

3. Once you're connected, run either of the following commands to download the script required to install the agent:

```
wget https://inspector-agent.amazonaws.com/linux/latest/
install
```

OR

```
curl -O https://inspector-agent.amazonaws.com/linux/latest/
install
```

You should get an output similar to the one shown below if you use the `wget` command:

```
sh-5.2$ cd ~
sh-5.2$ wget https://inspector-agent.amazonaws.com/linux/latest/install
--2024-04-01 11:18:01--  https://inspector-agent.amazonaws.com/linux/latest/install
Resolving inspector-agent.amazonaws.com (inspector-agent.amazonaws.com)... 3.160.19.138, 2600:9000:25f3:e400:4:6195:f553:e781, 2600:9000:25f3:1c00:4:6195:f553:e781, ...
Connecting to inspector-agent.amazonaws.com (inspector-agent.amazonaws.com)|3.160.19.138|:443... connected.
HTTP request sent, awaiting response... 200 OK
Length: 31083 (30K) [binary/octet-stream]
Saving to: 'install'

install                       100%[===================================================================================>]  30.35K  --.-KB/s    in 0s

2024-04-01 11:18:01 (308 MB/s) - 'install' saved [31083/31083]
```

Figure 11.33: wget code output

4. Once the Inspector agent is downloaded, you need to run the script by entering the `sudo bash install` command.

Now that the agent is installed, you can configure Amazon Inspector to perform a vulnerability scan on the EC2 instance.

Enabling Amazon Inspector across the Organization

While Amazon Inspector Classic focused on the EC2 service, the service has since evolved to help protect more AWS services.

To enable Amazon Inspector across multiple AWS accounts, you can use AWS Organizations to manage your accounts. With AWS Organizations, you can create groups of accounts that share resources and policies. You can enable Amazon Inspector on each account that you plan to have Inspector check. You need to remember, however, that Inspector is a regional service and needs to be enabled for each Region in which it will be used.

With **Amazon Inspector Deep Inspection**, you can have another account, such as the security account in your organization, run the inspections. If you are managing the security across multiple accounts, then your central management and governance process becomes more streamlined when using a delegated administrator account and leveraging cross-account IAM access. This allows you to manage the security assessments for all your organization's accounts from a single location.

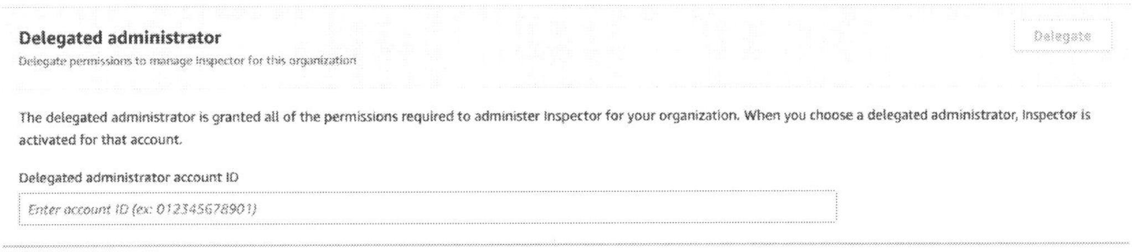

Delegated administrator   Delegate
Delegate permissions to manage Inspector for this organization

The delegated administrator is granted all of the permissions required to administer Inspector for your organization. When you choose a delegated administrator, Inspector is activated for that account.

Delegated administrator account ID

Enter account ID (ex: 012345678901)

Figure 11.34: Delegated administrator screen for Amazon Inspector

Now you are familiar with how the new Amazon Inspector continuously scans for vulnerabilities across your organization and can directly compare this to the previous version of Amazon Inspector after having walked through implementing the Inspector agent on the EC2 instance that you spun up earlier in this chapter.

Summary

In this chapter, you learned how to create key pairs for your EC2 instances so that you could securely access your instances over either the SSH or RDP protocols. Then, you examined how to securely access your private AWS infrastructure using a hardened bastion server or the AWS Session Manager service.

You also saw how to take your previously configured EC2 instance and then install the Amazon Inspector agent on it so that the latter can inform you if it finds any vulnerabilities.

In *Chapter 12, Managing Key Infrastructure*, you will examine the Amazon-managed encryption service KMS. You will go through steps to create your customer-managed keys and learn how different permissions can be set so that users from various groups in your organization can access data using those keys. You will also see how keys can be either rotated automatically or manually based on the needs of your organization.

Further Reading

For additional information on the AWS shared responsibility model and more comprehensive understanding of AWS security, please look at the following resources:

- Tips for securing your EC2 instances: `https://packt.link/cWtCg`
- Amazon Inspector FAQs: `https://packt.link/FSfts`
- AWS Systems Manager FAQs: `https://packt.link/gbQKd`
- Amazon Detective FAQs: `https://packt.link/eqhB9`

Exam Readiness Drill – Chapter Review Questions

Apart from a solid understanding of key concepts, being able to think quickly under time pressure is a skill that will help you ace your certification exam. That is why working on these skills early on in your learning journey is key.

Chapter review questions are designed to improve your test-taking skills progressively with each chapter you learn and review your understanding of key concepts in the chapter at the same time. You'll find these at the end of each chapter.

> **How To Access These Resources**
>
> To learn how to access these resources, head over to the chapter titled *Chapter 21, Accessing the Online Practice Resources*.

To open the Chapter Review Questions for this chapter, perform the following steps:

1. Click the link – `https://packt.link/SCSC02E2_CH11`

   Alternatively, you can scan the following QR code (*Figure 11.35*):

Figure 11.35: QR code that opens Chapter Review Questions for logged-in users

2.   Once you log in, you'll see a page similar to the one shown in *Figure 11.36*:

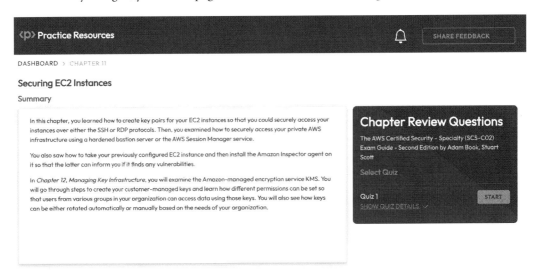

Figure 11.36: Chapter Review Questions for Chapter 11

3.   Once ready, start the following practice drills, re-attempting the quiz multiple times.

Exam Readiness Drill

For the first three attempts, don't worry about the time limit.

ATTEMPT 1

The first time, aim for at least **40%**. Look at the answers you got wrong and read the relevant sections in the chapter again to fix your learning gaps.

ATTEMPT 2

The second time, aim for at least **60%**. Look at the answers you got wrong and read the relevant sections in the chapter again to fix any remaining learning gaps.

ATTEMPT 3

The third time, aim for at least **75%**. Once you score **75%** or more, you start working on your timing.

> **Tip**
> You may take more than three attempts to reach 75%. That's okay. Just review the relevant sections in the chapter till you get there.

Working On Timing

Target: Your aim is to keep the score the same while trying to answer these questions as quickly as possible. Here's an example of how your next attempts should look like:

Attempt	Score	Time Taken
Attempt 5	77%	21 mins 30 seconds
Attempt 6	78%	18 mins 34 seconds
Attempt 7	76%	14 mins 44 seconds

Table 11.2: Sample timing practice drills on the online platform

> **Note**
> The time limits shown in the above table are just examples. Set your own time limits with each attempt based on the time limit of the quiz on the website.

With each new attempt, your score should stay above 75% while your time taken to complete should **decrease**. Repeat as many attempts as you want till you feel confident dealing with the time pressure.

12
Managing Key Infrastructure

Encrypting your data may be the most critical of all the security measures you take in your environment. Once data is encrypted, only those with authorization to use the key that decrypts the data may access those files and pieces of information to read and view their contents.

As a security professional, you are often the one that others in the organization come to with questions on how to facilitate data encryption using the company's standards. This is why it's essential that you are familiar with the workings of **Key Management Service** (**KMS**) and the API calls that encompass this service.

Throughout this chapter, you will gain basic knowledge of encryption and a substantial understanding of the services that manage and provide encryption for AWS accounts and environments. This will allow you to manage, rotate, and protect encryption keys and ensure that data is being encrypted.

> **Note**
>
> With the *AWS Certified Security Specialty exam*, robust knowledge of the KMS service, in particular, is a must. There will be multiple times when the service will be either front and center of the question (or answer) or will be a crucial component to consider as part of the solution. You need a solid understanding of this concept to place yourself in the best position for success.

The following main topics will be covered in this chapter:

- Working with Amazon KMS
- Understanding the difference between Amazon-managed keys and customer-managed Keys
- Cross-region key management
- Checking the compliance of KMS keys with AWS Artifact
- Implementing CloudHSM

Technical Requirements

You require an active AWS account and the ability to create a KMS key and a new CloudHSM cluster. This means that if you do not own the account in which you are performing the practice exercises, then you will need an IAM role attached to your user that allows the creation, manipulation, and deletion of KMS keys. You will need a VPC with multiple Availability Zones to set up the CloudHSM cluster.

A Basic Overview of Encryption

In today's world, data protection and privacy are of the utmost importance, not just to individuals but also to large organizations dealing with customer data on a large scale. When data is not encrypted, that data is considered **plaintext**, meaning that anyone who has access to the data can view it without any restrictions. If none of this data is sensitive, then storing it in plaintext form is not an issue. However, if the data contains sensitive or confidential information, it should be encrypted.

Encryption is the process that ensures the confidentiality and security of sensitive data. It involves transforming data into an unreadable format using an encryption algorithm and a cryptographic key. This makes the data unintelligible to unauthorized parties, protecting it from unauthorized access and interception.

Encryption provides a critical layer of protection for sensitive data, such as customer information, financial data, and trade secrets. It safeguards against data breaches and unauthorized access and ensures compliance with privacy regulations. By implementing encryption, you significantly reduce the risk of data compromise and enhance the security posture of your organization.

Imagine the data as a message that must be securely transmitted or stored. Encryption acts as a lock for this message, transforming it into a form that can only be understood with the correct key. The encryption algorithm performs mathematical operations on the data according to the key's instructions, turning it into a jumbled, scrambled version called ciphertext.

With encryption, even if someone intercepts the ciphertext, they won't be able to make sense of it without the correct key. Only authorized users or parties who possess the key can decrypt the ciphertext and convert it back to its original, readable form—the plaintext version.

You should now have a basic understanding of the process of encryption. In the next section, you will learn the difference between symmetric and asymmetric encryption keys.

Symmetric Encryption versus Asymmetric Encryption

It is important for you to have a robust understanding of the difference between symmetric and asymmetric encryption keys, as this will help you understand how KMS works as you advance through the chapter. KMS uses both **symmetric** and **asymmetric** encryption.

One of the simplest ways to remember the differences between symmetric and asymmetric encryption is that symmetric encryption uses the same key to both encrypt and decrypt data. It's like having a single key that locks and unlocks a door. With symmetric encryption, the encryption and decryption operations are fast and efficient, making it suitable for encrypting large amounts of data. However, there is a challenge when it comes to securely sharing the encryption key: how do you share it in a secure manner? To maintain the confidentially of the data, the encryption key needs to be securely distributed to authorized parties so it does not fall into the wrong hands. This is where a service such as KMS comes into play as it secures a symmetric key's distribution. Examples of common symmetric encryption algorithms are **Advanced Encryption Standard (AES)**, **Digital Encryption Standard (DES)**, and Triple DES.

> **Note**
>
> The easiest way to remember the types of encryption for the exam is as follows:
>
> **Symmetric** = **S**ame key encrypts and decrypts
>
> **Asymmetric** = **A** pair of keys is needed

Asymmetric encryption, also known as **public-key encryption**, employs a pair of mathematically related keys: **public** and **private** keys. The public key is widely distributed and used for encryption, while the private key is kept secret and used for decryption. It's like having a lock and a unique key that only you possess. Asymmetric encryption solves the challenge of securely sharing encryption keys in symmetric encryption. The public key can be freely distributed, allowing anyone to encrypt data, but only the possessor of the private key can decrypt it. This makes asymmetric encryption suitable for secure communication between two parties who have never interacted before or when multiple parties need to exchange information securely.

Figure 12.1 presents a graphical representation of asymmetric encryption.

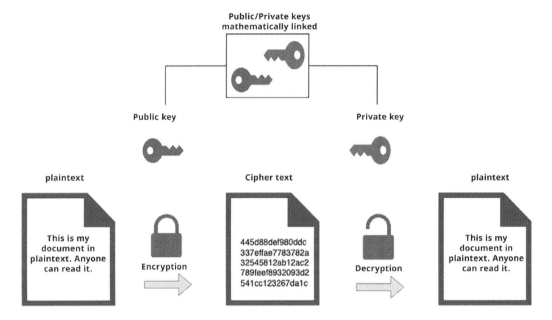

Figure 12.1: Asymmetric encryption flow

With an understanding of how both symmetric and asymmetric encryption keys work, you can now apply that knowledge as you start to dive deeper into the components of AWS KMS.

Working with AWS KMS

Before you start to review KMS in depth, you should first become familiar with the different components of the service and how they interact with each other. The following is a list of components that you should have a complete understanding of. They are explained in detail in the following sections:

- Customer Master Keys
- Data Encryption Keys
- Key Material
- Key Policies
- Grants

Customer Master Keys

Customer Master Keys (CMKs) are an essential component of KMS as they contain the key material for both encrypting and decrypting data.

Think of the CMK as a keychain that holds the keys to lock and unlock your valuable belongings. In this case, the belongings are your data, and the keys represent the cryptographic information needed to secure the data.

The CMKs are created and managed within KMS and provide a secure and convenient way to generate and control encryption keys. Encryption keys act as the guardians of your sensitive data, ensuring that only authorized parties can access and decipher it. CMKs securely store the encryption keys used for data protection. KMS uses industry-standard security practices to safeguard CMKs, ensuring they remain protected from unauthorized access or tampering. Below is a key list of points to understand about CMKs:

- CMKs are used in AWS to manage encryption keys for protecting sensitive data.

- CMKs enable encryption and decryption of data, ensuring that only authorized parties can access and decipher it.

- CMKs are securely stored and protected by KMS, following industry-standard security practices.

- Fine-grained access control allows you to control who can use the CMKs for encryption and decryption operations.

- CMKs seamlessly integrate with various AWS services, making it easy to encrypt data within those services.

- CMKs can be used to encrypt and decrypt data within AWS or in your applications outside of AWS.

- KMS offers different types of CMKs, including AWS-managed keys and customer-managed keys, each with specific characteristics and capabilities.

- CMKs support envelope encryption: a data key is generated and used for encrypting the data, and then that key is encrypted with the CMK for added security.

- Key usage, audit trails, and key events are logged and can be monitored through AWS CloudTrail and AWS CloudWatch.

> **Note**
>
> For a full comparison between symmetric and asymmetric CMKs, please see the following resource at `https://packt.link/kUYaQ`.

It is possible to store your CMKs in a custom key store instead of the KMS key store. These custom key stores can be created using an AWS CloudHSM cluster you own and manage. Having your own CloudHSM allows you to have direct control over the **Hardware Security Modules** (**HSMs**) that are responsible for generating the key material. You will read about CloudHSM later in this chapter, in the *Exploring CloudHSM* section.

There are two different types of CMKs used by KMS that you need to be familiar with:

- AWS-managed
- Customer-managed

AWS-Managed CMKs

AWS-managed CMKs are owned and used by AWS services to encrypt your data. They do not reside within your KMS console or within your account, and you cannot even track their usage or see the audit trail of when they were used and by whom. They are completely independent of your AWS account. However, because they can be used by services within your AWS account, those services can use those keys to encrypt your data within your account.

AWS-managed CMKs are encryption keys created and maintained by KMS. They are a convenient option for quickly implementing encryption without the need to manage the underlying key infrastructure. Unlike AWS-owned CMKs, AWS-managed keys are rotated at least once every year, whereas the rotation of AWS-owned CMKs can vary. You, as a user or key administrator, have no power to rotate the keys and the keys themselves are Region-specific.

AWS-managed CMKs are automatically rotated by AWS at least once per year. The exact rotation can vary, but AWS aims to rotate these keys on an annual basis to enhance security and align with best practices.

Examples of AWS-managed CMKs include the following:

- **AWS-managed CMKs for Amazon S3**: These CMKs are used for server-side data encryption in S3 buckets.
- **AWS KMS Default CMK**: This CMK is automatically created and managed by KMS as the default encryption key for AWS services that support KMS encryption, such as Amazon EBS, Amazon RDS, and Amazon Redshift.

Customer-Managed Keys

The other type of key the KMS service offers is the customer-managed key. These keys provide the most significant level of flexibility and control. Unlike AWS-managed CMKs, with customer-managed keys, you have total control and governance over these keys.

Customer-managed keys in KMS are encryption keys you create and manage within the AWS environment. These keys provide you with complete control over the lifecycle and usage of the keys, offering greater flexibility and customization.

With customer-managed keys, you can define key policies, set rotation schedules, and manage key permissions according to your specific security requirements. This level of control allows you to align the key management practices with your organization's policies and compliance needs.

Customer-managed keys are not tied to any specific AWS service or feature, and you can use them for encryption in various AWS services or even in your own applications running outside of AWS. This allows you to encrypt data stored in AWS and still have full control over the key. This means that you can carry out activities including setting up specific keys for specific groups or roles and can see the full audit log for each key created.

It's important to note that while you have more control over managing these keys, it also means that you bear the responsibility for adequately safeguarding and protecting them. KMS provides the tools and security measures required to ensure the integrity and confidentially of your customer-managed keys.

Which type of KMS key you use can often depend on you or your organization's security policy. If the policy requires that data be encrypted at rest while using a certain service or services in AWS, then the AWS-managed keys will suffice. Using these keys also allows you and your organization to keep costs down since there are no monthly fees associated with AWS-owned keys.

On the other hand, if your security policy dictates that, in the event of an incident, you must be able to rotate the KMS key on demand, or that your organization must be the owner of the key, then in that case a customer-managed key is the best choice.

With an understanding of the different types of CMKs, you will now learn about data encryption keys and how they work hand in hand with CMKs to encrypt the actual data.

Data Encryption Keys

AWS KMS **Data Encryption Keys** (**DEKs**) are cryptographic keys generated by KMS for encrypting data. DEKs are used in conjunction with customer-managed Keys to protect sensitive information. They are typically short-lived and utilized for specific encryption operations. DEKs are designed to be efficient and provide an extra layer of security by encrypting data and then encrypting the DEK itself with the customer-managed key.

Here is a list of the key facts about DEKs:

- DEKs are generated and managed by KMS to perform the encryption and decryption of data.

- DEKs are used in conjunction with customer-managed keys to encrypt and decrypt data securely.

- DEKs are randomly generated and are unique to each encryption operation, adding an extra layer of security.

- DEKs are used for envelope encryption, where the data is encrypted using the DEK, and then the DEK is encrypted with the customer-managed key for added security.

- DEKs provide fast and efficient encryption and decryption operations, allowing secure and high-performance data protection.

- DEKs can be used with various AWS services and features that support KMS encryption, such as Amazon S3, Amazon EBS, and Amazon RDS.

- KMS manages the lifecycle and security of DEKs, ensuring that they are generated securely and stored temporarily during the encryption and decryption process.

- DEKs are an integral part of the encryption workflow in KMS, providing a secure and scalable solution for protecting sensitive data.

- DEKs are symmetric keys. This means that the same key is used for both encryption and decryption.

Figure 12.2 demonstrates an example of DEKs being used within AWS services. It shows how the encryption process works for Amazon S3 server-side encryption with KMS-managed keys, known as SSE-KMS.

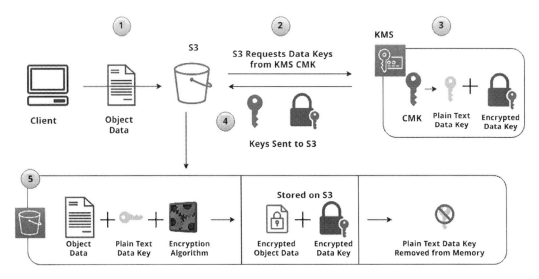

Figure 12.2: Encryption process of objects in S3 with SS3-KMS

The process shown in the preceding diagram is explained in detail in the points below:

1. First, the client identifies the object(s) that they will upload to S3, indicating SS3-KMS as the encryption mechanism, selecting either an AWS-managed or customer-managed CMK.

2. Amazon S3 responds by initiating a request to generate DEKs from KMS to allow S3 to encrypt the data submitted by the client.

3. Using the CMK selected during *step 1*, KMS then generates two data keys, a plaintext data key and an encrypted version of that same data key.

4. KMS sends both of these data keys back to S3 to allow S3 to begin the encryption process using the plaintext data key.

5. At this stage, S3 then encrypts the data with the plaintext version of the data key and stores the resulting encrypted object alongside the encrypted version of the data key. The plaintext data key is then deleted and removed from memory.

Now that you have seen how the encryption process works using DEKs, you will look at the actual key material that is used to compose customer-managed keys.

Key Material

AWS creates the key material for the KMS key. The key material is the data used to encrypt and decrypt your sensitive data. As the customer, you cannot extract, export, view, or manage this key material. You can delete the key but cannot delete the key material.

The key material data is stored within your CMK. With DEKs, the CMK material is used to encrypt a version of the data key and decrypt an encrypted version of the data key.

When you create your CMK, KMS automatically creates new key material for that CMK. However, when creating your own customer-managed CMKs, you can choose to create your CMK without any key material and then import your own key material into the key. This must be done with a symmetric encryption key.

Importing Your Own Key Material

Mostly, when creating a new KMS key, you will get AWS to create the key material. However, there are certain times when you may want to have complete control over the key material that is used by KMS. This could include situations in which you already have existing cryptographic keys generated and managed outside of AWS that you want to import into KMS or when you need to use specific cryptographic algorithms to meet regulatory compliance.

For the situations described above, when creating your symmetric key in the KMS service, you can choose `External (Import Key material)` under `Advanced options` and then import the material.

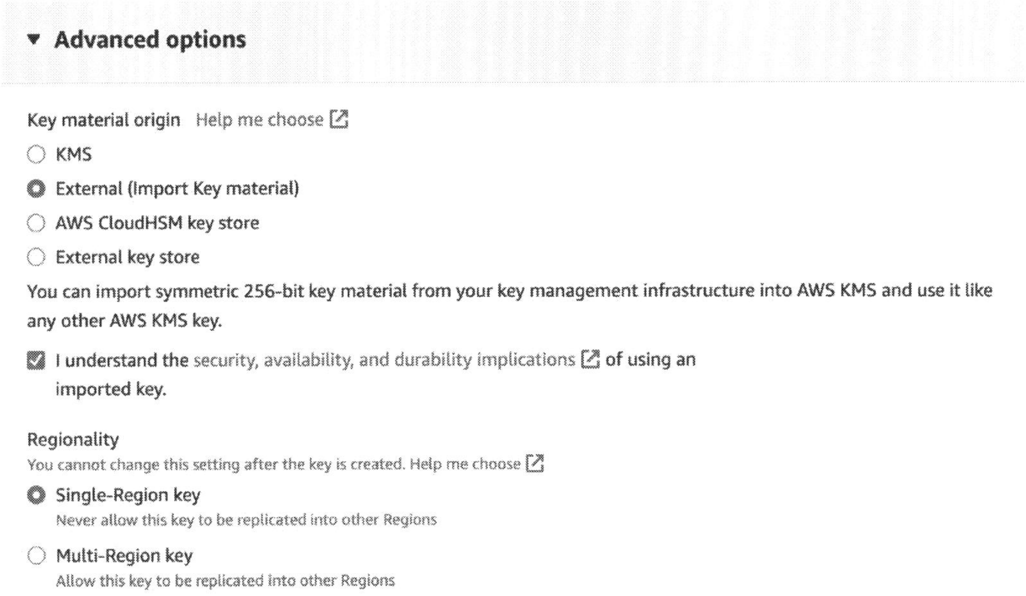

▼ Advanced options

Key material origin   Help me choose ↗

○ KMS

◉ External (Import Key material)

○ AWS CloudHSM key store

○ External key store

You can import symmetric 256-bit key material from your key management infrastructure into AWS KMS and use it like any other AWS KMS key.

☑ I understand the security, availability, and durability implications ↗ of using an imported key.

Regionality
You cannot change this setting after the key is created. Help me choose ↗

◉ Single-Region key
  Never allow this key to be replicated into other Regions

○ Multi-Region key
  Allow this key to be replicated into other Regions

Figure 12.3: Importing key material

When doing this, you must select the checkbox to confirm that you understand the security, availability, and durability implications of using an imported key.

You will then be asked to download the public token and import a token for your CMK. This is required in order to perform two functions:

1. The public key is used to encrypt your key material before uploading it to KMS.

2. Then, KMS will decrypt the uploaded key using the private key associated with that same public key.

The imported token consists of metadata to ensure that the key material was uploaded and imported correctly.

There are a couple of additional points to consider when performing this import. The key material must be in binary format when encrypting it with the public key. Also, when importing the key back into your CMK, you can add an expiry date for the key material, at which point it will be deleted, rendering the CMK unusable.

If the key material is deleted automatically through this expiration date or manually in any way, the CMK can no longer be used for encryption. The only way to reinstate that same CMK is to import that same key material again, whereas if you were to delete the CMK, it would be impossible to reinstate it.

It is important to note that if you use imported key material for your KMS key, you must manually rotate it on the schedule established for your organization.

Key Policies

AWS KMS key policies are a means of controlling access to KMS keys. Each KMS key is associated with a key policy that consists of statements defining who has permission to use the key and what actions they can perform. Key policies help enforce secure and granular access control to cryptographic keys. They allow you to specify which IAM users, roles, AWS accounts, or AWS services can access the key and define the allowed key operations, such as encryption, decryption, and key rotation. Key policies provide an additional layer of security and enable you to implement fine-grained access control over your KMS keys to protect sensitive data and ensure compliance with regulatory requirements.

Grants

KMS grants are a mechanism KMS provides to control and manage access to cryptographic operations and keys. Simply, they let you specify who can perform specific functions, such as encrypting or decrypting data using KMS keys.

When granting access, you can define the principal (AWS **Identity and Access Management** (**IAM**) user, role, or AWS account) to whom you want to provide access. You can also specify the actions that the principal is allowed to perform, such as encryption, decryption, or re-encryption of data. Additionally, you can set constraints, such as specifying a time frame during which the access is granted.

KMS grants provide fine-grained control over access to your keys, enabling you to enforce security and compliance requirements. By using grants, you can ensure that only authorized entities can perform cryptographic operations using your KMS keys, enhancing the overall security of your data and applications.

Envelope Encryption and KMS

One of the key concepts in KMS is **envelope encryption**. When AWS encrypts your data, your data is secure, but your key must also be protected. AWS does this by encrypting your data with a data key and then encrypting the data key with another key. The top-level plaintext data key is known as the master key.

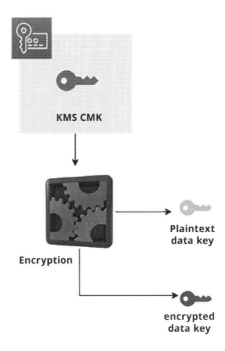

Figure 12.4: KMS creating an encrypted data key from a plaintext data key

Envelope encryption in KMS is used to enhance data encryption security by combining multiple encryption keys. Envelope encryption provides an added layer of protection for sensitive data stored in AWS services or applications.

Here's how envelope encryption works in AWS KMS:

1. **Master Key**: AWS KMS uses a master key, also known as a customer master key, to protect data encryption keys. The customer master key is a symmetric key managed by KMS.

2. **DEK**: A unique DEK is generated when data needs to be encrypted. DEKs are random and specific to each piece of data that requires encryption.

3. **Enveloping the DEK**: The DEK is then used to encrypt the actual data (such as files or database records). However, instead of storing the DEK directly with the data, the DEK is encrypted with the master key.

4. **Storing the Encrypted DEK**: The encrypted DEK, also known as the envelope key, is stored alongside the encrypted data. This way, the DEK remains protected.

5. **Decrypting the Envelope Key**: The encrypted DEK (envelope key) is retrieved from storage when data needs to be decrypted. The envelope key is passed to KMS along with the appropriate permissions to decrypt the data.

6. **Decrypting the Data**: Finally, the DEK decrypts the data, allowing access to the original plaintext content.

Using envelope encryption, KMS ensures that sensitive DEKs remain protected and separate from the encrypted data. This approach adds an extra layer of security, as the master key never leaves KMS, reducing the risk of unauthorized access to sensitive encryption keys.

Additionally, envelope encryption enables granular access control. By using AWS IAM policies, you can control who has permission to encrypt and decrypt data using specific customer master keys, providing additional control and security over data encryption operations.

Having reviewed envelope encryption and its usage in KMS, you can now proceed to examine the different roles used in key management in KMS.

The Roles of Key Management and Usage in KMS

In KMS, several roles are involved in key management and key usage. These roles help enforce secure access control and proper management of cryptographic keys. They are discussed here:

- **Key Administrators**: Key Administrators have the highest level of access and control over the keys. They can create, delete, and manage customer master keys. Key Administrators can also define key policies, which determine who can use and manage the keys and configure key rotation schedules.

- **Key Users**: Key Users are granted permission to use CMKs for cryptographic operations such as encryption, decryption, and signing. They can generate DEKs using CMKs and perform cryptographic operations using these keys. Key Users have limited control over the keys themselves but have access to their functionality.

- **Key Managers**: Key Managers have the combined capabilities of Key Administrators and Users. They can create and manage CMKs and use the keys for cryptographic operations. Key Managers can also define key policies and set key rotation schedules.

- **IAM Users and Roles**: AWS IAM allows you to create IAM users and roles with specific permissions to access and manage KMS keys. IAM users and roles can be granted permission to administer and use CMKs based on defined policies. IAM policies can be attached to users or roles to grant granular access control over KMS keys.

It's important to note that these roles are assigned through IAM policies and permissions. IAM policies determine what actions each role can perform and on which CMKs. By adequately configuring IAM policies, you can enforce the principle of least privilege, ensuring that users and roles have only the necessary permissions to perform their designated tasks.

These roles help separate responsibilities, ensuring that individuals or systems only have access to the required key management and usage capabilities. By following the principle of separation of duties and assigning roles appropriately, you can maintain a secure and controlled key management environment in KMS.

Now that you know the different roles in play when you create and use KMS keys, you will see how they come together next as you create a new KMS key.

Creating a Key in KMS

Previously in this chapter, you read about customer-managed keys. The following steps will teach you how to create your own customer-managed key in KMS:

1. Sign in to the AWS Management Console and navigate to KMS. You can go there quickly by using the following URL: `https://packt.link/rpBkc`.

2. From the menu on the left, click on the option named `Customer managed keys`.

3. Once you are on the `Customer managed keys` page, click the orange `Create key` button near the top.

4. You should now be on the `Configure key` page. You will be presented with two sets of options on this page. For `Key type`, choose `Symmetric`; for `Key usage`, select `Encrypt and decrypt`.

Configure key

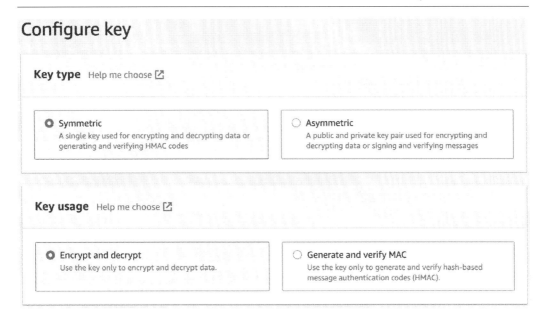

Figure 12.5: Configuring a key in KMS

5.   Then, move down to the `Advanced options` part of the screen. Click on the arrow to reveal the choices for the advanced options. Under the heading `Regionality`, choose `Multi-Region key`. (If you do not select this, you will not be able to use this key for the exercise later in this chapter.) Once you have made these selections, click the `Next` button at the bottom of the screen.

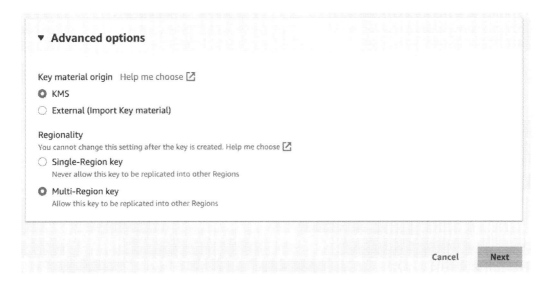

Figure 12.6: Advanced options in KMS for creating a key

6.   After configuring your key, you should be on the Add labels screen. The most important step here is to give your key a name to distinguish it from other keys you may create later. Name your key Chapter12-USEAST2. This tells you the Region where you created the key, which will be helpful later in the chapter. If you like, you can give your key a description. Otherwise, scroll to the bottom of the page and click the Next button.

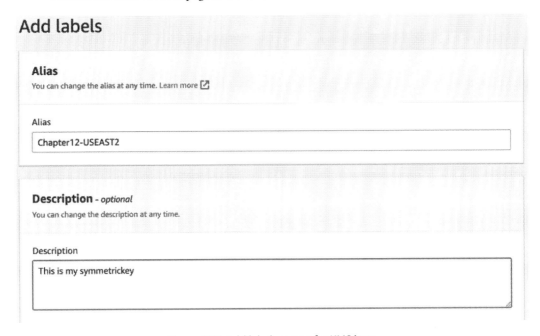

Figure 12.7: Add labels screen for KMS keys

7.   Now you will be on the Define key administrative permissions screen. You will need to add your own IAM user to the key administrators. This way, you can delete the key after you are done with this chapter or you are finished with the key—whichever comes first. If you do not add your own user to the list of users with administrative permissions, then the only way to modify the users who can manage the key would be to add users with the root account. Ensure that the checkbox is selected under the Key deletion heading next to Allow key administrators to delete this key. Once you have chosen your IAM user as a key administrator, click the orange Next button at the bottom of the page.

Key deletion

☑ Allow key administrators to delete this key.

Figure 12.8: Key deletion option in KMS

8. After choosing the key administrators, move to the `Define key usage permissions` screen. These users and roles will be allowed access to the key for encryption and decryption purposes. You are going through a simple exercise here, so select your IAM user for permission to use the KMS key you are creating. Once you have selected your user, click the `Next` button at the bottom of the screen.

9. You will now be on the `Review` screen. Scroll down until you find the `Finish` button. However, take notice of the key policy in JSON right above the `Finish` button. You can add more conditions to the policy before creating the key. Click the `Finish` button to create your key.

Using the AWS Management Console, you have made your own KMS symmetric key. If you followed the instructions, you are both the administrator of the key and the authorized user of the key. In the next section, you will learn how, as the key administrator, you can narrow the scope of what your new KMS key can be used for.

Scoping Key Policies for KMS Keys

Key policies serve as the fundamental means to govern access to KMS keys. Each key is governed by a single key policy, providing a central approach to managing access permissions. This key policy specifies who has permission to access and use the keys, including actions such as encryption, decryption, and key management. Through this singular policy, administrators can enforce granular control over key usage, defining which AWS identities or accounts are authorized to interact with the key and also specifying the scope of their permissions.

The primary function of the key policy is to determine who can use the key to perform cryptographic operations such as `encrypt`, `decrypt`, `GenerateDataKey`, and other operations. In addition, the key policy sets the permissions for who can administer the CMK to perform functions such as deleting/revoking the CMK and importing key material into the CMK.

The policy is considered a resource-based policy as it is tied to the CMK, and, as a result, it is only possible to use a CMK if it has a configured key policy attached.

Much like IAM policies, key policies are JSON-based and appear much like other IAM access policies from a syntax and structure point of view, so if you are familiar with IAM policies, then key policies will be easy to understand.

The key policies also allow you to configure access to and use of the CMKs in a variety of ways. Therefore, you can set up the accessibility to CMKs in the following manner:

- **Via key policies**: All access is governed by the key policy alone.

- **Via key policies and IAM**: Access is governed by the key policy in addition to IAM identity-based policies, allowing you to manage access via groups and other IAM features.

- **Via key policies and grants**: Access is governed by the key policy with the added ability to delegate access to others to use the CMKs.

The key point to remember here is that, without a key policy, you are unable to control access to your CMKs.

After reading about the theory of key policies, you will see how they come into action based on the exercise you did to create your KMS key earlier.

Using Only Key Policies to Control Access

When you created your KMS key in the earlier exercise, you selected your user as both the key administrator and the key user. You had the option to see the key policy before you created the key in *step 9* of the exercise, and you even had the opportunity to edit the policy before the KMS key was created.

A sample of the policy that was attached to the key would have looked something like this:

```
{
        "Sid": "Allow access for Key Administrators",
        "Effect": "Allow",
        "Principal": {
            "AWS": [
                "arn:aws:iam::1234567890:user/adam
            ]
        },
        "Action": [
            "kms:Create*",
            "kms:Describe*",
            "kms:Enable*",
            "kms:List*",
            "kms:Put*",
            "kms:Update*",
            "kms:Revoke*",
```

```
                "kms:Disable*",
                "kms:Get*",
                "kms:Delete*",
                "kms:TagResource",
                "kms:UntagResource",
                "kms:ScheduleKeyDeletion",
                "kms:CancelKeyDeletion",
                "kms:ReplicateKey",
                "kms:UpdatePrimaryRegion"
            ],
            "Resource": "*"
    }
```

As you can see, the **Statement Identifier** (`Sid`) identifies the section as `Allow access for Key Administrators`. It lists the user selected during the key creation process along with the ARN. You can see the entire range of actions this user can perform as an administrator. One point to note is that although key administrators cannot use the CMK, they do have access to update the key policy and add themselves as a user.

You have now seen the full Key Administrator policy in JSON format. Next, you will see how to narrow the policy scope using conditions.

Adding a Condition to the Key Policy

You can use the condition statement to restrict items and access as your policies become more scoped. To add a condition to limit usage to users in your AWS organization, you can use the `aws:PrincipalOrgId` condition key. Here is an abbreviated key policy showing where you would place the condition in the policy:

```
{
  "Version": "2012-10-17",
  "Id": "key-policy",
  "Statement": [
    {
      "Sid": "RestrictAWSOrgUsers",
      "Effect": "Allow",
      "Principal": {
        "AWS": "*"
      },
      "Action": "kms:*",
      "Resource": "*",
      "Condition": {
        "StringEquals": {
```

```
        "aws:PrincipalOrgID": "o-abc123456789"
      }
    }
  }
 ]
}
```

Although this isn't the full key policy, as shown in the previous section's example, it could place this condition on the Key Administrator's or Key User's statement identifier.

Adding a condition like this will ensure that even if you implement cross-account access on your KMS key, only users who are part of your organization will be allowed access.

You have now seen a full key policy and how to restrict key policies using a condition statement. But what if you want to use the same CMK in multiple regions? The next section will show you how.

Cross-Region Key Management

While having the ability to create and manage KMS keys on a one-by-one basis is a useful feature to have, either through the AWS Management Console or programmatically from the CLI, once your accounts start to spread out geographically, keeping track of which keys encrypt items in which regions can become burdensome. Luckily, AWS has listened to customer feedback and has introduced functionality in KMS that allows users like yourself to replicate a KMS key from one region to another.

There are some best practices that you should be aware of when starting to manage your KMS keys across multiple regions:

- **Turn on the KMS multi-Region replication**: KMS provides the option to enable multi-region replication for customer master keys. By enabling this feature, KMS automatically replicates your CMKs to other regions, allowing you to use the same CMK for encryption and decryption in different regions.

- **Choose a primary Region for creating and managing your CMKs**: Designate one region as the primary region for managing your CMKs. This region will be responsible for key creation, rotation, and updates. Other regions will replicate the CMKs for local use but won't be involved in key management.

- **Keep consistency in key policies**: Maintain consistency in key policies across regions. Key policies define who can access and use the CMKs, and ensuring consistent policies across regions helps maintain a unified security posture.

- **Understand data transfer and latency**: Take into account data transfer costs and latency when using CMKs across regions. Replicating CMKs across regions incurs additional data transfer charges, and encryption/decryption operations might experience additional latency due to cross-region communication.

- **Have a working knowledge of your compliance and data residency**: Make sure you understand regulatory and compliance requirements related to key management and data residency across regions. Ensure that your key management practices align with these requirements and consider regional restrictions if applicable.

The following section will take you through an exercise of replicating the KMS key you created earlier in another region.

Replicating a KMS Key in Another Region

1. Sign in to the AWS Management Console and navigate to KMS. You can go there quickly using the following URL: `https://packt.link/gfq6B`

2. Ensure you are in the Region where you previously created your KMS key.

3. From the menu on the left, click on `Customer managed keys`.

4. In the main window, find the KMS key you created and select it by clicking on its name. Remember, this must be the key that you chose to be a multi-Region key in the advanced options.

5. You should now be on the key's `Detail` page. Under the `General configuration` details, there will be a menu bar with options on the main screen. Click on the menu option labeled `Regionality`.

Figure 12.9: Details page for KMS replication

6. In the `Regionality` section, you can find the `Related multi-Region keys`. Click the button labeled `Create new replica keys` to create a new copy of your KMS key in a different region.

7. You will find yourself on the `Create new replica keys` page. Use the drop-down list to choose another region to replicate your KMS key. This example replicates the key in `us-west-2` `(Oregon)`. After you have selected your secondary region(s), click on the `Next` button.

Figure 12.10: Selecting replica Region screen for KMS

8. On the `Add Labels` page, you can change the alias of the key in the secondary region. However, for simplicity, scroll down to the bottom of the page and click the `Next` button.

9. On the `Key administrators` page, add or remove key administrators for the replica key if required. Then, scroll down to the bottom of the page and click the `Next` button.

10. Change which users and roles have permission to use the key on the `Define replica key usage permissions` page if required. Then, scroll down to the bottom of the page and click on the orange `Next` button.

11. Finally, you should be on the `Review` page. Look over your settings to ensure they are what you want them to be. Then, click on the `Create new replica keys` button when you're satisfied to create your new replica key.

After following the last exercise and taking note of the best practices for cross-region KMS key management, you should be able to replicate the KMS keys in your accounts to multiple regions should the need arise. The next section discusses the AWS Artifact service and how it helps you check that your keys conform to your regulations and compliance standards.

Checking the Compliance of KMS keys with AWS Artifact

Depending on your line of business or the types of compliance and regulations your organization needs to deal with, you may need to check if the encryption you use with KMS meets the compliance standards. Further, meeting compliance standards doesn't just concern the encryption service you're using but all the AWS services you use in your solution. So, where do you find the answers to questions about compliance quickly and easily?

AWS Artifact is a service that provides a central repository of AWS compliance-related documents and agreements. It provides easy access to various documents, including security and compliance reports, certifications, and service-specific agreements.

The AWS Artifact service aims to streamline and simplify the process of understanding and assessing the security and compliance posture of AWS services. It consolidates many required documents for compliance audits, assessments, and due diligence processes.

Some of the key features of the AWS Artifact service are the following:

- **Document Repository**: AWS Artifact serves as a centralized repository where customers can access and download compliance-related documents. These documents include AWS compliance reports (such as HIPPA reports), third-party auditor reports, AWS service-specific reports, and agreements (such as the AWS Customer Agreement).

- **Security and Compliance Reports**: AWS Artifact provides access to various security and compliance reports demonstrating AWS's adherence to industry standards and best practices. These reports include **System and Organization Controls (SOC)** reports, **Payment Card Industry Data Security Standard (PCI DSS)** reports, and ISO certifications.

- **Agreements and Contracts**: The service also provides access to essential agreements and contracts that govern the user of AWS services. This includes the AWS Customer Agreement, **Business Associate Addendum (BAA)** for HIPAA compliance, and the AWS Service Terms, among others.

- **On-Demand Access**: Customers can access AWS Artifact documents on demand, making it convenient for compliance teams, auditors, and customers to obtain the necessary information and documentation when needed.

- **Compliance Audits and Assessments**: AWS Artifact assists organizations in meeting their compliance requirements by providing relevant documentation and reports for audits and assessments. It simplifies the process of obtaining and managing compliance-related documents, saving time and effort for customers.

Note that while AWS Artifact provides access to compliance-related documents and agreements, it does not directly perform compliance assessments or audits. Instead, it serves as a central repository and resource for customers to obtain the necessary documentation and information to support their compliance efforts within the AWS ecosystem.

After checking through the documentation of AWS Artifact, you may find that the FIPS-140 Level 2 validation that KMS provides is insufficient for the types of compliance your company requires. In that case, there is another option for creating and managing your own encryption keys at a higher level of validation: CloudHSM.

Exploring CloudHSM

AWS CloudHSM is another managed service for data encryption. Being fully managed, many aspects of implementing and maintaining the HSM are abstracted, such as hardware provisioning, patching, and backups. CloudHSM also has the great advantage of automatically scaling on demand.

HSM stands for **Hardware Security Module**. It is specialized security hardware validated to FIPS 140-2 Level 3. HSMs can be used to generate and create your own encryption keys.

CloudHSM is required when you and your organization warrant additional control and administrative power over your encryption compared with KMS. Although KMS is supported by its own FIPS-enabled HSM, you have no control over those modules. Further, AWS cannot access your keys or any cryptographic material within your HSMs.

With certain compliance and regulatory requirements, you will be obliged to use an HSM to generate your keys or an HSM might be required to be used as a cryptographic key store. In addition to simply generating keys and storing them, an HSM also allows you to carry out the following tasks:

- The use of different encryption algorithms to cater to both symmetric keys and asymmetric keys
- The management of symmetric and asymmetric cryptographic keys, including importing and exporting keys
- Signing and verifying signatures
- The ability to use a cryptographic hash function to compute hash-based message authentication codes

As mentioned previously, CloudHSM can integrate with KMS, which means CloudHSM is used as a custom key store.

A custom key store allows you to store CMKs outside of KMS and within a CloudHSM cluster that you have created. You might want to use CloudHSM as a custom key store in KMS if your key material can't be stored within a shared environment. Additionally, you might need to ensure that your key material is backed up in multiple AWS regions.

Having gained a basic understanding of CloudHSM, you can now explore CloudHSM clusters in depth.

CloudHSM Clusters

When you deploy your CloudHSM instance, it is deployed as a cluster, and by default, this cluster size is 6 per account, per region. However, you can configure your cluster to have a single HSM up or up to 28 HSMs. The more HSMs you have, the better the performance of encrypting and decrypting items will be. To prevent complications with key synchronization, CloudHSM manages those key synchronizations for you. If you add additional HSMs to your cluster after the initial creation, CloudHSM will take a backup of all your users, policies, and keys. It will then deploy that backup on the new HSM within your cluster.

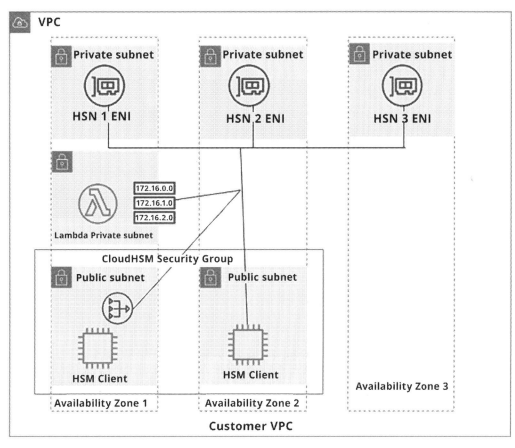

Figure 12.11: CloudHSM high availability cluster

One important point to note is that when you configure your cluster and you specify your subnets/Availability Zones as locations, what happens is that an **Elastic Network Interface** (**ENI**) is deployed in your subnets. These ENIs are then linked to an HSM in a VPC owned and managed by AWS.

You can see in *Figure 12.11* that three HSMs have been deployed across three different availability zones in the CloudHSM cluster. Each of these HSMs in turn gets a corresponding ENI in the customer's VPC. The private subnet allows connectivity between the public and private subnets and the use of the keys generated by the CloudHSM cluster from any Lambdas residing in that private subnet. With the Lambdas taking advantage of the NAT gateway in the public subnet, CloudHSM can talk to any VPC endpoints, such as AWS S3, RDS, or CloudWatch Logs, that have been established for the VPC. Redundant Amazon Linux instances have been configured in two Availability Zones so authorized humans can connect to the HSM cluster and obtain cryptographic credentials.

The following are the critical features of CloudHSM clusters:

- **High availability**: CloudHSM clusters are designed to provide high availability for your cryptographic operations. Each HSM appliance within the cluster is deployed in a separate AWS AZ to ensure redundancy and fault tolerance. In the event of an HSM failure or AZ outage, the remaining HSMs in the cluster continue to handle cryptographic operations, ensuring uninterrupted service.

- **Load balancing**: CloudHSM clusters employ load-balancing techniques to distribute cryptographic workloads across the HSM appliances within the cluster. This helps evenly distribute the computational load and ensures optimal performance and resource utilization. Load balancing also contributes to scaling the cluster's capacity to handle increased demand.

- **Synchronization and replication**: The HSM instance within a CloudHSM cluster synchronizes its configurations, keys, and cryptographic operations. Changes made to the cluster, such as key generation, deletion, or updates, are replicated across all HSMs within the cluster. This synchronization ensures consistent and uniform access to keys and cryptographic operations regardless of the specific HSM instance.

- **Scaling and capacity**: CloudHSM clusters can scale your cryptographic capacity based on your needs. You can add or remove HSM instances to the cluster as your organization requires, allowing you to scale up or down depending on workload demands. Scaling a cluster provides additional processing power and storage capacity, enabling you to handle increased cryptographic workloads or accommodate the growth of your applications.

- **Managed by AWS**: CloudHSM clusters are fully managed by AWS. AWS takes care of the underlying infrastructure, including hardware maintenance, patching, and monitoring, allowing you to focus on using the HSMs for key management and cryptographic operations. This managed service approach simplifies the operational aspects of maintaining and securing the HSM appliances.

- **Integration with AWS services**: CloudHSM clusters seamlessly integrate with various AWS services, enabling you to secure and manage keys for encrypting data within the AWS ecosystem. For example, you can use CloudHSM keys with KMS for encryption, CloudTrail for auditing the usage of the keys, and other services that support the use of CloudHSM.

CloudHSM clusters in AWS provide a highly available and scalable solution for managing cryptographic operations and key management. They offer redundancy, load balancing, synchronization, and the ability to scale capacity. CloudHSM clusters are managed by AWS, making it easier to integrate them with other AWS services and focus on securing your sensitive data and cryptographic operations. The following section will look at specific use cases for CloudHSM.

Use cases for CloudHSM/HSMs

You need to know when CloudHSM is appropriate in case you need to make recommendations to your customers and employer and if any scenarios come up in the AWS Security Specialty exam. The following are different use cases that might be presented in either questions or answer scenarios on the AWS Security exam:

- **Key management**: Dedicated HSMs excel in managing cryptographic keys securely. They offer a dedicated, tamper-resistant hardware environment to generate, store, and manage encryption keys for sensitive data. This is particularly valuable for industries with strict compliance and regulatory requirements, such as finance, healthcare, and government sectors.

- **Public Key Infrastructure (PKI)**: HSMs are crucial in PKI systems. They can generate and securely store the private keys used for digital certificates, ensuring the integrity and confidentiality of the keys. HSMs also provide the necessary cryptographic operations for certificate signing and validation, protecting the trust and security of digital identities.

- **Digital Rights Management (DRM)**: Dedicated HSMs are used in DRM systems to protect digital content and enforce usage rights. HSMs securely store encryption keys to encrypt and decrypt media files, ensuring only authorized parties can access and use the protected content.

- **Code signing**: HSMs can be utilized for code signing processes, which involve digitally signing software or firmware to ensure its authenticity and integrity. By securely storing the private signing keys in an HSM, organizations can mitigate the risk of key compromise and ensure the trustworthiness of the signed code.

- **High-security applications**: Dedicated HSMs are ideal for applications that demand the highest level of security and protection. This includes cryptographic operations for secure communications, secure database encryption, secure messaging, secure remote access, and secure payment processing.

Having explored where to use specialized HSMs, especially CloudHSM, you are now ready to learn the process of standing up a CloudHSM cluster.

Standing Up CloudHSM

The following steps will take you through creating a CloudHSM cluster, which is a straightforward process:

1. From within the AWS Management Console, search for the CloudHSM service or use the following URL to get there quickly: `https://packt.link/Pqqrd`.

2. Once you're on the CloudHSM home page, click the `Create cluster` button.

Figure 12.12: Create cluster button for CloudHSM

You will be brought to the cluster configuration page. Here, you will need to choose a VPC where you will place your cluster. If you have your VPC named `MyVPC` up and running from *Chapter 10, Configuring Infrastructure Security*, you can use it for this exercise.

3. Select the VPC named `MyVPC` from the drop-down list under the `VPC` heading in the first section of the page.

Figure 12.13: VPC selection screen for CloudHSM

4. Next, move on to the page's AZ(s) section. If you are using MyVPC from the template in *Chapter 10*, there will only be one AZ to choose from.

> **Note**
>
> In a production environment, you want to have at least three AZs for redundancy, and preferably three. Selecting the one AZ here is sufficient since you are simply getting familiar with how to stand up a CloudHSM cluster.

Choose the subnet ID that aligns with your private subnet from the drop-down box.

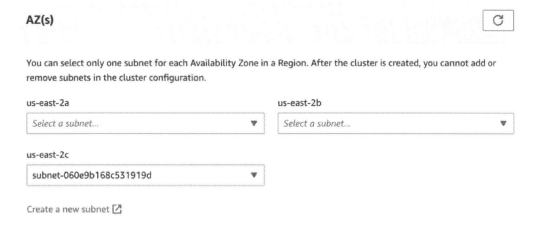

Figure 12.14: Subnet selection screen

5. Moving on to the Cluster source section of the page, keep the default setting of Create a new cluster. Then, click the Next button.

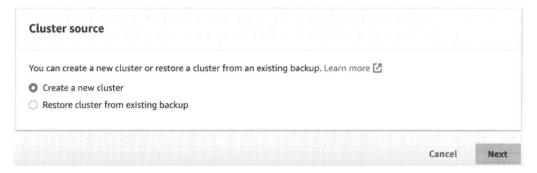

Figure 12.15: Cluster source selection screen

6. The next section to configure is `Backup retention period`. CloudHSM makes backups of your users, key materials and certificates, and HSM configurations and policies at least once every 24 hours. You will configure how long to save those backups on this screen. The default is 90 days. Set this to 7 days, the minimum for this exercise. Click the `Next` button once you have configured your backup retention policy.

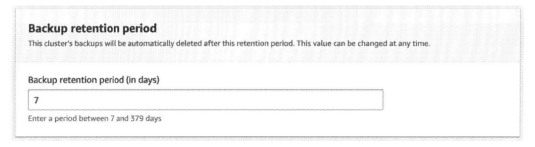

Figure 12.16: Backup retention selection screen

7. You should now be on the `Add Tags` page; click the `Next` button to move on.

8. Finally, you will be on the `Review` page. Here, review your cluster settings and the VPC and subnets. Once you are satisfied with everything, click the `Create cluster` button. You might see a warning telling you that once your cluster is created, you cannot change its VPC or subnets:

 You cannot change VPC or subnets after a cluster is created
Review the information above carefully. You cannot modify VPC or subnet settings after you create the cluster. You can only create HSMs for this cluster within the specified subnets. You can only access HSMs within the specified VPC. To revise cluster settings, click Previous. To confirm and proceed with cluster creation, click Create cluster.

Figure 12.17: VPC/subnet warning screen

You have seen how easy it is to create your own CloudHSM cluster. Your cluster is only in the initialization state at this point. Next, you will see the different types of users and which of those users can help activate your newly created CloudHSM cluster.

AWS CloudHSM Users

After setting up the CloudHSM cluster, you need to examine the various user types CloudHSM offers and the differences between them; for instance, different users have additional permissions. The user types are as follows:

- **Precrypto Office**
- **Crypto Office**
- **Crypto User**
- **Appliance User**

Precrypto Office User

When you create your first HSM within your cluster, the HSM will contain a **Precrypto Office (PRECO)** user with a default username and password. When your first HSM is set up, you must connect and log in to the HSM to activate it. Until you do so, your HSM will remain in an initialized state.

When connecting to the HSM, you must use the PRECO credentials and change its user password. Doing so will activate your HSM, and your PRECO user will become a Crypto Office user. PRECO's only role, and therefore it's only granted permission, is to change its own password and perform read-only operations on the HSM.

Crypto Office User

A **Crypto Office (CO)** user has more permissions than a PRECO user. A CO user can perform user management tasks, such as user creation and deletion and password changes. It can also perform several administrative-level operations, including the following:

- Zeroize the data on the HSM, which allows the CO to delete keys, certificates, and data on the HSM.
- Identify the number of HSMs within the cluster.
- Obtain the JSM metadata, including IP address, model, serial number, firmware, and device IDs.
- View synchronization statuses across HSMs in the cluster.

Crypto User

A **Crypto User (CU)** can perform cryptographic functions within AWS CloudHSM, including the following:

- Perform encryption and decryption
- The ability to create, delete, wrap, unwrap, and modify attributes of keys

- Signing and verifying

- Generating digests and **Keyed-Hash Message Authentication Codes** (**HMACs**)

Also, like the CO, CUs can zeroize data and basic cluster information such as the IP address and serial number.

Appliance User

The **Appliance User** (**AU**) is a user that exists on all HSMs and is used to carry out the cloning and synchronization actions of your HSMs. The CloudHSM service calls upon the AU to ensure that the synchronization of your HSMs within your cluster is maintained.

The AU carries the same permissions as the CO from a permissions perspective. However, it cannot change passwords or add/remove any other users.

The different users and their permissions are presented in *Table 12.1* so you can quickly compare them for your understanding.

Operations	PRECO	CO	CU	AU
Obtain basic cluster information (number of HSMs in the cluster, IP address, serial number, etc.)	NO	YES	YES	YES
Zeroize HSMs	NO	YES	YES	YES
Change own password	YES	YES	YES	YES
Change any user's password	NO	YES	NO	NO
Add and remove users	NO	YES	NO	NO
Get synchronization status	NO	YES	YES	YES
Key management operations	NO	NO	YES	NO
Encrypt, decrypt, sign, verify, generate, and digest HMACs	NO	NO	YES	NO

Table 12.1: Comparison between different users of CloudHSM

The previous section took you through all the important features and services offered by CloudHSM. The next section presents a comparison between the two encryption services: CloudHSM and KMS.

Comparing CloudHSM to KMS

CloudHSM and KMS are both services provided by AWS for managing cryptographic keys and enhancing the security of your applications and data. The choice between CloudHSM and AWS depends on several factors.

You should use **CloudHSM** if any of the following conditions apply:

- **Stringent security requirements**: CloudHSM is ideal when you require the highest level of control and assurance over your cryptographic keys. It provides dedicated HSMs that offer physical tamper resistance and meet stringent security standards. If you have specific compliance requirements or operate in regulated industries that mandate the use of dedicated HSMs, then CloudHSM is a suitable choice.

- **Custom cryptographic operations**: CloudHSM is beneficial when you require custom cryptographic operations beyond what KMS provides. With CloudHSM, you have direct control over the HSM applications, which allows you to perform complex cryptographic operations, such as specialized algorithms or key derivation functions tailored to your specific application requirements.

- You have specific **compliance requirements**: If you must comply with industry or regulatory standards that explicitly require using dedicated HSMs, such as FIPs 140-2 Level 3, CloudHSM is the appropriate choice. CloudHSM helps you meet these requirements by providing certified hardware and enabling auditable controls for key management and cryptographic operations.

You should use **KMS** if the following conditions apply:

- You and your organization need **simplified key management**: KMS provides a managed key management service that simplifies the management of cryptographic keys. It provides a fully managed, scalable, and highly available service, allowing you to create, manage easily, and control keys without the operational overhead of managing HSM appliances.

- You want to **integrate with AWS services easily**: KMS seamlessly integrates with various AWS services, making it convenient for encrypting and decrypting data within the AWS ecosystem. It simplifies key management for services such as Amazon S3, Amazon RDS, and AWS Lambda. If you primarily use AWS services and require a centralized key management solution within AWS, KMS is suitable.

- You need **flexible key policies and access control**: KMS offers fine-grained access control through key policies and IAM roles, allowing you to define who can access and use the keys. It provides a flexible and scalable solution for managing access to keys and implementing least privilege principles.

- You desire **ease of use and scalability**: KMS is designed to be easy to use and highly scalable. You can quickly create and manage keys using the AWS Management Console, CLI, or SDKs. KMS handles the underlying infrastructure and scales automatically, ensuring high availability and performance.

To recap, you should use CloudHSM when you require dedicated HSMs for stringent security requirements, custom cryptographic operations, or compliance mandates. You should use KMS when you require a managed key management service that simplifies key management, integrates well with other AWS services, and offers flexible access control.

Summary

In this chapter, you looked at the leading service for encrypting data at rest in AWS, Key Management Service, or KMS. You were given a basic introduction to encryption, and the difference between symmetric and asymmetric encryption keys was explained. You learned all about the major components of the KMS service: customer-managed keys, data encryption keys, key material, key policies, and grants.

You saw how the AWS Artifact service can help you check the compliance of the KMS keys you are using and the compliance of other services. You also learned how AWS Artifact is a self-service document repository that can help you with auditing or if you need to look up something that could be found in the customer agreement.

In *Chapter 13, Access Management*, you will review a new section regarding IAM. This section will begin with access management and discuss how you can allow users access to your systems natively with the IAM service, along with creating groups of users.

Further Reading

For additional information on the AWS shared responsibility model and an underlying foundation to AWS security, please look at the following resources:

- AWS KMS FAQs: `https://packt.link/kK77E`

- Demystifying KMS keys operations, **bring your own key** (**BYOK**), custom key store, and ciphertext portability: `https://packt.link/Y2jb9`

- AWS KMS Best Practices (whitepaper): `https://packt.link/5fsOY`

- AWS CloudHSM FAQs: `https://packt.link/IbDTH`

- AWS Artifact FAQs: `https://packt.link/jjdei`

Exam Readiness Drill – Chapter Review Questions

Apart from a solid understanding of key concepts, being able to think quickly under time pressure is a skill that will help you ace your certification exam. That is why working on these skills early on in your learning journey is key.

Chapter review questions are designed to improve your test-taking skills progressively with each chapter you learn and review your understanding of key concepts in the chapter at the same time. You'll find these at the end of each chapter.

> **How To Access These Resources**
>
> To learn how to access these resources, head over to the chapter titled *Chapter 21, Accessing the Online Practice Resources*.

To open the Chapter Review Questions for this chapter, perform the following steps:

1. Click the link – `https://packt.link/SCSC02E2_CH12`

    Alternatively, you can scan the following QR code (*Figure 12.18*):

Figure 12.18: QR code that opens Chapter Review Questions for logged-in users

2. Once you log in, you'll see a page similar to the one shown in *Figure 12.19*:

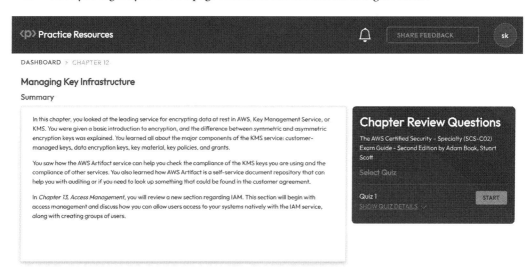

Figure 12.19: Chapter Review Questions for Chapter 12

3. Once ready, start the following practice drills, re-attempting the quiz multiple times.

Exam Readiness Drill

For the first three attempts, don't worry about the time limit.

ATTEMPT 1

The first time, aim for at least **40%**. Look at the answers you got wrong and read the relevant sections in the chapter again to fix your learning gaps.

ATTEMPT 2

The second time, aim for at least **60%**. Look at the answers you got wrong and read the relevant sections in the chapter again to fix any remaining learning gaps.

ATTEMPT 3

The third time, aim for at least **75%**. Once you score **75%** or more, you start working on your timing.

> **Tip**
>
> You may take more than three attempts to reach 75%. That's okay. Just review the relevant sections in the chapter till you get there.

Working On Timing

Target: Your aim is to keep the score the same while trying to answer these questions as quickly as possible. Here's an example of how your next attempts should look like:

Attempt	Score	Time Taken
Attempt 5	77%	21 mins 30 seconds
Attempt 6	78%	18 mins 34 seconds
Attempt 7	76%	14 mins 44 seconds

Table 12.2: Sample timing practice drills on the online platform

> **Note**
>
> The time limits shown in the above table are just examples. Set your own time limits with each attempt based on the time limit of the quiz on the website.

With each new attempt, your score should stay above 75% while your time taken to complete should **decrease**. Repeat as many attempts as you want till you feel confident dealing with the time pressure.

13

Access Management

The previous chapters focused more on what gets protected. This chapter begins the discussion on the *who*, which is not who gets protected but rather what permissions users and groups are allocated. Access management starts with segmenting users into groups so that they can be managed more effectively.

This chapter will help you with confidently implementing and managing access controls across various authentication mechanisms and will ensure you have a thorough understanding of all principles of permission-based access policies. You will also learn about some of the specific services and features in place that are designed to enrich and enhance the access control method selected.

In this chapter, you will learn how identities in the AWS **Identity and Access Management** system are authenticated and authorized. This allows the identities to perform their tasks in an appropriate manner that then becomes auditable.

The following main topics will be covered in this chapter:

- Understanding the **Identity and Access Management (IAM)** service
- Provisioning users, groups, and roles in IAM
- Configuring **Multi-Factor Authentication (MFA)**
- Understanding IAM Identity Center

Technical Requirements

You will need access to the AWS Management Console with an active account and AWS CLI access. You will also need access to a device on which you can install the Google Authenticator application.

Understanding the Identity and Access Management (IAM) Service

AWS IAM is a service provided by AWS that helps you control who can access your AWS resources and what they can do with them. It allows you to manage user accounts, set up permissions, and ensure the security of your AWS infrastructure.

Suppose you want to create a new user for your team member named `Alice`. You can do this quickly and easily with the AWS CLI using the following command:

```
aws iam create-user --user-name Alice
```

After your user `Alice` has been created, you would need to assign her permissions based on her job role and function. In this case, you could give `Alice` access to the Amazon S3 service, which she could use to put and retrieve files:

```
aws iam attach-user-policy --user-name Alice --policy-arn
arn:aws:iam::aws:policy/AmazonS3FullAccess
```

After attaching the managed S3 policy to user `Alice`, you realize it would be better to make sure that `Alice` only has permission to access the specific buckets that she would be working with. To ensure this, you create a custom policy instead like the following:

```
// CustomS3Policy.json
{
  "Version": "2012-10-17",
  "Statement": [
    {
      "Effect": "Allow",
      "Action": "s3:ListBucket",
      "Resource": "arn:aws:s3:::example-bucket"
    },
    {
      "Effect": "Allow",
      "Action": ["s3:GetObject", "s3:PutObject"],
      "Resource": "arn:aws:s3:::example-bucket/*"
    }
  ]
}
```

After creating the custom policy, you could then create the custom policy in AWS IAM and attach it to user `Alice` using the following commands:

```
aws iam create-policy --policy-name CustomS3Policy --policy-document
file://CustomS3Policy.json
aws iam detach-user-policy --user-name Alice --policy-arn
arn:aws:iam::aws:policy/AmazonS3FullAccess
aws iam attach-user-policy --user-name Alice --policy-arn
arn:aws:iam::123456789012:policy/CustomS3Policy
```

Notice that you first detached the AWS-managed S3 policy that gave full access before attaching the custom policy that gave scoped access.

With IAM, you can create and manage user accounts for different team members or applications. Each user is assigned a unique set of security credentials, such as access keys or passwords, which they can use to interact with AWS resources.

IAM uses a concept called "policies" to define permissions. Policies are like rulebooks that specify actions allowed or denied in specific AWS resources. You can create custom policies or choose from predefined ones to grant or restrict access as needed.

To simplify management, you can organize users into logical units called "groups" and assign permissions to these groups. This way, you can easily control access for multiple users at once.

IAM also supports **Multi-Factor Authentication** (**MFA**), which adds an extra layer of security. MFA requires users to provide an additional authentication factor (such as a temporary code from a virtual hardware device) when signing in.

Another essential feature of IAM is its support for roles and federation. Roles allow you to delegate users access to AWS resources without assigning long-term credentials. Federation enables you to integrate with your existing **Identity Provider** (**IdP**), such as Microsoft Active Directory, so your team members can use their existing credentials to access AWS resources.

IAM enables comprehensive logging of user activity and API calls, which helps you monitor and audit actions performed within your account. This is essential for maintaining security and compliance.

In the next section, you will be introduced to the key terms used in IAM.

Terms to Understand for IAM

To gain a comprehensive understanding of IAM, there is some terminology that you need to become familiar with, some of which you have already encountered in this book. This section highlights these key terms and provides their definitions. These don't need to be memorized for the *Security Specialty* exam per se, as there will be no direct questions on the terminology. However, they appear frequently in the questions, so knowing their meaning is critical so you fully understand the question or answer. These terms are listed here:

- **Principal**: An application or person that uses either the AWS root account user, an IAM user, or an IAM role to authenticate to the specified account and make requests. This is someone or something that can take action on an AWS resource.

- **Resources**: A resource is any item that you can work with inside an AWS account. Examples of a resource are a Lambda function, an EC2 instance, or a **Relational Data Service** (**RDS**) database.

- **Entities**: An entity can be an IAM user, a federated user, or a user coming in from an IdP. It could also be an assumed IAM role in the context of AWS, and it is simply the IAM resource object that AWS uses for authentication.

- **Identities**: The resources used to identify who is using the services are known as identities in IAM. These are your users, groups, and roles.

With a grasp of the overall IAM service and terminology, you will next be introduced to two concepts that are easy to confuse: authentication and authorization.

Authorization versus Authentication

Authorization and authentication are crucial in IAM. Even though the two terms seem incredibly similar and are used in conjunction quite frequently, it is essential to understand the difference between them as you move further into access and identity management. Understanding these differences is crucial for building secure and effective systems as these two concepts serve distinct but complementary roles in the realm of information security:

- **Authentication**: Authentication is the process of verifying who you claim to be. The system asks who you are, and you will often respond with a username and password. However, there can be times when you respond with a secure session token, such as an access token or a **JSON Web Token** (**JWT**). Authentication is about answering the questions *Who are you?* and *Can you verify who you say you are?*

- **Authorization**: Authorization takes place after authentication and establishes what you are allowed to do. Rules and policies govern what you are authorized to access. In the world of computing, this can be relayed through a token, such as a bearer token or JWT that grants you access to services or **Application Programming Interfaces** (**APIs**).

The processes of authentication and authorization are illustrated in *Figure 13.1*:

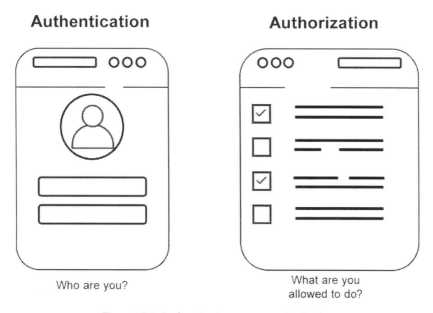

Figure 13.1: Authentication versus authorization

It can be easy to confuse authentication and authorization since they seem similar. However, think of authentication as your picture identification, such as a photo ID, and authorization as a badge that allows you to access a building or a specific room, such as a server room.

You need an ID badge to enter many large office buildings. In most cases, you are required to wear the badge at all times so it can be scanned to show that you are **authenticated** to be in the building without being stopped by security. As you move to the elevator, you might need to scan your badge to access your work floor. Your ID badge contains an RFID chip tied back to the policy system and your user profile. Scanning it lets the central system know which floors you can access. If you work on the fifth floor, you are **authorized** to press button number 5 and then travel up to the fifth floor. There might be other doors in the building to which you may or may not have access based on your level of authorization.

You can also think of a badge with a photo on one side and an RFID chip embedded inside. The photo provides authentication, and the chip allows for authorization. These might also come in the form of two distinct items, such as an ID badge coupled with a password or fingerprint to access a particular system.

Ways in Which IAM Can Authenticate with a Principal

IAM has several ways in which it can authenticate with a principal, outlined as follows:

- **Username and password**: A username and password are the way to enter the AWS Management Console.

- **Access key and secret access key**: These are long-term security credentials that can be associated with users or the root user. They can be rotated, and a maximum of two access keys can be associated with any user at any time.

- **Session token**: You can use an assumed role to take advantage of the **Security Token Service (STS)** to pass a token that will allow you or your application to gain access.

Best Practices for Using IAM

Throughout the years, AWS has developed (and revised) the best practices for using IAM in the most secure way possible. By following these best practices and guidelines, you place your organization and the accounts contained within that organization in a much better security posture. These best practices are as follows:

- Require human users to use federation with an IdP to access AWS using temporary credentials.

- Require workloads to use temporary credentials with IAM roles to access AWS.

- Require MFA.

- Safeguard your root user credentials. Do not use them for day-to-day operational tasks.

- Apply only the amount of permissions that a user or role needs (**least privilege**).

- Start with AWS-managed policies and then scope toward least-privileged permissions.

- Use the IAM Access Analyzer tool to generate least-privilege policies based on access activity.

- Regularly review and remove accounts for users, roles, permissions, and unused policies.

- Use conditions in IAM policies to further restrict access.

- Verify public and cross-account access to your resources using IAM Access Analyzer.

- Set up permission guardrails across multiple accounts.

- Use permission boundaries to delegate permissions management within an account.

These are the official *Security Best Practices in IAM* published by AWS, last updated on July 14, 2022, and can be found with further guidance at the following URL: `https://packt.link/ypJN5`.

It is suggested that you understand these guidelines for the *Certified Security Specialty Certification* exam. Understanding these best practices will help you navigate the IAM service to create roles, groups, and accounts. The next section will focus a bit more on the root account.

The Root Account

When you create a new account, you are automatically provided with a root account and a corresponding root user. The root account's power and privilege make it vulnerable to credential compromise, which would put your entire AWS account and all of the contained resources at risk. The most common risk arises with creating a set of (long-term) credentials, that is, the access key and secret key, for the root user and storing these credentials incorrectly, such as in an unencrypted text file on a developer's machine. This would risk credential exposure of the root account. Once a nefarious user gains access to the credentials, either through malware, phishing, or other means, they could locate and obtain those stored root credentials and have unrestricted account access. It doesn't just have a potential ending there. The holder of the root credentials will also have the ability to turn off CloudTrail logging, therefore stopping all recording of API activity before doing things such as data exfiltration or service disruption.

Due to this risk, it's best to not use this account for daily administration and operations. Instead, you should create another user account with the necessary administrative privileges to control your resources from within your account.

This section highlighted the security privileges of the root account and why you need to keep it secure. You are now ready to examine users, groups, and roles and how to configure and implement accounts that you can use for daily operational tasks.

Users versus Roles versus Groups in IAM

It is important for you to understand the differences between users, groups, and roles and their overall purposes within access control. This will help you architect and implement the most appropriate and effective access control for users and identities.

In AWS IAM, **users** represent individual identities, such as team members or applications, that interact with AWS resources. Each user is assigned a unique username and security credentials, which can include passwords or access keys. Users can be granted specific permissions to access and perform actions on AWS resources. For example, you can create a user named Emma and permit them to manage EC2 instances. Users are typically used to grant access to specific individuals or applications within your environment.

Roles, on the other hand, are used to grant temporary permissions to entities assuming those IAM roles, such as users or AWS services. Roles are not assigned to specific individuals but are assumed by trusted entities when needed. They enable secure delegation of access without the need to share long-term credentials. For example, you can create a Lambda Developer role and then define the permissions required to develop and deploy AWS Lambda functions. Then, users or services can assume this role temporarily to gain the necessary permissions. Roles are beneficial in scenarios where users or services need to access AWS resources on an as-needed basis that does not grant permanent access keys or passwords.

Groups are logical collections of users. Instead of assigning permissions to individual users, you can create groups and set permissions to those groups. This approach helps simplify permissions management, especially when multiple users require the same level of access to AWS resources. For example, you can create a `DatabaseAdmins` group that contains permissions to manage specific AWS services. You can then add multiple users to that group, and they will inherit the permissions assigned to it. By using groups, you can easily manage and update permissions for multiple users at once, ensuring consistent access.

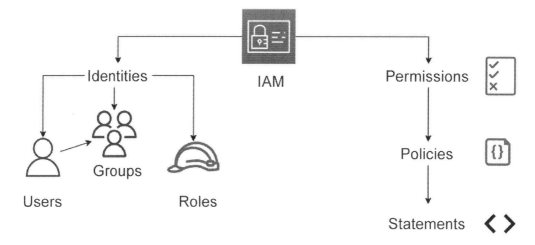

Figure 13.2: IAM identities

Figure 13.2 shows the hierarchy of IAM. Identities are composed of users, groups, and roles, and groups are made up of one or more users. IAM authorizes its identities using permissions, which comprise policies, and policies are made up of statements.

With an understanding of the different identities that can authenticate using the IAM service and how they get their authorizations, you are ready to take the next step—creating some groups in your account to hold a set of permissions.

Creating a Group

Inside your organization's AWS account, you will have added the users who will be accessing, administrating, and developing items within that account. You will want to organize these users based on their roles to simplify permissions management. Instead of assigning permissions individually to each user, creating groups that represent different roles is a better way to manage permissions. You can then assign users to one or more of the groups that you have created.

Groups within IAM are objects associated with a set of permissions, allowing any users who are members of that group to inherit those permissions. The group itself does not have any credentials associated with it. Instead, it is just a construct to facilitate the management of the users inside.

As you begin to lay out your accounts, before you add users with disparate policies, you should have at least a basic idea of how you want your groups to be organized in your account. The most fundamental three groups are **Admins**, **Developers**, and **Billing**, and these are all roles that would have **Role-Based Access Control** (**RBAC**)-based permissions tied to their groups.

Take the following steps to make the groups shown in *Table 13.1* and then associate the managed policies with them as shown:

Group Name	Managed Policy Name
AWSAdmins	AdministratorAccess
Billing	Billing
Developers	AmazonEC2FullAccess, CloudWatchFullAccess

Table 13.1: Association of IAM groups and AWS-managed IAM policies

1. Open up your terminal console to use your AWS CLI to create the groups.

2. Now type the following command so that you can create the first group (`AWSAdmins`):

```
aws iam create-group --group-name AWSAdmins
```

If the preceding command executed successfully, you should get a value returned as shown here (to get a table output like the following, use the `--table` flag at the end of your CLI statement):

```
---------------------------------------------------------------
|                        CreateGroup                          |
+-------------------------------------------------------------+
|                          Group                              |
+------------+------------------------------------------------+|
|  Arn       |   arn:aws:iam::182968331794:group/AWSadmins    |
|  CreateDate|   2023-06-02T19:44:14+00:00                    |
|  GroupId   |   AGPASVGODFYJD7LFYYS3F                        |
|  GroupName |   AWSadmins                                     |
|  Path      |   /                                             |
+------------+------------------------------------------------|
```

3. With the first group created, repeat *step 2* using the `aws iam create-group` command for the other groups listed in *Table 13.1*. Once you have finished creating the groups, move on to the next step.

4. With the preceding groups created, check all the groups in your account using the following command:

```
aws iam list-groups
```

You should see the CLI return a listing of all the groups in your account, which now includes AWSadmins, Billing, and Developers.

5. Attach a policy to your group. You are using the CLI and need to find out the **Amazon Resource Name (ARN)** for the managed policy you want to attach to your first group, AWSadmins. You can do this easily with a combination of the CLI and the grep command, as shown below:

```
aws iam list-policies --scope AWS --output json | grep
'AdministratorAccess'
```

Notice the use of the --scope AWS flag when searching through the policies. This flag means that you want to search through the policies owned and managed by AWS, not any custom policies you have written yourself. The --json output flag was also used in this command so that the output would be returned compacted on a line-by-line basis. This way, you can quickly read through the policies' names and grab the ARN for your clipboard in just a few steps.

> **Note**
>
> If you would like to read more about the options for the aws iam list-policies command, you can find all flags available on the documentation page here: https://packt.link/PS0L4.

The output that comes back should be just a few policies, like the ones shown here:

```
            "PolicyName": "AdministratorAccess",
            "Arn": "arn:aws:iam::aws:policy/AdministratorAccess",
            "PolicyName": "AdministratorAccess-Amplify",
            "Arn": "arn:aws:iam::aws:policy/AdministratorAccess-
Amplify",
            "PolicyName": "AdministratorAccess-AWSElasticBeanstalk",
            "Arn": "arn:aws:iam::aws:policy/AdministratorAccess-
AWSElasticBeanstalk",
            "PolicyName": "AWSAuditManagerAdministratorAccess",
            "Arn": "arn:aws:iam::aws:policy/
AWSAuditManagerAdministratorAccess",
```

6. Although four total policies were returned, the policy you want to attach to your *AWSadmins* group will be the first one, named AdminstratorAccess. Copy the ARN from that policy (arn:aws:iam::aws:policy/AdministratorAccess) to your clipboard for the next step so you can attach it to the group.

7. With the ARN for the policy now on your clipboard, attach it to the group you created earlier with the `attach-group-policy` command, as shown:

```
aws iam attach-group-policy --policy-arn
arn:aws:iam::aws:policy/AdministratorAccess --group-name
AWSadmins
```

Executing this command will not give you any return or feedback showing success.

8. To see whether the policy was successfully attached to the *AWSadmins* group, use the following:

```
aws iam list-attached-group-policies --group-name AWSadmins
```

The output should show you the policy name of `AdministratorAccess` and the associated policy ARN.

You are done creating your Administrator group for the moment. You can repeat the same steps to add policies for the other groups you created. You can search for the policy names in the table at the beginning of this exercise using the process shown in *step 5*.

> **Note**
>
> You are adding an AWS-managed policy to your group at this point, but in the next chapter, *Chapter 14, Working with Access Policies*, you will go through the process of constructing custom policies for your users and groups. Both types of policies are essential for managing your users and roles.

You just saw how quickly you were able to add groups and then attach a pre-created policy to one of those groups from the AWS CLI. In the next section, you will again use one of the groups you created, the `Admins` group. You will create a new user and then add that user to that group.

Creating a User

Users within IAM are objects defined as identities that can log in and authenticate using specified credentials as an associated password. Additional authentication may also be used in the form of MFA. Once authenticated, the user can access resources defined by their associated permissions.

You are automatically provided with a root account user when you create your account. In order to administer and provide access to the other users in your organization, you will need to create other accounts, as shown in the following walk-through:

1. Open your terminal command prompt from the last exercise so that you can go through the process of creating your user. To keep it simple, this example uses the name of the new user, `Packt`. However, you can change it to meet your needs if you desire.

2. Begin the process of creating a user with the `create-user` command, as shown:

```
aws iam create-user --user-name Packt
```

Once you create the user, you should get a return from the CLI similar to the following:

```
{
    "User": {
        "Path": "/",
        "UserName": "Packt",
        "UserId": "AIDASVGODFYJAFS705EVJ",
        "Arn": "arn:aws:iam::1234567890:user/Packt",
        "CreateDate": "2023-06-04T15:31:08+00:00"
    }
}
```

Your user is created but has no permissions at this point. You created the groups in the last exercise that hold the permission, so you can simply add the user to one of the groups.

3. Use the following command to display the `AWSadmins` group that was created earlier:

```
aws iam add-user-to-group --user-name Packt --group-name
AWSadmins
```

Similar to when you added the permissions to the group, there will be no return or feedback when this command has been run successfully.

Now that your user has a set of permissions, they need a way to log in to the AWS Management Console to gain access. You could use the `change-password` command and set a static password for them. However, that would reveal this new user's permanent password. The next step is a better alternative.

4. Use the `create-login-profile` command, set a temporary password, and then require the user to change their password upon initial login. See the following example command:

```
aws iam create-login-profile --user-name Packt --password Ch@
ng3mE --password-reset-required
```

You should see confirmation of the login profile created after running the command.

Your new user should be ready to use and log in to the AWS Management Console, and when you log in with the `Packt` user for the first time, that user will be prompted to change their password.

You must change your password to continue

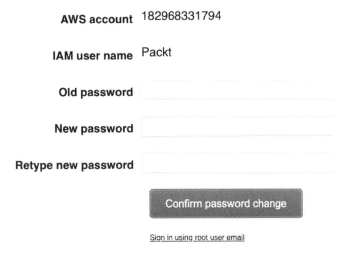

AWS account   182968331794

IAM user name   Packt

Old password

New password

Retype new password

Confirm password change

Sign in using root user email

Figure 13.3: New user login screen

Now you are familiar with how to create your user and add any previously created policy to that user. Next, you will log in to the AWS Management Console as a new user to further secure the account with MFA.

Adding Multi-Factor Authentication to Your User

A secure password is good, but adding a secondary form of authentication, especially on accounts with elevated access, is crucial.

Imagine you have an administrator for one of your AWS accounts with extensive privileges, but without MFA enabled. This administrator has a strong password, as per your organization's policy, but if their credentials are somehow compromised, then an attacker gains immediate access to the account. The administrator's password could be compromised through a phishing attack, keylogging, or some other means. With only the password needed for access, the attacker can now log in to the AWS Management Console or use the AWS CLI using the stolen credentials. Since it's an administrator account, the attacker has unrestricted access to sensitive resources, critical infrastructure, and the ability to make configuration changes. In this case, having a secondary form of authentication that the attacker cannot bypass would render any attempts to use the stolen password futile.

The following exercise will teach you how to add a second form of authentication to a user account. To perform this exercise, you will need the username and temporary password (if you still need to change it by logging in) for the user you created in the previous exercise. You must also install the *Google Authenticator* application on a mobile device or tablet to perform the MFA:

1. Log in to the AWS Management Console using the user you created in the `AWSadmin` group. If you followed the exercise's recommendations, this username will be `Packt`.

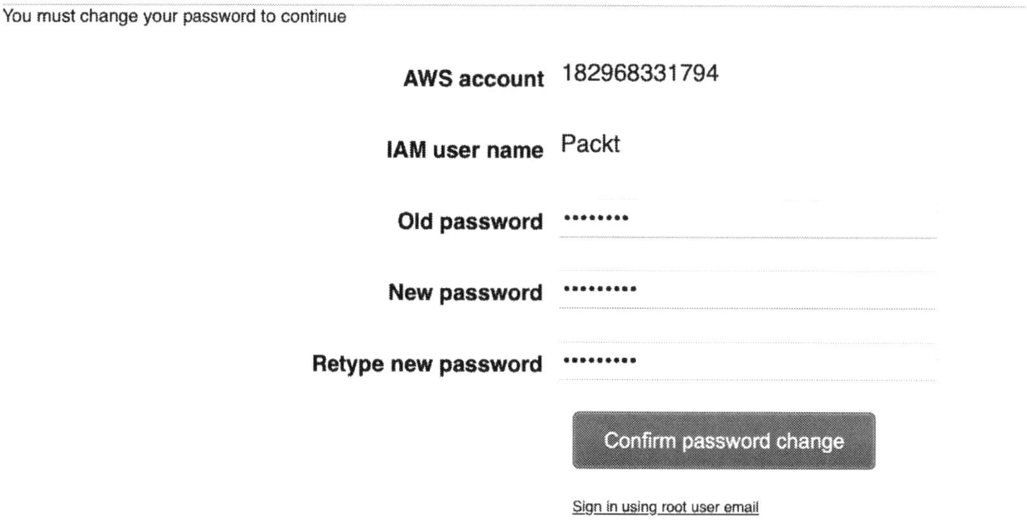

You must change your password to continue
_____

AWS account	182968331794
IAM user name	Packt
Old password	········
New password	·········
Retype new password	·········

Confirm password change

Sign in using root user email

Figure 13.4: User login screen

You will need to enter the old/temporary password that you added in the CLI before resetting the user with a new password. Once you change the password, you can use the AWS Management Console normally without restriction or a lockout screen appearing.

2. Next, navigate to the IAM service using the search bar at the top of the AWS Management Console.

3. Once in the IAM console, find and click on `Users` under the `Access management` subsection in the menu on the left.

Figure 13.5: IAM console menu

4. Scroll down on the main page until you come to the Users heading. Use the search box to type in the name of the user you are looking for, in this case, Packt. This will filter out the other users so you can focus on this single user.

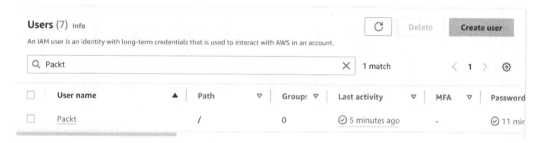

Figure 13.6: Users management screen

You can see from the provided screenshot the last activity (in this case, the last activity was when the user was just created), and the user is a member of the AWS admins group and does not currently have MFA set up for their account.

5. Click on the username to be taken to the user's details page.

6. Scroll down the page until you find the `Multi-factor authentication (MFA)` section. In this section, there will be two buttons labeled `Assign MFA device`. Click on either of the buttons to start configuring MFA for this user's account.

Figure 13.7: MFA section

Once you have clicked the `Add MFA device` button, you must fill out some details about your MFA device.

7. If you use Google Authenticator on a mobile device to perform MFA, name the device `Google Auth`. You will also need to select `Authenticator App` in the `Select MFA device` section. After making these selections, scroll down and press the `Next` button.

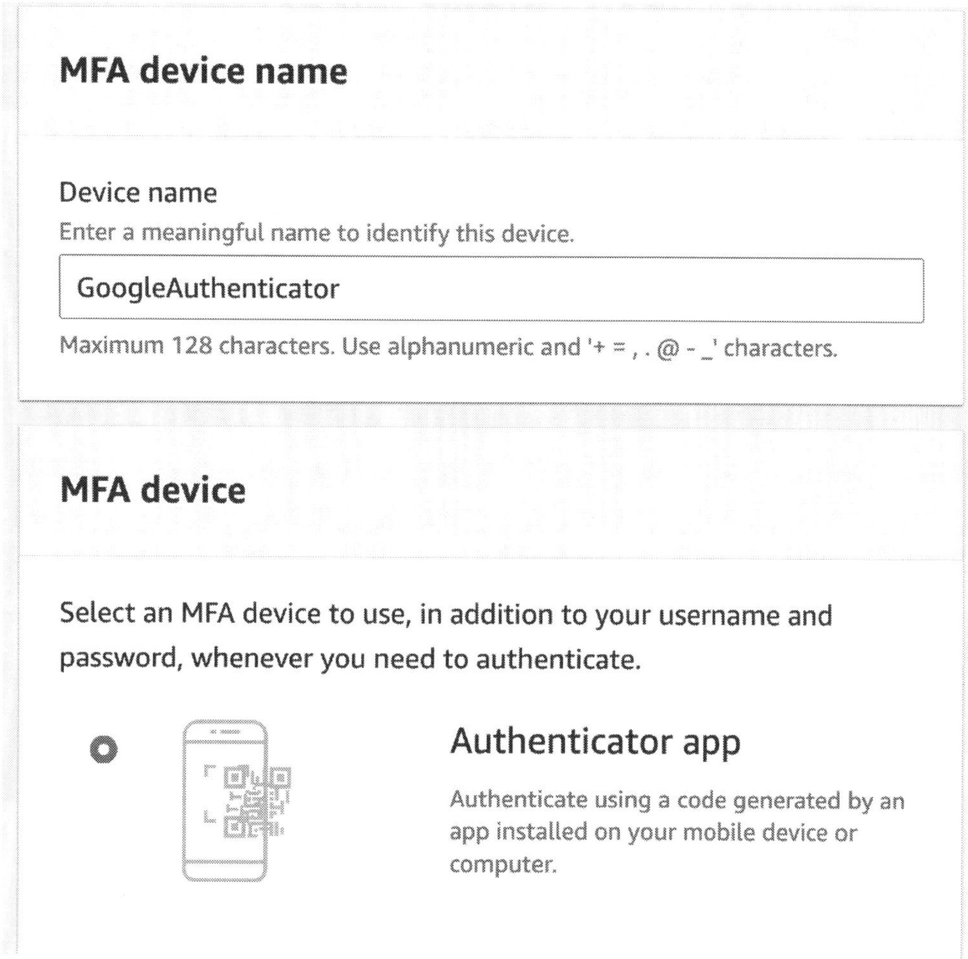

MFA device name

Device name

Enter a meaningful name to identify this device.

> GoogleAuthenticator

Maximum 128 characters. Use alphanumeric and '+ = , . @ - _' characters.

MFA device

Select an MFA device to use, in addition to your username and password, whenever you need to authenticate.

Authenticator app

Authenticate using a code generated by an app installed on your mobile device or computer.

Figure 13.8: MFA setup screen

8. You should now be on the Set up device page. Scroll down to click on the link labeled Show QR code. This will display a QR code.

9. Scan the QR code with your device's camera while in the Google Authenticator application. You will then see the AWS ID appear on your device screen.

10. Next, enter the next two consecutive codes shown on the app into the AWS Management Console screen for your user. Once you have done this, press the Add MFA button to complete the process.

Open your authenticator app, choose **Show QR code** on this page, then use the app to scan the code. Alternatively, you can type a secret key. Show secret key

Fill in two consecutive codes from your MFA device.

Figure 13.9: QR code for configuring MFA on the device

You have just gone through the process of adding enhanced security protection to a new user's account so that password protection is not their only form of authentication. Next, you will learn about STS and how using short-term credentials can help mitigate the risk associated with lost long-term credentials.

Security Token Service

AWS STS acts as a trusted intermediary that issues temporary security credentials to users or applications when they need to access AWS resources. These temporary credentials have a limited lifespan, typically ranging from a few minutes to a few hours. Such credentials reduce the risk of unauthorized access if credentials are compromised and also minimize the window of opportunity for attackers to exploit stolen records.

AWS STS allows you to implement the principle of least privilege, granting users or applications only the necessary permissions required for their tasks. By defining fine-grained access policies for temporary credentials, you ensure that individuals or applications only have access to the specific resources they need, thereby reducing the potential impact of any security breaches.

Further, credentials automatically expire after a defined period and require users or applications to re-authenticate and obtain new credentials for continued access. This mitigates the risk of unauthorized access due to forgotten or unrevoked long-term credentials.

AWS STS integrates with external IdPs using standard protocols such as SAML and ODIC. This allows your organization to leverage existing identity management systems, such as Microsoft Active Directory, for AWS IAM. Integrating with your identity federation infrastructure enables you to centralize user management, simplify your user onboarding and offboarding processes, and enhance the user experience.

Further, AWS STS is highly scalable and can handle high volumes of authentication requests. It can be seamlessly integrated into your existing AWS infrastructure, including applications and services, using the AWS SDKs and APIs. This scalability and flexibility make it suitable for organizations of all sizes, thereby accommodating growth and evolving access requirements.

Obtaining Credentials with STS

Figure 13.10 details how STS works.

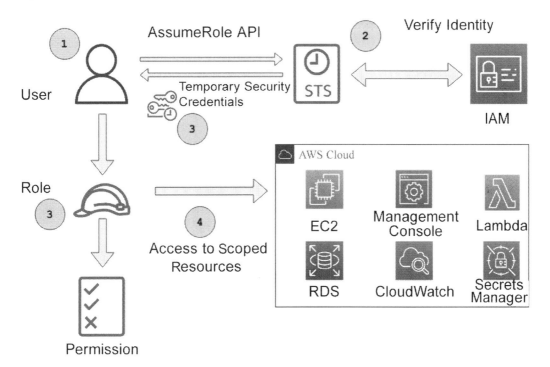

Figure 13.10: STS authorization flow

Refer to the numbers in the preceding diagram and then read the details of the process in the corresponding steps here:

1. **Request for temporary security credentials**: A user (or application) makes a request to AWS STS to obtain temporary security credentials. This request can be made programmatically using the AWS SDK, AWS Management Console, or API calls. For a user, it can also be done using the CLI.

2. **Verify the requester's identity**: AWS STS verifies the requestor's identity before issuing the temporary credentials. This verification process can involve authenticating the requestor using long-term AWS credentials associated with an IAM user or role.

3. **Generate temporary security credentials**: Once the requester's identity is verified, AWS STS generates temporary security credentials consisting of an access key ID, a secret access key, and a session token. These credentials are unique to the requester and have limited permissions based on the access policies associated with the IAM user or role.

4. **Access to AWS resources**: With the temporary credentials in hand, the requester can now use them to access AWS resources. For example, they can make API calls, interact with AWS services, or access resources through the AWS Management Console.

5. **Credential expiration and renewal**: Temporary credentials have an expiration time, after which they become invalid. If the requester needs continued access, they need to obtain new credentials by re-requesting them from AWS STS. This expiration and renewal process ensures that access to AWS resources is time-limited, reducing the risk of unauthorized access due to compromised credentials.

To recap, AWS STS issues temporary security credentials with limited access privileges to users or applications. These temporary credentials enhance security, follow the principle of least privilege, and integrate with identity federation systems.

In the next section, you will learn how to manage users across your organization using IAM Identity Center.

IAM Identity Center

IAM Identity Center is an AWS service that allows companies to manage the security of the sign-in process for their workforce users. It provides **Single Sign-On (SSO)** access to applications, multi-account permissions, and a simple web portal. With IAM Identity Center, your organization can create and manage its users' access to all AWS accounts and applications from a central location. The service also enables users to create workforce users and groups within IAM Identity Center or synchronize them with an existing identity source, such as Microsoft Active Directory Domain Services or external IdPs such as Okta Universal Directory or Microsoft Entra ID (formerly Azure AD).

The following are the main features of IAM Identity Center:

- Multi-Account Permissions
- Workforce Identities
- Application Assignments for SAML Applications
- Identity Center-Enabled Applications
- AWS Access Portal

IAM Identity Center simplifies managing permissions across multiple AWS accounts. You can centrally plan and implement IAM permissions, creating fine-grained access-based controls for job functions or custom requirements. By assigning these permissions to workforce users, you can control their access to specific accounts efficiently.

IAM Identity Center also allows you to create and manage human users within your organization, known as workforce identities. You can also synchronize with existing users and groups for external identity sources such as Microsoft Active Directory or Okta Universal Directory. This ensures consistent access across all of your AWS accounts and applications.

With application assignments, you can grant SSO access to SAML 2.0 applications such as Salesforce and Microsoft 365 for your users in IAM Identity Center. Users can conveniently access these applications from a unified location, eliminating the need for separate federation setups.

AWS applications and services such as Amazon Managed Grafana, Amazon Monitron, and Amazon SageMaker Studio notebooks also seamlessly integrate with IAM Identity Center. These applications automatically connect to IAM Identity Center for sign-in and user application directory services. Users benefit from a consistent SSO experience, and sharing application resources becomes more streamlined due to a shared view of users, groups, and memberships.

Summary

This chapter discussed the IAM service. You saw how authentication and authorization form the basis of IAM and discovered some of the best practices for using IAM. You completed an exercise of creating a group in IAM, creating a new user, adding a policy to that user, and then adding that user to the previously created group.

You also saw how STS could be used to create temporary security credentials, which are more secure than providing long-term security credentials for both users and roles. Finally, you reviewed AWS IAM Identity Center and how it can help manage user accounts across many accounts in an AWS organization and provide consolidated access to those same users to SaaS applications outside of your AWS environment.

In *Chapter 14, Working with Access Policies*, you will examine the policies and constructs used in IAM policies, service control policies, and other policies.

Further Reading

For additional information on the AWS Shared Responsibility Model and the underlying foundation of AWS security, please check out the following resources:

- AWS Identity and Access Management (IAM) FAQs: `https://packt.link/51G7g`

- You can now assign multiple MFA devices in IAM: `https://packt.link/ySmO1`

- AWS Simple Token Service API reference: `https://packt.link/rKu35`

- AWS IAM Identity Center FAQs: `https://packt.link/1xzoF`

Exam Readiness Drill – Chapter Review Questions

Apart from a solid understanding of key concepts, being able to think quickly under time pressure is a skill that will help you ace your certification exam. That is why working on these skills early on in your learning journey is key.

Chapter review questions are designed to improve your test-taking skills progressively with each chapter you learn and review your understanding of key concepts in the chapter at the same time. You'll find these at the end of each chapter.

> **How To Access These Resources**
>
> To learn how to access these resources, head over to the chapter titled *Chapter 21, Accessing the Online Practice Resources*.

To open the Chapter Review Questions for this chapter, perform the following steps:

1. Click the link – `https://packt.link/SCSC02E2_CH13`

    Alternatively, you can scan the following QR code (*Figure 13.11*):

Figure 13.11: QR code that opens Chapter Review Questions for logged-in users

2.   Once you log in, you'll see a page similar to the one shown in *Figure 13.12*:

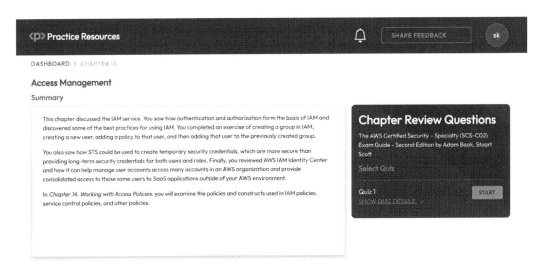

Figure 13.12: Chapter Review Questions for Chapter 13

3.   Once ready, start the following practice drills, re-attempting the quiz multiple times.

Exam Readiness Drill

For the first three attempts, don't worry about the time limit.

ATTEMPT 1

The first time, aim for at least **40%**. Look at the answers you got wrong and read the relevant sections in the chapter again to fix your learning gaps.

ATTEMPT 2

The second time, aim for at least **60%**. Look at the answers you got wrong and read the relevant sections in the chapter again to fix any remaining learning gaps.

ATTEMPT 3

The third time, aim for at least **75%**. Once you score **75%** or more, you start working on your timing.

> **Tip**
>
> You may take more than three attempts to reach 75%. That's okay. Just review the relevant sections in the chapter till you get there.

Working On Timing

Target: Your aim is to keep the score the same while trying to answer these questions as quickly as possible. Here's an example of how your next attempts should look like:

Attempt	Score	Time Taken
Attempt 5	77%	21 mins 30 seconds
Attempt 6	78%	18 mins 34 seconds
Attempt 7	76%	14 mins 44 seconds

Table 13.2: Sample timing practice drills on the online platform

> **Note**
>
> The time limits shown in the above table are just examples. Set your own time limits with each attempt based on the time limit of the quiz on the website.

With each new attempt, your score should stay above 75% while your time taken to complete should **decrease**. Repeat as many attempts as you want till you feel confident dealing with the time pressure.

Section 5:
Identity and Access Management

Having understood how to create your environment and securely create resources to run and connect to your applications, you now need to learn how to appropriately create and manage the users that will work in that environment. This process starts with the **Identity and Access (IAM)** service in AWS, which is covered in this section. This section comprises the following chapters:

- *Chapter 13, Access Management*

- *Chapter 14, Working with Access Policies*

- *Chapter 15, Federated and Mobile Access*

- *Chapter 16, Using Active Directory Services to Manage Access*

You will often find that there are times when you need to allow external users access to certain resources in your account, either from another AWS account or users who are simply there to use your application but do not need extended access to the environment. If you have an on-premises environment, then you may already be managing users and their permissions via Active Directory. Instead of duplicating the users in multiple systems, you can use Federation to streamline the process and help ensure that when a user leaves the organization or has a change in duties, permission creep does not leave them expanded capabilities that were unintended. These concepts are covered in detail in *Chapters 15 and 16*.

One of the major parts of IAM is the ability to craft the individual, group, and role policies that are used to provide the least privileged access that allows users to perform their necessary duties. The ability to understand how users, groups, and roles are provided access is covered in *Chapter 13*. As an AWS security professional, you need to have the ability to read, write, and test both straightforward and complex policies. You must also know what an effective set of permissions looks like once you combine any **Service Control Policies** (**SCP**) set in place at the organizational level, an identity-based policy, and any permissions boundaries. *Chapter 14* will walk you through how to craft individual policies, not only for the IAM service but also for other services as well. All of the aforementioned concepts will be discussed in detail in the upcoming chapters.

14
Working with Access Policies

After creating the users and groups who can access the services in your accounts, the next step in the process is to craft the policies that provide only the access necessary for each user, group, and role to perform their tasks. In the previous chapter, you reviewed how you could quickly provide access using a pre-crafted policy that AWS manages.

As an AWS security professional, it is most likely that one of your duties will be to write and tune the policies that grant and restrict access to the resources held in the account and AWS Organizations. You need to have a comprehensive understanding of how to provide both access and denial to services for the users, groups, and roles in your account.

You should also be familiar with the tools that can show you whether you have provided the policies that your entities need or a set of permissions that is too large or too narrow for the duties that they are trying to perform. You will learn about the tool present in the IAM services console that performs that task later in this chapter, under the section labeled *Access Advisor*.

Finally, how do you handle access requests from other accounts? This can also fall under your responsibility as an AWS security specialist. There are a few different options available to you depending on whether the secondary account needs access to multiple services or only the data stored on the S3 service.

You will cover the following main topics in this chapter:

- Understanding the difference between policy types
- Identifying policy structure and syntax
- How to configure cross-account access using IAM policies
- Policy evaluation
- Using bucket policies to control access to S3

Technical Requirements

To complete all the steps detailed in this chapter, you must have access to two separate AWS accounts and administrative access to the IAM service. You will also need access to a code or text editor, such as Visual Studio Code or Notepad++, to compose and edit the policy files.

Understanding the Differences between Access Policy Types

Policies are associated with users, groups, roles, or resources and define who or what can or cannot access AWS resources. You may already be familiar with some policy types, but AWS supports several different types of policies, including the following:

- Identity-based policies

- Resource-based policies

- **Access control lists** (ACLs)

- **Simple Storage Service** (S3) bucket policies

- Organization **service control policies** (SCPs)

The following sections discuss each type of policy in greater detail.

Identity-Based Policies

If you have been using AWS for any length of time, then you will be most familiar with this type of policy. Identity-based IAM policies in AWS are a way to manage permissions and control access for individual users, groups, or roles within your AWS accounts. You can attach these policies to identities created within the IAM service. These policies then define what actions those identities can perform and what resources they can access.

For example, suppose a group had a policy attached to it that allows full Amazon S3 access. The group users would be granted permissions based on this and any other policies bound to the group, which makes the policy an identity-based policy. By using identity-based IAM policies, you can ensure that each user, group, or role in your AWS account has the appropriate level of access to AWS resources. They help enforce security, control resource usage, and adhere to the principle of least privilege.

In the case of an identity-based policy that would help enforce security, control resource usage, and adhere to the principle of least privilege, consider the following scenario. Your company hosts multiple Amazon S3 buckets for different purposes, ranging from marketing assets to sensitive financial reports. By crafting specific identity-based policies, the organization ensures that access permissions align with team roles. For instance, the marketing team is granted read-only access to the `Marketing` bucket, the finance team receives read and write permissions for the `FinancialReports` bucket, and the sales team gains full access to the `OrderStatements` bucket. IAM groups are created associating these policies with corresponding teams, facilitating easy management and modification of permissions as the organization evolves. This approach not only enhances security by adhering to the principle of least privilege but also allows efficient resource usage, adaptability to changing roles, and streamlined auditing for compliance purposes.

Identity-based policies can be AWS managed, customer managed, or **inline policies**. The three types of identity-based policies are discussed in detail here:

- **AWS-managed policies**: These are predefined, ready-to-use policies that can be found within IAM. AWS-managed IAM policies are created and maintained by AWS experts and thus adhere to the best security and access control practices. These policies are designed to provide secure and granular access to AWS services and resources. They are automatically updated by AWS when new services or actions are added or when security best practices change. This means you don't have to spend time and effort manually managing and updating the policy versions.

  You can filter out only the AWS-managed policies from the IAM service from the AWS Management Console. Navigate to `Policies` and use the search bar to select the filter options. Then choose the `AWS managed` policy type.

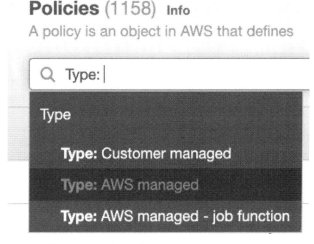

Figure 14.1: The Policies management screen

The preceding screenshot shows how you can select the AWS-managed policies. Once selected, it will then filter out any customer-managed policies that you might have previously created.

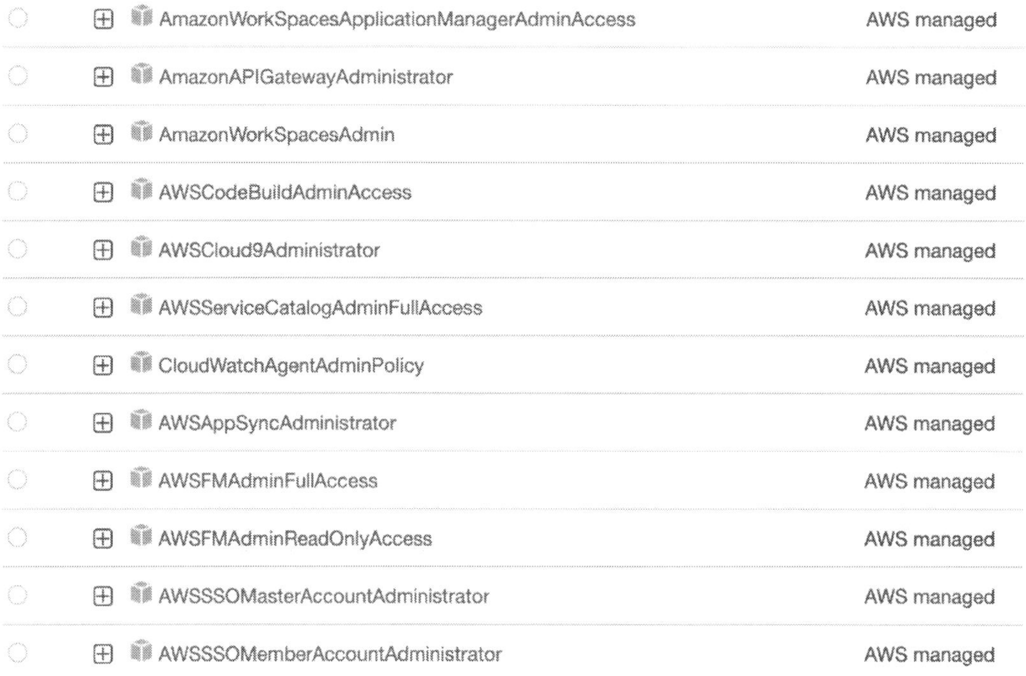

○	⊞ ◫ AmazonWorkSpacesApplicationManagerAdminAccess	AWS managed
○	⊞ ◫ AmazonAPIGatewayAdministrator	AWS managed
○	⊞ ◫ AmazonWorkSpacesAdmin	AWS managed
○	⊞ ◫ AWSCodeBuildAdminAccess	AWS managed
○	⊞ ◫ AWSCloud9Administrator	AWS managed
○	⊞ ◫ AWSServiceCatalogAdminFullAccess	AWS managed
○	⊞ ◫ CloudWatchAgentAdminPolicy	AWS managed
○	⊞ ◫ AWSAppSyncAdministrator	AWS managed
○	⊞ ◫ AWSFMAdminFullAccess	AWS managed
○	⊞ ◫ AWSFMAdminReadOnlyAccess	AWS managed
○	⊞ ◫ AWSSSOMasterAccountAdministrator	AWS managed
○	⊞ ◫ AWSSSOMemberAccountAdministrator	AWS managed

Figure 14.2: List of AWS-managed policies in the AWS account

Once you have the AWS-managed policy filter on, you can combine that with a search of the service or types of permissions you are trying to provide to your user, group, or role. In the preceding screenshot, a filter has been applied so that only policies containing the Admin name will appear in the search results.

- **Customer-managed policies**: These are policies that you have customized to fit your specific need for a user, group, or role. For instance, there might not be an AWS-managed policy that specifically meets your organization's needs. As a result, you may need to either copy and customize an existing managed policy or create your policy from scratch. You can use the visual editor to do so or write it yourself using the **JavaScript Object Notation (JSON)** format. Customer-managed identity-based policies give you much more granular control over how you want to manage identity access than AWS-managed policies.

- **Inline policies**: These are different from both AWS and customer-managed policies in the sense that inline policies are embedded directly into the identity object. For example, customer-managed policies are stored in IAM as separate objects and can then be assigned to multiple identities, such as groups, roles, and users. Inline policies are *not* stored as individual objects; they only exist within the entity that they are created in—users or roles. *Figure 14.3* presents a diagrammatic representation of the differences between managed and inline policies.

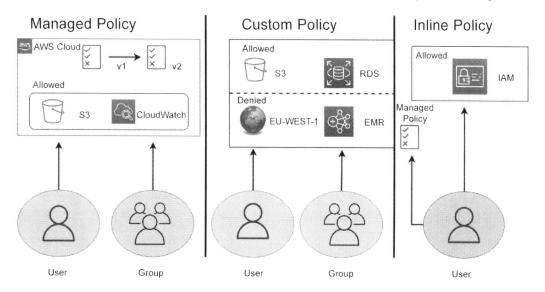

Figure 14.3: Managed versus inline policies in IAM

It is recommended to use managed policies instead of inline policies whenever possible. Managed policies are easily visible within IAM, while inline policies are embedded within identities and not as easily visible. Managed policies, as their name suggests, are managed by AWS, and therefore are updated by the AWS service team as new services are added to the platform or as other best practices are discovered. This takes an element of micromanagement and responsibility off of you and your team. However, conversely, a permission to a service might be added (or possibly removed) that you had not expected. All in all, using a managed policy if available is preferable in most cases since it will save you from looking up all the possible services needed for the role and having any future services updated automatically.

Resource-Based Policies

AWS resource-based policies are a powerful IAM feature that allows you to control access to specific AWS resources. These policies are attached directly to the resources themselves and define who can access and perform actions on them. Resource-based policies provide fine-grained access control, allowing you to specify the permissions, conditions, and restrictions for each resource. This level of control enables you to delegate access, collaborate with other AWS accounts, and securely share resources, all while maintaining centralized management.

In AWS IAM, the concepts of resource and identity are fundamental for effectively managing access and permissions. An identity in IAM represents the entity requesting access or performing actions within the AWS environment. An identity can be a user, role, group, or service that has assumed a service role. On the other hand, a resource denotes the AWS entities upon which actions can be taken, or access can be granted. These resources can be diverse, including EC2 instances, S3 buckets, DynamoDB tables, and Lambda functions.

Examples of resource-based policies include S3 bucket policies for controlling access to S3 buckets and Lambda function policies for defining permissions for invoking serverless functions. By leveraging resource-based policies, you can enforce robust security measures and ensure that only authorized entities can interact with your AWS resources.

Another significant offering by AWS when it comes to access control and permissions management is **permissions boundaries**.

Permissions Boundaries

AWS IAM permission boundaries are an advanced feature that allows you to set the maximum permission an IAM entity (user or role) can have. They act as a limiting factor to restrict the permissions an IAM policy can grant, even if the policy attached to the entity allows expanded access.

You need to understand the following key points about permissions boundaries:

- They can be used for controlling maximum permissions.
- They are used to limit policy permissions.
- They are a separate policy from the IAM policy.
- They *do not* grant any permissions.

IAM permissions boundaries are used to control the upper limit of permissions for an IAM entity. They enforce a least-privilege model by preventing an entity from being granted excessive permissions that could potentially compromise security. When a permission boundary is applied to an IAM entity, it acts as a barrier to policy permissions. Even if an IAM policy allows certain actions or access to specific resources, the permission boundary will limit those permissions to its defined scope.

IAM permissions boundaries are separate from the IAM policies attached to an entity. While IAM policies also restrict permissions, they are defined in a separate IAM policy document as opposed to permission boundaries. Permission boundaries are beneficial when you want to delegate control to different teams or departments within your organization while still maintaining some level of control over their maximum permissions. They help prevent accidental or intentional escalation of privileges by placing a boundary on the permissions an entity can be granted. Further, when working with complex permission structures or implementing a multi-account strategy, permission boundaries can help you simplify permissions management across multiple IAM entities. They provide a centralized way to control and limit permissions across different roles or users.

> **Note**
>
> Permission boundaries do not grant permissions themselves; they only restrict the maximum permissions that can be granted. Additionally, permission boundaries cannot be used to grant additional permissions beyond what is already allowed by an entity's identity-based policies.

Having gained a conceptual understanding of permissions boundaries, you are ready to go through the exercise of creating a permissions boundary for one of the groups you created earlier in your account.

Creating a Permissions Boundary

To gain a better understanding of permissions boundaries, go through the following steps to create a permissions boundary policy:

1. Open up the IAM service in the AWS Management Console. You can navigate there quickly by using the following URL: `https://packt.link/hDp3I`.

2. On the left-hand side menu in the IAM service, under the heading `Access management`, select `Policies`.

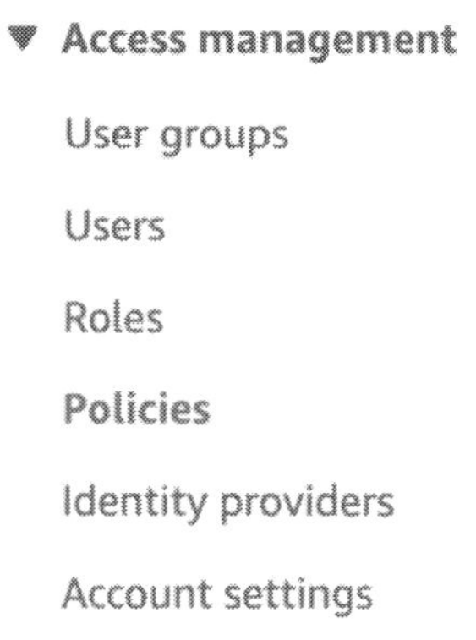

▼ **Access management**

    User groups

    Users

    Roles

    Policies

    Identity providers

    Account settings

Figure 14.4: The IAM menu

3. Once on the `Policies` main page, click on the button labeled `Create policy`.

4. Once in the policy editor, click the `JSON` button on the top to switch to JSON. Change `Effect` from `Allow` to `Deny`. Set the action as `Billing -> All resources`. At the end, your policy should look like the following:

```
{
    "Version": "2012-10-17",
    "Statement": [
        {
            "Sid": "Statement1",
            "Effect": "Deny",
            "Action": [
                "billing:*"
            ],
            "Resource": [
                "*"
            ]
        }
    ]
}
```

5. Once you have crafted this policy, scroll down to the bottom of the page and click `Next`.

6. On the `Review and create` screen, enter the new policy name as `PB-Billing-Deny`. Once you have done that, scroll down to the bottom of the page and press the `Create policy` button.

Policy details

Policy name
Enter a meaningful name to identify this policy.

PB-Billing-Deny

Maximum 128 characters. Use alphanumeric and '+=,.@-_' characters.

Figure 14.5: The Policy details screen

7. Now, from within the IAM management console, select the user or role you would like to attach the permissions boundary to. In this example, you will see a user who has been given the `AdministratorAccess` AWS-managed policy permissions. To restrict this user's access either temporarily or permanently, you could use the permissions boundary you just created. Once you click on the user's name, you should be taken to the user's summary page.

Figure 14.6: The Summary screen for the user

8. Scroll down until you see the box labeled `Permissions boundary`. Click on the arrow on the left of the `Permissions boundary` header to expand the box.

Figure 14.7: The Permissions boundary screen

9. Click on the button labeled `Set permissions boundary`. This will bring you to a new screen where you can choose a policy to set as the boundary.

10. Search for the policy you just created by typing `PB` in the search box. Once you find your `PB-Billing-Deny` policy, select it and then press the `Set boundary` button.

Figure 14.8: The Permissions policies screen

Now that you know how to create a permissions boundary and attach it to a policy, you will review how the combination of SCP, permission boundaries, and identity-based policies all come together to form effective permissions.

Seeing Where Effective Permissions Reside

When using IAM, it's crucial to understand how policy requests are evaluated based on the service's internal logic. To help with this, here are the rules you should keep in mind:

- By default, all requests are denied (unless you are the root user).
- If any service has been explicitly denied, this explicit denial rule takes precedence, even if another rule has the service allowed.
- An explicit allow in a policy will override the default implicit deny.
- If an SCP, session policy, or permissions boundary grants access to a service, it will override the implicit deny.

For a deeper understanding of how the rules are processed, it is suggested that you read the official documentation from AWS on how rules are processed, which can be found at the following URL: `https://packt.link/i9hhb`.

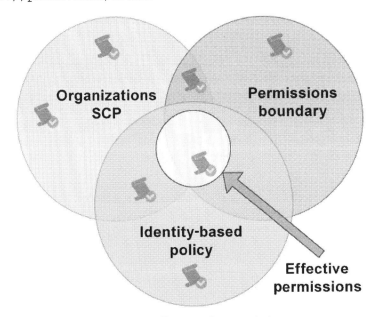

Figure 14.9: Effective policy permissions

Figure 14.9 is a Venn diagram of three circles with `Organizations SCP` (circle on the left), `Permissions boundary` (circle on the right), and `Identity-based policy` (circle at the bottom). With an identity-based policy, the user or group is granted permissions for that effective user. However, other identity policies at play can limit, or in some cases expand, the user's effective permissions. The center where all the policies intersect (highlighted by the arrow in the diagram) is the effective permission set for the user.

You now have an idea of where the effective permissions lie after combining multiple types of policies. Next, you will focus on policies applied at the organizational level: SCPs.

Understanding SCPs

SCPs in AWS provide fine-grained control over the permissions and actions that can be performed within an AWS organization. SCPs allow organizations to establish centralized governance and enforce security policies across multiple accounts.

SCPs provide six key benefits, discussed as follows:

- **Centralized governance**: SCPs enable organizations to define and enforce security policies centrally. By creating and attaching SPCs at the root level of an organization, you can establish a standard set of rules that apply to all accounts within the organization. This ensures consistent security configurations and helps maintain compliance with organizational standards.

- **The ability to limit access to AWS services and actions**: They also allow you to restrict access to specific AWS services and actions. You can define policies that deny or allow permissions for various services, API calls, or particular actions within those services. This enables you to tailor the level of access granted to different groups based on their specific needs, reducing the risk of unauthorized or accidental actions.

- **Enforcement of AWS services and actions**: SCPs also help enforce security best practices and compliance requirements across the organization. You can minimize the attack surface and mitigate potential risks by restricting access to certain services or actions through SCPs. They also play a crucial role in meeting regulatory or industry-specific compliance standards by enforcing policies that govern data privacy, access controls, and other security measures.

- **Segregation of duties**: SCPs facilitate the segregation of duties within the organization. By restricting certain actions to specific groups or accounts, you can ensure that no single entity has excessive privileges. This helps maintain accountability and reduces the risk of unauthorized or malicious activities.

- **The prevention of accidental changes**: SCPs can be used to prevent accidental changes or actions that could impact critical resources or infrastructure. By carefully defining and restricting permissions, you can reduce the likelihood of unintended modifications or deletions of data or resources that could lead to service disruptions or data loss.

- **Layered access control**: SCPs work in conjunction with IAM policies. While IAM policies focus on individual accounts or users, SCPs provide an additional layer of control at the organizational level. This layered approach allows for a combination of granular access control at the account/ user level and broad policy enforcement at the organization level.

By leveraging SCPs in AWS, organizations can establish a robust security framework, ensure consistent governance, enforce compliance requirements, and mitigate the risk of unauthorized access or actions across their AWS accounts and services.

Identifying Policy Structure and Syntax

An AWS IAM policy consists of several parts that define the permissions and access control rules for AWS resources. The different components of an IAM policy are as follows:

- **Version**: The `Version` field specifies the version of the IAM policy language being used. The current version is typically set to `2012-10-17`.

- **ID**: The `ID` field provides a unique identifier for the policy. It is optional and is mainly used for reference or management purposes.

- **Statement**: The `Statement` field is an array that contains one or more policy statements. Each statement defines a specific permission or access control rule. Multiple statements can be used to define different permissions within the same policy.

- **Sid**: The `Sid` field is an optional identifier for a statement. It is commonly used for reference and auditing purposes.

- **Effect**: The `Effect` field specifies whether the statement allows or denies access. There are only two options: `Allow` or `Deny`.

- **Action**: The `Action` field lists the AWS service actions that are allowed or denied. Actions represent specific operations that can be performed on AWS resources, such as `s3:GetObject` or `ec2:DescribeInstances`.

- **Resource**: The `Resource` field specifies the **Amazon Resource Name** (**ARN**) or resource identifier to which the policy statement applies. It defines the AWS resources to which the specified actions are allowed or denied.

- **Condition**: The `Condition` field allows you to define additional constraints or requirements for evaluating the statement. Conditions are optional and provide contextual factors that must be met for the statement to allow or deny access.

A sample policy that could be used to allow a user to list all users, groups, and roles in IAM would look like the following:

```
{
    "Version": "2012-10-17",
    "Statement": [
        {
            "Sid": "ListAllUsers",
            "Action": [
                "access-analyzer:ValidatePolicy",
                "iam:ListUsers",
                "iam:ListGroups",
                "iam:ListPolicies",
                "iam:ListRoles"
```

```
          ],
          "Effect": "Allow",
          "Resource": "*"
          "Condition": {
            "Bool": {
              "aws:MultiFactorAuthPresent": "false"
            }
          }
        }
      ]
}
```

IAM policies play a central role in controlling access to AWS resources. By defining the appropriate statements with desired effects, actions, resources, and optional conditions, you can effectively manage permissions and enforce security and compliance requirements within your AWS environment.

In the next section, you will take an even closer look at the condition field and how it can limit access to the resources and identities you specify for access.

Understanding the Use of Conditions in IAM Policies

Conditions in IAM policies allow you to control access to AWS resources based on additional contextual factors beyond the fundamental identity or resource information. For instance, suppose your company requires any documents in a specific S3 bucket or folder to require MFA in order to perform delete actions. Using regular actions in the policy, you can add `s3:DeleteObject`, but adding the condition clause of `"Bool": {"aws:MultiFactorAuthPresent": "true"}` would ensure that only those users who had MFA tied to their user accounts would be allowed to perform the action. Conditions help you create fine-grained access control rules by specifying additional requirements that must be met for an IAM policy to allow or deny access. Here's how you can use conditions in IAM policies:

- **Policy structure**: Conditions are specified within the `Condition` element of an IAM policy statement. Each condition consists of a key-value pair that defines the condition. Multiple conditions can be specified within the `Condition` element.

- **Condition keys**: Condition keys are predefined attributes you can use to construct conditions in IAM policies. AWS provides a wide range of condition keys that cover various aspects of the request context, including the IP address, request source, user agent, and tags. You can find the list of condition list keys at the following URL: `https://packt.link/8INtM`.

- **Comparison operators**: Comparison operators evaluate the condition keys against the desired values. Common comparison operators include *StringEquals*, *StringNotEquals*, *StringLike*, *NumericEquals*, and *DateGreaterThan*. The appropriate operator depends on the condition key and the desired condition.

- **Values**: Values are the specific values against which the condition key is evaluated. For example, you can specify an IP address, a tag value, a date, or any relevant value that applies to the condition key.

- **Combining conditions**: Multiple conditions can be combined using logical operators such as *And*, *Or*, and *Not*. This allows you to create complex conditions by combining multiple condition keys and comparison operators.

Understanding by Example

Suppose you want to create an IAM policy that allows users to access an S3 bucket only if they are accessing it from a specific IP range. You can achieve this using conditions in the policy. See this example policy statement:

```json
{
  "Version": "2012-10-17",
  "Statement": [
    {
      "Sid": "AllowBucketAccess",
      "Effect": "Allow",
      "Action": "s3:GetObject",
      "Resource": "arn:aws:s3:::example-bucket/*",
      "Condition": {
        "IpAddress": {
          "aws:SourceIp": "192.168.0.0/24"
        }
      }
    }
  ]
}
```

In the preceding example, the `IpAddress` condition key is used to specify that `aws:SourceIp` (source IP address of the request) should be in the CIDR value `192.168.0.0/24` range. Only requests originating from this specific IP range will be allowed to perform the `s3:GetObject` action on the S3 bucket specified in the `Resource` field.

By leveraging conditions in IAM policies, you can enforce more granular access control rules based on contextual factors, which enables you to tailor permissions based on specific requirements and increase the security of your AWS resources.

Now that you know how to use a conditional clause within an IAM policy, you might be thinking about the different conditions available to you. The next section will show you how to construct conditional clauses using a variety of conditional operators.

Key Conditional Terms to Know

To ensure you're fully aware of all the tools at your disposal before you attempt to craft more complex policies, there are some conditional terms and operators you should be familiar with.

> **Note**
> The list of key terms provided is not all-inclusive. You also need not memorize each and every term from the list for the certification test.

The purpose of this section is to show you the different ways to narrow the scope of permissions within AWS accounts and organizations and help you become familiar with the operators and condition operators. Remember that these policies (as of the time of publication) are written in JSON.

Condition operators are broken down into the following categories:

- String
- Numeric
- Date and time
- Boolean
- Binary
- IP address
- ARN
- `IfExists` (check whether the key value exists and needs an additional value)
- `NullCheck` (check whether the key value exists and does not need another value)

Now that you're familiar with some of the conditional operators, you'll next look at how to use the string operator to perform conditional checks.

String Operators

Table 14.1 presents the string condition operators and describes their features.

Condition Operator	Description
StringEquals	Exact matching, case sensitive
StringNotEquals	Negated matching
StringLike	Case-sensitive matching
StringNotLike	Negated case-sensitive matching

Table 14.1: String condition operators and their description

Using a string condition operator in the policy clause of a condition statement allows you to find exactly matching or similar values from the values being examined. Take the following example for a policy created for a user (or group), where the user needs permission to access a bucket, but only in the case where the folder in the bucket matches that particular user's username:

```
{
    "Version": "2012-10-17",
    "Statement": [
      {
        "Effect": "Allow",
        "Action": "s3:ListBucket",
        "Resource": "arn:aws:s3:::packt-user-data",
        "Condition": {"StringLike": {"s3:prefix": [
          "",
          "home/",
          "home/${aws:username}/"
        ]}}
      },
      {
        "Effect": "Allow",
        "Action": "s3:*",
        "Resource": [
          "arn:aws:s3:::packt-user-data/home/${aws:username}",
          "arn:aws:s3:::packt-user-data/home/${aws:username}/*"
        ]
      }
    ]
}
```

You can see from a combination of the *Condition* and *Resource* sections of the statement that a user who has this policy attached can list the home directory of the bucket and then perform any actions in their own folder and child folders of their username directory. They would not have access to data if they used folders with other usernames.

The Bool Condition Operator

You can use the `Bool` Boolean condition operator to evaluate a condition and control access based on the result. The `Bool` operator allows you to perform logical comparisons, such as checking whether a condition is `true` or `false`. Examine the following example policy to see how it's used:

```
{
  "Version": "2012-10-17",
  "Statement": {
    "Effect": "Allow",
    "Action": "s3:GetObject",
    "Resource": "arn:aws:s3:::example-bucket/*",
    "Condition": {
      "Bool": {
        "aws:MultiFactorAuthPresent": "true"
      }
    }
  }
}
```

In this example, the IAM policy allows the `s3:GetObject` action on objects within the `example-bucket` bucket if the condition specified by the `Bool` operator is `true`. The condition checks whether the user has enabled MFA by evaluating the `aws:MultiFactorAuthPresent` condition key.

IP Address Condition Operators

When you are trying to restrict usage to either known or unknown IP addresses, there are two operators available to you: `IpAddress` and `NotIpAddress`. *Table 14.2* shows the two IP address conditions available:

Conditions Operator	Description
IpAddress	The specified IP addresses from the specified range
NotIpAddress	All IP addresses except for the IP addresses from the specified range

Table 14.2: The two IP address conditions available

You can utilize IP address condition operators to create condition elements that control access based on a comparison between a key and an IPv4 or IPv6 address or a range of addresses. These operators are beneficial for filtering out specific IP addresses and ranges when used with the `aws:SourceIp` key. The value provided must adhere to the standard CIDR format, such as `192.168.0.0/24` for IPv4 or `2001:DB8:1234:5678::/64` for IPv6 addresses. If you specify an address without the associated routing prefix (the part of the IP address that is denominated by the slash followed by the number at the end of the CIDR address, i.e., `/16` or `/24`), IAM automatically assigns the default prefix value of `/32`.

By leveraging IP address condition operators in your IAM policy, you can effectively restrict access based on specific IP addresses or ranges, ensuring that only authorized sources are granted access to the specified AWS resources.

> **Note**
>
> If you would like to see the full list of conditional keys available for use in IAM policies, then you can either look at the IAM condition keys, available at `https://packt.link/loj0z`, or the global condition keys at the following URL: `https://packt.link/nuimW`.

You've now reviewed how to craft IAM policies that have narrow scopes using conditional operators. In the next section, you will learn how to manage the different policies you have created as they change over time.

Managing your IAM policies

Over time, you are likely to accumulate and use a long list of policies, especially as you create your own custom identity-based policies with highly specific permission sets of a user, group, or role. Therefore, it's important to have an understanding of some of the features available to you within the IAM service and console that help you manage the roles that you create in your AWS accounts.

When you access a policy within the AWS Management Console—for example, a custom policy that you have created—you will be presented with a page that looks like the following:

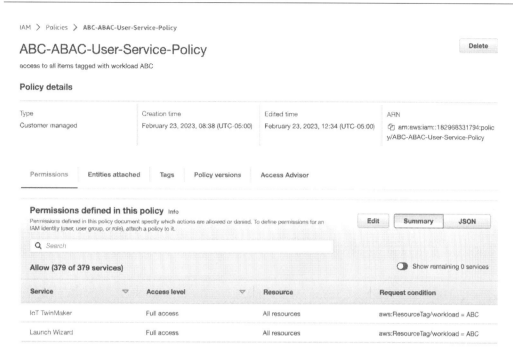

IAM > Policies > ABC-ABAC-User-Service-Policy

ABC-ABAC-User-Service-Policy

Delete

access to all items tagged with workload ABC

Policy details

Type	Creation time	Edited time	ARN
Customer managed	February 23, 2023, 08:38 (UTC-05:00)	February 23, 2023, 12:34 (UTC-05:00)	arn:aws:iam::182968331794:policy/ABC-ABAC-User-Service-Policy

Permissions | Entities attached | Tags | Policy versions | Access Advisor

Permissions defined in this policy Info

Permissions defined in this policy document specify which actions are allowed or denied. To define permissions for an IAM identity (user, user group, or role), attach a policy to it.

Edit | Summary | JSON

Q Search

Allow (379 of 379 services)

Show remaining 0 services

Service	Access level	Resource	Request condition
IoT TwinMaker	Full access	All resources	aws:ResourceTag/workload = ABC
Launch Wizard	Full access	All resources	aws:ResourceTag/workload = ABC

Figure 14.10: The Policy details screen

The page will display the policy ARN and the description of the policy that you added when you created the policy. Underneath the `Policy details` section, you will have the following tabs:

- **Permissions**
- **Entities attached**
- **Tags**
- **Policy versions**
- **Access Advisor**

Each of these tabs will help you gain a better understanding of how the policy is configured. The following sections discuss each of the tabs individually and detail the information and resources they provide.

Permissions

The `Permissions` tab is where you can view and manage the permissions associated with the policy. It displays the permissions attached to the policy and allows you to directly modify or remove them as needed. This allows you to make changes to the permission without the need to navigate to separate policy management sections, thereby streamlining the policy management process. The following screenshot shows all the permissions attached to the current policy.

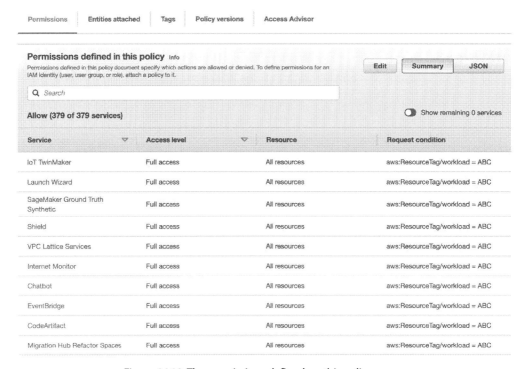

Figure 14.11: The permissions defined on this policy screen

Entities Attached

The `Entities attached` tab allows you to associate an entity (user, group, or role) with a policy as a set of permissions that the entity is allowed to perform. It also gives you the ability to use this policy as a permissions boundary for one or more entities. You can see from the following screenshot that the policy has now been attached to our user.

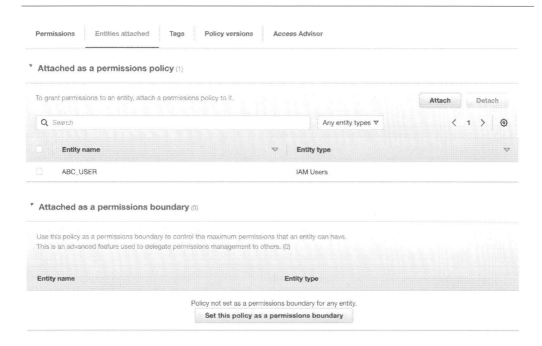

Figure 14.12: Entities attached to the policy

Tags

The Tags tab allows you to add key-value tag pairs to each specific IAM policy. The primary purpose of using tags in AWS (including for IAM entities) is to enable easier resource management and governance.

Tags enhance resource organization, allowing users to categorize and group resources based on common characteristics. This simplifies resource discovery and navigation, especially in large and complex environments. Also, tags facilitate cost allocation and tracking by providing granular insights into resource usage. Teams can use tags to analyze cost reports and identify the cost implications of specific resources or projects.

Another valuable feature of tags is that they support access control and governance by allowing policies to be applied based on tag values. This ensures that resources adhere to organizational policies and compliance standards. Finally, tags enhance automation and resource life cycle management, enabling the development of efficient, tag-aware workflows.

Figure 14.13 shows where the policy has been tagged with a key of `workload` and a value of ABC.

Figure 14.13: Policy tags

Policy Versions

This tab allows you to view, manage, and track different versions of an IAM policy. Each IAM policy version represents a specific iteration of the policy document. The tab displays all the versions associated with the selected IAM policy as well as the history of the changes made over time. You can compare different versions of an IAM policy side by side to understand the differences between the versions. The `Policy versions` tab also allows you to create new versions, delete unwanted versions, or set a specific version as the default one. The default version is used for evaluating policy permissions if a specific version is not specified in the IAM role or user policies.

The following screenshot shows multiple versions of the same policy as well as which version is the default version.

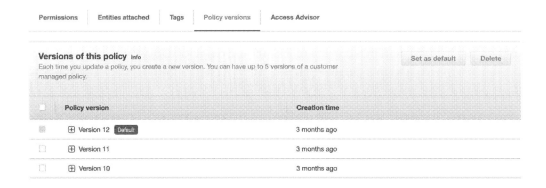

Figure 14.14: Policy versions

Access Advisor

The `Access Advisor` tab provides valuable insights into the permissions and access patterns of IAM entities, such as users, roles, and groups. The tab offers a comprehensive analysis of the services and actions accessed by IAM entities over a specified time period. It provides visibility into the exact API calls made by the entity, including information on the service, action, and the last time the action was accessed. Access Advisor helps identify unused or underutilized permissions assigned to an IAM entity. It highlights actions that the entity has not accessed within the specified time frame, suggesting potential opportunities to review and tighten the entity's permissions to adhere to the principle of least privilege. The insights provided by Access Advisor can be used for permission optimization. By reviewing the accessed actions and comparing them to the entity's intended responsibilities, you can fine-tune the permissions assigned to achieve a more streamlined and secure IAM environment.

Additionally, by examining the access history and usage patterns from the `Access Advisor` tab, you can perform security audits and detect any suspicious or unexpected activities associated with IAM entities. Unusual access patterns or unexpected API calls can indicate potential security risks, and `Access Advisor` helps you identify and investigate such anomalies.

The following screenshot shows the access history and services accessed by `ABC_USER`.

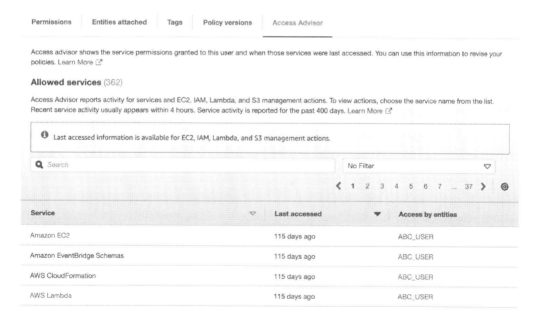

Figure 14.15: Access history and services accessed by the user

You have now reviewed how to use the IAM console to review your policies in depth. The next section will demonstrate how you provide access to a secondary account using cross-account access.

Configuring Cross-Account Access Using IAM Policies

Cross-account access in AWS provides a way for you to securely collaborate and share resources with other AWS accounts. By configuring cross-account access, you can grant permissions to trusted accounts, allowing them to access and manage specific resources in your account. This helps you facilitate collaboration with partners, vendors, or different teams within your organization.

With cross-account access, you establish a trust relationship between your account and the other trusted accounts. You create an IAM role in your account that defines the permissions you want to grant. Then, you specify the trusted accounts that are allowed to assume the role and then define the actions, resources, and conditions for access.

Once the role is assumed in the trusted account, the user or role in that account receives temporary security credentials with the permissions you defined. These credentials can be used to access resources, such as S3 buckets, EC2 instances, or other services, depending on the permissions that you have granted to the role.

By leveraging cross-account access in AWS, you can maintain a higher level of security and control. You can grant fine-grained permissions, allowing trusted accounts to access only the specific resources that they need while ensuring that sensitive data or critical infrastructure remains protected.

Cross-account access also promotes collaboration and simplifies resource sharing. You can securely work with external partners or enable different teams within your organization to access resources without the need to create multiple accounts or share credentials. It provides a more streamlined and controlled approach to sharing resources while maintaining a clear separation of responsibilities between accounts.

ACLs in AWS are primarily used to control access to network resources, such as Amazon S3 buckets and Amazon VPC subnets. While ACLs are not directly involved in configuring cross-account access, you can use the following AWS services in combination with ACLs to enable cross-account access using ACLs:

- **AWS IAM**: IAM is the key service for managing access to AWS resources. To enable cross-account access, you can use IAM roles and policies to define permissions for the trusted accounts. By creating IAM roles with appropriate permissions and attaching them to the trusted accounts, you can grant cross-account access. The IAM policies associated with the roles control what actions can be performed on the resources.

- **AWS S3 bucket policies**: When granting cross-account access to Amazon S3 buckets, you can use S3 bucket policies in conjunction with ACLs. The bucket policy allows you to specify the permissions for the trusted accounts or IAM roles from other accounts. The bucket policy defines who can access the bucket, what actions they can perform (such as list, read, or write), and which objects they can access. By combining the bucket policy and ACLs, you can configure granular access controls for cross-account access to S3 buckets.

- **VPC network ACLs and security groups**: In Amazon VPC, you can use network ACLs and security groups to control cross-account access to subnets and instances. Network ACLs define inbound and outbound traffic rules at the subnet level, allowing you to control access from specific IP addresses or CIDR blocks. Security groups, on the other hand, provide granular control over inbound and outbound traffic at the instance level. By configuring appropriate rules in network ACLs and security groups, you can enable cross-account access to resources within a VPC.

ACLs

Although they might seem similar in nomenclature, it's important not to confuse ACLs with **network access control lists** (**NACLs**), the latter of which are used to control network traffic. Amazon S3 employs ACLs that function similarly to resource-based policies. These ACLs can be associated with S3 buckets, and uniquely, they can also be linked to individual S3 objects, a capability not shared with S3 bucket policies.

ACLs are primarily used in relation to Amazon S3 buckets. S3 ACLs are a legacy method for controlling access to S3 buckets and objects, although it is recommended to use S3 bucket policies or IAM policies for more robust and fine-grained access control. The following list discusses how ACLs are used specifically in relation to S3:

- **Controlling bucket-level access**: S3 ACLs can be used to control access at the bucket level. You can specify permissions for different AWS accounts or predefined groups (e.g., authorized users, all users, etc.), to determine who can perform specific actions on the entire bucket. This includes actions such as listing objects, uploading objects, or deleting objects.

- **Managing object-level permissions**: S3 ACLs can also be used to manage access to individual objects (i.e., the files stored in your bucket) within a bucket. You can select object-level permissions using ACLs to grant or revoke access for specific AWS accounts or predefined groups. This allows you to control read, write, and delete access on a per-object basis.

- **Combining with IAM policies**: Although not commonly used together, S3 ACLs can be combined with IAM policies to provide additional access control options. IAM policies define permissions for IAM users, groups, or roles and can be used in conjunction with S3 ACLs to set more granular access controls. An example of this would be where you have an S3 bucket where you want to grant a specific set of users read access to that bucket. Within that bucket, suppose there is a folder that only certain users of that group would have permission to write to. In this case, you could then grant the read access with an IAM policy, most likely with a user attribute condition where the users belong to the same group, and then the S3 ACL would be applied to the specific folder granting the write permission only to the specific users who need that authorization.

It's important to note that S3 bucket policies and IAM policies provide more flexible and robust access control mechanisms compared to ACLs. Bucket policies allow you to define permissions using a JSON-based policy language, and IAM policies provide centralized access management for AWS services, including S3.

When configuring ACLs, you have a number of options as to who can access the object or bucket via an ACL:

- **Access for other AWS accounts**: Using this option, you can enter the email address of the account owner or the canonical ID of the AWS account.

- **Public access**: This is a pre-configured S3 group created by AWS and allows anyone on the internet to gain access to the objects in your bucket. This should be used with extreme caution, as there is a risk of data exposure by AWS accounts due to public access policies on S3 buckets. Ensure that no sensitive or confidential data is stored within an object or bucket that has public access.

- **S3 log delivery group**: This is another pre-configured S3 group created by AWS. This option allows write permission to the bucket for S3 server access logging. If this logging is configured, these logs can be useful from a security and audit perspective.

To gain a better perspective of these options, complete the following short, interactive learning exercise with the S3 service:

1. Log in to the AWS Management Console and navigate to S3. You can do this quickly by using the following URL: `https://packt.link/kTONa`.

2. Select a previously created bucket that you would like to configure the permissions for. This example here uses `packt-object-test`. Click on the bucket name to view a menu of options for the bucket.

Figure 14.16: List of S3 buckets

3. Once inside your selected bucket, you should see a horizontal menu of options for the bucket. Click on the menu item named `Permissions`.

4. Inside the permissions settings, scroll down the page until you find the heading labeled `Access control list (ACL)`.

    You will see the default ACL applied to the bucket, which allows bucket objects to be listed and written from the account that owns the bucket, along with the ability to both read and write the bucket ACL.

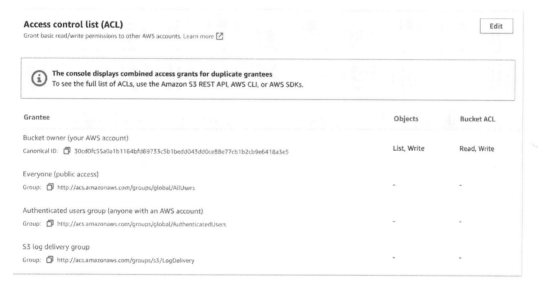

Figure 14.17: Permission in S3 bucket

5. Click on the `Edit` button in the top-left corner of the ACL box.

    You will now be on the screen that allows you the ability to modify the permissions of this bucket's ACL. Take notice of certain sections where you can allow access to the authenticated users group; this is any user with an AWS account.

6. Click on the button at the bottom of the access control list labeled Add grantee. You will see an extra set of options appear for allowing access from another AWS account; however, you will need their canonical ID to provide access.

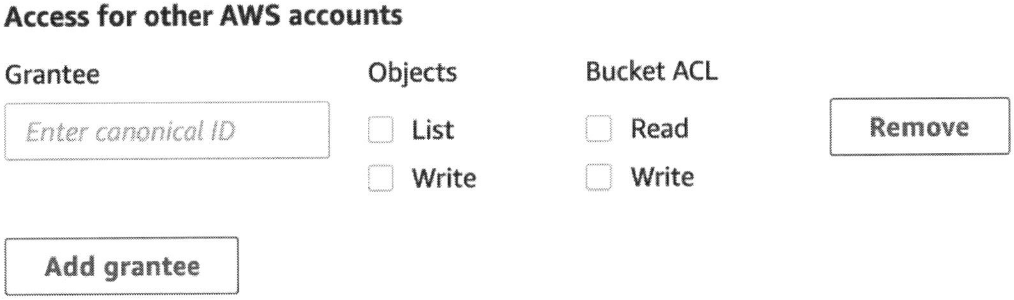

Access for other AWS accounts

Grantee	Objects	Bucket ACL	
Enter canonical ID	☐ List ☐ Write	☐ Read ☐ Write	Remove

Add grantee

Figure 14.18: Setting permissions for S3

Understanding Canonical IDs

In AWS, a canonical ID is a unique identifier assigned to an AWS account or user. It is a string of characters that serves as a globally unique identifier for the account or user within the AWS ecosystem. Canonical IDs are primarily used in specific scenarios, such as managing access control for Amazon S3 bucket permissions.

Here's an example of a canonical ID:

b035577b325d98aa1e72ca0000EXAMPLE

When working with Amazon S3 bucket permissions, the canonical ID is used to grant or deny access to specific AWS accounts or users. It provides a more reliable and secure way to specify access permissions compared to using AWS account numbers or user-friendly names, as those can potentially change over time. This is also often done for security and privacy reasons, as the canonical ID doesn't reveal the account's identity to external parties.

For example, in an S3 bucket policy, you might have a statement like the following:

```
{
  "Effect": "Allow",
  "Principal": {
    "CanonicalUser": "b035577b325d98aa1e72ca0000EXAMPLE"
  },
  "Action": "s3:GetObject",
  "Resource": "arn:aws:s3:::abcuser-bucket/*"
}
```

Canonical IDs are also typically used when configuring bucket policies or ACLs in Amazon S3. When granting permissions to another account or user, you can specify their canonical ID to ensure that the permissions are correctly applied to the intended account or user.

It's important to note that canonical IDs are not visible or accessible to AWS account holders by default. They are internal identifiers used by AWS for authentication and authorization purposes. If you need to retrieve the canonical ID for your own account, you can contact AWS support for assistance.

Using Roles to Provide Cross-Account Access

Roles and role assumptions are secure methods for granting limited access to third parties who have their own AWS account but require restricted access to your account. This could include third-party partners or auditors who need read-only access. By creating a role in your AWS account and allowing trusted third-party accounts to assume that role, you can control and monitor the access they have. Role assumption enables you to collaborate effectively with external parties while maintaining control over the level of access that they are granted, ensuring the security and confidentiality of your resources.

For this exercise, you will need two accounts, as follows:

Account A: This will be the account where you will create a role that will be assumed.

Account B: This will be the account will be working in and will use one of your previously created users to assume the role created by Account A from this other account, Account B.

Before you start, it would be a good idea to know the account numbers and have them in a text document labeled `Account A` and `Account B`. This will make things easier as you get through the process of setting up the role. If you don't know your AWS account number then the easiest way to find it is to click on your username at the top of the main menu. In the drop-down menu that appears, one of the items is `account`, with your account number.

You will start the process with `Account A` (the new account) and create the role to be assumed as follows:

1. Sign in to the console with a user on `Account A` who has either admin user privileges or the ability to create IAM users and roles.
2. Navigate to the IAM service at `https://packt.link/ctDkD`.
3. In the left-hand side menu, click `Roles`.
4. Once the `Roles` screen appears in the main window, click the button labeled `Create role`.

5.   The type of trusted identity you want to choose on the next screen is `Another AWS account`, as illustrated in the following screenshot:

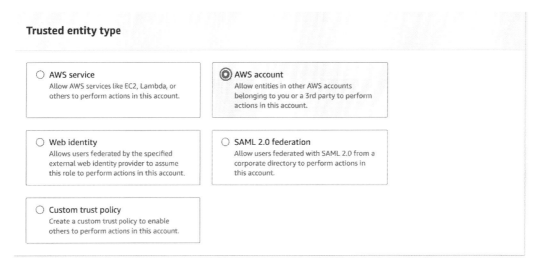

Figure 14.19: Role creation screen

6.   Enter the account number of `Account B` into the account field and then press the `Next: Permissions` button at the bottom of the page.

7.   On the `Attach permissions policies` page, type `S3FullAccess` into the search box. This should bring up the `AmazonS3FullAccess` policy. Click the box next to this policy name. After you have checked the box, click the button labeled `Next: Tags` at the bottom of the page, as illustrated in the following screenshot:

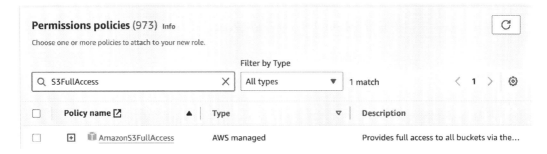

Figure 14.20: Policy selection screen

8. You will not be adding any tags in this exercise, so just click the button at the bottom of the screen that says `Next: Review`.

9. Once you get to the `Review` page, name your role `AssumeS3`. If you would like to type a description, you can do so (see the example description in the following screenshot), but this is not necessary. Make sure that everything looks correct, and then click the `Create role` button at the bottom.

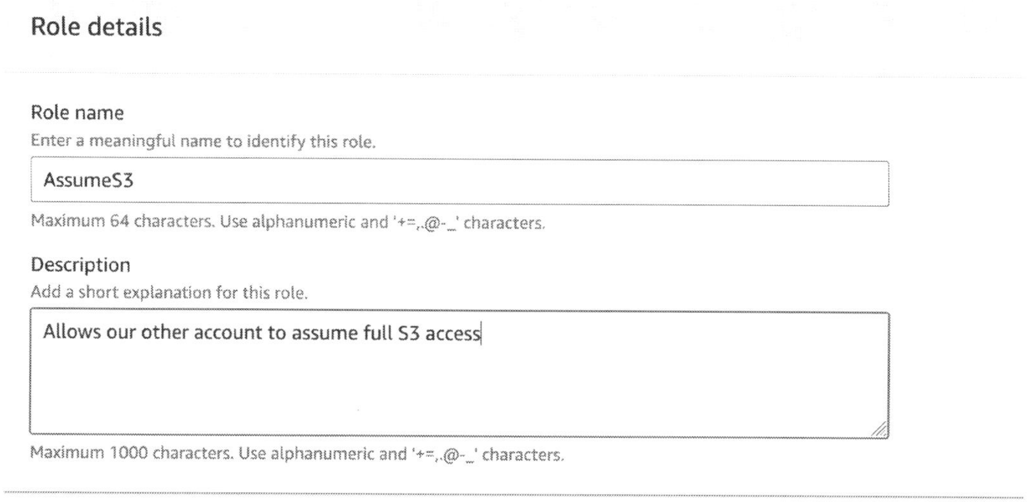

Role details

Role name

Enter a meaningful name to identify this role.

> AssumeS3

Maximum 64 characters. Use alphanumeric and '+=,.@-_' characters.

Description

Add a short explanation for this role.

> Allows our other account to assume full S3 access

Maximum 1000 characters. Use alphanumeric and '+=,.@-_' characters.

Figure 14.21: Create role screen

Now that you have your role set up in `Account A`, you can log out of this account and then log back in to `Account B`. You can use this new role to switch from your main role to the `AssumeS3` role in `Account A` by following these steps:

1. Once you have logged in, click on your name in the top-right corner to open the drop-down menu (you did this previously to find your account numbers).

2. In the drop-down menu, click on the item labeled Switch Roles, as illustrated in the following screenshot:

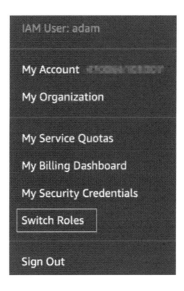

Figure 14.22: User menu in AWS

3. Now, on the Switch Roles screen, click the button labeled Switch Role.

4. On the next screen, you will be presented with three textboxes to fill out, as follows:

    A. In the box labeled Account, cut and paste the account number from Account A.

    B. In the box labeled Role, type in the name of the role you created previously (AssumeS3).

    C. In the box labeled Display Name, type in AccountA_S3, as illustrated in the following screenshot:

Figure 14.23: Role switching screen

With this information entered, you are now ready to switch roles.

5. After entering all the information, click the `Switch Role` button.

6. You should now be in `Account A` with the `AssumeS3` permissions signified by the color at the top of the menu bar, along with the display name of the role, as illustrated in the following screenshot:

Figure 14.24: Color-coded account name

You now have an understanding of how roles can help you manage the permissions in your own account, as well as giving you the ability to take on a defined permission set in another account.

Summary

This chapter discussed the different types of access policies used in AWS. These included SCPs, identity-based policies, resource-based policies, and permissions boundaries. You saw some of the granular constructs of creating policies, especially in the case of conditions, and how you can use those constructs to narrow down the scope of the permissions of a policy to the least-privileged access.

You also reviewed how to provide access to a secondary account using roles rather than separate accounts. Using this method can allow you to provide access to third parties who need access to your account for a specific reason and already have their own AWS accounts and IAM users. In addition to using roles, you also learned how using ACLs can enable cross-account access for different types of resources.

In *Chapter 15, Federated and Mobile Access,* you will examine what federated access is as well as how to allow access to your account from mobile devices using identity providers. You will learn how to use the AWS Cognito service and learn the differences between user pools and identity pools.

Further Reading

For additional information on the AWS Shared Responsibility Model and the underlying foundation of AWS security, please check out the following resources:

*   Introduction to AWS Security: `https://packt.link/ZiGxG`

*   Example IAM identity-based policies: `https://packt.link/uv4tF`

*   IAM JSON policy elements: Condition operators: `https://packt.link/QFj56`

Exam Readiness Drill – Chapter Review Questions

Apart from a solid understanding of key concepts, being able to think quickly under time pressure is a skill that will help you ace your certification exam. That is why working on these skills early on in your learning journey is key.

Chapter review questions are designed to improve your test-taking skills progressively with each chapter you learn and review your understanding of key concepts in the chapter at the same time. You'll find these at the end of each chapter.

> **How To Access These Resources**
>
> To learn how to access these resources, head over to the chapter titled *Chapter 21, Accessing the Online Practice Resources*.

To open the Chapter Review Questions for this chapter, perform the following steps:

1. Click the link – `https://packt.link/SCSC02E2_CH14`

    Alternatively, you can scan the following QR code (*Figure 14.25*):

Figure 14.25: QR code that opens Chapter Review Questions for logged-in users

2.   Once you log in, you'll see a page similar to the one shown in *Figure 14.26*:

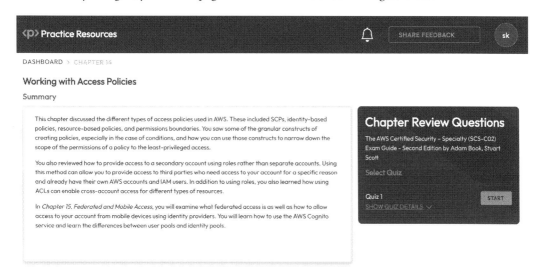

Figure 14.26: Chapter Review Questions for Chapter 14

3.   Once ready, start the following practice drills, re-attempting the quiz multiple times.

Exam Readiness Drill

For the first three attempts, don't worry about the time limit.

ATTEMPT 1

The first time, aim for at least **40%**. Look at the answers you got wrong and read the relevant sections in the chapter again to fix your learning gaps.

ATTEMPT 2

The second time, aim for at least **60%**. Look at the answers you got wrong and read the relevant sections in the chapter again to fix any remaining learning gaps.

ATTEMPT 3

The third time, aim for at least **75%**. Once you score **75%** or more, you start working on your timing.

> **Tip**
> You may take more than three attempts to reach 75%. That's okay. Just review the relevant sections in the chapter till you get there.

Working On Timing

Target: Your aim is to keep the score the same while trying to answer these questions as quickly as possible. Here's an example of how your next attempts should look like:

Attempt	Score	Time Taken
Attempt 5	77%	21 mins 30 seconds
Attempt 6	78%	18 mins 34 seconds
Attempt 7	76%	14 mins 44 seconds

Table 14.3: Sample timing practice drills on the online platform

> **Note**
> The time limits shown in the above table are just examples. Set your own time limits with each attempt based on the time limit of the quiz on the website.

With each new attempt, your score should stay above 75% while your time taken to complete should **decrease**. Repeat as many attempts as you want till you feel confident dealing with the time pressure.

15

Federated and Mobile Access

Even though this is not explicitly called out as one of the items in the exam outline, knowing how to connect your accounts via federated methods will be useful when answering the exam questions. Understanding the concepts of the **Security Assertion Markup Language** (**SAML**) and **identity providers** (**IdPs**) and how they simplify secure access to your accounts is key. There may be standalone questions related to these concepts or they may be embedded within questions on other topics. This chapter will cover the necessary aspects of these important topics so that when these items come up, both in the exam and in your real-life tasks, you will have the understanding needed to tackle them with confidence.

The following main topics will be covered in this chapter:

- What is federated access?
- Enabling SSO with corporate account identities using SAML
- Social federation
- Amazon Cognito

Technical Requirements

You must have a basic understanding of AWS services and networking concepts.

What Is Federated Access?

In the context of AWS, **federated access** refers to a mechanism that allows users to access AWS resources using their existing identity and credentials from an external IdP. It enables users to authenticate and authorize their access to AWS services without the need for separate AWS-specific credentials.

In a typical federated access scenario, the user's identity is managed by an external IdP, such as Microsoft Azure Active Directory, Okta, or an on-premises identity system. The IdP serves as a trusted authority that authenticates the user and issues security tokens to represent the user's identity.

When a user attempts to access AWS resources, they are redirected to the IdP for authentication. Once the user's identity is verified, the IdP issues an access token or security assertion, such as a SAML token or an **OpenID Connect (OIDC)** token. This token contains the necessary information to identify the user and specify their access rights.

The user then presents this token to AWS for verification. AWS validates the token with the IdP to ensure its authenticity and checks the access privileges associated with the user's identity. If the token is valid and the user is authorized, AWS grants access to the requested resources.

With a basic understanding of what federated access is and how it works, it should be clear now why you would want to federate your account with access to your SAML-enabled provider. However, you might wonder whether there are times when it doesn't make sense to use federation. There are, and the next section presents some of those exact scenarios.

Reasons Not to Use Federated Access with Your AWS Account

While federated access offers numerous benefits, there are certain scenarios where it may not be the best choice for managing access to your AWS account. Some of the reasons why it may not be suitable for you are as follows:

- **Dependency on an external IdP**: Federated access relies on an external IdP for user authentication and authorization. If the IdP experiences an outage or has connectivity issues, it may impact your users' ability to access AWS resources. Therefore, this dependency introduces an additional layer of complexity and potential points of failure in the authentication process.

- **Limited control and flexibility**: When using federated access, your control and flexibility over user management and access policies are limited by the capabilities and configurations of the chosen IdP. You may face constraints in terms of customizing IAM policies, fine-grained permissions, and other AWS-specific features. If you require granular control over access management or have specific requirements that the IdP cannot fulfill, federated access may not be the ideal solution.

- **Complexity of setup and maintenance**: Setting up federated access involves configuring trust relationships between AWS and the IdP, mapping roles, and ensuring that the integration of the two works smoothly. This process can be more complex and time-consuming compared to creating and managing AWS IAM users directly. Additionally, ongoing maintenance, updates, and troubleshooting may be required to keep the federated access infrastructure operational.

- **Performance considerations**: Federated access introduces additional network communication and verification steps between AWS and the IdP during the authentication process. Depending on the scale and latency of your environment, this can result in increased authentication times and potentially impact the overall performance of your applications and servers.

- **Unique use case requirements**: Certain use cases, such as scripting or programmatic access to AWS resources, may not align well with federated access. IAM users with long-term access keys are often more suitable for automated processes, scripts, or third-party tools that require programmatic access to AWS APIs.

- **Complexity for third-party applications**: If you use third-party applications or services that integrate with AWS, they might require AWS IAM user credentials instead of federated access. These applications may not support federated access or may have limitations in their integration capabilities, which could restrict your ability to use federated access in these scenarios.

While federated access provides many benefits, it may not be the best fit for every situation. Consider the factors presented to your unique situation when deciding to adopt federated access for your AWS account.

In the next section, you will see how to enable **single sign-on** (**SSO**) with a corporate account using SAML.

Enabling SSO with Corporate Account Identities Using SAML

IAM Identity Center enables identity federation using the widely adopted SAML 2.0 standard. SAML 2.0 allows the secure exchange of user information between an IdP and a **service provider** (**SP**). With IAM Identity Center, authorized users can enjoy federated SSO access to applications within the AWS Management Console.

By integrating SAML IdP capabilities into your managed Microsoft AD or IAM Identity Center identity store, users can seamlessly sign in to SAML-supported services. This includes the AWS Management Console and popular third-party applications such as Microsoft 365, SAP Concur, and Salesforce. IAM Identity Center leverages the exchanged SAML assertions to facilitate a smooth and secure user experience across multiple platforms.

While SAML is primarily used within an enterprise environment, you may want to have outside users gain specific access to data or services in your account. Social federation can be of help in such situations. The next section will discuss social federation, showing how you can authenticate to your service using pre-existing accounts from social media or third-party IdPs.

Using Social Federation

Social federation allows you to build your applications to request temporary credentials. In simple terms, social federation refers to the ability to use your existing social media accounts, such as Google or Facebook, to log in to other websites or services without creating new usernames or passwords. It makes the sign-in process more convenient and streamlined.

Social federation works by establishing a connection between the website or app you want to access and your social media account. When you choose to sign in with your social media account, the website, service, or app requests permission from the social media platform to verify your identity. Once your identity is confirmed, you are granted access to the website or app without having to create or manage another set of credentials.

Social federation typically utilizes OIDC or **OAuth** as tokens to facilitate seamless and secure authentication and authorization processes across multiple platforms and applications, including AWS resources. OIDC provides authentication services, allowing users to log in to different platforms using their existing social media or IdP accounts. At the same time, OAuth enables authorization by granting access to specific resources or functionalities based on user permissions.

The advantage of social federation is that it simplifies the sign-in process, eliminates the need to remember multiple usernames and passwords, and saves time when you are accessing different online services. It also provides a level of trust and familiarity when you are using accounts from well-known social media platforms.

With a basic understanding of how social federation works, you will next see how the Amazon Cognito service can use social federation to easily incorporate accounts and logins already owned by your user base to gain measured access to specific areas of your AWS account.

Understanding the Amazon Cognito Service

Amazon Cognito is a service that simplifies and secures user authentication and management in various applications, such as web, mobile, and **Internet of Things** (**IoT**) applications. The benefits of the Cognito service can be summed up as follows:

- **User experience and engagement**: Amazon Cognito helps improve the user experience in applications by providing a seamless and secure authentication process. It ensures that users can easily register and sign in to your applications using their preferred methods, such as usernames and passwords or social media accounts. This enhances user engagement and satisfaction, increasing your applications' adoption and usage.

- **Security and compliance**: Cognito offers robust security features to protect user accounts and sensitive data. It supports **multi-factor authentication** (**MFA**), ensuring an extra layer of security beyond passwords. It also helps organizations comply with security and privacy regulations by securely storing and managing user information. With Cognito, you can provide users with a safe and trusted environment for accessing your applications.

- **Accelerated development**: By utilizing Cognito, your development team can save valuable time and effort on building complex user management functionalities from scratch. Cognito provides **pre-built authentication components, customizable UIs**, and **integration with social media logins**. This enables your team to focus more on core business functionality and accelerates the development of your applications.

- **Scalability and flexibility**: Cognito is designed to handle millions of users, making it suitable for applications with high user volumes or rapidly growing user bases. It seamlessly scales to meet the demands of your applications without compromising performance or security. Additionally, Cognito offers flexibility in integrating with other AWS services and third-party applications, allowing you to leverage existing infrastructure and systems.

- **SSO capabilities**: Cognito supports SSO, which means that users can access multiple applications with a single set of credentials. This streamlines the user experience by eliminating the need to remember multiple usernames and passwords. It also simplifies user onboarding and offboarding processes, ensuring efficient management of user access across various applications.

- **Cross-platform compatibility**: Cognito provides **software development kits** (SDKs) for various platforms, including web, mobile, and IoT devices. This allows your applications to provide a consistent and secure user experience across different platforms, enhancing usability and compatibility across your entire customer journey.

After learning about how Amazon Cognito simplifies user authentication and management along with enhancing security, you might be wondering about some specific situations where you would use Amazon Cognito. The following section will take you through specific scenarios in which Cognito would be a good fit.

When to Use Amazon Cognito

Previous sections of this chapter have described the capabilities of Amazon Cognito but you have yet to learn in which situations implementing Amazon Cognito in your application makes the most sense. The following points discuss some common use cases:

- **Web and mobile applications**: Amazon Cognito is frequently used in web and mobile applications to handle user registration, sign-in, and profile management. It provides out-of-the-box authentication features, customizable UI components, and integration with social IdPs, allowing developers to quickly implement secure user authentication flows.

- **SSO solutions**: Cognito can be utilized to build SSO solutions, enabling users to sign in once and access multiple applications seamlessly. It acts as the central IdP, handling authentication across different services and granting users access based on their authenticated identity.

- **Secure APIs**: Cognito can be employed to secure APIs by acting as an authentication layer. It integrates with Amazon API Gateway, allowing developers to enforce authentication and authorization policies for API endpoints. This ensures that only authenticated and authorized users can access sensitive API resources.

- **Enterprise applications**: In enterprise environments, Cognito can manage user identities and access control for internal applications. It allows organizations to integrate with existing identity systems, such as AD, LDAP, or SAML-based systems, enabling seamless user authentication and management across various applications.

- **Serverless applications**: With the rise of serverless architectures, Cognito can be utilized to handle user authentication and authorization in serverless applications. It seamlessly integrates with AWS Lambda and other serverless services, enabling secure access control and user management without the need to manage infrastructure.

- **Multi-platform application development**: Cognito is suitable for scenarios where developers need to build applications that span multiple platforms, such as web, mobile, and IoT. It provides SDKs and libraries for various platforms, making it easier to implement consistent authentication.

User Pools

Amazon Cognito user pools are one of two primary components of Amazon Cognito. They allow you to create and manage user identities, handle user registration and sign-in, and securely authenticate users.

With user pools, you can set up customizable sign-up and sign-in pages for your applications, support different authentication methods (such as linking username/password, social login, or corporate identities), and manage user profile information. They also offer security features such as MFA and integration with AWS services.

Furthermore, user pools take care of user registration, authentication, and profile management, making it easier for developers to handle user accounts and security in their applications without reinventing the wheel. Once a user is authenticated via the user pool, either from the user pool itself or via a third-party IdP, Amazon Cognito will generate tokens that manage the access to your cloud-based or mobile application.

It is also possible to enable additional features using user pools, such as MFA to provide additional security to your user base. You can also create user pool groups and assign different permissions to each. This provides greater access control and prevents all users from having the same access, which might pose a security risk.

As part of the authentication response, when a user successfully authenticates with a user pool, Amazon Cognito generates a **JSON Web Token** (**JWT**). This JWT serves as proof of authentication and contains information about the user, such as their identity, user attributes, and authentication status. The JWT is typically used by the client application's subsequent requests for access to protected resources within the application.

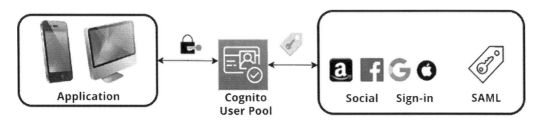

Figure 15.1: Cognito user pool authentication

When a user seeks authentication through Amazon Cognito using an IdP to access a user pool, as shown in *Figure 15.1* on the right-hand side, a streamlined process ensures security and ease of access. Initially, the user interacts with the application or service, shown on the far left, which then redirects the user to Amazon Cognito's authentication page. From there, the user selects the preferred IdP, such as Google or Facebook, providing credentials for authentication. Upon successful authentication, the IdP generates an authentication assertion, including user identity details, and sends it back to Amazon Cognito. Amazon Cognito validates the assertion, exchanging it for temporary AWS credentials and a JWT. This JWT holds pertinent user information and is used for subsequent authorization within the user pool, granting access to requested resources within the application or service.

User pools in Amazon Cognito provide the functionality of refreshing expired or expiring access tokens. When a user presents a refresh token, the Amazon Cognito service verifies its validity and issues a new access token. The new access token is a JWT that allows the user to continue accessing protected resources without re-entering their credentials.

Once your users are stored in a Cognito user pool, you need to provide them with a set of permissions that will enable them to access the AWS resources that your application uses. This is what you will learn about in the next section with Cognito identity pools.

Identity Pools

The second primary component of Amazon Cognito is identity pools. These pools serve as a means to access AWS services by providing the necessary credentials. Through an identity pool, you can generate unique identities for your users, granting them temporary access credentials to AWS services.

Examining the workflow depicted in *Figure 15.2*, you will observe that the user initiates the login process (typically through an application on their device) using a web-based IdP. After successful authentication with the web IdP, a `GetId` request is sent to Amazon Cognito for validation. Subsequently, the application proceeds with a `GetCredentialsForIdentity` request. Cognito, once again, validates this request. At this stage, Cognito communicates with **Security Token Service (STS)**, obtaining a short-lived token for the authorized services associated with the application. Finally, Cognito returns the acquired token to the application, as illustrated in the following diagram:

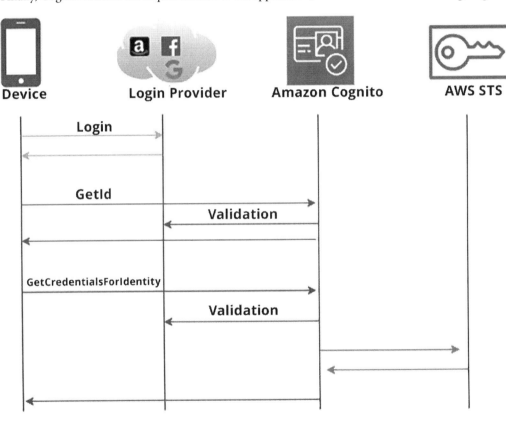

Figure 15.2: Authorization flow of a Cognito identity pool

> **Memory tip**
> User pools provide the authentication, whereas identity pools provide the authorization.

After examining how Cognito identity pools perform the authorization process, you will now explore how user pools work in conjunction with Amazon Cognito.

How User and Identity Pools Work Together

In Amazon Cognito, user pools and identity pools work together to provide a comprehensive solution for user management, authentication, and access to AWS resources. The following points summarize how they work together:

- **User pools**: User pools are used to manage identities and provide user authentication within your application. When you create a user pool, it acts as a user directory where users can sign up, sign in, and manage their profiles. User pools handle user registration and authentication and generate JWTs to authenticate and authorize access to your application's backend services.

- **Identity pools**: Identity pools allow you to grant your users temporary AWS credentials to access AWS resources. Identity pools enable users to sign in to your application using their *user pool credentials* or other IdPs (such as social media accounts or corporate identities). They act as a bridge between user authentication and AWS service access.

The interaction between user pools and identity pools usually follows these steps:

1. **User authentication**: Users sign in to your application using their credentials (username/password) or other IdPs (social logins, SAML, etc.). User pools handle the authentication process and return tokens (such as JWTs) to your application.

2. **Obtaining identity credentials**: After successful authentication with the user pool, your application can request temporary AWS credentials from the associated identity pool. These credentials are specific to the authenticated user and their authorized access to AWS resources.

3. **Access to AWS resources**: With the obtained temporary AWS credentials, your application can access AWS resources on behalf of the user. The identity pool ensures the user has appropriate permissions based on the configured IAM roles and policies.

By combining user and identity pools, you can achieve a seamless user experience with a unified authentication process while granting your users authorized access to AWS resources. User pools handle user authentication and management, while identity pools connect authenticated users with AWS services, providing temporary credentials for secure access.

It's important to note that user pools and identity pools are both managed by Amazon Cognito but serve different purposes.

Summary

In this chapter, you looked at federated access, what it is, and when (and when not) to use it. You also learned about SAML and how it is primarily used for enterprise federations where trusted entities exchange authentication and authorization data.

Finally, as the chapter wrapped up, you reviewed the Amazon Cognito service. You read in depth about the differences between user pools and identity pools and went through the job function for each pool type. You saw how, once a user is authenticated to a user pool, they are issued a JWT. You also learned how user data is stored in the JWT for later use in the user pool.

In the next chapter, you will look extensively at AWS Directory Service and the different varieties of it available to you in AWS.

Further Reading

For additional information on AWS security, please check out the following resources:

- AWS Cognito FAQs: `https://packt.link/oHgXr`

- The Web Identity Federation Playground (an interactive website to test authentication): `https://packt.link/8PVv9`

- The Shared Responsibility Model: `https://packt.link/NcebR`

Exam Readiness Drill – Chapter Review Questions

Apart from a solid understanding of key concepts, being able to think quickly under time pressure is a skill that will help you ace your certification exam. That is why working on these skills early on in your learning journey is key.

Chapter review questions are designed to improve your test-taking skills progressively with each chapter you learn and review your understanding of key concepts in the chapter at the same time. You'll find these at the end of each chapter.

> **How To Access These Resources**
>
> To learn how to access these resources, head over to the chapter titled *Chapter 21, Accessing the Online Practice Resources*.

To open the Chapter Review Questions for this chapter, perform the following steps:

1. Click the link – `https://packt.link/SCSC02E2_CH15`

   Alternatively, you can scan the following QR code (*Figure 15.3*):

Figure 15.3: QR code that opens Chapter Review Questions for logged-in users

2.   Once you log in, you'll see a page similar to the one shown in *Figure 15.4*:

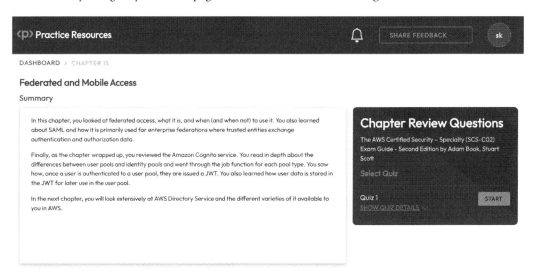

Figure 15.4: Chapter Review Questions for Chapter 15

3.   Once ready, start the following practice drills, re-attempting the quiz multiple times.

Exam Readiness Drill

For the first three attempts, don't worry about the time limit.

ATTEMPT 1

The first time, aim for at least **40%**. Look at the answers you got wrong and read the relevant sections in the chapter again to fix your learning gaps.

ATTEMPT 2

The second time, aim for at least **60%**. Look at the answers you got wrong and read the relevant sections in the chapter again to fix any remaining learning gaps.

ATTEMPT 3

The third time, aim for at least **75%**. Once you score **75%** or more, you start working on your timing.

> **Tip**
>
> You may take more than three attempts to reach 75%. That's okay. Just review the relevant sections in the chapter till you get there.

Working On Timing

Target: Your aim is to keep the score the same while trying to answer these questions as quickly as possible. Here's an example of how your next attempts should look like:

Attempt	Score	Time Taken
Attempt 5	77%	21 mins 30 seconds
Attempt 6	78%	18 mins 34 seconds
Attempt 7	76%	14 mins 44 seconds

Table 15.1: Sample timing practice drills on the online platform

> **Note**
>
> The time limits shown in the above table are just examples. Set your own time limits with each attempt based on the time limit of the quiz on the website.

With each new attempt, your score should stay above 75% while your time taken to complete should **decrease**. Repeat as many attempts as you want till you feel confident dealing with the time pressure.

16

Using Active Directory Services to Manage Access

As organizations grow, they look to manage users in a way that is more suitable for enterprise-level needs. This includes the **Identity and Access Management** (**IAM**) aspect of user and group management and items such as logging for a more robust security solution. Microsoft **Active Directory** (**AD**) is not only an enterprise-grade IAM solution used by organizations of all sizes but also a solution that, when it comes to the AWS cloud, comes in different versions with diverse offerings to meet the needs of customers.

AD in the cloud plays a crucial role in managing user identities and access to resources in your cloud-based infrastructure. It serves as a centralized authentication and authorization system that allows you to control who can access your cloud resources. AD enables you to create and manage user accounts, set up permissions, and define access policies for your cloud-based applications and services.

By integrating AD with your cloud environment, you can achieve a seamless and consistent user experience across both on-premises and cloud-based systems. Users can log in using their familiar credentials, eliminating the need for separate login credentials for different applications and services. This integration also simplifies user management, as you can leverage existing AD groups and policies to control access to your cloud resources if you match them with an appropriate role in AWS.

The following main topics will be covered in this chapter:

- Understanding the different Active Directory offerings in AWS
- Deciding which offering is right for your organization
- Connecting to a current on-premises Active Directory
- Security and Active Directory in AWS

Technical Requirements

There is a requirement to have a basic understanding of AWS services and networking concepts.

Understanding the Different Active Directory Offerings in AWS

AWS provides integration capabilities with Microsoft AD to enable seamless authentication and authorization of users in AWS environments. The integration allows you to extend your existing on-premises AD to AWS resources, such as EC2 instances, Amazon RDS databases, and AWS WorkSpaces.

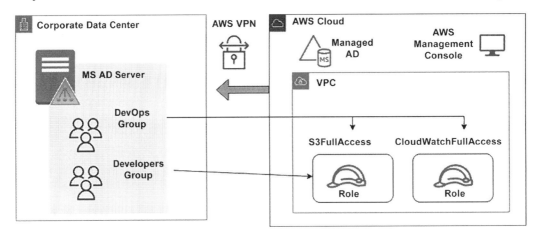

Figure 16.1: On-premises AD to managed AWS AD

Once you have set up a version of the AWS Directory Service, you establish a trust relationship between your on-premises AD and AWS. This trust relationship allows users in your on-premises AD to access AWS resources using their existing AD credentials. When users attempt to access an AWS resource, such as by logging in to an EC2 instance, AWS leverages the trust relationship with AD to authenticate the user. The user provides their AD credentials, which are validated against the on-premises AD. The user is then granted access to the requested resource if the credentials are verified.

AWS Managed Microsoft AD

AWS Managed Microsoft AD is a fully managed, highly available, and secure AD service provided by AWS. It is designed to be compatible with Microsoft AD and provides all the features and capabilities you would expect from an on-premises AD deployment. Critical features of AWS Managed Microsoft AD include the following:

- **Fully managed service**: AWS manages the underlying infrastructure, including hardware, software updates, backups, and high availability.

- **Microsoft AD compatibility**: AWS Managed Microsoft AD is compatible with Microsoft AD, allowing you to use familiar AD administration tools and techniques.

- **Multi-Availability Zone (AZ) deployment**: AWS Managed Microsoft AD automatically deploys across multiple AZs to ensure high availability and fault tolerance.

- **Trust relationships**: You can establish trust relationships between AWS Managed Microsoft AD and your on-premises AD, enabling seamless user access to AWS resources.

- **Group policy support**: AWS Managed Microsoft AD supports using **Group Policy Objects (GPOs)** to manage and enforce policies within the AD environment.

- **Lightweight Directory Access Protocol (LDAP) and Kerberos support**: AWS Managed Microsoft AD allows applications and services to authenticate and communicate using the LDAP and Kerberos protocols.

- **Integrated with AWS services**: AWS Managed Microsoft AD seamlessly integrates with other AWS services, such as Amazon RDS, Amazon EC2, and AWS IAM Identity Center (formerly known as AWS Single Sign-On).

Having just learned about the features that AWS Managed Microsoft AD provides, you might be wondering about the use cases in which it makes sense. Some use cases will be discussed in the next section.

Use Cases for AWS Managed Microsoft AD

AWS Managed Microsoft AD can be utilized in various ways to enhance IAM in a cloud environment. The following are some applications where AWS Managed Microsoft AD can be beneficial:

- **Centralized user management**: By leveraging AWS Managed Microsoft AD, organizations can centralize user management and authentication. It becomes the single source of truth for user accounts, allowing administrators to create, manage, and deactivate user accounts across multiple AWS services and applications. This simplifies the user onboarding and offboarding process and ensures consistent access controls.

- **Hybrid AD integration**: AWS Managed Microsoft AD enables seamless integration between on-premises AD and the AWS cloud. It allows you to synchronize user accounts, groups, and attributes to ensure a consistent directory structure across both environments. This facilitates hybrid identity scenarios, where users can utilize their existing AD credentials to access AWS resources and applications.

- **Resource forest architecture**: Organizations can utilize AWS Managed Microsoft AD as a dedicated resource forest. This approach keeps user accounts and administrative functions separate from the primary on-premises AD. It provides an isolated environment for managing access to cloud-specific resources while maintaining the existing on-premises directory structure.

- **Compliance and security**: AWS Managed Microsoft AD incorporates security features such as **Multi-Factor Authentication** (**MFA**), password policies, and audit logging, enhancing the overall security posture of the cloud environment. It also facilitates compliance with regulatory requirements by providing centralized access controls, user account management, and monitoring capabilities.

- **AWS service integration**: AWS Managed Microsoft AD integrates with several AWS services, enabling seamless authentication and authorization. For example, it can be an **Identity Provider** (**IDP**) for Amazon WorkSpaces, Amazon RDS, Amazon QuickSight, and other services, allowing users to access these resources using their AD credentials.

In this way, AWS Managed Microsoft AD offers a range of capabilities for centralized user management, hybrid AD integration, application integration, and enhanced security in the AWS cloud. It provides a robust foundation for managing user identities, ensuring secure access to resources, and simplifying the administration of cloud-based applications and services.

With a solid understanding of AWS Managed Microsoft AD under your belt, you can now proceed to learn about the other option for AD in AWS: AD Connector.

AWS AD Connector

AD Connector is another option that AWS provides for integrating your existing on-premises AD with AWS resources. AD Connector acts as a proxy service that enables secure communication between your on-premises AD and AWS. The key features of AWS AD Connector include the following:

- **Lightweight integration**: AD Connector allows users to access AWS resources using their existing AD credentials without replicating the entire directory to the cloud.

- **Secure connection**: AD Connector establishes a secure connection between your on-premises AD and AWS using encrypted LDAP communication.

- **User authentication**: Users can authenticate against their on-premises AD, and AD Connector verifies their credentials before granting access to AWS resources.

- **Simplified management**: Since AD Connector does not replicate the entire directory, it simplifies management and reduces administrative overhead.

- **No data sync**: AD Connector does not synchronize user group or group data to AWS, thereby reducing the risk of data duplication or inconsistencies.

- **Integration with IAM**: You can use AD Connector to grant AWS IAM roles and permissions to users in your on-premises AD.

In addition to this second managed AD service offered by AWS, there is one more service not quite like the others. This is the subject of the next section.

AWS Simple AD – Not Quite Active Directory

AWS Simple AD is a directory service offered by AWS that provides a Microsoft AD-compatible directory in the cloud. It is a simplified version of AD, specifically designed for small and mid-sized businesses, and it does not offer the full-featured set of AWS Managed Microsoft AD.

AWS Simple AD allows businesses to create and manage user accounts in the cloud. It's like having an online directory where you can store information about your employees and organize them into groups.

With AWS Simple AD, you can create user accounts for each employee and assign them a username and password. This allows them to log in to different applications and services your company uses, all with just one set of credentials. It thereby eliminates the need for employees to remember multiple usernames and passwords for various systems.

You can also create groups within Simple AD to organize your employees based on their roles or departments. For example, you can have a group for managers, a group for salespeople, and a group for IT staff. This makes managing permissions and access to different resources within your company easier. You can grant specific permissions to each group so that they have access to the tools and information they need to do their jobs.

Use Cases for Simple AD

A good use case for Simple AD is when a small or mid-sized business needs a basic directory service compatible with Microsoft AD in the cloud. The following are more use cases where AWS Simple AD would be a good fit:

- **Managing EC2 instances**: If you have Windows EC2 instances that need to join a domain or a Linux instance that you want to connect via LDAP, then Simple AD can help you manage those instances.

- **LDAP**: Simple AD supports LDAP, a widely used protocol for accessing directory services. If your organization relies on applications or services that use LDAP for authentication and authorization, Simple AD can serve as a cloud-based LDAP directory that those applications can leverage.

Although Simple AD is not a full-fledged version of AD, it can be helpful in certain situations, especially for testing purposes or for an organization trying to manage costs.

If you have a team of developers working on a cloud-based application that requires robust user authentication along with access control, this could be a case for Simple AD. To ensure that the application's security features are implemented correctly, the development team could collaborate with the security team to set up a testing environment in their AWS account. Simple AD could then be deployed as a managed directory service to simulate real-world authentication scenarios and test the application's integration with LDAP-compatible directories.

In the next section, you will look at how to decide which AD service is right for your organization.

Deciding Which Offering Is Right for Your Organization

With several different options available for AD in AWS, it can sometimes be confusing as to which of the service offerings to use. In this section, you will see a set of charts along with service quotas that should help clarify when the different versions of AD are the correct choice for your particular scenario.

As you have gone through this chapter, you have learned about three different major offerings that AWS provides you to connect your resources to a directory either based in the AWS cloud or relayed to it. While each of these provides the same type of end functionality, such as providing a domain name to an EC2 instance and allowing a user to log in to that instance with their domain-based username and password, the number of features and functionality that the three services offer can vary. *Table 16.1* presents a chart that will help you quickly grasp some of the major features (or features lacking) of the services discussed so that you are aware of the background if/when these services are mentioned in a test question.

	AWS Simple AD	**Managed Microsoft AD**	**AWS AD Connector**
Is a managed service	✓	✓	✓
Allows multi-Region deployment		✓	
Supports trust relationships		✓	✓
Has group policy management	✓	✓	✓
Connects to an on-premises directory		✓	✓
Can join computers and instances to the domain	✓	✓	✓
Can share the directory with multiple accounts		✓	

Table 16.1: Guide to the major features of AD services

The set of features presented in the preceding chart is not exhaustive. They do show, however, that each service allows the connection of computers and EC2 instances to the domain, is a managed service, and supports group policy management.

With a solid understanding of how the various AD services differ in AWS, you are ready to understand one-way and two-way trust relationships using Managed Microsoft AD.

Common Trust Scenarios with AWS Managed Microsoft AD

When establishing a trust relationship between an on-premises domain and AWS Managed Microsoft AD, it is essential to consider the specific requirements to determine the appropriate direction of trust deployment. You will see in the following two scenarios some common situations that arise.

For all scenarios, the initial choice is between a **Forest trust** or an **External trust**. A **forest** in AD is a group of domains that share a common schema, configuration, and global catalog. It enables organizations to establish a hierarchical structure for managing users, computers, and resources within a single namespace. A Forest trust establishes a trust relationship between two AD forests, allowing users to access resources in the other forest.

On the other hand, an External trust is a one-way or two-way authentication relationship between domains in different AD forests. It allows users in one forest to access resources in another forest while maintaining separate administrative boundaries and security policies. Unlike Forest trusts, External trusts do not merge domain namespaces or share a common schema, serving primarily as a means to establish communication and access between separate forest environments.

In most cases, it is recommended that you use a Forest trust as it fully supports Kerberos authentication without any limitations. However, if there is a specific requirement for an External trust, it can be implemented, but it's important to be aware of certain considerations.

> **Note**
>
> Kerberos authentication is a widely used network authentication protocol that allows users to securely verify their identities and gain access to resources within a networked environment. It employs encryption and mutual authentication to ensure the confidentiality and integrity of communication between clients and servers.

Scenario 1 – Allowing Allocated On-Premises Users Access to AWS Resources via Active Directory

In this scenario, you would establish a one-way trust between your on-premises AD domain controller in your corporate data center and an AWS Managed Microsoft AD in your AWS account. This one-way trust allows users who already have accounts in your on-premises environment *and* have been allocated to a group with permissions to the cloud environment to seamlessly access AWS resources without needing separate credentials or authentication mechanisms.

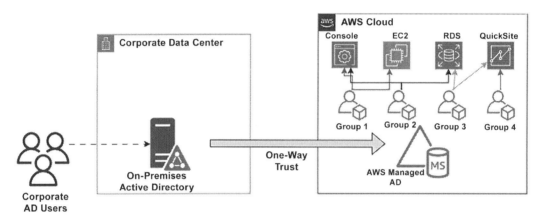

Figure 16.2: One-way trust with AWS managed Microsoft AD

The implementation would need the following steps to be completed:

1. Allocate the AWS Managed Microsoft AD to receive the one-way trust.

2. Configure a one-way incoming trust relationship from your on-premises AD domain controller to the AWS Managed Microsoft AD domain.

3. Configure the trust authentication settings to allow requests from the on-premises environment to the AWS environment while still restricting authentication requests back to the on-premises environment.

4. Synchronize the users and groups from the on-premises AD to the AWS Managed Microsoft AD using AWS Connector. While you do this, ensure that you maintain consistent identity management access throughout both environments.

5. Enforce access control policies in the AWS account/Organization/**Organizational Unit** (**OU**) based on group memberships and permissions.

In the end, after performing the steps, you would have unidirectional (one-way) authentication for your corporate users to access resources in AWS. In this setup, users in the on-premises domain can authenticate and access resources in the AWS environment, but users in AWS cannot authenticate against the on-premises domain.

Scenario 2 – Using AWS Managed Microsoft AD to Allow Different Departments in Different Accounts to Access Files

In this scenario, your organization has been broken down into multiple OUs that segment the groups of business, such as finance, sales, and development. Some of these units, such as finance and sales, need to collaborate and have access to certain documents stored in their accounts. You can, therefore, establish a two-way trust between the accounts.

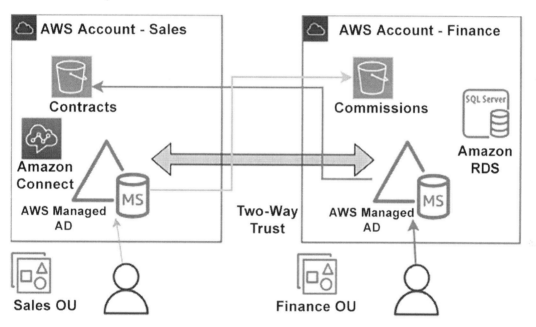

Figure 16.3: Two-way trust with AWS managed Microsoft AD

In this scenario, with the two-way trust in place, the sales department users can now authenticate against the AWS Managed Microsoft AD in their account. Once authenticated, they can access (either upload or download according to the permissions granted) the necessary documents in the finance AWS account. Similarly, finance department users can authenticate against their own domain in their finance account and can access sales documents and resources stored in the sales account.

AWS Managed Micrsoft AD simplifies access to resources across departments, eliminating the need for separate credentials and authentication mechanisms, and can scale seamlessly to accommodate changing requirements as your organization grows.

To help you understand this concept better, consider a two-way trust in Microsoft AD as a mutual agreement between two separate areas of your organization's network. If you had two different departments within your company, each with its own set of rules and access controls, a two-way trust would allow employees from both departments to securely access files or applications in each other's areas. Basically, two-way trust simplifies access for employees who need to work across different parts of the company, ensuring they can securely access the resources they need to do their jobs effectively.

With AWS Managed Microsoft AD configured with two-way trust, you can access the following services:

- The AWS Management Console
- Amazon EC2 instances
- Amazon RDS for SQL Server
- Amazon WorkSpaces/WorkDocs/WorkMail
- Amazon QuickSight
- Amazon Connect
- Amazon Chime
- Amazon FSx for Windows File Server
- Amazon IAM Identity Center (formerly known as AWS SSO – Single Sign-On)
- AWS Directory Service

After reviewing the previous scenarios, you should have a better idea of which of the AD services provided by AWS would best suit your organization's needs. With that in mind, in the next section, you will see how to use your on-premises AD as an IdP and connect it to AWS.

Connecting to a Current On-Premises Active Directory

In *Chapter 15, Federated and Mobile Access*, you learned about IdP along with SAML. In the upcoming exercise, you will need to recall what you previously learned in order to use your on-premises AD as an IdP to allow your users to authenticate to AWS.

To begin with, you need to configure your enterprise network as a SAML provider to AWS. For this configuration, do the following:

1. Configure Microsoft AD with a SAML IdP, for example, Windows AD Domain Services.

2. Create a `metadata.xml` document via your IdP, which is a key document in the configuration. This `metadata.xml` document also includes authentication keys.

3. Using your organization's portal, you must ensure that any requests to access the AWS Management Console are routed to the correct AWS SAML endpoint, allowing those users to authenticate via SAML assertions.

> **Note**
>
> To help you with this part of the configuration, please visit the following URL, which will help you integrate third-party SAML solution providers with AWS: `https://packt.link/02uOL`.

Once you have created your `metadata.xml` document, you need to create a SAML provider via the IAM service. To do this, you can use the following steps as a guide:

1. Log in to the AWS Management Console and navigate to the IAM service. You can get there quickly by using the following link: `https://packt.link/mn40V`.

2. On the left-hand menu, choose `Identity providers` under the `Access management` heading.

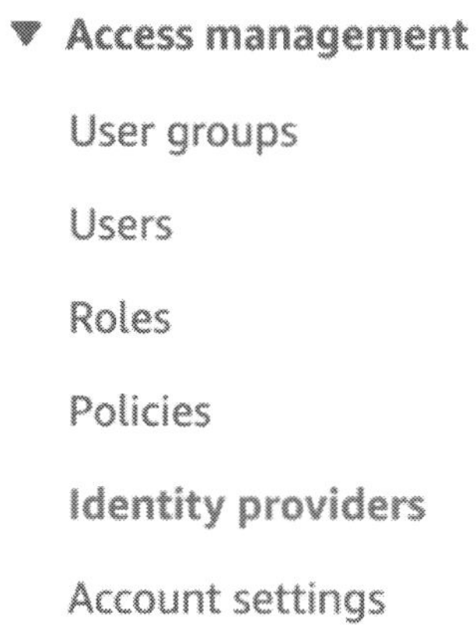

▼ **Access management**

   User groups

   Users

   Roles

   Policies

   Identity providers

   Account settings

Figure 16.4: Access management menu

3. Once on the main `Identity providers` screen, click the `Add provider` button.

4. This will take you to the page where you can enter your provider information. Keep the default provider type selected as `SAML`.

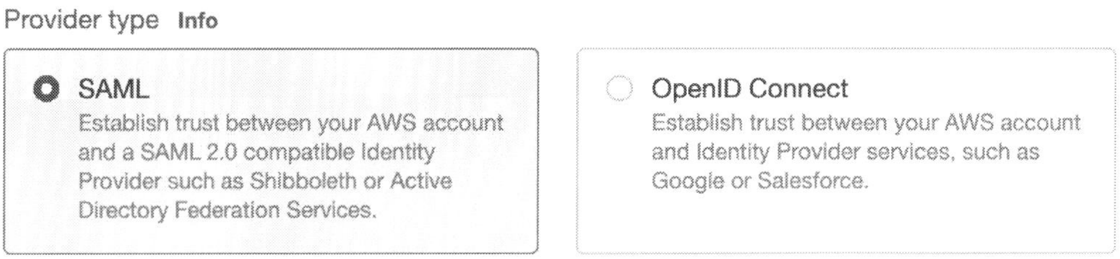

Provider type

● SAML	○ OpenID Connect
Establish trust between your AWS account and a SAML 2.0 compatible Identity Provider such as Shibboleth or Active Directory Federation Services.	Establish trust between your AWS account and Identity Provider services, such as Google or Salesforce.

Figure 16.5: Identity provider selection screen

5. Enter a name for the provider. This should be something that lets you know which AD server you are using as the IdP. After you have set the provider name, upload your `metadata.xml` file.

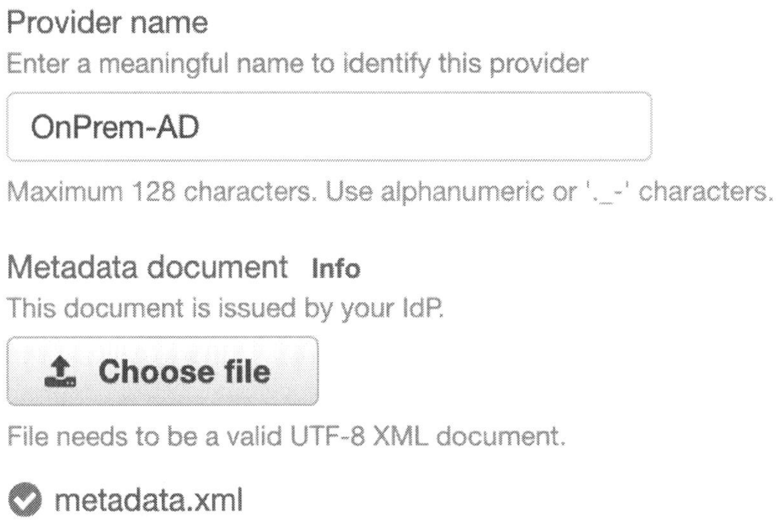

Provider name

Enter a meaningful name to identify this provider

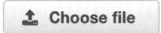
OnPrem-AD

Maximum 128 characters. Use alphanumeric or '._-' characters.

Metadata document Info

This document is issued by your IdP.

⬆ **Choose file**

File needs to be a valid UTF-8 XML document.

✅ metadata.xml

Figure 16.6: Identity provider details screen

6. After setting the name and uploading the `metadata.xml` file, scroll down to the bottom of the page and click on the `Add provider` button.

7. Once your SAML provider has been created within IAM, you must create one or more roles from within IAM that your federated users will assume to gain permissions within your AWS environment. When creating the role(s), select the `SAML 2.0 federation` option.

Trusted entity type

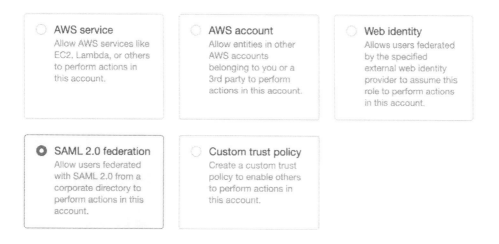

○ AWS service
Allow AWS services like EC2, Lambda, or others to perform actions in this account.

○ AWS account
Allow entities in other AWS accounts belonging to you or a 3rd party to perform actions in this account.

○ Web identity
Allows users federated by the specified external web identity provider to assume this role to perform actions in this account.

◉ SAML 2.0 federation
Allow users federated with SAML 2.0 from a corporate directory to perform actions in this account.

○ Custom trust policy
Create a custom trust policy to enable others to perform actions in this account.

Figure 16.7: Trusted identity type selection screen

8. Once you have selected your SAML provider created in the previous steps, continue to add permissions to the role. The permissions policy of the role will dictate the permission federated users will gain when authenticated; it follows the same configuration as any other role. The role's trust policy creates a trust relationship between the IdP and IAM organizations. In this trust policy, the IdP you created in IAM is used as a principal for the federation.

You just learned how to connect your on-premises AD with AWS using SAML and federation. In the next section, you will learn techniques for keeping your AD systems secure in AWS. Many of these techniques can be ported over to AD systems running on-premises as well.

Security and Active Directory in AWS

Securing AD in AWS involves implementing a combination of best practices and security measures to protect the directory service and its associated resources. These best practices are discussed here:

*   Apply the principle of least privilege by granting users and groups only the minimum necessary privileges within AD. This helps prevent the misuse of excessive permissions.

- Implement MFA as an extra layer of security. Enabling MFA for all user accounts requires users to provide additional authentication beyond their passwords, such as a code from a mobile app or a hardware token.

- Regularly updating and patching AD is critical. This task may be taken care of for you if you use one of the managed options provided by AWS. However, if you are managing your own AD server in AWS, then keeping the system up to date with the latest security patches and updates helps address identified vulnerabilities and enhances overall security.

- Implement robust security monitoring using logging and monitoring solutions such as AWS CloudWatch. Enable auditing for critical events such as authentication attempts, privilege changes, and object modifications. This enables timely detection and response to potential security incidents.

- Employ network security measures such as security groups and **Network Access Control Lists** (**NACLs**) to restrict access to the AD infrastructure. Using secure protocols such as LDAP is essential for communication and enforcing secure network configurations.

- Enforce strong password policies within AD. Implement requirements for password complexity, length, and expiration. Educate your users about password best practices to prevent easy guessing or cracking of passwords.

- Regularly back up the AD database and system state to ensure data integrity and availability. Periodically test the restore process to validate the effectiveness of the backup strategy.

- Limit the exposure of the domain controllers to only necessary network segments. Minimize direct internet access to domain controllers and restrict access to authorized administrators to reduce the risk of unauthorized access.

- Perform regular security assessments, including vulnerability assessments and penetration testing, to identify and remediate any security weaknesses within the AD environment.

- Finally, conduct training and awareness programs to educate users and administrators about security best practices. This includes raising awareness about social engineering threats and emphasizing the importance of maintaining a secure AD environment.

With the foundational understanding of how to keep an AD system in the AWS cloud secure, we move on in the next section to practical steps on how to create that secure environment.

Securing AWS Directory Services

When using one of the AWS managed AD services offerings, such as AD Connector or Managed Microsoft AD, it's important to follow security best practices to protect your directory and associated resources. The following are some key security recommendations:

- **Network security**:

    - Implement network segmentation to isolate the AD Connector environment from other systems and networks.

    - Use security groups and NACLs to control inbound and outbound access to either AD Connector or Managed Microsoft AD.

    - Restrict access to directory services from trusted networks and limited exposure to the public internet.

- **Secure connectivity**:

    - Use a **Virtual Private Network** (**VPN**) or AWS Direct Connect to establish a secure and private connection between your on-premises network and the AWS VPC hosting AD Connector.

    - Encrypt communication channels using **Secure Sockets Layer/Transport Layer Security** (**SSL/TLS**) or IPsec protocols to ensure data privacy and integrity.

- **Authentication and access control**:

    - Enforce strong passwords and implement MFA for all user accounts to add an extra layer of security.

    - Use least privilege principles and grant users only the permissions necessary to perform their tasks with AD Connector.

    - Regularly review and audit user accounts, groups, and access rights to ensure they align with your organization's security policies.

- **Monitoring and logging**:

    - Enable logging and monitoring for either AD Connector or Managed Microsoft AD and analyze the logs for potentially suspicious activities, such as failed login attempts or privilege escalations.

    - Utilize AWS CloudTrail to capture API calls and events related to your AD, to make sure an audit trail is present for investigations and compliance platforms.

- **Secure communication protocols**:

  - Ensure that secure communication protocols, such as LDAPS (LDAP over SSL/TLS), are used to encrypt data transmission between your on-premises AD and AD Connector.

- **Security**:

  - Conduct regular security assessments, such as vulnerability scanning and penetration testing, to identify and remediate any security weaknesses or vulnerabilities in your AD environment.

  - Consider engaging third-party security experts to perform independent assessments for a comprehensive evaluation.

- **Security awareness and training**:

  - Educate users and administrators about security best practices, including password hygiene, social engineering threats, and the importance of protecting sensitive data.

  - Regularly provide security assessment awareness training to ensure all stakeholders understand their roles and responsibilities in maintaining a secure AD environment.

By following the aforementioned security best practices, you can enhance the security posture of either your Managed Microsoft AD or AD Connector in AWS and protect your organization's critical data.

Summary

In this chapter, you examined the different varieties of Microsoft AD that are available in AWS. This included learning about the ways to connect your on-premises AD to AWS: Managed Microsoft AD and AD Connector. You also read about examples of both one-way trust and two-way trust. You looked at securing AD in AWS both from a practical and logistical standpoint. Finally, you also went through a detailed comparison chart of all the services that emphasized how they differ from one another.

Chapter 17 marks the beginning of the final section of this book and will address the best practices of data protection. This section begins with protecting data in flight and at rest. In this chapter, you will learn how to secure data stored in S3 buckets and EBS volumes so that any resting data is protected. You will also learn about techniques to keep your data safe while it is traveling to and from different services.

Further Reading

For additional information on the AWS Shared Responsibility Model and to gain a better understanding of AWS security, please look at the following resources:

- AWS Directory Service FAQs: `https://packt.link/ikEZK`

- How to connect your On-Premises Active Directory to AWS using AD Connector: `https://packt.link/oIZDz`

Exam Readiness Drill – Chapter Review Questions

Apart from a solid understanding of key concepts, being able to think quickly under time pressure is a skill that will help you ace your certification exam. That is why working on these skills early on in your learning journey is key.

Chapter review questions are designed to improve your test-taking skills progressively with each chapter you learn and review your understanding of key concepts in the chapter at the same time. You'll find these at the end of each chapter.

> **How To Access These Resources**
>
> To learn how to access these resources, head over to the chapter titled *Chapter 21, Accessing the Online Practice Resources*.

To open the Chapter Review Questions for this chapter, perform the following steps:

1. Click the link – `https://packt.link/SCSC02E2_CH16`

   Alternatively, you can scan the following QR code (*Figure 16.8*):

Figure 16.8: QR code that opens Chapter Review Questions for logged-in users

2. Once you log in, you'll see a page similar to the one shown in *Figure 16.9*:

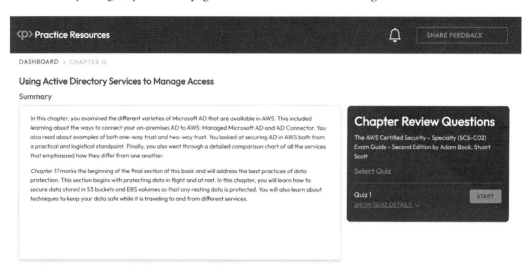

Figure 16.9: Chapter Review Questions for Chapter 16

3. Once ready, start the following practice drills, re-attempting the quiz multiple times.

Exam Readiness Drill

For the first three attempts, don't worry about the time limit.

ATTEMPT 1

The first time, aim for at least **40%**. Look at the answers you got wrong and read the relevant sections in the chapter again to fix your learning gaps.

ATTEMPT 2

The second time, aim for at least **60%**. Look at the answers you got wrong and read the relevant sections in the chapter again to fix any remaining learning gaps.

ATTEMPT 3

The third time, aim for at least **75%**. Once you score **75%** or more, you start working on your timing.

> **Tip**
> You may take more than three attempts to reach 75%. That's okay. Just review the relevant sections in the chapter till you get there.

Working On Timing

Target: Your aim is to keep the score the same while trying to answer these questions as quickly as possible. Here's an example of how your next attempts should look like:

Attempt	Score	Time Taken
Attempt 5	77%	21 mins 30 seconds
Attempt 6	78%	18 mins 34 seconds
Attempt 7	76%	14 mins 44 seconds

Table 16.2: Sample timing practice drills on the online platform

> **Note**
> The time limits shown in the above table are just examples. Set your own time limits with each attempt based on the time limit of the quiz on the website.

With each new attempt, your score should stay above 75% while your time taken to complete should **decrease**. Repeat as many attempts as you want till you feel confident dealing with the time pressure.

Section 6:
Data Protection

So far, you have invested time in setting up your AWS account using secure best practices, added your users to least privileged roles, and made sure that any services that you are using are following secure guidelines. After performing all these operations, you can begin to feel confident that the data and applications running in your accounts have a much better chance of being protected than before.

Your organization's data differentiates it from others in its own industry as well as competing industries. You, as the security professional, must take the final precautions so that there are no opportunities for someone to capture and reassemble the data packets traveling between endpoints, which would otherwise put your intellectual property at risk. You also don't want your users or customers to fall victim to any incident where their personally identifiable information is exposed. Through the final section of this book, as you prepare for the *AWS Security Specialty* certification, you will learn about techniques to protect your data as well as to make secure connections for both you and your customers to your environments.

This section comprises the following chapters:

- *Chapter 17: Protecting Data in Flight and at Rest*
- *Chapter 18: Securely Connecting to Your AWS Environment*
- *Chapter 19: Using Certificates and Certificate Services in AWS*
- *Chapter 20: Managing Secrets Securely in AWS*

You need to protect your organization's and customers' data via encryption. The methods to do so are covered in *Chapter 17*. In that chapter, you will learn about encrypting EBS volumes for EC2 instances as S3 buckets when the data is not moving and techniques for finding sensitive data using tools such as **Amazon Macie**.

Chapter 18 shows you how to ensure that your secured data stays that way using secure connection techniques such as SSL connections, bastion servers, and System Manager's Session Manager. In *Chapter 19*, you will learn all about secure certificates, both public and private. You will even see how to create your own private certificate store. *Chapter 20* will show you how to use native tools that Amazon provides to keep secrets, such as database usernames and passwords, out of your code bases and even techniques to rotate them automatically. The upcoming chapters will take you through all the preceding concepts, wrapping up this final domain.

17

Protecting Data in Flight and at Rest

Data protection is one of the six domains in the *AWS Certified Security Specialty Exam*. Hence, understanding the concepts and execution of protecting data at rest, that is, when it is not in use on disk, and in flight, when it is being transferred from service to service or service to user, is imperative to successfully pass this test.

Storing non-encrypted data in the cloud poses significant security risks, leaving sensitive data vulnerable to unauthorized access, interception, and exploitation by malicious actors. Similarly, transmitting non-encrypted data from AWS (or any cloud provider) to another source, including an end user, exposes sensitive data to interception and eavesdropping, potentially resulting in unauthorized access and data breaches. Essentially, without encryption, critical information such as passwords, financial details, and personal data can be intercepted by malicious actors, compromising data integrity and confidentiality.

You will often be storing confidential and sensitive information when using data storage services such as **Elastic Block Store (EBS)**, **Elastic File System (EFS)**, **Simple Storage Service (S3)**, **DynamoDB**, and **Relational Database Service (RDS)**, which store data for you in AWS. You, therefore, need to understand the methods for protecting the data that is being stored in these services. You will learn how to implement encryption across these services as this chapter takes you through encryption at rest and in transit.

Your data will likely be stored on various services within your AWS account. Although many of the previously mentioned services use standard components to encrypt the data stored at rest, such as **Key Management Service (KMS)**, each has varying specifics that need to be understood to protect the data adequately.

The following main topics will be covered in this chapter:

- Protecting data stored on EBS volumes with encryption

- Protecting data stored on the EFS service with encryption

- S3 encryption and protection options

- Securing database data stored on RDS

- Protecting NoSQL data in DynamoDB

Technical Requirements

There is a requirement to have access to the AWS Management Console with an active account and AWS CLI access. Some of the exercises in this chapter suggest that you have completed previous exercises to create items such as KMS keys and a **Virtual Private Cloud** (**VPC**). However, you can perform the exercises in the chapter even without completing the previous exercises.

Data Encryption Introduction

Several factors govern the increased emphasis on data encryption in recent times. One such significant factor is the need for compliance with industry-specific regulations that your company must adhere to. Additionally, internal compliance governance may also require data encryption as a mandatory measure. Furthermore, adopting encryption can be a proactive approach to enhancing security by introducing an extra layer of protection to your environment. Regardless of the specific driver or reason, the ultimate objective remains the same—to establish a more secure platform for your customers with effective data protection.

In order to achieve the ultimate goal of encryption, it is important to limit unauthorized physical and logical access to data.

There are three states that data can reside in and that you will need to be aware of when looking at data and encryption:

- **Data in transit**: This is the transfer of data between devices, networks, or systems, usually over a network. In this state, data is vulnerable to interception or tampering.

- **Data at rest**: This refers to data stored persistently in storage, such as S3 buckets, EBS drives, RDS databases, or EFS filesystems, and that is not being actively processed.

- **Data in use**: This refers to the active manipulation of data in a system's memory or processing units during computation or analysis tasks.

Following Amazon's recommendation, maximizing encryption in your environment is advisable. This entails encrypting data at rest, ensuring its security while stored, and in transit, that is, safeguarding it during the transmission between clients and servers.

With an understanding of what you will be learning in this chapter, it's time to move on to the first section, in which you will explore how encryption secures data at rest on EBS volumes.

Keeping Data Stored on EBS Volumes Secure with Encryption

Encrypting EBS volumes in AWS provides an added layer of security by protecting the data stored within these volumes in the following ways:

- Data stored on the EBS volumes is transformed into an unreadable format. This helps safeguard sensitive data from unauthorized access, such as in the cases of data breaches or physical theft of storage devices.

- After you enable encryption for EBS volumes, AWS automatically generates an encryption key for you or allows you to **bring your own key** (**BYOK**). The encryption key is used to encrypt the data on the volume. By managing the encryption keys securely, you can control and restrict access to the encrypted data, ensuring only authorized users or services can decrypt and access the information.

- AWS's encryption of EBS volumes is seamlessly integrated into the EC2 service, the main service to which EBS belongs. It doesn't require any modifications to your applications or configurations. You can enable encryption when creating a new EBS volume or encrypt existing volumes without interrupting the availability or performance of your running instances.

- Encrypting your EBS volumes can help you meet your organization's compliance or regulatory requirements. These can include items such as the **Health Insurance Portability and Accountability Act** (**HIPAA**) or the **Payment Card Industry Data Security Standard** (**PCI DSS**). Encryption is often a crucial element in demonstrating the security and privacy of data, which is essential for compliance in many industries.

Now that you understand how encryption keeps data secure on your EBS volumes, you are ready to learn about the process of encrypting EBS volumes in different states and gain some valuable hands-on practice.

Encrypting an EBS Volume

In this section, you will review the following scenarios in which you can implement EBS encryption:

- How to configure encryption as you create a new EBS volume

- How to create an encrypted EBS volume from an unencrypted snapshot

- How to re-encrypt an existing EBS volume using a new **customer master key** (**CMK**)

- How to apply default encryption to a volume

Once you begin using EBS volumes, you might need to implement encryption at different stages. The following subsections will take you through the processes involved.

Encrypting a New EBS Volume

To encrypt a new EBS volume, follow these simple steps:

1. Log on to the AWS Management Console and navigate to the EC2 service. You can do so quickly by using the following URL: `https://packt.link/yhY5l`.

2. Once on the EC2 main page, use the left-hand menu to find the main menu item heading of `Elastic Block Store`. Click on the menu item named `Volumes` under the main heading.

▼ **Elastic Block Store**

Volumes

Snapshots

Lifecycle Manager

Figure 17.1: Elastic Block Store menu

3. Click on the `Create volume` button near the top right of the screen to start creating a new volume.

   This brings you to the `Volume settings` screen. You should be presented with a number of options, including `Volume type`, `Size` (for the volume), `Availability Zone`, and optional `Snapshot ID` to create the volume from. These options are shown in the following screenshot:

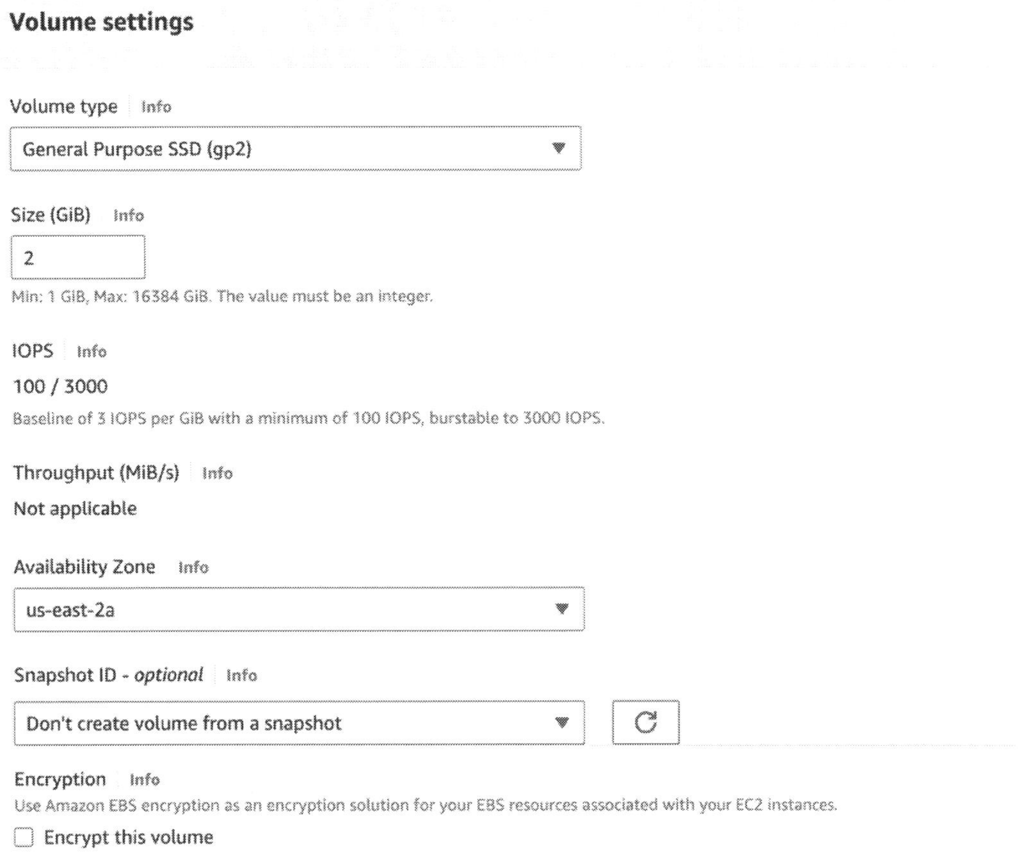

Volume settings

Volume type   Info

```
General Purpose SSD (gp2)                                    ▼
```

Size (GiB)   Info

```
2
```

Min: 1 GiB, Max: 16384 GiB. The value must be an integer.

IOPS   Info

100 / 3000

Baseline of 3 IOPS per GiB with a minimum of 100 IOPS, burstable to 3000 IOPS.

Throughput (MiB/s)   Info

Not applicable

Availability Zone   Info

```
us-east-2a                                                  ▼
```

Snapshot ID - *optional*   Info

```
Don't create volume from a snapshot         ▼          ↻
```

Encryption   Info

Use Amazon EBS encryption as an encryption solution for your EBS resources associated with your EC2 instances.

☐ Encrypt this volume

Figure 17.2: EBS volume settings

4. Select your desired Volume Type, Size (in GB), and Availability Zone options for these settings. To apply encryption, select the checkbox under the Encryption label, and this will provide you with additional options, including your choice of KMS key to encrypt the volume, as covered in the next step.

5.   First select your master key setting, which is effectively your CMK. If you have already created a customer-managed key within KMS (you might already have one created if you did the exercise in *Chapter 12*), then you can select that key here. Alternatively, you can select an AWS-managed key instead. For simplicity's sake, this example will use an AWS-managed key.

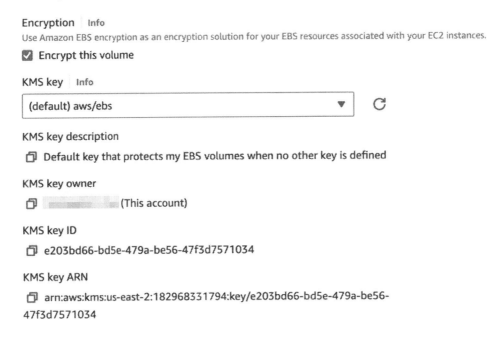

Figure 17.3: EBS encryption screen

> **Note**
> The data keys generated and encrypted by the CMK are stored alongside the encrypted data on your volumes. This data key is also then copied by any snapshots that are created to maintain encryption.

6.   When you have selected your CMK to use for encryption via KMS, select the Create Volume button. You will see a success message upon creation of the volume.

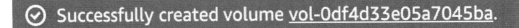

Figure 17.4: Success message upon volume creation

If a snapshot was taken of this volume, that snapshot would also be automatically encrypted using the same CMK.

Creating an Encrypted EBS Volume from an Unencrypted Snapshot

To create an encrypted volume from an unencrypted snapshot, follow these steps:

1. Log on to the AWS Management Console and navigate to the EC2 service. You can do so quickly by using the following URL: `https://packt.link/yhY5l`.

2. On the left-hand menu, find and click on the `Snapshots` menu item under the `Elastic Block Store` heading.

3. Once on the `Snapshots` screen, look at the current snapshots for the Region that you are in. Use the horizontal scroll bar to scroll across to the right until you find the `Encryption` heading. You are going to want to perform this exercise on an EBS snapshot that is not currently encrypted, so make sure that the snapshot you are about to select has the `Not encrypted` label.

Snapshot status ▽	Started ▽	Progress ▽	Encryption ▽
⊘ Completed	2023/03/19 15:33 GMT-4	⊘ Available (100%)	Not encrypted
⊘ Completed	2023/03/19 15:30 GMT-4	⊘ Available (100%)	Not encrypted
⊘ Completed	2022/09/02 14:10 GMT-4	⊘ Available (100%)	Encrypted
⊘ Completed	2023/03/07 12:35 GMT-5	⊘ Available (100%)	Not encrypted

Figure 17.5: EBS volume snapshot

4. Once you have selected the snapshot you want to use for this exercise, click on the white `Actions` button near the top and choose the menu item labeled `Create volume from the snapshot` in the drop-down menu.

   You should now be on the `Create volume` page. For this exercise, you are not interested in changing any of the configurations on this page until you get down to the `Encryption` heading. The box should be unchecked but click the box next to `Encrypt this volume`.

Encryption   Info

Use Amazon EBS encryption as an encryption solution for your EBS resources associated with your EC2 instances.

☐ Encrypt this volume

Figure 17.6: Encrypt this volume checkbox

5. Once you click on the box under the Encryption heading, a set of options will appear, as in the previous exercise, to create an encrypted volume. Choose whether you will use a KMS key or the (default) aws/ebs key.

Figure 17.7: EBS volume encryption

6. After selecting the encryption key for your new EBS volume, scroll down to the bottom of the page and click on the orange Create Volume button.

How to Re-Encrypt an Existing EBS Volume Using a New CMK

If you had previously created an encrypted volume, but now have the need to change the key used to encrypt that volume, say that you want to move away from a deprecated key or the default AWS key, then you can follow these steps:

1. Log on to the AWS Management Console and navigate to the EC2 service. You can do so quickly by using the following URL: https://packt.link/yhY5l.

2. On the left-hand menu, find and click on the Volumes menu item under the Elastic Block Store heading.

3. Find the volume for which you want to change the encryption key and select it.

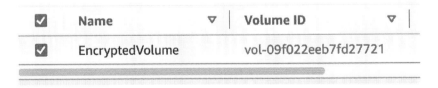

Figure 17.8: Selecting the encrypted volume

4.   From the `Actions` drop-down menu, choose `Create snapshot`.

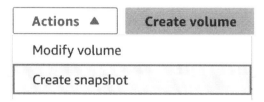

Figure 17.9: Actions menu

5.   Add a description for your snapshot so you can find it, then scroll to the bottom of the page and press the `Create snapshot` button.

6.   Once the snapshot has been created, go to the left-hand menu and click on `Snapshots` under `Elastic Block Store`.

7.   This will bring you to the list of snapshots for the Region. Find the snapshot you just created and select it. Once selected, choose the `Actions` menu at the top and then click on `Create volume from snapshot`.

You can then create the new volume and change the KMS key.

How to Apply Default Encryption for an EBS Volume

If you want to add encryption to the volume, but don't want to pay for or manage KMS keys, you can do this by following these steps:

1.   Log on to the AWS Management Console and navigate to the EC2 service. You can do so quickly by using the following URL: `https://packt.link/yhY5l`.

2.   On the left-hand menu, find and click on the `Volumes` menu item under the `Elastic Block Store` heading.

3.   Click on the `Create volume` button near the top right of the screen to start creating a new volume.

4.   Select your desired `Volume Type`, `Size` (in GB), and `Availability Zone` options. To apply the default encryption, select the checkbox under the `Encryption` label, and this will provide you with additional options, as you will see in the following steps, such as the ability to choose the default encryption key for the volume.

5. When the KMS key drop-down menu appears, choose the option for the (default) aws/ebs key.

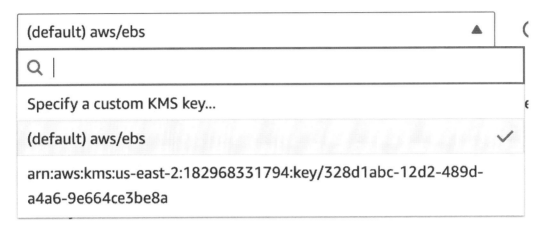

Figure 17.10: Defaultaws/ebs option

6. Click the Create volume button.

> **Note**
> If you have created a volume that was previously unencrypted, you cannot encrypt that volume. You can create a snapshot of that volume and then create a new volume that is encrypted either with default encryption or a custom KMS key.

EBS volumes are a great way of storing data, but they are limited to a single AZ. There are times when you need to have your data available in more than one availability zone at a time in a single Region. A good example of this is if you are sharing your data with a service such as Elastic Container Service, where the containers span multiple Availability Zones as they spin up and down. After learning how to encrypt EBS volumes, you will learn how to add encryption to EFS in the next section.

Encrypting Amazon EFS

Amazon EFS is used for file-level storage and has the capacity to support access for thousands of instances at once. Being a file-level storage system, it behaves much like most other filesystems and utilizes standard filesystem semantics; for example, it adheres to a file hierarchy structure with folders and subfolders, and you can easily rename and lock files, and so on. It also provides low-latency access, making this a great service for many of your file storage needs, from home directories to big data analytics.

With a storage service, there will of course be times when you will need to encrypt your data for additional protection, and EFS supports both in-transit and at-rest encryption.

Situations When You Should Use Encryption with EFS

Encrypting Amazon EFS is recommended in various scenarios to enhance the security and protection of your data. In particular, encrypting Amazon EFS may be an effective approach to the following:

- **Compliance requirements**: If your organization operates in an industry that requires specific data protection standards or compliance regulations, encrypting Amazon EFS helps ensure adherence to those requirements. Encryption adds an extra layer of security to sensitive data, providing an additional safeguard against unauthorized access.

- **Sensitive data**: When dealing with sensitive or confidential data, it is crucial to encrypt Amazon EFS to prevent unauthorized disclosure or data breaches. Sensitive data can include **personally identifiable information** (**PII**), financial records, medical data, or intellectual property. Encryption protects such information, even in the event of unauthorized access to the underlying storage infrastructure.

- **Data in transit**: Encrypting Amazon EFS is particularly important when transferring data between the EFS filesystem and other resources or services. Encryption helps protect data during transit, preventing potential interception or unauthorized access.

- **Shared filesystems**: If you are using Amazon EFS to store data that is shared among multiple users or accounts, encrypting the filesystems provides an added layer of security. It ensures that only authorized entities with the necessary encryption keys can access the data, even if there are security vulnerabilities in other parts of the shared infrastructure.

The following subsection expands upon how to enable encryption at rest when using EFS before moving on to how EFS also supports encryption in transit.

Encrypting EFS at Rest

Amazon EFS is automatically encrypted upon creation using a shared KMS key. With this managed service, there is no way to change keys or choose a non-encrypted EFS filesystem.

Follow these steps to create an EFS filesystem that is protected by encryption:

1. Log in to the AWS Management Console and navigate to the EFS service. You can use the following URL: `https://packt.link/vJxsL`.

2. Once at the EFS service, click on the menu item named `File systems`.

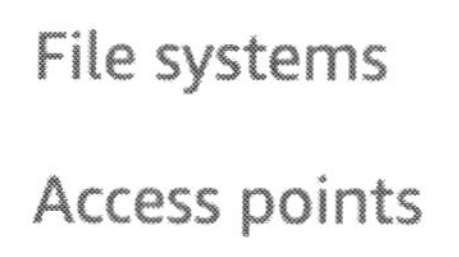

File systems

Access points

Figure 17.11: File systems menu

3. Once `File systems` is on the main screen, click on the button labeled `Create file system`.

    You should now see a `Create file system` window pop up.

4. Select the VPC in which you want to create your EFS. Optionally, you can choose to add a name to your filesystem to quickly identify it. You can see from the following screenshot that the default VPC was chosen and that the filesystem was named `chapter_17`.

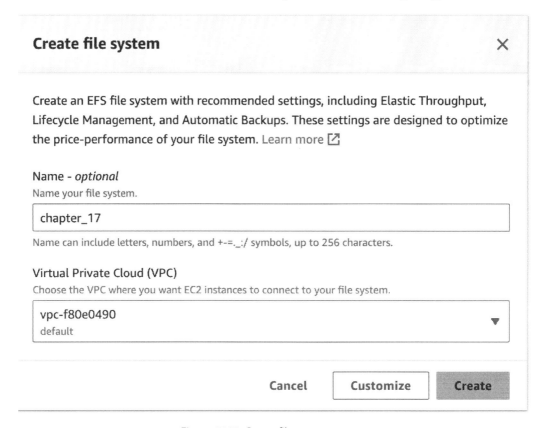

Figure 17.12: Create file system screen

5. Once you have made these selections for your new filesystem, press the `Create` button.

The successful creation of your EFS filesystem should return you to the main EFS page. The new filesystem that you just created should appear under the list of filesystems. Under the `Encrypted` heading, you will see that your filesystem is already encrypted.

Name	File system ID	Encrypted	Total size	Size in Standard / One Zone	Size in Standard-IA / One Zone-IA	Provisioned Throughput (MiB/s)
chapter_17	fs-0d12ccadfc 623895d	⊘ Encrypted	6.00 KiB	6.00 KiB	0 Bytes	-

Figure 17.13: List of EFS filesystems

You just went through the process of creating a new EFS volume for storing files that could be used to connect to EC2 instances, Fargate containers, or Elastic Container Service. In the next section, you will learn how to protect the objects you have stored on the blob storage system in AWS—S3.

S3 Data Protection and Encryption Options

S3 provides the capability to encrypt objects at rest, with the default option being storing objects unencrypted. However, if your environment requires compliance, it is highly likely that encrypting stored objects will be necessary.

When you determine that encryption is necessary for your S3-stored objects, you can consider server-side and client-side encryption. Before deciding, it's essential to ask yourself some key questions, as follows:

- Do you need to manage the encryption key?

  - Is there a compliance policy you must follow with strict rotation guidelines?

- Where will the encryption key be stored?

  - Will you be using AWS KMS to store the key or do you have something else in mind that your organization uses (such as CloudHSM or a third-party solution)?

- Who will be responsible for the encryption and decryption of the data?

  - Will it be a service-based role performed by an application or end user?

After you have thought about the fundamental reasons for how you would like your S3 data to be encrypted, and how your keys will be managed, you next need to enforce those items. The next section will explain how you go about enforcing those policies.

Enforcing Encryption of Data in Transit to S3

To enhance the security of your network traffic going to the S3 service, it is recommended that you employ HTTPS (Transport Layer Security, or TLS) to protect against eavesdropping and tampering attempts, such as man-in-the-middle attacks. AWS advises configuring your S3 bucket policies to permit only encrypted connections over HTTPS (TLS) using the `aws:SecureTransport` condition.

Additionally, it's beneficial to implement continuous monitoring by utilizing the `s3-bucket-ssl-requests-only` managed rule within AWS Config. This rule helps ensure that SSL/TLS encryption is consistently enforced for requests made to your S3 buckets, providing ongoing detection of and control over potential security vulnerabilities.

Using Gateway Endpoints to Protect Data in Transit

Gateway endpoints in AWS provide a secure and efficient way to protect data in Amazon S3. These endpoints act as a gateway or entry point for accessing S3 buckets from within your VPC without the need for internet traffic. By leveraging gateway endpoints, data transfers between your VPC and S3 can occur privately and securely over the AWS network.

When you create a gateway endpoint for S3, it establishes a direct connection between your VPC and S3, bypassing the internet gateway. Gateway endpoints use **PrivateLink** technology, which ensures that data transferred between your VPC and S3 remains within the AWS network without traversing the internet. This eliminates the exposure of your data to the public internet, minimizing the attack surface and reducing the risk of unauthorized access or interception.

By utilizing gateway endpoints, you can enforce granular access control policies and leverage VPC security features, such as security groups and **network access control lists** (**ACLs**), to secure the data flow between your VPC and S3. Additionally, you can monitor and log the traffic through the endpoint using Amazon CloudWatch and AWS CloudTrail, thereby also gaining visibility and auditability of your data transfers.

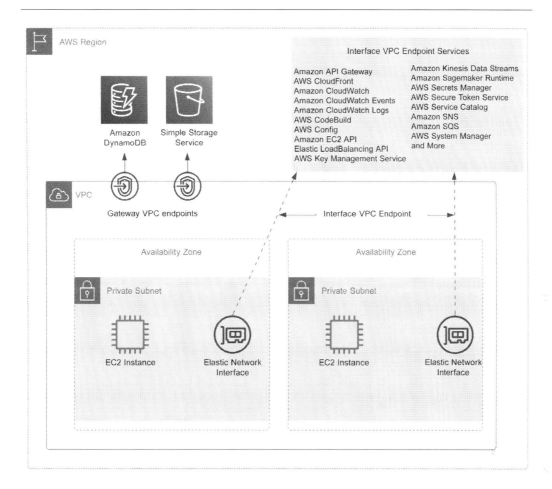

Figure 17.14: VPC showing gateway and interface endpoints

Additionally, data can be protected in transit with other services using VPC interface endpoints. Similar to gateway endpoints, VPC interface endpoints also utilize AWS PrivateLink to establish a private and secure connection between your VPC and certain AWS services. They allow you to connect to AWS services such as CloudWatch or Systems Manager without the need to traverse the public internet. PrivateLink technology utilizes AWS-managed **Network Load Balancers** (**NLBs**) and **Endpoint Network Interfaces** (**ENIs**) within your VPC.

Having gained a basic understanding of how endpoints help keep your data secure during transit, you will learn how to set up a gateway endpoint in the next exercise to help you better understand the intricacies of gateway endpoints.

Creating an S3 Gateway Endpoint

To create a gateway endpoint and securely transmit data to and from your S3 bucket from your VPC, use the following steps:

1. Use the AWS Management Console to navigate to the VPC service. You can get there quickly by using the following URL: `https://packt.link/xhTTK`.

2. Once at the VPC service, use the left-hand menu under the `Virtual private cloud` heading and click on the menu item named `Endpoints`.

Elastic IPs

Managed prefix lists

Endpoints

Endpoint services

NAT gateways

Peering connections

Figure 17.15: Virtual private cloud menu

3. After you have reached the main `Endpoints` page, click on the button labeled `Create endpoint` in the top-right corner of the page.

   You should now be on the screen named `Create Endpoint`.

4. Give your endpoint a name, such as `S3-Chapter17`, and choose the service category of `AWS services`.

Endpoint settings

Name tag - *optional*
Creates a tag with a key of 'Name' and a value that you specify.

S3-Chapter17

Service category
Select the service category

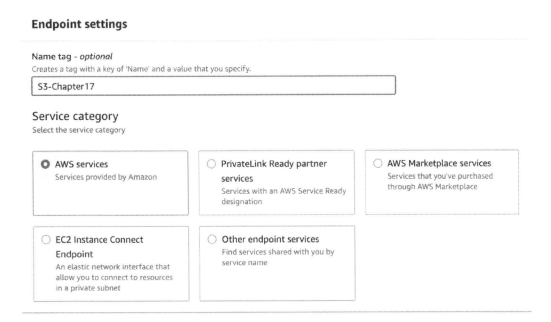

Figure 17.16: S3 Endpoint settings

5.   With the endpoint name and service category set, scroll down to the `Services` heading. The easiest way to find the S3 service is to type `S3` in the search box. When the results come up, choose `com.amazonaws.s3-global.accesspoint`. Select the radio button next to the service name.

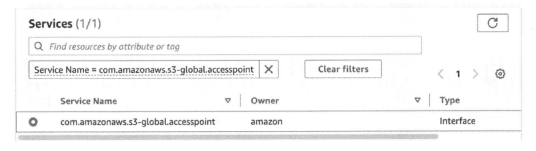

Figure 17.17: S3 service screen

6.   After selecting S3 as the service, move to the section labeled VPC. Here you must select one of your VPCs to attach the gateway endpoint. You can choose either the default VPC or a previously created VPC to attach your endpoint.

Figure 17.18: VPC selection screen

7.   Next, scroll down to the Subnets and Security groups sections, respectively. Allow access to any subnets as well as any particular security groups that would need access to the endpoint. Remember the rule of least privilege access.

8.   Once you have made your selections, scroll down to the bottom of the page and click on the Create endpoint button.

With your gateway endpoint in place, any transfers from resources residing in that particular VPC to any S3 bucket will no longer use the public internet but rather will travel through the AWS private network instead.

Transferring your S3 objects using secure gateway endpoints ensures better protection during transit. This reduces the risk of external parties intercepting your data, making it safer than transferring over the public internet. In the next section, you will see how you can use object locks to protect data your organization has stored on S3 to prevent tampering and deletion.

Understanding Object Lock in Amazon S3

Object Lock in Amazon S3 provides additional data protection by allowing you to force retention policies on objects stored in S3 buckets. It helps prevent the accidental deletion or modification of objects, ensuring data immutability and compliance with regulatory requirements.

When you enable Object Lock on an S3 bucket, you can set a retention period for individual objects or the entire bucket. The objects cannot be deleted or modified during this retention period, which ensures data integrity and protection against unauthorized tampering.

There are two types of Object Lock modes available in Amazon S3:

- **Governance mode**: In this mode, the retention settings can only be modified or removed by users with specific permissions. This rule helps protect objects from being deleted or modified by most users, including those with elevated privileges.

- **Compliance mode**: In compliance mode, the retention settings are locked and cannot be overridden or deleted by any user, including the root account. It ensures strict data immutability and compliance with regulations that require tamper-proof data storage.

By utilizing Object Lock, you can safeguard critical data against accidental or malicious deletion, ensuring that objects remain unaltered for the defined retention period. This feature is particularly useful in industries such as finance, healthcare, and legal, where data immutability and long-term retention are crucial for compliance purposes.

It's also important to note that Object Lock works at the object level, and once the retention period is set, it cannot be shortened or removed until the specified duration has elapsed, thus maximizing the benefits of a reliable and tamper-proof mechanism to protect your data in S3.

While Object Lock can be a helpful feature when dealing with compliance requirements, it's not the only type of lock that is available for S3 objects. In the next section, you will learn about S3 legal hold, which does not have specific time constraints.

S3 Legal Hold

Legal hold is a feature in Amazon S3 that allows you to place a legal hold on objects stored in your S3 buckets. It is designed to help you preserve data and prevent its deletion or modification for legal and compliance purposes, such as litigation or regulatory investigations.

When you enable legal hold on an object in S3, it protects the object from being deleted or modified, even if someone has the necessary permissions to perform those actions. This ensures the object's content and metadata remain intact and unaltered during the legal hold period.

Legal hold operates independently of the retention settings provided by Object Lock. While Object Lock enforces a predefined retention period on objects, legal hold provides a mechanism to extend the protection indefinitely until the hold is released.

The key features of legal hold in Amazon S3 include the following:

- **Immutability**: Once an object is placed under legal hold, it cannot be deleted or modified until the hold is removed, ensuring data integrity and preservation.

- **Granularity**: Legal hold can be applied at the object level, allowing you to selectively protect specific objects within a bucket.

- **Durability**: Legal hold settings persist even if the object is replicated to different storage classes or across multiple AWS Regions, ensuring that the hold remains intact regardless of data movements.

- **Auditability**: Amazon S3 records events related to legal hold operations, providing an audit trail for compliance and regulatory purposes.

You won't find yourself using the legal hold feature very frequently; however, it can effectively protect the data needed for different types of investigations or legal proceedings from any type of tampering or manipulation if the need arises.

In the next section, you will learn how Amazon Macie helps you find where PII resides on your systems.

Using Amazon Macie to Discover PII

Amazon Macie is an advanced data security service provided by AWS, the primary goal of which is to help organizations discover, classify, and protect their sensitive data. Macie uses machine learning and artificial intelligence to automatically identify and categorize sensitive data, such as PII, intellectual property, financial data, and more.

The primary function of Amazon Macie is to automate the process of finding sensitive data stored in your account, specifically in S3 buckets. The Macie service can do this even if the data has been encrypted while stored at rest provided that you grant the service permissions to the key(s) that are protecting the data.

Amazon Macie's data classification capabilities can be combined with AWS Lake Formation and AWS Glue to automatically redact sensitive data within files stored in Amazon S3 buckets once Amazon Macie has classified it. If your company is subject to regulations such as GDPR in Europe or the **General Data Protection Law** (**LGPD**) in Brazil, then this is the type of automation that can keep you in compliance.

Macie also offers several key features to enhance data security. Through automated data discovery, it locates sensitive data within your AWS environment, including data in Amazon S3 buckets and Amazon EBS volumes. It does so by employing sophisticated algorithms to recognize patterns and structures that are characteristic of different types of sensitive data.

The service also includes powerful data classification capabilities. Macie can assign labels and metadata tags to your data, which further facilitates the management of sensitive information. This classification enables you to enforce data access controls, monitor data usage, and implement appropriate security measures based on the sensitivity of the data.

Additionally, Macie provides data access monitoring and alerts. It continuously analyzes data access patterns, detects unusual or suspicious activities, and generates alerts to notify you of potential security risks. Suppose you are managing your accounts in AWS through AWS Organizations. In that case, you can use a delegated administrator account to set up the Macie service in a centralized location, such as the security account. You can then have this delegated administrator account manage and consume the alerts for all the accounts in the organization.

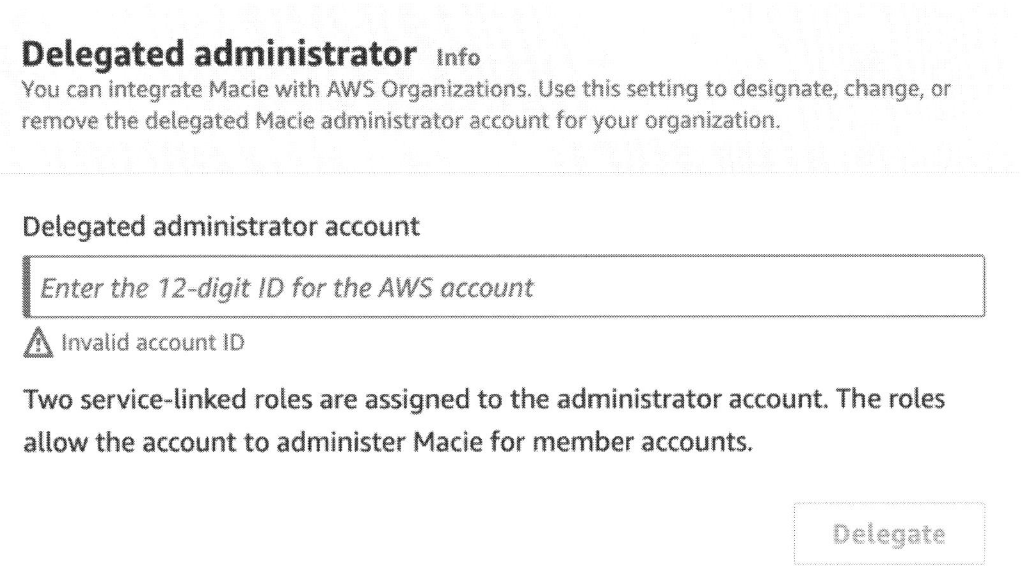

Delegated administrator Info

You can integrate Macie with AWS Organizations. Use this setting to designate, change, or remove the delegated Macie administrator account for your organization.

Delegated administrator account

> Enter the 12-digit ID for the AWS account

⚠ Invalid account ID

Two service-linked roles are assigned to the administrator account. The roles allow the account to administer Macie for member accounts.

Delegate

Figure 17.19: Delegated administrator screen for Macie

Essentially, incorporating Amazon Macie can help you and your organization achieve better visibility and control over sensitive data. This is especially important for organizations that are dealing with compliance requirements, and you will learn how Macie can help you with these requirements in the next subsection.

Maintaining Compliance with Amazon Macie

Amazon Macie is a managed service backed by machine learning that automatically detects, protects, and classifies sensitive data within your S3 buckets. It continuously reviews and monitors data object access patterns in S3 and the associated CloudTrail log data to identify and spot any irregular or suspicious activity outside of what can be considered regular operations.

Some of the valuable features of Amazon Macie include the following:

- **Natural language processing** (**NLP**) functionality, which allows the user to interpret techniques to interpret data stored in S3 helping to classify it. To learn more about NLP, please visit `https://packt.link/jVhHD`.

- Macie's ability to spot changes to specific security policies and ACLs that might affect who has access to your S3 bucket.

- The Amazon Macie service has the ability to categorize information, including sensitive security data such as PII, **protected health information** (**PHI**) data, access keys, and API keys. Customized configuration allows you to set up and assign business value to certain types of data using a risk score. Depending on your business and what's considered critical, you can set your own values on what you consider a risk.

One of the key components of Amazon Macie is how it classifies data to help determine its level of sensitivity and criticality to your business. In the next section, you will take a deeper look into Macie's data classifications.

Classifying Data Using Amazon Macie

Amazon Macie employs various techniques to classify data based on its content and context. The classification process involves analyzing the data and application machine learning algorithms to recognize patterns, structures, and characteristics that indicate different types of sensitive information. Here's how Amazon Macie classifies data:

- **Content analysis**: Macie examines the content of files and documents to identify patterns and specific data elements. It analyzes text, metadata, file types, and file formats to extract information that indicates sensitive data.

- **Natural Language Processing** (**NLP**): Macie utilizes NLP techniques to understand the context of the text and identify sensitive information based on language patterns. It can recognize keywords, phrases, or combinations of words that indicate sensitive data, including financial, legal, or proprietary information.

- **Machine learning models**: Macie employs pre-trained machine learning models that have been trained on large datasets to recognize common types of sensitive information. These models continuously learn and improve over time, enabling Macie to enhance its accuracy in identifying different data categories.

- **Data fingerprints**: Macie creates unique data fingerprints or data signatures for known sensitive data types. These fingerprints are generated by analyzing the content and structure of data elements. Macie can then match these fingerprints against the data it scans to identify similar patterns and classify the data accordingly.

- **Customization and training**: Macie allows you to customize and train the classification process based on your specific data types and business needs. You can define custom data types, keywords, or regular expressions to teach Macie to recognize and classify data unique to your organization or theory.

You now have an understanding of how, through a combination of all the techniques listed previously, Amazon Macie automatically classifies data accurately, enabling you to gain better visibility into your data, implement data access security controls, and apply appropriate security measures to protect your sensitive information. Next, you will learn about the difference between managed and custom identifiers that help you classify your sensitive data.

Managed Data Identifiers versus Custom Data Identifiers

In Amazon Macie, there are two different approaches to identifying and classifying sensitive data: **managed data identifiers** and **custom data identifiers**. Managed data identifiers in Macie are pre-built patterns, rules, or templates provided by AWS. These identifiers are designed to recognize and classify common types of sensitive data, such as credit card numbers, social security numbers, email addresses, or financial account numbers. Macie's managed data identifiers cover many data types and help identify sensitive information based on established patterns and structures.

AWS regularly updates and maintains the managed data identifiers to ensure they remain effective and accurate. Macie leverages machine learning algorithms and pattern-matching techniques to match the content of files and documents against these predefined managed data identifiers.

Custom data identifiers allow you to define and create your own patterns, keywords, regular expressions, or context-specific rules to identify specific types of sensitive data that are unique to your organization or industry. An example of this could be a regular expression pattern designed to detect credit card numbers stored in Amazon S3 buckets from among unstructured data. A custom identifier might search for patterns matching the format of credit card numbers such as *XXXX-XXXX-XXXX-XXXX*, helping to identify and classify sensitive information and ensure compliance with data protection regulations. With custom data identifiers, you can essentially tailor Macie's classification capabilities to recognize and classify data elements that are specific to your business needs. This empowers you to identify sensitive information that the predefined managed data identifiers may or may not cover.

Using a combination of managed data identifiers and custom data identifiers, you can enhance Macie's ability to accurately identify and classify sensitive data within your environment. The managed data identifiers provide a comprehensive set of predefined patterns, while custom data identifiers allow you to tailor the classification process to meet your unique data identification needs.

Now that you understand how Amazon Macie can help protect the data you have stored at rest by detecting and classifying sensitive data, you are ready to move on to another source of data storage in the next section—databases with the RDS service.

Protecting Data Stored in Relational Database Service on AWS

AWS RDS is a fully managed database service that simplifies the deployment, management, and scalability of relational databases in the cloud. With a strong emphasis on security, AWS RDS offers several features to protect your data. It provides encryption at rest to secure data stored on RDS instances, allowing you to encrypt your databases using AWS KMS or customer-managed keys. Encryption in transit ensures secure communication between your applications and RDS instances through **SSL/TLS encryption**.

RDS also integrates with other AWS services such as Amazon VPC, enabling you to isolate your databases within a private subnet and control network access. Regular automated backups, multi-AZ deployments, and built-in monitoring further enhance the security and reliability of your RDS database.

It is crucial to implement strong access control measures to safeguard data on RDS. AWS **Identity and Access Management** (**IAM**) can be used to help grant the appropriate permissions and limit access to RDS instances. Restricting access to authorized users and employing least privilege principals help prevent unauthorized access to sensitive data.

You have seen how data in RDS can be protected at rest. The next step is to grasp how to protect data in transit. The following subsection will explain techniques to accomplish this.

Protecting Data in Transit to and from RDS

Secure communication protocols protect data integrity by ensuring that information exchanged between applications and RDS remains unchanged during transit. You can employ encryption and authorization mechanisms provided by SSL/TLS protocols to detect and prevent tampering and ensure the data's integrity.

Using encryption for the transmission of your data also mitigates the risk of eavesdropping, a tactic in which attackers attempt to capture and monitor sensitive data in transit. Encrypted data, even if intercepted, is meaningless without the encryption keys. This significantly reduces the risk of data exposure.

Protecting data in transit is also essential for meeting regulatory and compliance requirements. Many industry-specific regulations, such as HIPAA or PCI-DSS, mandate the use of encryption during data transmission to ensure the privacy and security of sensitive information. By implementing encryption in transit, organizations can demonstrate adherence to these requirements.

To ensure secure communications between your applications and your database on RDS, it is vital to encrypt the data using SSL/TLS. Amazon RDS simplifies this process by automatically creating an SSL certificate and installing it on the database instance during the provisioning of a database instance.

You can establish encrypted connections for MySQL by launching the MySQL client with the `--ssl_ca` parameter, which references the public key. This enables the encryption of connections between your application and the database instance.

For SQL Server, you need to download the public key and import the certificate into your Windows operating system. This step allows you to utilize SSL/TLS encryption for secure communication between your application and the database instance.

In the case of RDS for Oracle, native network encryption can be utilized. You can enable encryption for data transmission by adding the native network encryption option to an option group and associating it with the database instances.

Once this encrypted connection, integrated with Oracle's native network, is established, all data transferred between the database instance and your application will be securely encrypted during transfer, protecting it from potential interception or unauthorized access.

Furthermore, you have the option to enforce encrypted connections by configuring your database instance to only accept encrypted connections, thereby adding an additional layer of security to your data communication.

In this section, you've observed how encryption works with RDS. The next will demonstrate how to encrypt and protect the NoSQL database in AWS—DynamoDB.

Protecting Data on Amazon DynamoDB

Amazon DynamoDB by AWS is a fully managed, NoSQL database service. It offers fast, scalable, and flexible storage for applications that require low-latency access to large volumes of structured data. DynamoDB provides built-in encryption-at-rest capabilities that enhance the security of your data.

DynamoDB also supports **Secure Sockets Layer/Transport Layer Security** (**SSL/TLS**) encryption protocols for secure communication. When you enable SSL/TLS encryption, it establishes an encrypted channel between your applications and DynamoDB, protecting data during transmission.

DynamoDB Encryption Options

DynamoDB uses keys stored in AWS KMS to ensure that all data is encrypted while at rest. This feature reduces the complexity and operational burden associated with protecting sensitive data, as encryption keys are managed centrally by KMS. By seamlessly integrating encryption into DynamoDB, AWS KMS allows granular control over encryption keys, enabling key administrators to define access policies and revoke permissions as needed, further enhancing the security of data stored in DynamoDB.

DynamoDB encryption at rest offers an additional layer of data protection, encrypting not only the primary key but also local and global secondary indexes, streams, global tables, backups, and **DynamoDB Accelerator** (**DAX**) clusters whenever the data is stored in durable media.

It seamlessly integrates with AWS KMS, allowing you to manage the encryption keys used to encrypt your tables. When creating a new DynamoDB table, you can choose from the following three distinct KMS key types for table encryption:

- **AWS-owned key (default)**: This is the default encryption type where the key is owned by DynamoDB, incurring no additional charges.

- **AWS-managed key**: This key is stored in your account and managed by AWS KMS. This key is subject to AWS KMS charges.

- **Customer-managed key**: You retain complete control over this key, as it is stored in your account and is owned and managed by you. AWS KMS charges apply for this key type.

You can switch between these key types as needed. By selecting the appropriate encryption key type, you can tailor your encryption-at-rest configuration to meet your specific security requirements while leveraging the capabilities of AWS KMS.

Summary

In this chapter, you reviewed the different approaches to protecting data at rest and in transit. You examined the different processes of encrypting EBS volumes in their various states. This included creating a new encrypted EBS volume, creating an encrypted volume from an unencrypted snapshot, and even changing the current key on a volume. You then moved on to the block storage service offered by Amazon S3 and saw the different ways to protect data using this service, including using the Object Lock and legal hold features.

In *Chapter 18*, you will explore how users can securely connect to your Amazon environment. This includes creating secure connections for your organization so that the chances of data being captured in transit are minimized. You will also learn how to implement good practices for your users so that they can connect to your environment in a safe and secure manner.

Further Reading

For additional information on the AWS Shared Responsibility Model and an underlying foundation of AWS security knowledge, please check out the following resources:

- Security best practices for Amazon S3: `https://packt.link/sReZF`

- Must-know best practices for Amazon EBS encryption: `https://packt.link/tLmFC`

- DynamoDB encryption at rest: `https://packt.link/8t9cj`

- Data masking and granular access control using Amazon Macie and AWS Lake Formation: `https://packt.link/MLeYH`

Exam Readiness Drill – Chapter Review Questions

Apart from a solid understanding of key concepts, being able to think quickly under time pressure is a skill that will help you ace your certification exam. That is why working on these skills early on in your learning journey is key.

Chapter review questions are designed to improve your test-taking skills progressively with each chapter you learn and review your understanding of key concepts in the chapter at the same time. You'll find these at the end of each chapter.

> **How To Access These Resources**
>
> To learn how to access these resources, head over to the chapter titled *Chapter 21, Accessing the Online Practice Resources*.

To open the Chapter Review Questions for this chapter, perform the following steps:

1. Click the link – `https://packt.link/SCSC02E2_CH17`

   Alternatively, you can scan the following QR code (*Figure 17.20*):

Figure 17.20: QR code that opens Chapter Review Questions for logged-in users

2.   Once you log in, you'll see a page similar to the one shown in *Figure 17.21*:

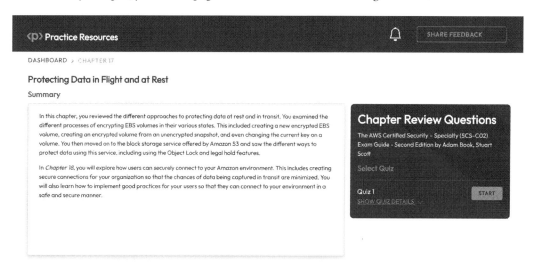

Figure 17.21: Chapter Review Questions for Chapter 17

3.   Once ready, start the following practice drills, re-attempting the quiz multiple times.

Exam Readiness Drill

For the first three attempts, don't worry about the time limit.

ATTEMPT 1

The first time, aim for at least **40%**. Look at the answers you got wrong and read the relevant sections in the chapter again to fix your learning gaps.

ATTEMPT 2

The second time, aim for at least **60%**. Look at the answers you got wrong and read the relevant sections in the chapter again to fix any remaining learning gaps.

ATTEMPT 3

The third time, aim for at least **75%**. Once you score **75%** or more, you start working on your timing.

> **Tip**
>
> You may take more than three attempts to reach 75%. That's okay. Just review the relevant sections in the chapter till you get there.

Working On Timing

Target: Your aim is to keep the score the same while trying to answer these questions as quickly as possible. Here's an example of how your next attempts should look like:

Attempt	Score	Time Taken
Attempt 5	77%	21 mins 30 seconds
Attempt 6	78%	18 mins 34 seconds
Attempt 7	76%	14 mins 44 seconds

Table 17.1: Sample timing practice drills on the online platform

> **Note**
>
> The time limits shown in the above table are just examples. Set your own time limits with each attempt based on the time limit of the quiz on the website.

With each new attempt, your score should stay above 75% while your time taken to complete should **decrease**. Repeat as many attempts as you want till you feel confident dealing with the time pressure.

18

Securely Connecting to Your AWS Environment

As you continue to work on securing your AWS environment so that your data is effectively protected both in transit and at rest, you need to ensure that the initial points of contact that your users have with your applications are also secure. As the primary users of the network, your corporate users are the ones most likely to interact with the AWS environment most frequently, especially for transactions that require elevated access.

This chapter explores various connectivity options and their associated security measures to establish and maintain secure connections between your personal or corporate environment and your AWS environment. You will examine the configuration of security features such as routing, security groups, and the permissions required to connect to your AWS environment through AWS **Virtual Private Network** (**VPN**) and/or **AWS DirectConnect**. By delving into these topics, you will gain insights into establishing robust and secure connections that meet your specific needs and enable seamless interaction between your environments.

The following main topics will be covered in this chapter:

- Understanding your connection
- AWS VPN
- AWS Direct Connect
- AWS CloudHub

Technical Requirements

You need to have a basic understanding of AWS services and networking concepts for this chapter. You will also need access to an active AWS account with a user with the appropriate permissions to create and edit items with AWS VPC. You will also need to have an AWS VPC stood up.

Understanding Your Connection

If you are part of an organization developing solutions on AWS, accessing your resources and services over the internet is straightforward. Many users accomplish this through the AWS Management Console, which you might have already interacted with while completing the exercises in this book. Using the AWS Management Console, you can easily deploy and configure the infrastructure and services you have designed for your environment.

From a logical standpoint, connecting to your AWS environment from your on-premises setup via the internet can be visualized as follows:

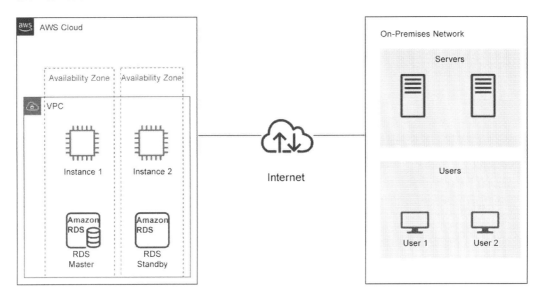

Figure 18.1: Connecting an on-premises network to AWS VPC

As shown in *Figure 18.1*, just using a basic setup where the servers and users connect to the instance in your AWS account directly via the internet leaves you open to bad actors sniffing the traffic during the different server hops that it takes before it reaches its final destination. You want to provide a secure environment for your users and the data that they are working on, so you need to establish a more secure connection to your resources.

Now that you understand the basic connection you initially used to connect to AWS infrastructure and services, you should consider methods to improve the security of this connection. In the next section, you will look at the first option, the easiest of the two to implement: AWS VPN.

Understanding AWS VPN

AWS VPN is a service that enables secure and encrypted communication between your corporate network and your AWS resources. It establishes a VPN connection over the internet, allowing you to securely access your AWS infrastructure as if it were an extension of your corporate network. With AWS VPN, you can maintain the confidentiality and integrity of your data while seamlessly connecting to and managing your resources in the cloud.

A Quick Overview of VPNs

A VPN is a secure connection that allows users to access a private network, such as AWS, over the internet by using an encrypted connection from a user's device and that private network. It creates a private network **tunnel** within the public network, allowing users to securely transmit data between their devices and a remote network or resource. VPNs provide confidentiality, integrity, and privacy by encrypting data and ensuring that it remains protected from unauthorized access. They enable users to access resources and services as if they were directly connected to the private network even when they are physically located outside of it. VPNs are commonly used to enhance security and privacy when accessing sensitive information or when connecting to remote networks, such as corporate networks or cloud environments.

Many times, a company needs its employees, especially remote employees, to securely access corporate resources in the cloud, such as company databases or internal applications. A VPN connection is used to establish a secure tunnel between the employee's device and the corporate network. This allows remote workers to securely transmit sensitive data over the internet, ensuring the confidentiality and integrity of their information while accessing cloud-hosted resources from any location.

When a VPN connection is established, the user's data is encrypted and encapsulated within the VPN tunnel. This ensures that the information remains protected from eavesdropping, interception, or tampering by unauthorized individuals or entities. VPNs use encryption protocols to secure the data, making it difficult for third parties to track or monitor their online accounts.

One of the most common uses for a VPN is when employees are working from remote locations, either at home or at a client's location, and need a secure connection back to their own company's file servers. The VPN keeps the transmissions secure and encrypted, regardless of whether the network they are working on is public or protected by another company.

VPNs are commonly used for various purposes, including the following:

- **Remote access**: VPNs allow remote workers to securely access your organization's internal network, systems, and resources from outside locations.

- **Secure access over public Wi-Fi**: Using a VPN connection protects sensitive data and communications when you are connected to public Wi-Fi networks, which are often insecure and prone to hacking.

- **Bypassing geographical restrictions**: The use of a VPN can enable your users to access content or services that may be inaccessible to them otherwise due to their geographic location. By connecting to a VPN server in a different country, those users can appear in traffic logs as if they are accessing the internet from that location.

- **Enhancing security**: A VPN adds an extra layer of security to online activities such as transferring financial information, data that contains personally identifiable information, or even company trade secrets as data transmitted over a VPN is encrypted.

As you can see from the following diagram, the VPN gateway is located on the AWS side of your environment. The customer gateway is located at your on-premises physical environment, either at your data center, office, or remote location where you are connecting from.

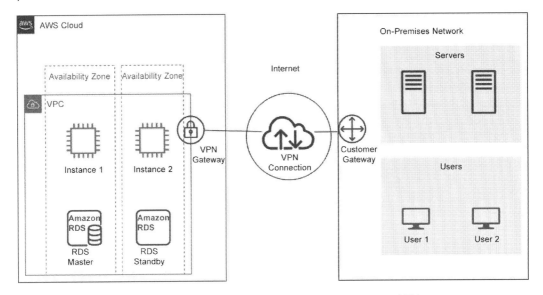

Figure 18.2: VPN connection connecting a customer gateway to a VPN gateway

As this is a managed service, the VPN gateway component (which resides within AWS) is implemented and designed with redundancy in mind and actually consists of two endpoints. Both these endpoints are located in different data centers for resiliency (this has not been depicted in *Figure 18.2* for simplicity purposes).

In addition to this, the VPN connection itself consists of two IPsec tunnels. The next subsection will give you a better understanding of IPsec tunnels and their common use cases.

Understanding IPsec tunnels

An **IPsec tunnel** (short for **Internet Protocol Security tunnel**) is a secure and encrypted connection established between two networks or devices over the internet. IPsec tunnels are designed to protect the confidentiality and integrity of the data transmitted. Using a combination of authentication, encryption, and data integrity checks, IPsec creates a virtual encrypted tunnel through which data travels, shielding it from potential eavesdropping or tampering. This technology is widely employed for site-to-site connections, remote access scenarios, and cloud integrations (such as in the case of a VPN connection), ensuring that sensitive information remains private and secure throughout its journey.

IPsec tunnels play a pivotal role in modern network security by providing a robust shield against cyber threats. Acting like a virtual tunnel with fortified walls, it employs the following tools:

- Encryption to render data unreadable to unauthorized parties
- Authentication mechanisms to validate the identities of communicating entities, thwarting any attempts at unauthorized access
- Data integrity checks to guarantee that the information remains unaltered during transit

In this manner, IPsec tunnels serve as a cornerstone for safeguarding digital communications, enabling organizations to establish trusted connections and protect sensitive data across various network scenarios.

IPsec tunnels are commonly used for various purposes, including the following:

- **Site-to-Site VPNs**: IPsec tunnels are widely used to establish secure connections between different network locations, such as connecting branch offices to a central corporate network.
- **Remote access VPNs**: IPsec is used to provide secure remote access for individual users or devices connecting to a corporate network from external locations.
- **Cloud connectivity**: IPsec tunnels are used to create secure connections between on-premises networks and cloud environments, such as connecting to VPCs in AWS.
- **IoT and connected devices**: IPsec tunnels can secure communications between the **Internet of Things** (**IoT**) devices, ensuring data privacy and protection.

IPsec tunnels are a key factor in any VPN's security, and that includes AWS VPN. With an understanding of how IPsec tunnels are used throughout various applications in the real world, you will next look at some pros and cons of the AWS VPN service, which will help you make the most informed decision possible.

Pros and Cons of AWS VPN

As you prepare to use AWS VPN to connect your current network to your VPC, there are a few pros and cons that you should be aware of.

First, take a look at the pros of using VPN:

- **Secure connectivity**: AWS VPN provides a secure and encrypted connection between your corporate network and AWS resources. It ensures that data transmitted between the two environments remains confidential and protected from unauthorized access.

- **Flexibility and scalability**: AWS VPN offers flexibility in establishing connections. It allows you to connect multiple sites or branch offices to AWS, providing a unified network environment. Additionally, it scales easily to accommodate growing business needs, by enabling you to add or remove VPN connections as required.

- **Cost-efficiency**: Using AWS VPN eliminates the need to invest in expensive hardware or dedicated leased lines. It leverages the existing internet infrastructure to establish secure connections, reducing capital expenditures and maintenance costs associated with traditional networking solutions.

- **Ease of management**: AWS VPN integrates seamlessly with other AWS services, simplifying management and monitoring. It can be configured and controlled through the AWS Management Console or using APIs, so you can conveniently set up, modify, and track the VPN connections.

Now that you have seen the positive aspects of using VPN, you should also review some of the negative aspects that could affect your environment when using VPN. They are presented here:

- **Dependence on internet connectivity**: Since AWS VPN relies on the internet to establish connections, the quality and reliability of the internet connection in question can impact performance. If the corporate network or AWS resources experience connectivity issues, it can affect the VPN connection as well.

- **Potential latency**: The VPN connection introduces additional overhead due to encryption and encapsulation, which can result in increased latency compared to a direct network connection. While the impact is generally minimal, certain latency-sensitive applications may experience performance degradation. These can include applications such as databases stored in AWS, **customer relation management** (**CRM**) systems, and voice-over-IP calling systems.

- **Network configuration complexity**: Setting up and configuring AWS VPN may require some networking knowledge and expertise. This task can be time-consuming as it cannot all be done from the AWS console; you need to submit a request for the dedicated connection. This includes selecting the AWS Direct Connect Partner provider, connection bandwidth, and the location of AWS Direct Connect. Proper planning and understanding of network requirements, IP addressing, and routing are essential to ensure a smooth and secure connection.

- **Data security risk**: AWS operates over the public internet, which is a shared infrastructure. Although the connection is encrypted, it is important to assess and manage security risks associated with transmitting data over public networks.

Having an understanding of the pros and cons of using AWS VPN in your environment will help you understand the different use cases as they are presented in various questions in the AWS Certified Security Specialty exam. In the next section, you will go through the process of setting up a VPN connection to gain a better understanding of the components and steps required to create a VPN connection with one of your AWS VPCs in your account.

Using AWS VPN in your environment

Setting up an AWS VPN involves several steps to establish a secure and encrypted connection between your on-premises network and your AWS environment.

> **Note**
> You will need to know the IP address from your home network/office network where you are going to establish the VPN, as this will be used in the step for creating the customer gateway. If you do not know this information, then you should use one of the sites available online to look up your external facing IP address.

The following steps will take you through the basic setup involved when establishing a VPN connection:

1. In the AWS Management Console, navigate to the VPN service. You can use the following link for quick access: `https://packt.link/kGc5x`.

2. On the left-hand navigation bar, scroll down until you reach the section named `Virtual private network (VPN)`. Click on the link named `Virtual private gateways`.

▼ **Virtual private network (VPN)**

Customer gateways

Virtual private gateways

Site-to-Site VPN connections

Client VPN endpoints

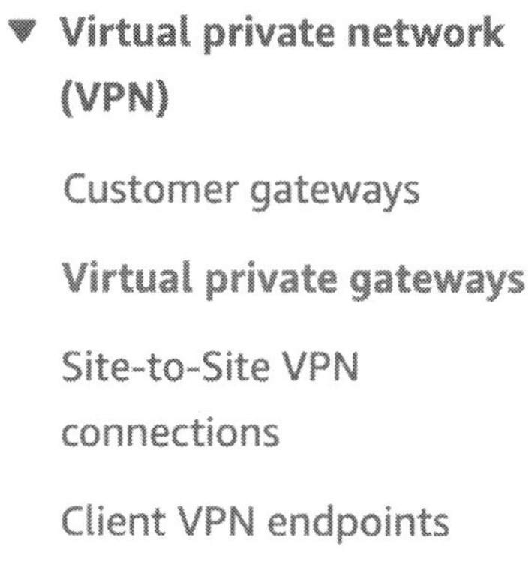

Figure 18.3: VPN menu

3. Once Virtual private gateways appears in the main section of the page, click on the button labeled Create virtual private gateway. There should always be an orange button at the top, and if you haven't created any previous virtual private gateways, there will be a white button in the middle of the screen.

4. After you click the button, a screen will appear to provide the details of the virtual private gateway. A good name for this one would be something like Chapter18-Demo-VPG. Fill this in, but keep the rest of the default settings, such as Autonomous System Number (ASN) as Amazon default ASN.

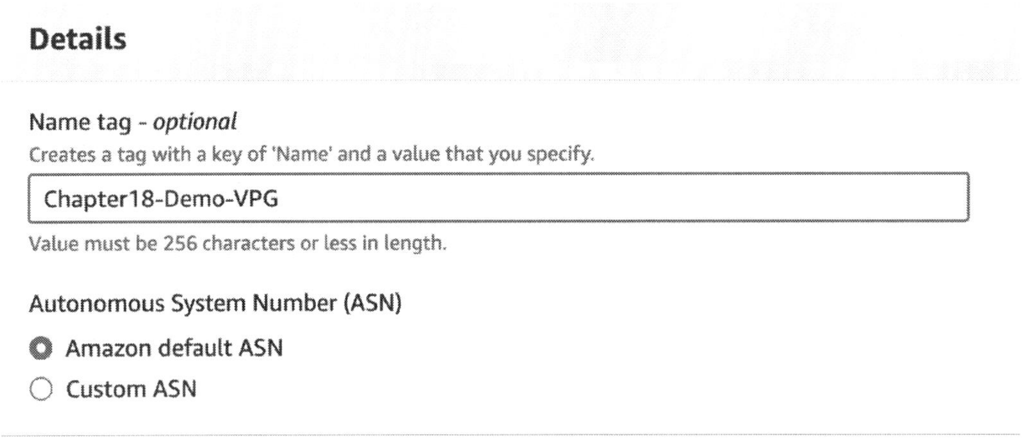

Details

Name tag - *optional*

Creates a tag with a key of 'Name' and a value that you specify.

Chapter18-Demo-VPG

Value must be 256 characters or less in length.

Autonomous System Number (ASN)

◉ Amazon default ASN

◯ Custom ASN

Figure 18.4: Virtual private gateway details screen

5. Once you have filled in the name of the virtual private gateway, scroll down to the bottom of the page and click the button labeled Create virtual private gateway.

    You should now be back on the main virtual private gateways screen, where you should be able to see your newly created virtual private gateway. It will be in the Detached state. You will attach it to your VPN in the next step.

Name ✎	▽	Virtual private gateway ID	▽	State	Type	▽	VPC
◯ Chapter18-Demo-VPG		vgw-0acc6481d2b72265a		⊖ Detached	ipsec.1		–

Figure 18.5: The newly created virtual gateway

6. Now, you will need to attach the virtual private gateway to the VPC. Select the radio button next to the name of the virtual private gateway. Once the drop-down menu appears, click on the option named Attach to VPC.

7. On the Attach to VPC page, under Details, use the drop-down menu to choose which one of your VPCs you want to have your virtual private gateway connected to. Once selected, click on the Attach to VPC button.

    After you press the button, you will be taken back to the Virtual private gateways screen, where you should see your virtual private gateway in an Attaching state.

| ○ | Chapter18-Demo-VPG | vgw-0acc6481d2b72265a | ☉ Attaching | ipsec.1 |

Figure 18.6: Virtual private gateway attaching state

8. Go back to the left-hand menu and, once again, under the Virtual private network heading, click on the sub-menu item named Customer gateways.

9. When the Customer gateways main window appears, click on the button labeled Create customer gateway.

10. When the Create customer gateway page appears, in the Details section, enter Chapter18-CustomerGateway as the optional name tag.

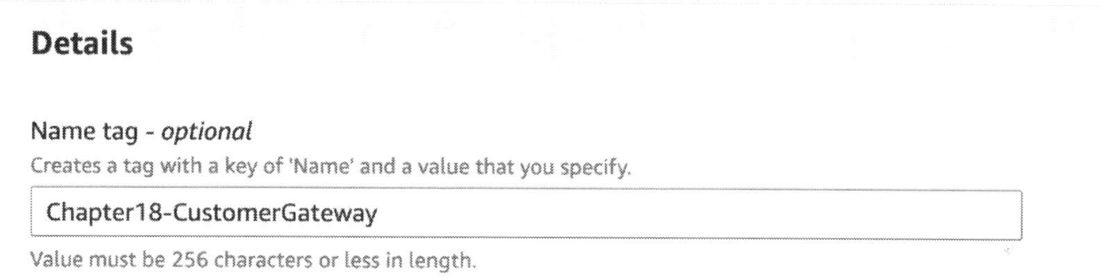

Details

Name tag - *optional*
Creates a tag with a key of 'Name' and a value that you specify.

Chapter18-CustomerGateway

Value must be 256 characters or less in length.

Figure 18.7: Virtual private gateway tag screen

11. Then scroll down to the label named IP address. Here, enter either your own public IP address or your organization's public IP address.

IP address   Info
Specify the IP address for your customer gateway device's external interface.

192.0.2.1

Figure 18.8: IP address field

12. Optionally, you can scroll down to the field named `Device` and enter a name for your device, such as `Netgear router`.

13. Finally, scroll down to the bottom of the page and click on the `Create customer gateway` button.

By following all of the steps here, you will have created a VPN connection from your on-premises location to your Amazon VPC. Using the VPN will help make sure that any traffic that you send to the VPC stays encrypted and secure. In the next subsection, you will look at the different routing options for VPNs.

Configuring VPN Routing Options

Once you have created your VPN by establishing your virtual private gateway and attaching a customer gateway, you can begin adding routing configuration to your subnets to allow you to route traffic to your corporate site via the VPN Site-to-Site connection.

Have a look at the example in the following diagram:

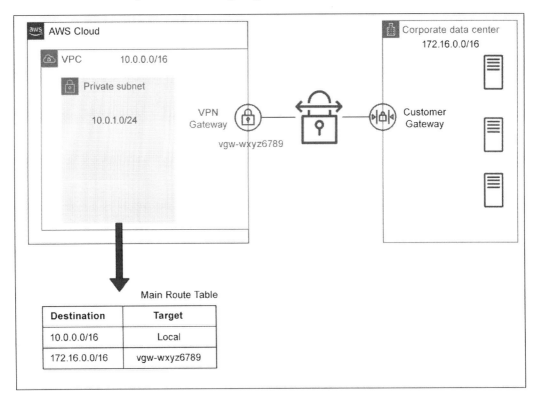

Figure 18.9: VPN routing example

As you can see in *Figure 18.9*, AWS VPC has a `10.0.1.0/24` subnet within the VPC CIDR block of `10.0.0.0/16`. The main route table has a manually added static route pointing to the network address space within the corporate data center on the other side of the VPN connection. You will notice that this route has been added with the destination pointing to our VPN gateway (`vpn-wxyz6789`). As a result of this, any traffic destined for this network will travel via the VPN gateway.

A key element in AWS routing is the principle of the *longest prefix match*, and having an understanding of this principle will help you troubleshoot routing issues. The *longest prefix match* determines how routes are prioritized in directing traffic to a target, especially when a route table has overlapping CIDR blocks—how will AWS determine where to send the traffic? Well, AWS will use the destination that has the most precise destination network listed; this approach is known as the *longest prefix match*. With the longest prefix match, using the same VPC and subnet pictured in *Figure 18.9*, traffic within the same subnet (e.g., from `10.0.1.5` to `10.0.1.10`) will remain within the subnet and won't be routed outside. Traffic destined for addresses within the VPC but outside the subnet (e.g., from `10.0.1.5` to `10.0.2.10`) will be routed based on the longest prefix match in the route table associated with the subnet.

Using a VPN allows you to secure your transmissions to AWS over the public internet. In the next section, you will see how you can bypass the public internet and have your data travel directly through a dedicated connection using AWS Direct Connect.

Transmitting Data Directly with AWS Direct Connect

AWS Direct Connect provides a dedicated and private network connection that allows you to establish a direct link between your on-premises data center and the AWS cloud. This secure connection bypasses the public internet to ensure that your data is transmitted directly and privately to AWS services and resources.

When you set up AWS Direct Connect, you work with an AWS Direct Connect partner who will provide a physical connection from your data center to an AWS Direct Connect location. This connection is typically a high-speed, low-latency, and dedicated network link that provides a more reliable and consistent data transfer experience compared to using the public internet.

Once the physical connection is established, AWS provisions a virtual interface to associate with your AWS account. This virtual interface acts as a gateway that allows data to flow securely between your data center and your VPCs in AWS. You can create multiple virtual interfaces to segregate different types of traffic or to connect to multiple VPCs across different AWS Regions.

When data is transmitted from your data center to AWS, it enters the AWS network through the virtual interface and is routed directly to the specified AWS services and resources. Since the connection is private and dedicated, your data remains within the AWS network until it reaches its destination, which improves security and reduces exposure to potential internet threats.

One of the most prevalent use cases for using a Direct Connect connection is when you need to lower your latency speeds when transmitting your data to AWS Direct Connect. If you have migrated your company's workloads to AWS, especially items like VMware, then you need a speedy stable connection for your workforce when accessing those files and workloads. Users at a corporate office may notice a lag or wait time when trying to retrieve files and data from the cloud if many users are trying to perform multiple operations at the same time. Also, when you go over the public internet, there are multiple "hops" in the network before you reach your final destination. This is not the case when using Direct Connect. As its name suggests, it is a direct connection in a datacenter from your equipment to the AWS equipment, thereby making the transmissions faster and in many cases more secure since it is a direct route.

AWS Direct Connect provides several benefits, which you will learn about in the next subsection.

Benefits of Using AWS Direct Connect

AWS Direct Connect provides several benefits, including enhanced security, reduced data transfer costs, predictable network performance, and ease of compliance with regulatory requirements. By leveraging this dedicated and private connection, you can seamlessly integrate your on-premises environment with the AWS cloud, ensuring secure and efficient data transmission for your business-critical workloads and applications.

The following are the key benefits of Direct Connect explained in detail:

- **Enhanced security**: By bypassing the public internet, AWS Direct Connect ensures that your data is transmitted securely and remains protected from potential security threats. You can implement encryption to safeguard sensitive information further during transit.

- **Providing reliable and consistent performance**: With AWS Direct Connect, you can achieve low-latency and high-bandwidth connectivity, resulting in a more stable and predictable network performance. This is crucial for applications and services that demand real-time data transfer and is helpful when you are trying to migrate data and servers from on-premises systems to the cloud at a higher speed than you can achieve over normal internet lines.

- **Reduced data costs**: AWS Direct Connect enables you to transfer data between your on-premises environment and the AWS cloud infrastructure, and data transfer into AWS is not charged for any method. However, with data transfer out or data egress, Direct Connect presents an opportunity for savings if data is transferred in bulk. The price per GB of data egress can be up to one-fifth the price of transferring data over the public internet.

- **Seamless cloud integration**: The Direct Connect gateway allows you to connect multiple VPCs from different AWS Regions to a single Direct Connect connection. This simplifies network management and enables seamless communication between your on-premises resources and cloud-based applications hosted in separate VPCs.

- **Compliance and regulatory requirements**: AWS Direct Connect helps you meet compliance and regulatory requirements by providing a dedicated and secure connection for sensitive workloads and data.

- **Reduced network complexity**: By consolidating your connections through AWS Direct Connect, you can reduce network complexity, making it easier to manage and maintain your cloud network infrastructure.

- **Scalability and flexibility**: As your cloud needs evolve, AWS Direct Connect can easily scale to accommodate increased bandwidth requirements or additional connections to new AWS Regions.

Having learned about the benefits of Direct Connect, you also need to have an idea of the security features that it provides as well as where it falls short. These aspects are discussed in the following subsections.

How AWS Direct Connect Provides Security

AWS Direct Connect provides security through several mechanisms that help ensure the confidentiality, integrity, and availability of data as it travels between your on-premises data center and your AWS resources. This direct link bypasses the public internet, reducing exposure to potential security threats associated with transmitting data over the open internet.

Take a look at the list of ways in which AWS Direct Connect enhances security:

- **Using a private and dedicated connection**: AWS Direct Connect establishes a dedicated and private network connection between your on-premises environment and AWS. This dedicated connection ensures that the data transmitted between your organization's network and AWS remains isolated from other network traffic, reducing the risk of interception or tampering by unauthorized parties.

- **Encryption options with Direct Connect**: While AWS Direct Connect does not encrypt the data flowing over the connection, you can implement mechanisms at the application layer or use VPN technologies to encrypt the data in transit. This ensures that even if the data were intercepted, it would be unreadable without the appropriate decryption keys.

- **Authentication and access control**: AWS Direct Connect uses **Border Gateway Protocol** (**BGP**) for routing traffic between your network and AWS. BGP supports authentication, ensuring that only authorized networks can participate in the routing exchange. Additionally, AWS **Identity and Access Management** (**IAM**) can be used to control who has access to create, delete, or modify Direct Connect resources.

- **An added layer of physical security**: AWS Direct Connect locations are highly secure data centers operated by AWS and Direct Connect partners. These locations feature robust physical security measures, including access controls, surveillance, and monitoring, to prevent unauthorized access.

- **Monitoring via health checks and failover capabilities**: AWS Direct Connect monitors the health of your connections and endpoints. If an endpoint becomes unhealthy, traffic can be automatically redirected to healthy endpoints, ensuring high availability and minimizing disruptions.

- **Direct Connect gateway and virtual private interfaces**: The Direct Connect gateway allows you to connect multiple VPCs from different AWS Regions to a single Direct Connect connection. Private virtual interfaces can be configured to keep traffic within the AWS network, providing an additional layer of security.

- **Reduced exposure to the public internet**: Using AWS Direct Connect reduces the exposure of your data to the public internet, minimizing the risk of various internet-based attacks, such as **distributed denial of service (DDoS)** attacks.

It's important to note, however, that while AWS Direct Connect enhances security, the overall security of your applications and data also depends on how you configure and manage your network, endpoints, and resources in the AWS environment. Implementing best security practices, utilizing encryption, and regularly reviewing your network architecture can further enhance the security posture of your cloud infrastructure.

You just learned about the advantages of using an AWS Direct Connect connection from your corporate location. But what happens when you have multiple corporate offices each of which has a Direct Connect connection and all of them are trying to connect to the same account? This is where the Direct Connect gateway comes in. In the next section, you will learn about the Direct Connect gateway, which is helpful in the situation described.

Direct Connect Gateway

AWS Direct Connect gateways simplify and enhance the connectivity between your on-premises data centers and multiple Amazon VPCs within the AWS environment. Think of it as a central hub that consolidates and manages the connections between your organization's various networking resources. With an AWS Direct Connect gateway, you can establish private and dedicated network connections to AWS, bypassing the public internet for improved security, reliability, and lower latency.

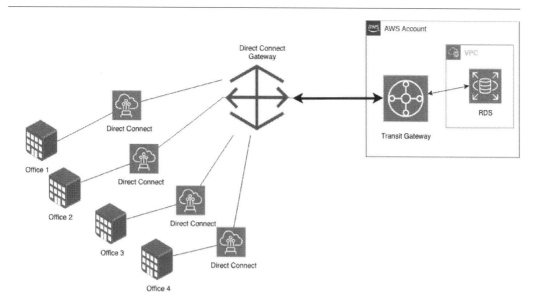

Figure 18.10: AWS Direct Connect gateway

Imagine your company has different locations around the country or around the globe, each with its own dedicated or shared Direct Connect connection. The data that the company is working with is in either one account or multiple accounts within the same organization. The users within your organization need to collaborate. In this case, the Direct Connect gateway will simplify the networking setup by allowing you to associate all of the Direct Connect connections together.

The Security Benefits of the AWS Direct Connect Gateway

The AWS Direct Connect gateway provides several security benefits that contribute to a robust and secure network infrastructure. First, by establishing private, dedicated connections to AWS resources, Direct Connect gateway helps bypass the public internet, reducing exposure to potential security threats associated with internet-based traffic. This private connectivity ensures that data traveling between your on-premises data centers and AWS remains within a secure, controlled environment.

Additionally, the Direct Connect gateway enhances security by enabling the implementation of private network architectures. With the ability to connect multiple VPCs to your on-premises network through a centralized gateway, you can establish consistent security policies and control across these connections. This centralized management simplifies the enforcement of security measures, such as access controls and encryption, ensuring a uniform and robust security posture across your entire network.

Furthermore, the Direct Connect gateway supports the use of **Virtual LANs (VLANs)** to isolate logically and segment network traffic, providing an additional layer of security. This segmentation helps prevent unauthorized access and enhances network visibility and control. Overall, the Direct Connect gateway plays a crucial role in creating a secure and efficient hybrid cloud environment, where data transfer between your on-premises infrastructure and AWS services is not only optimized but also protected against potential security threats.

Along with the AWS Direct Connect gateway, there is another hub-and-spoke model service that allows you to connect to multiple VPCs from a single location, even if you don't have the Direct Connect service. In the next section, you will learn about how you can still connect to multiple VPCs using AWS CloudHub.

Understanding the Purpose of AWS CloudHub

AWS VPN CloudHub is a managed service that allows you to connect multiple AWS Site-to-Site VPN connections securely. This enables your sites to communicate with each other and not just with resources in your VPC. You can see from the following image that CloudHub allows connectivity from multiple remote locations (just like the Direct Connect gateway) but does so using VPN connections instead of Direct Connect circuits.

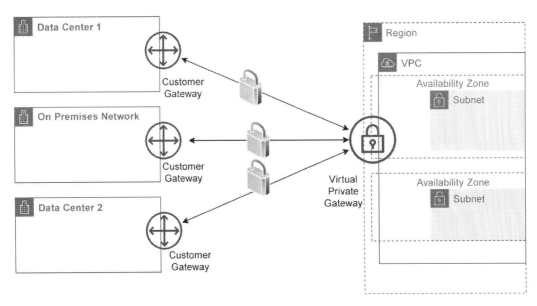

Figure 18.11: The hub-and-spoke model of AWS CloudHub

AWS VPN CloudHub operates on a simple hub-and-spoke model, as shown in *Figure 18.11*, that you can use with or without a VPC. In this approach, the VPN connection is the hub, and the remote offices act as the spokes. In the hub-and-spoke design of CloudHub, the AWS account is the hub and the remote offices are the spokes. It is more cost-effective than multiple Direct Connect connections and is extremely useful in cases where you need a redundant connection for your on-premises networks.

The benefits of using AWS VPN CloudHub include the following:

- **Scalability**: AWS VPN CloudHub can scale to meet the needs of your organization, even as your traffic grows.

- **Reliability**: AWS VPN CloudHub is a highly reliable resource that is backed by the AWS commitment to uptime.

- **Ease of use**: AWS VPN CloudHub is easy to set up and manage, even for novice users.

- **Security**: AWS VPN CloudHub uses industry-standard encryption to protect your data in transit and at rest and employs IPSec to secure connections.

- **Cost-effectiveness**: AWS VPN CloudHub is a cost-effective way to connect to your sites securely. If you are using a VPN in your organization and have multiple locations that need connecting to a single account, then AWS CloudHub is a viable option.

Amazon VPN CloudHub employs an Amazon VPC virtual private gateway coupled with several customer gateways. Each customer gateway utilizes distinct BGP **autonomous system numbers** (**ASNs**). It's essential to ensure non-overlapping IP ranges among the remote sites. Your gateways effectively broadcast the relevant routes (BGP prefixes) across their VPN connections. These route advertisements are then received and subsequently propagated to each BGP peer, enabling seamless bi-directional data transmission between the different sites.

Summary

In this chapter, you looked at the different ways you can secure the connections you and your company make into your AWS environment. You started by reviewing the default connection from an on-premises network to AWS that is simply a connection over the internet, which is an insecure manner of operation. You were then introduced to the two main services that can help you protect your data in transit: AWS VPN and AWS Direct Connect.

In the final section of this chapter, you looked at AWS VPN CloudHub and how it can connect multiple remote sites to a VPN connection using a hub-and-spoke model, thereby simplifying your networking and security tasks for connectivity for remote offices.

In the next chapter, we will look at how to further protect data in transit by using and creating certificates using the AWS Certificate Manager service.

Further Reading

For additional information on the AWS Shared Responsibility Model and the underlying foundation of AWS security, please look at the following resources:

- AWS VPN FAQs: `https://packt.link/s0Whv`
- AWS Direct Connect FAQs: `https://packt.link/KOUcO`
- AWS VPN CloudHub Documentation: `https://packt.link/hKLUh`
- Connect your VPC to remote networks using AWS VPN: `https://packt.link/IciRm`

Exam Readiness Drill – Chapter Review Questions

Apart from a solid understanding of key concepts, being able to think quickly under time pressure is a skill that will help you ace your certification exam. That is why working on these skills early on in your learning journey is key.

Chapter review questions are designed to improve your test-taking skills progressively with each chapter you learn and review your understanding of key concepts in the chapter at the same time. You'll find these at the end of each chapter.

> **How To Access These Resources**
>
> To learn how to access these resources, head over to the chapter titled *Chapter 21, Accessing the Online Practice Resources*.

To open the Chapter Review Questions for this chapter, perform the following steps:

1. Click the link – `https://packt.link/SCSC02E2_CH18`

    Alternatively, you can scan the following QR code (*Figure 18.12*):

Figure 18.12: QR code that opens Chapter Review Questions for logged-in users

2. Once you log in, you'll see a page similar to the one shown in *Figure 18.13*:

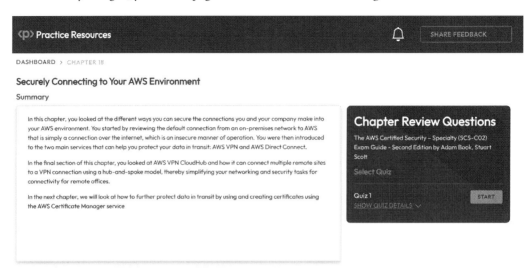

Figure 18.13: Chapter Review Questions for Chapter 18

3. Once ready, start the following practice drills, re-attempting the quiz multiple times.

Exam Readiness Drill

For the first three attempts, don't worry about the time limit.

ATTEMPT 1

The first time, aim for at least **40%**. Look at the answers you got wrong and read the relevant sections in the chapter again to fix your learning gaps.

ATTEMPT 2

The second time, aim for at least **60%**. Look at the answers you got wrong and read the relevant sections in the chapter again to fix any remaining learning gaps.

ATTEMPT 3

The third time, aim for at least **75%**. Once you score **75%** or more, you start working on your timing.

> **Tip**
>
> You may take more than three attempts to reach 75%. That's okay. Just review the relevant sections in the chapter till you get there.

Working On Timing

Target: Your aim is to keep the score the same while trying to answer these questions as quickly as possible. Here's an example of how your next attempts should look like:

Attempt	Score	Time Taken
Attempt 5	77%	21 mins 30 seconds
Attempt 6	78%	18 mins 34 seconds
Attempt 7	76%	14 mins 44 seconds

Table 18.1: Sample timing practice drills on the online platform

> **Note**
>
> The time limits shown in the above table are just examples. Set your own time limits with each attempt based on the time limit of the quiz on the website.

With each new attempt, your score should stay above 75% while your time taken to complete should **decrease**. Repeat as many attempts as you want till you feel confident dealing with the time pressure.

19

Using Certificates and Certificate Services in AWS

When users go online, either on the public internet or on a private intranet, they expect a secure connection so they can trust that the data they are sending is safe. These connections are secured by SSL and TLS certificates, and it is often up to the security team of any organization to manage, install, and rotate these certificates. **AWS Certificate Manager** (**ACM**) helps take out many manual steps of creating, configuring, and installing security certificates and integrates almost seamlessly for many services that interact with client-facing components.

The following main topics will be covered in this chapter:

- A basic overview of the different types of secure certificates used
- Understanding the certificate types used in the ACM service
- Use cases for the ACM service
- Using public certificates with the ACM service
- Creating and managing private **certificate authorities** (**CAs**) in ACM
- Manage the security configuration of your **Elastic Load Balancers** (**ELB**) using SSL/TLS certificates via Certificate Manager

Technical Requirements

You must have a basic understanding of AWS services and networking concepts.

AWS Certificate Manager (ACM) Overview

ACM is a valuable service that simplifies and enhances the security of your web applications and websites. Think of ACM as a trusted guardian for your online presence. Its main job is to provide you with digital certificates, which are like special keys that ensure the safety and privacy of data as it travels between your servers and your users' web browsers. These certificates are crucial because they encrypt sensitive information, such as login credentials and payment details, ensuring that even if someone tries to eavesdrop on the data, they can't decipher it.

One significant benefit of using ACM is the level of trust it establishes with web browsers and devices. ACM certificates are issued by globally recognized **Certificate Authorities** (**CAs**), which means that when browsers see your certificates, they automatically trust your websites (and applications). It's like having a universally accepted ID card for your online presence, which is vital in building trust with your users.

ACM also simplifies the process of obtaining and managing these certificates. You request a certificate from ACM by specifying the domain names or web addresses you want to secure. ACM then verifies that you indeed own or control those domain names, adding an essential layer of security. Once verified, ACM issues the certificate, handles all the technical complexities, such as creating encryption keys, and automatically renews certificates when needed. This means you can focus on your application's functionality while ACM handles security seamlessly.

In essence, ACM is like a reliable security partner for your web applications, ensuring that your user's data is shielded from prying eyes and your online presence is trustworthy. It simplifies the complex world of SSL/TLS certificates, making them accessible to all levels of expertise and helping you maintain the highest security standards for your digital assets.

With this initial understanding of the ACM service and the different types of security certificates it offers, you can proceed to examine how these certificates are utilized in various scenarios in the next section. This will help you both for the exam and as you perform your day-to-day responsibilities.

Certificate Types in ACM

To work closely with ACM, you need to have an understanding of the different types of certificates that the service uses. The SSL/TLS certificate is a digital security certificate that provides secure, encrypted communication over the internet. This certificate is primarily used to establish a secure connection between a client (e.g., a web browser) and a server (e.g., a website) or between servers. Security certificates are crucial to ensure data privacy and integrity during online transactions, data transfers, and other sensitive communications.

A CA, such as ACM, is responsible for issuing and digitally signing SSL/TLS certificates. They establish trust in the certificates they issue, ensuring that users can rely on their authenticity.

ACM supports three primary types of security certificates:

- **Public certificates**: Public certificates are used to secure websites and other publicly accessible web applications. They are issued by a public CA and are trusted by all major web browsers.

- **Private certificates**: Private certificates are used to secure private networks and applications. They are issued by a private CA and trusted only by devices and applications configured to trust that CA.

- **Wildcard certificates**: Wildcard certificates can secure multiple domain names with a single certificate. For example, a wildcard certificate for `*.example.com` can be used to secure `example.com`, `www.example.com`, `mobile.example.com`, and any other subdomain of `example.com`. A wildcard certificate can be issued by either a public or private CA.

In addition to those three primary types of certificates, ACM also supports several specialized certificate types, including the following:

- **Domain Validation (DV) certificates**: DV certificates are the most common certificates. They are issued based on the applicant's domain ownership and do not require any manual intervention.

- **Organization Validation (OV) certificates**: OV certificates require the applicant to provide additional information about their organization, such as their legal name and address. The CA then verifies this information before the certificate is issued.

- **Extended Validation (EV) certificates**: EV certificates require the applicant to undergo a rigorous vetting process by the CA. This process includes verifying the applicant's legal name, address, and identity.

The type of certificate that you will need will depend on your needs. If you are just looking to add more legitimacy and trust to your website, then a DV certificate would be fine. However, if you are in the type of industry that performs e-commerce, then your organization needs to take the next step up to an OV certificate. Furthermore, if your enterprise is dealing with financial transactions, banking, or handling sensitive information, then this is when you need to apply for an EV certificate.

In the next section, you will learn how to differentiate between public and private certificates generated by ACM.

Determining the Difference between Public and Private Certificates

As mentioned in the previous section, public certificates are used to secure websites and other publicly accessible web applications. They are issued by a CA and trusted by all major web browsers. They validate the website's identity to visitors and ensure encrypted communication; this is commonly indicated by the padlock icon in web browsers next to the URL address. Public certificates can be obtained from various sources, including ACM and commercial CAs. ACM allows AWS customers to request and manage public certificates easily and for free.

Private certificates secure private networks and applications such as internal websites, VPNs, APIs, internal servers, IoT devices, and other sensitive resources. As mentioned earlier, they are issued by a private CA and trusted only by devices and applications configured to trust that CA. They authenticate and encrypt data traffic between these resources, enhancing security within the organization's private network, often without public internet access or public trust requirements. To request a private certificate from ACM, you must first create a private CA. Once you have created a private CA, you can request certificates from ACM for your devices and applications.

Now that you have a foundational understanding of the difference between public and private certificates, you are ready to learn about ACM (the service in AWS that generates, stores, and manages those certificates) in depth, both with respect to public and private applications.

Gaining a Deeper Understanding of the ACM Service and Its Uses

While the primary use case of ACM is to provide SSL/TLS certificates for public and private websites, it also offers a valuable feature called **AWS Private CA** (previously ACM Private CA). The true functionality of the service comes in the fact that it provides a centralized platform for requesting, provisioning, and deploying SSL/TLS certificates, eliminating the need for manual management tasks. With ACM, you can easily obtain certificates for the AWS resources running in your environment such as ELB, **CloudFront distributions**, and **API Gateway endpoints**, facilitating secure communication between clients and these services. ACM offers features such as automatic certificate renewal, which ensures that certificates are continuously updated to maintain security and compliance.

ACM also offers a user-friendly interface and robust features and one of the key features is its simplicity and ease of use. You can request and manage certificates through the AWS Management Console, CLI, or API. This can suit your needs whether you are just starting or are an experienced AWS user. ACM also provides certificate tagging capabilities, enabling you to organize and manage your certificates efficiently. Furthermore, ACM supports certificate validation through DNS or email validation, ensuring the legitimacy of certificate requests. As a service, ACM simplifies SSL/TLS certificate management, enhances security, and helps you maintain compliance with industry standards.

While the core ACM service is focused on SSL/TLS certificates on public websites, AWS Private CA expands its capabilities to serve a broader range of security needs within an organization. It's a versatile tool for managing private certificates, enhancing security, and ensuring the trust and integrity of various digital interactions beyond web communication.

The following section will discuss the offerings of ACM with regard to public certificates.

Using Public Certificates with the ACM Service

ACM is valuable for managing and provisioning public certificates, especially in securing web applications or websites. When you host a website or application that requires secure communications over HTTPS, ACM can simplify the obtainment and renewal of SSL/TLS certificates.

ACM also handles the complexity involved in certificate management, handling tasks such as certificate issuance, renewal, and integration with AWS services such as Elastic Load Balancing and Amazon CloudFront so that you can focus on building and running your applications. At the same time, AWS ensures the seamless and secure management of your public certificates, enhancing the overall security posture of your online services.

The next few subsections will take you through some use cases where you would implement public certificates on AWS using ACM.

Real-World Uses for Public Certificates Created by ACM

The ACM service that creates public certificates has many capabilities that you should be aware of as well:

- **Securing websites**: ACM can be used to provision and manage SSL/TLS certificates for securing websites hosted on AWS services such as ELB, Amazon CloudFront, or Amazon API Gateway. This ensures that data transmitted between clients and the website is encrypted.

- **Security APIs**: APIs deployed on AWS API Gateway can use ACM to manage SSL/TLS certificates, ensuring encrypted communication between clients and API endpoints. This is essential for protecting sensitive data transmitted via API calls and maintaining compliance with security standards.

- **Securing custom applications**: Custom applications running on EC2 instances or other AWS services can use ACM to obtain and manage SSL/TLS certificates for securing communication channels. This helps prevent eavesdropping and data interception, ensuring the confidentiality and integrity of data transmitted over the internet.

In the next section, you will take a look at one of the most prevalent use cases for public certificates created by ACM – securing a website, especially one hosted on Amazon S3.

Securing Static Sites Hosted on Amazon S3

Static websites hosted on Amazon S3 are a cost-effective and scalable solution for delivering web content. These websites consist of fixed HTML, CSS, JavaScript, and media files that don't change dynamically. S3's high availability and content distribution capabilities combined with its easy setup and low operational costs make it an ideal choice for hosting brochure sites, landing pages, documentation, and other content-centric web assets. Static websites on S3 can also be easily enhanced with Amazon CloudFront for secure and speedy content delivery to users worldwide.

ACM is critical in securing a static website hosted on Amazon S3.

One of the primary ways ACM benefits your static website is by providing SSL/TLS certificates. When you associate an ACM certificate with your S3 website, it enables HTTPS, which encrypts the data transmitted between your visitors' browsers and your S3-hosted site. This encryption ensures that sensitive information, such as login credentials or personal data, remains confidential during transit, enhancing the overall security posture of your website. This process is shown in *Figure 19.1*.

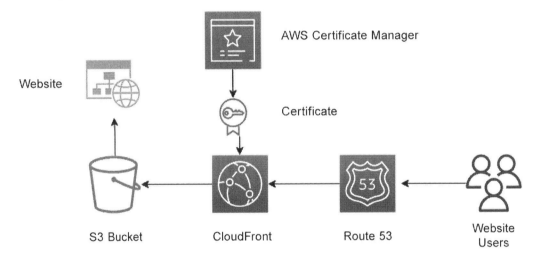

Figure 19.1: ACM certificate securing static website on S3

ACM takes the hassle out of certificate management by automatically renewing certificates before expiration to ensure uninterrupted, secure website access. This automated renewal process eliminates the risk of certificate lapse, which could lead to security warnings for your visitors or even site downtime. Thus, with ACM, you can rest assured that your security certificates are always up to date and focus on creating and maintaining your static content.

Securing an Elastic Load Balancer with a Certificate Issued by ACM

When setting up your ELBs, you can categorize them as internal or internet-facing. Internal load balancers exclusively employ private IP addresses, serving requests originating from within your VPC. In contrast, internet-facing ELBs have a distinct configuration. They possess public DNS names, which resolve to publicly reachable IP addresses alongside their internal IP addresses used exclusively within your VPC. This differentiation ensures that internet-facing ELBs are accessible from both the public internet and your private VPC network.

Therefore, just like you do with other various services that interact with the public internet, you will want to consider implementing encryption with ELB to enhance the security of your solution and reduce potential threats to your infrastructure. When working with ELBs, you can accomplish this by employing server certificates.

When you opt for the HTTPS protocol as a listener while setting up your ELB, there is additional configuration involved in the second step of the setup process to handle encryption. You have to specify a server certificate and security policies. HTTPS is essentially the secure, encrypted variant of the HTTP protocol. By employing the HTTPS protocol, your load balancer can serve encrypted requests originating from external hosts, enhancing the security of your data transmission.

Internet-facing ELBs have public DNS names that resolve to the internet. As a best security practice, ensure that the traffic going to your websites and web applications from these load balancers goes through a secure protocol.

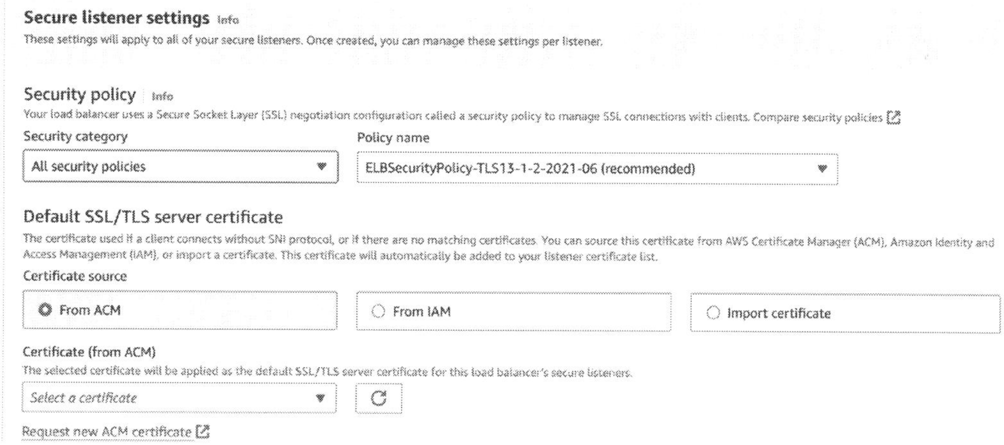

Figure 19.2: Secure listener settings for ELB

When utilizing a secure protocol in `Secure listener settings` for your ELB, choosing a certificate for an association is essential. *Figure 19.2* shows an application load balancer, in which the certificate enables the ELB to terminate incoming encrypted requests from external hosts. As part of this process, the ELB decrypts the incoming request before forwarding the now-decrypted request to your designated target group. This ensures a seamless and secure flow of information within your system.

As emphasized in the earlier screenshot, AWS recommends leveraging ACM to create and manage your SSL/TLS public certificates. This preference is primarily attributed to ACM's seamless integration with the ELB service, which ensures a streamlined and efficient process for securing your web application or websites.

Issuing a Security Certificate via ACM

Suppose your company is running, and owns, the domain name `example.com`, and they decide that they want to run a store called `https://shop.example.com` and a site where their salespeople could upload their reports, at the URL named `https://expenses.example.com`. Your company would then need to protect both of these websites with a single wildcard certificate.

In such cases, you could use the ACM service to issue a security certificate. The following steps will walk you through the process of doing that:

1. Sign in to the AWS Management Console and navigate to the ACM service. You can use the following URL to get there quickly: `https://packt.link/yViz6`.

2. Click the `Request a certificate` button in the ACM dashboard to begin the certificate issuance process.

3. On the `Request certificate` page, under `Certificate type`, make sure that the radio button has been selected next to `Request a public certificate`. After ensuring this, you can click the `Next` button at the bottom of the page.

Figure 19.3: Certificate type selection screen for ACM

4.   You should now be on the `Request public certificate` page. Enter the domain names (e.g., `*.example.com`) or subdomains you want to include in the certificate request in the `Fully qualified domain name` box. If you want to add a secondary domain to the same certificate, click the button labeled `Add another name to this certificate`.

Domain names

Provide one or more domain names for your certificate.

Fully qualified domain name   Info

*.example.com

Add another name to this certificate

You can add additional names to this certificate. For example, if you're requesting a certificate for "www.example.com", you might want to add the name "example.com" so that customers can reach your site by either name.

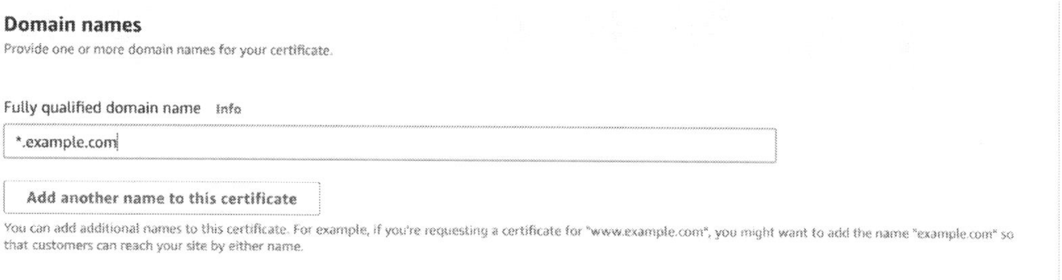

Figure 19.4: Adding domains to the certificate

> **Note**
>
> As you will see in the next step, any domain (or subdomain) you enter must be verified to show that you own the rights to create a certificate for that domain. Before Amazon CA can issue a certificate, ACM requires the verification of your ownership or control over all the specified domain names. Opting for the preferred method of DNS validation involves ACM furnishing you with one or more **Canonical Name (CNAME)** records that need to be incorporated into your domain DNS database. These records encapsulate a distinctive key-value pair, acting as conclusive evidence of your domain control. Adding these records to the DNS reinforces the validation process and ensures a secure and verifiable confirmation of your ownership or control over the specified domain.

5.   Scroll down on the page until you see `Validation method`. You have two options with this section. The preferred method is `DNS Validation`, which is simpler; you just add an entry to your DNS record.

     The other option is `Email validation`, where ACM sends validation emails to a specific email address associated with the domain. You must respond to these emails to complete validation.

6. Select the DNS validation option for this exercise and go to the section labeled `Key algorithm`. Select the `RSA 2048` value.

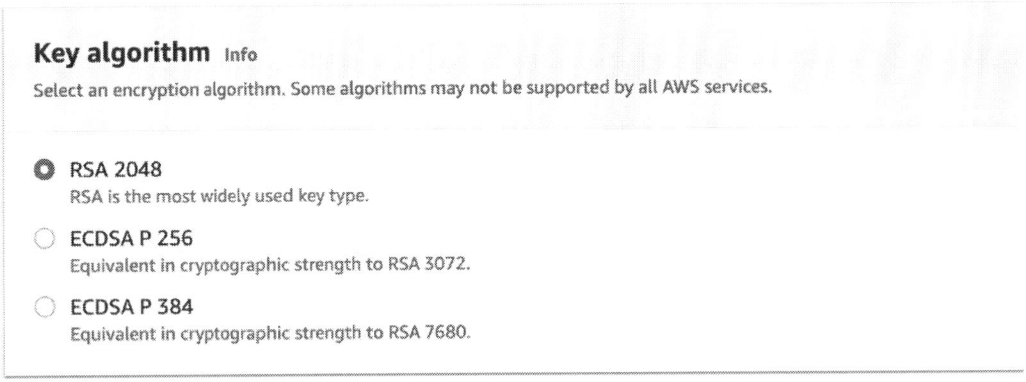

Key algorithm Info

Select an encryption algorithm. Some algorithms may not be supported by all AWS services.

● **RSA 2048**
RSA is the most widely used key type.

○ **ECDSA P 256**
Equivalent in cryptographic strength to RSA 3072.

○ **ECDSA P 384**
Equivalent in cryptographic strength to RSA 7680.

Figure 19.5: Key algorithm selection screen for ACM

7. Scroll down to the bottom of the page and click the `Request` button.

The DNS records may require several hours to get updated as per your service provider's processing time. During this period, the status of your certificate request will be displayed as `Pending`. Upon completion of the DNS record changes, the status will transition to `Issued`, indicating that your SSL certificate is now ready to use.

Having learned how to use ACM to issue secure certificates, you also need to be aware that each certificate is not valid in perpetuity. Each issued certificate has a validity period ranging from one to three years. In the next section, you will see how ACM can renew your expiring certificates automatically, keeping them valid as long as you need.

Allowing ACM to Manage the Renewal of Certificates

ACM's managed renewal feature is invaluable for organizations seeking streamlined and robust certificate management. Its primary strength lies in simplifying the often intricate and error-prone SSL/TLS certificate renewal process. By automating certificate renewals, ACM eliminates the need for manual tracking, reduces administrative overhead, and ensures that certificates are consistently up to date. This enhances security by preventing lapses due to expired certificates and boosts operational efficiency as IT teams can allocate their time and resources to more strategic tasks.

Furthermore, ACM's managed renewal feature fosters reliability and reduces the risk of service disruptions. Automatic renewals translate into consistent certificate validity, preventing unexpected downtime caused by expired certificates. Additionally, ACM's integration with AWS services means that certificates associated with these services are also renewed seamlessly, reinforcing the reliability and continuity of secure communication.

If you use DNS validation, ACM automatically renews your certificates, ensuring you stay protected without manual intervention. Alternatively, ACM will send you email notifications as your certificate's expiration date approaches so you can act promptly. These renewal services apply to both public and private ACM certificates.

Several factors determine eligibility for automated renewal:

- Certificates are `ELIGIBLE` for automatic renewal when they are associated with other AWS services, such as Elastic Load Balancing or CloudFront

- Certificates are `ELIGIBLE` if they have been exported at any time since their issuance or last renewal

- Private certificates issued using the ACM `RequestCertificate` API and subsequently exported or linked to other AWS services are also `ELIGIBLE` for automatic renewal

- The same eligibility applies to private certificates created via the management console and later exported or connected to other AWS services

However, automatic renewal is `NOT ELIGIBLE` for private certificates obtained through the AWS Private CA `IssueCertificate` API. You can manually renew certificates with a Private CA using ACM.

Additionally, certificates imported from external sources and those that have already expired are `NOT ELIGIBLE` for automatic renewal.

Overall, ACM's managed renewal feature embodies AWS's commitment to simplifying cloud security, allowing organizations to maintain the highest level of protection while minimizing complexity and cost. The next section will examine private CAs in ACM.

Private Certificate Authorities in AWS ACM

As mentioned earlier in this chapter, ACM offers the capability to set up private CAs for organizations seeking a reliable and secure way to manage digital certificates within their infrastructure. A private CA in ACM provides a dedicated and controlled environment for generating and maintaining digital certificates, ensuring the confidentiality and integrity of sensitive data transmissions. This service allows users to issue and manage certificates for internal resources, applications, and devices, providing a robust security layer within the AWS ecosystem. By leveraging private CAs in ACM, not only can users establish trust within their infrastructure, encrypt communications, and enhance overall data protection, but they can also confidently manage their certificate life cycle, streamline security practices, and meet compliance requirements, even for complex and dynamic cloud environments.

Creating and using a private CA in ACM offers several key advantages:

- **Enhanced security and control**: A private CA allows organizations to have dedicated control over issuing and managing digital certificates. This heightened control ensures that certificates are only issued to trusted entities within the organization, reducing the risk of unauthorized access.

- **Tailored certificate policies**: Users can define and enforce custom certificate policies and practices to align with their specific security requirements. This flexibility enables organizations to implement policies that suit their unique needs and regulatory compliance standards.

- **Internal resource protection**: Private CAs in ACM are particularly useful for securing internal resources, applications, and devices. This allows organizations to establish trust within their infrastructure, ensuring secure communication and data protection even within their private networks.

- **Streamlined certificate management**: Integration with AWS services allows seamless deployment and management of certificates across various AWS resources. This simplifies securing applications and services within the AWS ecosystem, enhancing operational efficiency.

- **Rapid incident response**: With a private CA, organizations can quickly respond to security incidents by revoking compromised or unauthorized certificates. This agility in managing the certificate life cycle contributes to a more robust security posture.

- **Compliance and auditing**: Using private CAs facilitates compliance with industry standards and regulatory requirements. Organizations can maintain a detailed certificate issuance and revocation record, supporting audit processes and ensuring adherence to security processes.

- **Centralized certificate management**: The centralization of certificate management within ACM simplifies the overall administration of certificates. This centralized control ensures consistency and uniformity in certificate deployment and updates.

- **Scalability**: Private CAs in ACM provide a scalable solution, allowing organizations to manage many certificates efficiently. This scalability is crucial for dynamic and growing cloud environments.

Using a private CA in ACM empowers organizations with a secure, flexible, and scalable solution for managing digital certificates.

The next section presents some real-world examples where it would make sense to utilize Private CA with ACM.

Real-World Uses for ACM Private CA

ACM Private CA is a service that extends ACM's functionality beyond website certificates. Setting up a private CA, while still much easier with the help of ACM, is more overhead than just creating a public certificate. Then why would you want to go through the cost and trouble of doing this? As you look through some of the following uses, you will see that there are specific use cases that allow companies such as your own to create a secure environment that has strict controls where they as the company have the power to regulate those controls – especially with regard to the certificates:

- **Custom private CAs**: ACM Private CA allows you to create and manage custom private CAs. This is particularly useful in environments where you must issue and manage your own private certificates for various purposes beyond websites, such as securing internal services, IoT devices, or VPN connections.

- **Secure internal communications**: You can use ACM Private CA to issue private certificates for securing communications between resources within your organization's network. For example, you can issue certificates for securing internal APIs, databases, email servers, and more.

- **Internet of things (IoT) device security**: ACM Private CA can be used to issue certificates for IoT devices. These certificates help ensure secure and authenticated communication between IoT devices and the cloud, safeguarding sensitive data and commands transmitted by these devices.

- **VPN and secure connections**: ACM Private CA can issue certificates for securing VPN connections, ensuring that data transferred between remote offices or between remote clients and a corporate network remains confidential and authenticated.

- **Code signing**: ACM Private CA certificates can be used for code signing, which is crucial for verifying the authenticity and integrity of software updates or applications before they are executed. This is a critical security measure for software development and distribution. The certificate itself does not sign the code, and you would need to use a code signing tool, but the certificate generated by ACM is used in the code signing process.

- **Secure email and document signing**: ACM Private CA certificates can also be used to sign emails and documents securely, providing the sender's authenticity, integrity, and content. This can be seen in PDF files to show that they are authentic and have not been tampered with after the original user has created the file. You can perform the signing of the document with software tools or manually with the help of certain languages such as Java.

- **Compliance and regulation**: ACM Private CA can assist organizations in meeting regulatory and compliance requirements, such as the **Health Insurance Portability and Accountability Act (HIPAA)**, **General Data Protection Regulation (GDPR)**, or industry-specific security standards, by providing a secure means of managing and issuing certificates for various purposes.

While that may seem like a lot of tasks available for a private certificate manager to perform, the next section will explain a real-world use case of using private certificates issued by ACM Private CA to help your understanding.

Using a Private Certificate from ACM in the Real World

Private certificates served by ACM are valuable in scenarios where secure communication within a private network is essential. One prominent use case is securing communications between microservices or instances within a **virtual private cloud** (**VPC**). By using ACM to manage private certificates, you ensure that the communication channels between these services are encrypted, enhancing the overall security of your microservice architecture.

For example, consider a microservices environment where instances must communicate securely over HTTPS within a VPC. This VPC could be hosting an ECS cluster that is running multiple services such as payment processing and inventory management. Using the Boto3 library, each microservice can interact with AWS services such as AWS Lambda or API Gateway to handle requests, ensuring data confidentially and integrity within the VPC environment. You can use ACM to generate and manage private certificates in this case. The following example Python code uses the AWS SDK (Boto3) to show how you might retrieve a private certificate from ACM:

```python
import boto3
# Specify the ARN of your private certificate in ACM
certificate_arn = "arn:aws:acm:region:account-id:certificate/
certificate-id"

# Create an ACM client
acm_client = boto3.client('acm')

# Retrieve the private certificate
response = acm_client.get_certificate(
    CertificateArn=certificate_arn
)

# Use the certificate data in your application
private_certificate_data = response['Certificate']['CertificatePem']
```

In this example, the private certificate is obtained from ACM using its ARN, and this certificate data can then be utilized in your application for secure communication between microservices.

Another use case is securing communication between on-premises servers and instances in the AWS cloud. Take the case of a financial firm where data resides both on-premises and in AWS in places such as S3 and RDS. A private certificate could be used to establish a trusted communication channel in such a hybrid environment. ACM allows you to manage private certificates that facilitate secure connections over VPN connections or Direct Connect links. This ensures that data transferred between your on-premises infrastructure and AWS resources remains encrypted and protected.

While the ability to create (and destroy) your own certificates within your organization whenever you need them can seem appealing, there are some downsides to running a private CA. In the next section, you will look at the potential challenges that can arise with using Private CA.

Disadvantages of Using Private CA with ACM

Using a private CA managed by ACM introduces some disadvantages. One notable drawback is the lack of direct control over the Private CA infrastructure. ACM abstracts much of the underlying management of Private CA, making it challenging for organizations to maintain granular control over the CA or customize its setup. This limitation may concern enterprises with specific security or compliance requirements that demand more hands-on management of their CA infrastructure. Examples of the types of organizations that would use a private CA would include financial institutions, healthcare providers, and government agencies.

Another disadvantage of a private CA managed by ACM is that it could introduce additional complexity in terms of configuration and setup. Organizations may need to navigate intricacies related to syncing the certificates between ACM and the private CA, potentially leading to certificate life cycle management and automation challenges.

Cost considerations can also play a role. While ACM is a managed service with no additional charges for certificate management, integrating a private CA adds costs that organizations need to be mindful of. At the time of publication, there was a charge of $400 (USD) per month per private CA for the general-purpose mode or $50 per month per private CA for the short-lived certificate mode.

Overall, while ACM is a highly convenient managed solution for public certificates, when it comes to opting for a private CA, organizations should weigh the disadvantages of limited control, added complexity, and associated costs.

A private CA managed by ACM might not be the optimal solution in specific use cases where detailed control, customization, or compatibility with certain requirements is essential. The following are some specific use cases that demonstrate this:

- **To gain advanced customization and control**: Organizations with highly specific requirements for customizing their CA infrastructure, including unique security policies, specialized cryptographic algorithms, or non-standard configurations, may find ACM's managed approach limiting. An independently managed private CA offers more flexibility for tailoring the CA environment to precise specifications.

- **To ensure integration with non-AWS environments**: In complex, multi-cloud, or hybrid environments where interoperability with non-AWS services or on-premises components is crucial, using AWS Private CA may pose challenges. Compatibility and seamless integration across diverse platforms might be better achieved with an independently managed private CA.

- **When using hardware security modules (HSMs)**: Organizations with stringent security requirements that involve the use of HSMs for secure key storage might find limitations in ACM's managed approach.

- **For unique compliance requirements**: Industries with specific compliance standards or regulatory frameworks that necessitate adherence to particular certificate policies and practices may find ACM's predefined policies insufficient.

- **For custom key storage solutions**: Organizations requiring specialized key storage solutions beyond the offerings provided by ACM may find an independently managed private CA more suitable. ACM abstracts many key management details, and if custom key storage solutions are a priority, a different approach may be needed.

- **For complex certificate life cycle management**: In cases requiring highly intricate or complex certificate life cycle management processes that go beyond ACM's automated features, an independently managed private CA offers more control over the entire certificate life cycle.

- **For specific cryptographic algorithm requirements**: Organizations with specific cryptographic algorithm requirements that are not supported or fully customizable within ACM may find an independently managed private CA more aligned with their cryptographic preference.

As you can see, organizations with use cases involving advanced customization, compatibility across diverse environments, specialized security requirements, or specific compliance needs may find that a private CA managed independently outside of ACM better addresses their unique requirements.

Summary

In this chapter, you looked at using and storing public and private trust certificates via the ACM service. You examined the difference between public and private certificates and how both can be used with the ACM service. You looked at how public certificates can help secure transmissions for public-facing websites and web apps being served from other AWS services, such as S3 buckets and ELBs.

You also looked at how a private CA could be managed from the ACM service, as well as use cases where using private certificates both does and does not make sense for you and your organization.

In the next chapter, we will discuss how to make your operating environment more secure by storing confidential information such as passwords and API tokens. This can be accomplished in several ways using AWS native services that will be discussed; you will also review some walk-through examples of how to use the services.

Further Reading

For additional information on AWS security, please look at the following resources:

- AWS Certificate Manager FAQs: `https://packt.link/1pm1A`

- AWS Private CA Pricing: `https://packt.link/Lawh3`

- Amazon Trust Services Repository: `https://packt.link/bk22H`

Exam Readiness Drill – Chapter Review Questions

Apart from a solid understanding of key concepts, being able to think quickly under time pressure is a skill that will help you ace your certification exam. That is why working on these skills early on in your learning journey is key.

Chapter review questions are designed to improve your test-taking skills progressively with each chapter you learn and review your understanding of key concepts in the chapter at the same time. You'll find these at the end of each chapter.

> **How To Access These Resources**
>
> To learn how to access these resources, head over to the chapter titled *Chapter 21, Accessing the Online Practice Resources*.

To open the Chapter Review Questions for this chapter, perform the following steps:

1. Click the link – `https://packt.link/SCSC02E2_CH19`

    Alternatively, you can scan the following QR code (*Figure 19.6*):

Figure 19.6: QR code that opens Chapter Review Questions for logged-in users

2. Once you log in, you'll see a page similar to the one shown in *Figure 19.7*:

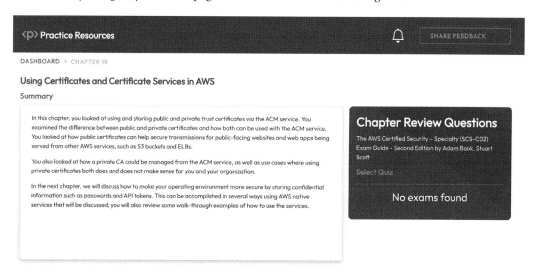

Figure 19.7: Chapter Review Questions for Chapter 19

3. Once ready, start the following practice drills, re-attempting the quiz multiple times.

Exam Readiness Drill

For the first three attempts, don't worry about the time limit.

ATTEMPT 1

The first time, aim for at least **40%**. Look at the answers you got wrong and read the relevant sections in the chapter again to fix your learning gaps.

ATTEMPT 2

The second time, aim for at least **60%**. Look at the answers you got wrong and read the relevant sections in the chapter again to fix any remaining learning gaps.

ATTEMPT 3

The third time, aim for at least **75%**. Once you score **75%** or more, you start working on your timing.

> **Tip**
>
> You may take more than three attempts to reach 75%. That's okay. Just review the relevant sections in the chapter till you get there.

Working On Timing

Target: Your aim is to keep the score the same while trying to answer these questions as quickly as possible. Here's an example of how your next attempts should look like:

Attempt	Score	Time Taken
Attempt 5	77%	21 mins 30 seconds
Attempt 6	78%	18 mins 34 seconds
Attempt 7	76%	14 mins 44 seconds

Table 19.1: Sample timing practice drills on the online platform

> **Note**
>
> The time limits shown in the above table are just examples. Set your own time limits with each attempt based on the time limit of the quiz on the website.

With each new attempt, your score should stay above 75% while your time taken to complete should **decrease**. Repeat as many attempts as you want till you feel confident dealing with the time pressure.

20

Managing Secrets Securely in AWS

As you and your organization navigate an increasingly dynamic digital landscape, ensuring the security of your sensitive information becomes paramount. This includes safeguarding your secrets, passwords, and other credentials in a manner that aligns with best practices and industry standards.

In AWS, you have both users and roles, used by services such as Lambda and EC2 instances, which have a need for secrets to authenticate against either local services such as a **Relational Database Service (RDS)** database or a third-party service such as an API, for example, Salesforce. If a security incident were to ever happen, then you would need a way to rotate your credentials so they can no longer be used and then see who accessed that secret from where. This is where a secrets management tool comes into play.

Implementing a modern secrets management solution that will automate the process, ensure encryption, restrict access to authorized individuals and entities, and even provide credential rotation is the best step toward securely managing your secrets. Luckily, there is more than one native solution to choose from in the AWS ecosystem of tools, two of which we will look at in depth in this chapter.

The following main topics will be covered in this chapter:

- Why you (and your developers) should store secrets securely
- Understanding the different secret storage systems in AWS
- Seeing the pros and cons of Secrets Manager versus Systems Manager Parameter Store
- Understanding how to audit which users and service roles have used a secret

The chapter will start with a short discussion on why you should store your secrets in a secure manner.

Technical Requirements

There is a requirement to have access to the AWS Management Console and an **Identity and Access Management** (**IAM**) user that can access both the Secrets Manager service and the Systems Manager service. You also need IAM permissions in the account you will be using to create (and destroy) an Amazon RDS database, which will be used in the exercises presented in this chapter.

Mitigating the Risk of Lost and Stolen Credentials

Cyber threats and data breaches have become pervasive risks in today's interconnected world. If your secrets and passwords are not effectively secured, you expose yourself and your organization to potential breaches that could compromise valuable data, disrupt operations, and tarnish your reputation.

To mitigate the risks to your data, you should focus on implementing a robust secrets management approach. This involves using tools such as **AWS Secrets Manager**, **Systems Manager Parameter Store**, or possibly a tool from a third-party vendor. These tools centralize the storage, retrieval, and rotation of credentials. Such solutions not only enhance security through encryption, access controls, and automated rotation but also streamline the management process, freeing up resources for other critical tasks.

By prioritizing security, you can align with regulatory requirements, bolster customer trust, and proactively address a potential source of vulnerabilities. You will enhance your overall security posture, maintain compliance, and ensure that only those users and services authorized to access the secret credentials have the required permissions.

Now you understand the reasons why you need to take action to reduce the opportunities for the credentials in your systems and accounts to be used by unauthorized users, both internally and externally. Often, when developers are trying to produce code that works, they get caught up in automated tools and processes pushed by the business and IT/security that hampers them from trying to perform their job function (to keep the company secure). However, AWS provides services that can help developers integrate security features seamlessly into their code, making it easier to manage secrets securely while developing features, products, or services.

In the next section, you will learn about the different services available in AWS that make this possible.

Secret Storage Systems in AWS

There are several ways to securely store secrets in AWS, each tailored to a specific use case and security requirements.

One standard method is to use **AWS Secrets Manager**, which is a fully managed service that centralizes the storage and management of secrets, such as database credentials, API keys, and encryption keys. It offers encryption, automatic rotation, and fine-grained access control, making it suitable for applications running on AWS services.

Another option is the **AWS Systems Manager Parameter Store**, which can securely store secrets and other configuration data. It supports encryption with AWS **Key Management Service** (**KMS**) keys, versioning, and hierarchical structuring for better organization.

If your organization requires hardware-based security, you can utilize the AWS **Hardware Security Module** (**HSM**) through **CloudHSM**. This service offers dedicated, tamper-resistant hardware for key storage and cryptographic operations, making it ideal for the protection of highly sensitive data and ensuring compliance with the necessary industry standards.

For serverless applications, **AWS Lambda** can store secrets using environment variables, which are encrypted at rest. While this is a lightweight approach, it's best suited for small-scale applications with minimal secrets.

Now that you have an overview of the different services available to manage your secrets securely in your AWS environment, you will take a deeper look at the inner workings of some of these solutions, starting with AWS Secrets Manager.

AWS Secrets Manager

AWS Secrets Manager simplifies the management of sensitive information such as API keys, database passwords, and encryption keys, by providing a centralized and secure repository with automation and fine-grained access control. Secrets Manager also offers logging capabilities to track when a role or user accesses a secret stored inside the services, providing visibility into secret usage for auditing and compliance purposes. It allows developers to store and retrieve these secrets securely, thus ensuring that robust security practices are in place.

What sets AWS Secrets Manager apart is its ability to automate the rotation of secrets. This means that instead of requiring manual updates for passwords or keys at regular intervals to reduce the risk of unauthorized access, the service will automatically handle this task. It integrates seamlessly with various AWS services, making it easier for you and your organization to protect sensitive data across your applications and services.

AWS Secrets Manager offers robust security features to safeguard your data effectively. First and foremost, it ensures that data at rest and in transit is encrypted. Access to stored secrets is controlled through AWS IAM policies, which means you can specify who has permission to retrieve or manage secrets. This fine-grained access control minimizes the risk of insider threats.

Second, it automates secret rotation, which significantly enhances your security posture. Secrets, such as database passwords or API keys, are automatically changed regularly. This automation reduces the likelihood of security breaches due to compromised credentials. Additionally, Secrets Manager provides a complete audit trail, allowing you to track and monitor who accesses secrets and when, which is crucial for compliance and security audits.

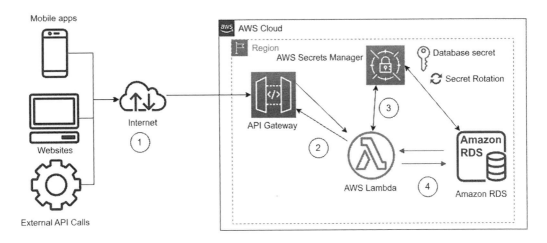

Figure 20.1: Secrets Manager overview

Further, the service operates with high availability, replicating secrets across multiple Availability Zones, which ensures reliability and continuity even in the event of hardware or software failures.

Overall, AWS Secrets Manager provides a comprehensive security feature suite that allows you to manage and protect your critical assets confidently.

With a foundational grasp of the AWS Secrets Manager service, you're now ready to explore in more detail the advantages and potential disadvantages of the Secrets Manager service in the next section.

Pros and Cons of the Secrets Manager Service

As you evaluate the options for secrets management in AWS, it's essential to recognize the positives and negatives of each service, whether you are choosing one for your organization or considering using a service to answer a question on the exam.

Here are some positive aspects of using AWS Secrets Manager:

- **Centralized management**: AWS Secrets Manager provides a centralized location to store and manage secrets, making handling sensitive information across different applications and services easier.

- **Security**: Secrets Manager offers robust security features, including encryption at rest and in transit, fine-grained access control, and integration with AWS IAM for user and resource authentication.

- **Automated rotation**: One of the critical features of Secrets Manager is its ability to automate the rotation of secrets. This enhances security by automatically changing credentials regularly, reducing the risk of unauthorized access.

- **Integration with AWS services**: Secrets Manager seamlessly integrates with various AWS services, including Amazon RDS, Amazon Redshift, and Amazon EC2 instances. This makes it easier to manage and update the credentials used by these services.

- **Audit trail**: AWS Secrets Manager provides an audit trail, allowing you to track who accessed which secret and when. This can be invaluable for compliance and security auditing.

- **High availability**: Secrets Manager is designed for high availability and reliability. Your secrets are replicated across multiple Availability Zones to ensure availability even in the case of hardware or software failures.

- **Ease of use**: The service is user-friendly and offers a simple API for integration into applications and services. This reduces the complexity of managing secrets manually.

The following are some potential cons of AWS Secrets Manager:

- **Cost**: While the cost of using AWS Secrets Manager is generally reasonable, this is something to consider if you are managing a large number of secrets or performing frequent secret rotations.

- **Vendor lock-in**: Using AWS Secrets Manager ties you to the AWS ecosystem. If you decide to migrate to another cloud provider or go back to using on-premises infrastructure, then you might need to reconfigure how secrets are managed.

- **Limited to AWS resources**: While Secrets Manager integrates seamlessly with many AWS services, it might not be as straightforward to use with non-AWS services or custom applications hosted outside AWS.

- **Potential latency**: Accessing secrets from Secrets Manager could introduce a slight bit of latency compared to accessing secrets stored locally. However, this latency is usually negligible for most use cases.

- **Learning curve**: While AWS Secrets Manager aims to simplify secrets management, there is still a learning curve associated with understanding its features, best practices, and integration with other AWS services.

- **Potential overhead**: For simple use cases, the added automation and features of Secrets Manager might introduce unnecessary complexity and overhead.

You now have an idea about where the Secrets Manager service excels and where it may also fall a little short of expectations. The next section will take you through the implementation of Secrets Manager in your infrastructure.

Creating, Storing, and Retrieving a Secret in AWS Secrets Manager

In this subsection, you will learn how to use the AWS Secrets Manager service to both store and retrieve secrets through the AWS Management Console.

Before you can store a secret using Secrets Manager, you'll need to set up a small RDS database so that you can create a username and password (which will be the secret to store and ultimately rotate) during this exercise. After this database has been created, you can move on to the next steps of creating, storing, and retrieving the secret. The following steps will teach you how to create a new RDS database:

1. Log in to the AWS Management Console and then navigate to the RDS. You can get there quickly by using the following URL: `https://console.aws.amazon.com/rds/`.

2. Once you are on the RDS main page, click on the button labeled `Create database`.

3. You should now be on the page with the title `Create database`. At the top of the page, under `Choose a database creation method`, select the radio button next to the option named `Easy create`.

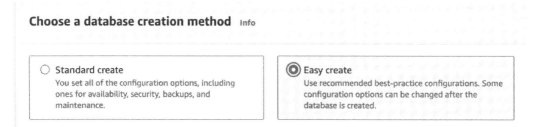

Figure 20.2: Create database

4. Next, move down the page to the box titled `Configuration`. Use the following options to set up your database quickly. What you should select/type is in `CodeType`:

- Engine type – `MySQL`

- Edition – `MySQL Community`

- Database instance size – `Free tier`

- Database instance identifier – `secrets-rotation`
- Master username – `admin`
- Autogenerate a password – check this box

5. After you have filled in your configuration settings, scroll down to the bottom of the page and click on the `Create database` button to start the creation of your database.

6. While your database is being created, look for a button near the top of the screen named `View credential details`. Click on this button to display the autogenerated password that was created for your admin user.

7. When the popup appears, copy the master password to something such as Notepad or a temporary file, as you will need to store this master password in Secrets Manager in the next step. This is the only time you will be able to access this created credential until you store it.

With your sample RDS database created, you are ready to move on to creating your secret in the Secrets Manager service.

The following steps will show you how to create a secret in AWS Secrets Manager and then store it:

1. Start by logging in to the AWS Management Console and then navigate to the Secrets Manager service. You can do this quickly by using the following URL: `https://console.aws.amazon.com/secretsmanager/landing`.

2. Once on the main Secrets Manager page, click on the button labeled `Store a new secret`. This should be located on the right-hand side of the screen.

3. You will now be presented with the type of secret that you want to store. Since you previously created an RDS database, you will choose the RDS option; however, take note of the different options available under `Secret type`.

Figure 20.3: Secret type selection screen

4. After selecting the secret type, move down the page until you reach the section labeled `Credentials`. Go back to the note that you saved in the previous section when you created the database and were shown the administrative username and password. Enter those values in the `User name` and `Password` fields.

Figure 20.4: Credentials screen for Secrets Manager

5. Scrolling down to the next box (named `Encryption key`) on the page allows you to select a custom KMS key for encryption. However, for this exercise, stay with the default value of the `aws/secretsmanager` encryption key.

6. Continue to scroll down the page until you reach a box named `Database`. If you created the prerequisite database for this exercise, then you should see the database instance named `secrets-rotation` in the list of available databases. Select this database by clicking on the radio button next to it.

Figure 20.5: Database selection screen

7. After selecting your database, scroll to the bottom of the page and click on the Next button to continue.

8. After clicking the Next button, you should be brought to a page named Configure Secret. This is where you will name the secret in a meaningful fashion so that both your human users and your service roles can understand it. Name your secret test/rds/MySQL. (A description is not needed, but you are welcome to add one.)

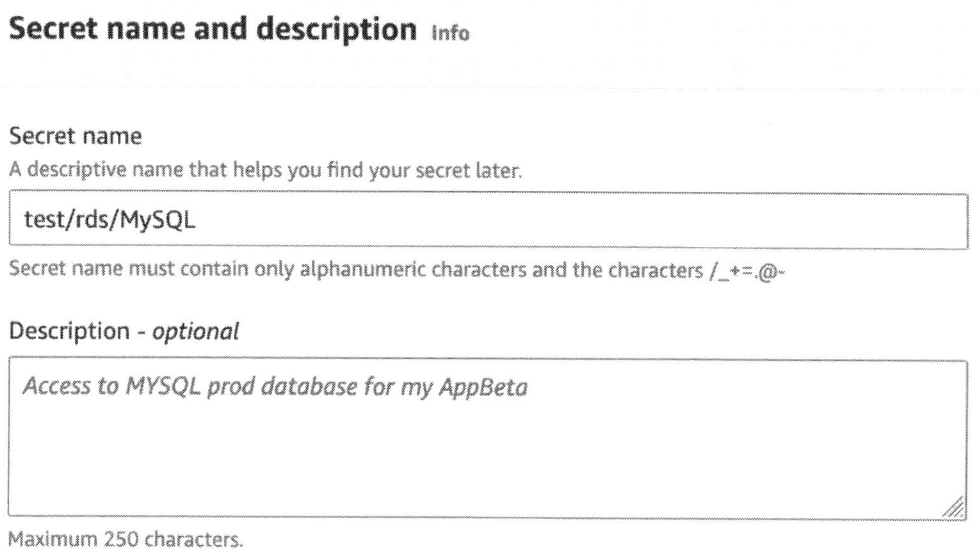

Secret name and description Info

Secret name

A descriptive name that helps you find your secret later.

```
test/rds/MySQL
```

Secret name must contain only alphanumeric characters and the characters /_+=.@-

Description - *optional*

```
Access to MYSQL prod database for my AppBeta
```

Maximum 250 characters.

Figure 20.6: Secret name and description screen

9. After you have added the secret name, scroll down to the bottom of the page and click on Next.

Now, you should be on the Configure rotation page. This is where you can set up the password that you just stored to be changed on a schedule. Although this is an optional step, you will go through the process here so that you are familiar with the process and the functionality available to you in AWS Secrets Manager.

10. At the top of the page, click on the toggle button to turn on `Automatic rotation` for the secret.

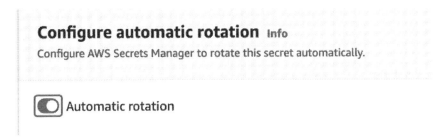

Figure 20.7: Automatic rotation toggle switch

11. Scroll down until you reach the box named `Rotation schedule`. Click the radio button next to `Schedule Expression`. Then, in the `Schedule expression` box, enter the rate (30 days). Keep the checkbox checked at the bottom where it says `Rotate immediately when the secret is stored. The next rotation will begin on your schedule.`. This will set your secret to rotate automatically every 30 days.

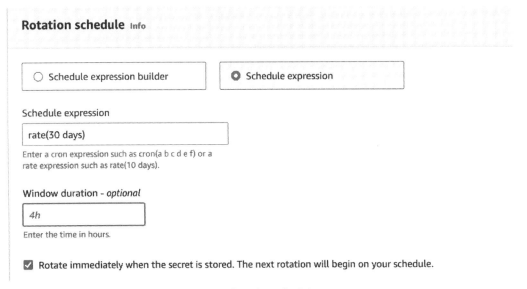

Figure 20.8: Rotation schedule screen

12. Under `Rotation function`, make sure that the radio button is checked for the selection of `Create a rotation function`. You will need to give your function a name, something such as `chapter20-mysql-rotation`.

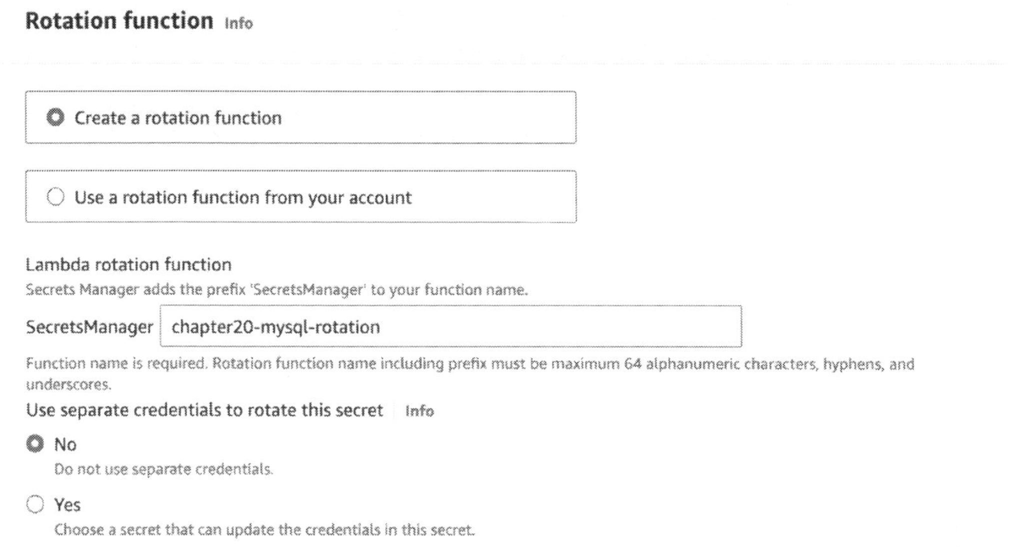

Rotation function Info

○ Create a rotation function

○ Use a rotation function from your account

Lambda rotation function
Secrets Manager adds the prefix 'SecretsManager' to your function name.

SecretsManager | chapter20-mysql-rotation

Function name is required. Rotation function name including prefix must be maximum 64 alphanumeric characters, hyphens, and underscores.

Use separate credentials to rotate this secret   Info

○ No
   Do not use separate credentials.

○ Yes
   Choose a secret that can update the credentials in this secret.

Figure 20.9: Rotation function screen

Scroll down to the bottom of the page and click the orange Next button.

13. You should now be on the Review page. Take a look at your settings as you scroll down the page and then click on Store at the bottom of the page.

You just learned how to create and store a secret in AWS Secrets Manager. The type of secret that you originally created was one for an RDS database. You then put that secret on an automated rotation schedule so that it automatically rotates every 30 days. In the next section, you will explore how to retrieve the secret that you just stored.

Retrieving the Secret from Secrets Manager

Your secret is now safely stored in the AWS Secrets Manager service, but to access that secret later, in order to access the database, you'll need to use the AWS CLI by performing the following steps:

1. Open up your terminal instance so that you can access your command-line interface.

2. Use the following command to list the current secrets stored in your account:

```
aws secretsmanager list-secrets --region us-east-2
```

> **Note**
> if you did not create your secret in the Ohio/us-east-2 region, then substitute the Region you used for that value.

This should return you something like the following:

```
SECRETLIST        arn:aws:secretsmanager:us-east-
2:123456789012:secret:test/rds/MySQL-GZEnNT        2023-
09-04T10:35:04.126000-04:00        2023-09-03T20:00:00-
04:00        2023-09-04T10:38:49.554000-04:00        test/rds/
MySQL   2023-09-05T19:59:59-04:00        True     arn:aws:lambda:us-east-
2:182968331794:function:SecretsManagerc20-mysql-rotation
ROTATIONRULES    30        rate(30 days)
241F1740-B356-4DA6-8450-F3C7CFD22786      AWSCURRENT
D218B954-9695-4642-AFE5-A16676003478      AWSPENDING
```

You can then see from the output that the secret's **Amazon Resource Name (ARN)** is arn:aws:secretsmanager:us-east-2:123456789012:secret:test/rds/MySQL-GZEnNT. Use this value in the next command to access the actual stored secret.

3. Use the following command to access the secret once you have determined the secret's ARN:

```
aws secret-manager get-secret value --secret-id:
arn:aws:secretsmanager:us-east-2:123456789012:secret:test/rds/
MySQL-GZEnNT –region us-east-2
```

If everything was entered incorrectly, then you should get a return that looks like the following:

```
arn:aws:secretsmanager:us-east-2:182968331794:secret:test/rds/MySQL-
GZEnNT        2023-09-04T10:35:04.159000-04:00                test/rds/
MySQL  {"username":"admin","password":"grEcyvTAprziNpsRxbYYgrEcyvTAp
rziNpsRxbYY","engine":"mysql","host":"secrets-rotation.c1hz2weoab5l.
us-east-2.rds.amazonaws.com","port":3306,"dbInstanceIdentifier":"secre
ts-rotation"}        241f1740-b356-4da6-8450-f3c7cfd22786
VERSIONSTAGES   AWSCURRENT
```

At this point, you can log in to the MySQL server using the console or a third-party program using the credentials provided to you.

Now that you have seen how to retrieve the secret that you have stored in AWS Secrets Manager, you can next practice manually rotating a secret in case of a security incident.

Secrets Rotation in AWS Secrets Manager

In the earlier setup exercise, you learned how you can set a secret to rotate automatically. However, it may be necessary to do this manually in various situations, primarily those in which automatic rotation is not feasible or when immediate action is required. The following are some use cases when manual rotation becomes necessary:

- **When using an unsupported service**: AWS Secrets Manager supports automatic rotation for several database services, such as AWS RDS, DynamoDB, and Redshift. However, if you're using a non-supported or custom service, you will need to implement manual rotation.

- **When dealing with legacy systems**: Older systems or applications may not be compatible with the automatic rotation features of AWS Secrets Manager. In such cases, manual rotation is often the only option.

- **When using third-party services**: When dealing with third-party services that rely on API keys or tokens, AWS Secrets Manager may not have the necessary integration. Manual rotation becomes necessary to ensure these credentials are updated regularly.

- **When dealing with an emergency response**: In situations where a security breach is suspected or an exposed secret is compromised, immediate manual rotation is essential to minimize the risk and secure the system.

- **During the testing and verification process**: During initial setup or when significant changes are made to a rotation process, manual rotation can be used for testing and verification before transitioning to automated rotation.

- **When using non-standard secrets**: For secrets that do not conform to the usual username-password pattern, such as SSH keys or certificates, manual rotation might be required as these require different handling procedures.

Rotating a Secret with Rotation Configuration

If you set up a rotation for the secret when you originally stored the secret in AWS Secrets Manager, using the prebuilt Lambda function is a simple way to rotate the previously stored password. The prebuilt Lambda function that AWS provides automates all the steps of rotating the secret. These include the following:

- Creating a new version of the secret

- Changing the credentials for the service or database

- Performing a test with the new credentials

- Moving the new credentials to the latest version ID in Secrets Manager

Rotate your function with the prebuilt Lambda function using the following steps:

1. Navigate to the AWS Secrets Manager service.

2. Find the name of the secret that you want to rotate and then click on it.

Figure 20.10: Secret name

3. Once on the `Secret details` page, scroll down until you see the box named `Rotation configuration`. On the right-hand side of the top of the box will be a button named `Rotate Secret immediately`. Click the button to rotate the secret.

You may use the previously described CLI process to view the secret value or scroll up a bit on the page until you see the box named `Secret value`. In this box, there will be a `Retrieve secret value` button that you can click to view your secret value.

Rotating a Secret Manually

As you previously read, there are instances when you just cannot wait for the automated process to rotate the secret. If you feel that the service itself is not performing the task or that the password or token has been changed by an external entity, then you will need to rotate the secret inside of AWS Secrets Manager in a manual fashion.

The process is much like the previous set of steps; however, with this process, it is up to you to change the values in the application and database and then store those changed values with the corresponding secret in AWS Secrets Manager. You would first have to retrieve the secret stored, and once it is displayed on the CLI, then you would have the opportunity to edit its value.

You have just seen multiple ways to rotate secrets stored in AWS Secrets Manager, both with a manual process and with the Lambda function that is connected to the secret if automated rotation has been enabled. There are cases when you and others in your organization may want to use the same secret in more than one AWS Region. The following section will explain how this is possible with the replication capabilities of AWS Secrets Manager.

Using AWS Secrets Manager in Multiple Regions

Using Secrets Manager, you are able to securely store, retrieve, manage, and rotate your sensitive information, including database credentials and API keys.

When you create a secret within Secrets Manager, it is established and managed within a specific AWS Region of your choice. While this regional scoping is a recommended security practice, specific scenarios such as disaster recovery and cross-regional redundancy might necessitate the replication of secrets across multiple regions. Secrets Manager has the capability to allow you to effortlessly replicate your organization's secrets to one or more Regions if this is part of your strategy.

As you can see in *Figure 20.11*, your architecture would be spread across two separate regions, in this case, and a first RDS instance (running the MySQL engine for the following example) would be configured to replicate to the secondary Region. Secrets Manager stores the secrets for the RDS, which is replicated in the other region.

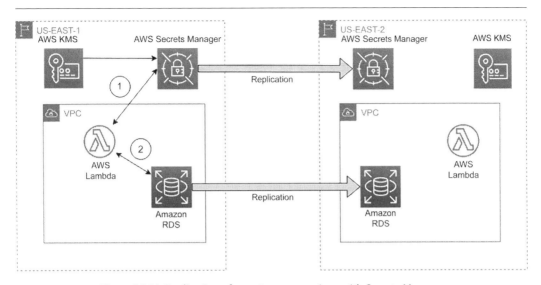

Figure 20.11: Replication of secrets across regions with Secrets Manager

Using AWS Secrets Manager allows you and your team members to store confidential passphrases and other need-to-know information in a single service and use it across the multiple regions that your organization is situated in. This strategy also works well in the case of disaster recovery for the need to fail over from a primary to a secondary Region and to reuse the secrets for applications or databases from the primary Region. All of this high availability does come with extra costs associated with it, so that is also something to keep in mind for those who are on a strict budget.

With a solid understanding of the Secrets Manager service, you can now move on to an alternative service that is both native to AWS and can be used to securely store and track the use of secret information for your team in the next section, Systems Manager Parameter Store.

AWS Systems Manager Parameter Store

AWS Systems Manager Parameter Store is a versatile service offered by AWS that is designed to simplify the management of configuration data, secrets, and application parameters. It acts as a secure and centralized repository for storing and retrieving this information, making it an invaluable tool for developers and system administrators. Parameter Store supports multiple data types, including plaintext and encrypted values, which can be managed through a straightforward API or the AWS Management Console.

One of its key features is robust security, offering the option to encrypt sensitive data using AWS KMS keys, ensuring data-at-rest protection. With hierarchical structuring, you can organize parameters efficiently to enhance manageability. Additionally, versioning allows you to track changes and revert to previous values if needed. Parameter Store integrates seamlessly with other AWS services, enabling applications running on AWS to securely access configuration data and secrets without exposing them directly in the code or environment variables.

AWS Parameter Store also streamlines the process of managing and securing critical information to promote best practices in configuration management and security while improving the overall efficiency of AWS-based applications and systems.

With AWS Parameter Store, secrets are stored as parameters. When you edit the value of a parameter in Parameter Store, a new version of the parameter is created, and the previous versions are also retained. The first version of a parameter is assigned `Version 1`. When you change the value of the parameter, the version number is automatically incremented by 1. You can view the details of all versions of a parameter, including the values, in its history.

You now have a basic understanding of how the Parameter Store service works. Similar to many other AWS services, Parameter Store also comes with its own positive and negative aspects. You will notice that the list of pros and cons may seem similar to the ones explained previously in this chapter for the AWS Secrets Manager service. However, there are differences that you need to be attuned to as you read through them.

Pros and Cons of SSM Parameter Store

Previously, in this chapter, you looked at the benefits and drawbacks of the AWS Secrets Manager service. While the Parameter Store service has many similar traits to Secrets Manager, be sure to read through the list to see the nuances of how they differ.

The following are some advantages of using Systems Manager Parameter Store:

- **Secure storage**: AWS Systems Manager Parameter Store provides secure storage for sensitive information. Parameters can be stored as `SecureString`, which is encrypted with AWS KMS keys, adding an additional layer of security.

- **Integration with AWS services**: Parameter Store seamlessly integrates with other AWS services, making accessing and using secrets in various AWS applications and resources easy.

- **Hierarchical structure**: It supports a hierarchical structure for organizing parameters, making it easier to manage and search for secrets within a well-organized hierarchy.

- **Version control**: Parameter Store maintains a version history of parameter values, enabling you to track changes and revert to the previous version if needed.

- **Fine-grained access control**: You can control access to parameters using AWS IAM policies to specify who can read or modify specific parameters.

- **Secure parameter rotation**: You can automate parameter rotation with AWS Lambda functions or other automated tools, ensuring that secrets are regularly updated, which is a best practice for security.

- **Attractive pricing**: There is a very generous free tier for SSM Parameter Store, including API calls. At the time of writing, Parameter Store allows storing secrets for free if your organization has under 10,000 parameters. Pricing for API calls is grouped into batches of 10,000 as well.

As mentioned earlier, there are some disadvantages of the Parameter Store service. The following points highlight these disadvantages and also show you how this service differs from AWS Secrets Manager:

- **Limited to AWS**: Parameter Store is primarily designed for use within the AWS ecosystem. While it can store any type of data, including secrets, integrating with non-AWS systems or applications hosted outside of AWS may not be as straightforward.

- **Complexity for non-AWS users**: If your organization uses multiple cloud providers or has on-premises infrastructure, managing secrets across different environments may require additional complexity and tooling.

- **No built-in audit trail**: Unlike AWS Secrets Manager, Parameter Store does not provide a built-in audit trail for who accessed secrets and when. You might need to implement additional logging and monitoring solutions for this.

- **Limited automation**: While you can automate parameter rotation, it may require more custom scripting and management compared to the automated rotation features provided by AWS Secrets Manager.

- **No native secret detection**: Parameter Store does not have native features for detecting sensitive data patterns or secrets within parameters, which some other solutions might offer.

- **Learning curve**: As with any AWS service, there is a learning curve associated with understanding how to use Parameter Store effectively and securely.

Now that you have an overview of the different characteristics of the Systems Manager Parameter Store service, you can proceed to learn about the specific permissions from the IAM service that are relevant to scoping permissions secrets and variables stored in the Parameter Store service.

Understanding the IAM Permissions Used with Parameter Store

One necessity of your role as a security specialist is a deep understanding of IAM permissions as they pertain to the different services in AWS. Knowing how to scope the least privileged access for users and roles is a crucial component when studying for the AWS Certified Security Specialty exam and performing tasks that correspond to your daily responsibilities. The following is a list of the permissions that specifically pertain to Systems Manager Parameter Store:

- `DeleteParameter`: This permission allows you to delete a parameter from the system. If you want to create a new parameter with the same name, you will need to wait for at least 30 seconds for the service to purge the previous name so that it can be reused.

- `DeleteParameters`: Much like the `DeleteParameter` permission, this allows you to delete a list of parameters from the system, multiple values at a time. If you would like to reuse any of the previous names, you will need to wait at least 30 seconds for the system to purge the names so they can be reused.

- `DescribeParameters`: Granting a user or service this permission allows the service to return information about zero or more parameters. A `MaxResults` flag may be passed so that only a certain number of parameters would be returned simultaneously. This permission only describes the parameter, such as name, last modified date, and type (i.e., `String` or `SecureString`). It does not return the parameter's value.

- `GetParameter`: This permission allows users to get the complete information about a specific parameter, including the stored value, by supplying the parameter name.

- `GetParameters`: This permission allows users to get the full information about a list of named parameters, including stored values.

- `GetParameterHistory`: This permission retrieves a history of the changes for a specified parameter, including modified dates, the user who modified them, and the value history.

- `GetParametersByPath`: This retrieves the basic information (name, type, value, and version) for all the values stored in a particular path. For example, if the value of `/app1/dev` were passed, any parameters stored in that hierarchy would be returned.

- `PutParameter`: A user with this permission can place or modify a parameter in the service.

With an understanding of the different IAM permissions used in conjunction with the Systems Manager Parameter Store service, you are ready to go through the exercise of storing and retrieving a secret with the service.

Storing and Retrieving a Secret in Parameter Store

It's time for you to go through the process of storing and retrieving a secure secret in Systems Manager Parameter Store so that you can see how the service differs from AWS Secrets Manager. You will use the same MySQL username and password you created previously in this chapter as part of the prerequisites for the AWS Secrets Manager exercises. If you went through the full process of that exercise, then the password that was originally given to you by the RDS service will no longer be valid since the Secrets Manager service will have rotated the password at this point. You therefore have two options:

- You can retrieve the current password from AWS Secrets Manager; however, note that the Parameter Store service will not automatically rotate the secret without a Lambda function and connection to that Lambda function (which is outside the scope of this chapter).

- You can use the original username and password you stored when creating the RDS database and not test its connection to the database. Only test the process of retrieving the password.

Note that only a single item will be stored in a single parameter. When it comes to values such as usernames and passwords, this means that the username would need to be saved in one parameter, and the password in another. This contrasts with the Secrets Manager service, where the username and password can be stored together and retrieved in a single API/CLI call.

Follow these steps to store a secret securely in Parameter Store:

1. Log on to the Systems Manager service using the AWS Management Console. You can get there quickly using the following URL: `https://console.aws.amazon.com/systems-manager/`.

2. Once on the Systems Manager main page, find the `Application Management` main heading on the left-hand menu. Underneath this heading, click on the `Parameter Store` menu item.

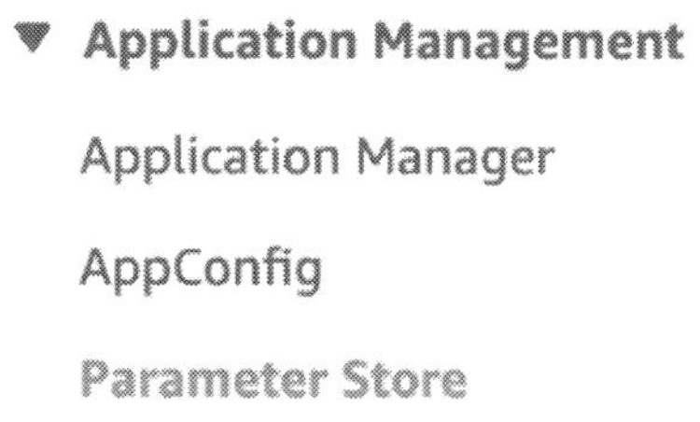

▼ **Application Management**

    Application Manager

    AppConfig

    Parameter Store

Figure 20.12: Application Management menu

3. You should now be on the page with the `My parameters` heading. Click on the button labeled `Create parameter` near the top right-hand side of the screen.

4. After clicking on the `Create parameter` button, you will be on the `Create parameter` page. The first section will be labeled `Parameter details`. Here, enter a name for the parameter; use `ps-mysql-pass` for the parameter name.

Parameter details

Name

🔍 ps-mysql-pass

Figure 20.13: Parameter details field

5. Move down the page to the `Tier` heading and ensure the radio button is selected for the `Standard` setting.

Tier
Parameter Store offers standard and advanced parameters.

⦿ **Standard**
Limit of 10,000 parameters. Parameter value size up to 4 KB.
Parameter policies are not available. No additional charge.

◯ **Advanced**
Can create more than 10,000 parameters. Parameter value size up to 8 KB. Parameter policies are available. Charges apply

Figure 20.14: Tier selection screen in Parameter Store

6. Next, move down the page to the `Type` heading. Here, since you are saving a database password, you will need to set the value as `SecureString`. This encrypts the value when it stores it. Once you have changed the type to `SecureString`, you will see the options for `KMS key source` appear. Keep the default settings as `My current account` and the `KMS Key ID` value of `alias/aws/ssm` to use the service's KMS key.

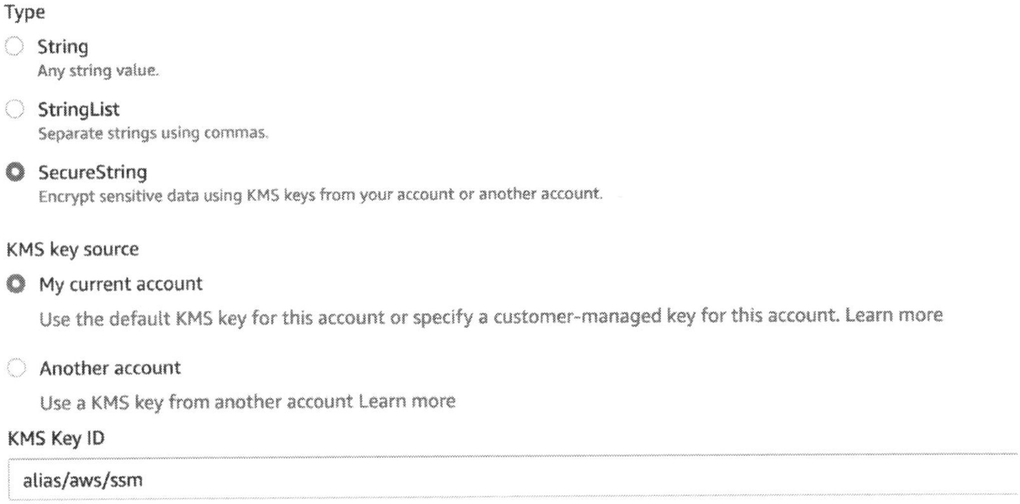

Type

◯ **String**
Any string value.

◯ **StringList**
Separate strings using commas.

⦿ **SecureString**
Encrypt sensitive data using KMS keys from your account or another account.

KMS key source

⦿ **My current account**
Use the default KMS key for this account or specify a customer-managed key for this account. Learn more

◯ **Another account**
Use a KMS key from another account Learn more

KMS Key ID

alias/aws/ssm

Figure 20.15: KMS key type setting

> **Note**
> If you were going to save the corresponding username that went along with this password in Parameter Store instead of an environment variable, you could store that as the type of `String` instead of `SecureString`.

7. Now, enter the value that you want the Parameter Store service to store for you securely. Enter the database password that you have saved from the previous exercise into the textbox.

8. After entering the value, scroll down to the bottom of the page and click on the orange `Create parameter` button.

You've now gone through the process of storing a secure secret/password in Systems Manager Parameter Store.

Next, you will see how easy it is to retrieve the value of something that has been stored in the Parameter Store service.

After you have stored the value of the confidential secret in the Parameter Store service, then at some point, you or someone on your team will need to access this secret parameter that has been stored in the service. Use the steps outlined as follows to retrieve the secret's value from the AWS Management Console:

1. Navigate to the AWS Systems Manager service.

2. Using the left-hand navigation menu, choose the `Parameter Store` option under the heading of `Application Management`.

3. Once on the Parameter Store main page, click on the name of the parameter/secret for which you would like to retrieve the value.

4. This will bring you to the overview page for the parameter. Find the value where you should see a row of asterisks underneath. Click on Show, and the secret will be displayed.

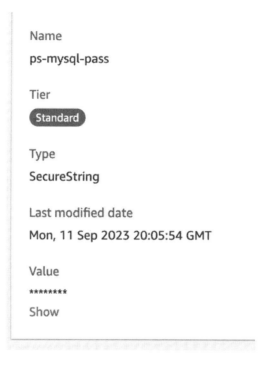

Figure 20.16: Overview page for parameter

You now know how to both store and retrieve secret values stored in AWS Systems Manager Parameter Store. However, in case of an audit or incident, as a security professional, it's also part of your responsibility to access the logs of who has used, added, or modified those secrets. The next section will explain how you can accomplish this task using the previous services mentioned in this chapter.

How Providing an Auditable Trail from Secret Usage Helps in Security and Compliance

Auditing AWS CloudTrail for those who used a secret in AWS Secrets Manager or AWS Systems Manager Parameter Store is a critical security practice that ensures transparency and accountability in your AWS environment. This audit trail serves several vital purposes.

First, it provides visibility and accountability. Knowing who accessed sensitive secrets is crucial for security and compliance. By auditing CloudTrail, you can track and attribute secret access to specific IAM users or roles. In case of unauthorized or suspicious access, this information helps you quickly identify and respond to security incidents.

Second, it aids in compliance and regulatory requirements. Many industry-specific regulations and compliance standards (e.g., PCI DSS and HIPAA) require organizations to maintain records of who accessed sensitive data. Auditing the access to secrets through CloudTrail helps demonstrate compliance with these standards during audits or assessments.

Furthermore, it contributes to incident investigation and forensics. In the unfortunate event of a security breach or data leak, having an audit trail of access to secrets can be invaluable. It assists in reconstructing the sequence of events, understanding the scope of the breach, and identifying potential security gaps that need mitigation.

Finally, it supports operational insights. Auditing access to secrets can also provide operational insights into how your applications and services utilize secrets. This information can help optimize your infrastructure, improve security policies, and streamline access management.

You have just learned how the secrets management tools in AWS provide an auditable trail for compliance when users or roles access a secret. An auditable trail can quickly help investigators obtain the necessary information during a forensic investigation.

Summary

In this chapter, you examined how to use the native services of AWS Secrets Manager and Systems Manager Parameter Store to store secret material, such as passwords and API keys, securely. You gained insights into why centralized secrets management is a critical part of a strong security strategy, both from a risk perspective and from the ability to audit the use of the secrets.

You learned how to store the secrets using different native AWS services, including AWS Secrets Manager and Systems Manager Parameter Store, and how to retrieve those secrets once they had been stored in the respective service(s).

This chapter marks the end of this comprehensive guide on the AWS Certified Security Specialty exam. This book covered all six domains of the exam, starting with the fundamentals of the AWS Shared Responsibility Model. You learned about what you are responsible for securing and what AWS is responsible for securing. You also reviewed the fundamental services that AWS provides and how attacks can happen once your organization moves its workloads and data to a cloud environment.

Incident response was discussed in the context of how to deal with incidents in AWS. You were introduced to the tools that help remediate the compliance and security posture of your account in AWS Config, GuardDuty, and Security Hub, respectively.

You then dove into logging and monitoring, exploring the kinds of logs generated by different AWS services. After that, you explored the main service used to capture log events, CloudWatch, and looked at how logs and metrics are used in the service. But what good are logs if you can't find the information you are looking for? The section on logging concluded by showing you how to search and parse your logs for information relevant to your needs at that moment.

Securing accounts is something that each AWS security specialist needs a solid understanding of, which is what you learned about in the *Infrastructure Security* section. You examined security techniques from both an account and infrastructure level. You also learned about managing key infrastructure.

Securing your AWS accounts is about not only the infrastructure but also managing permissions, which involves giving your users only the permissions that they need to perform their job duties. You explored this in the *Identity and Access Management* section. You examined IAM policies and how they were constructed, **Service Control Policies** (**SCPs**) and how they provide guardrails around your accounts, and even how to allow outside users measured access to your accounts by using federation.

In the final section, you learned about data protection, learning how to connect to your AWS environment in a secure fashion, along with learning about secure certificates and the AWS Certificate Manager service so that you can generate your own certificates.

Further Reading

For additional information on the AWS Shared Responsibility Model and an underlying foundation of knowledge of AWS security, please check out the following resources:

- AWS Secrets Manager FAQs: `https://packt.link/HVlmi`

- AWS Systems Manager Parameter Store FAQs: `https://packt.link/9N4YQ`

- Replicating secrets in multiple regions with AWS Secrets Manager: `https://packt.link/NnPuC`

- Auditing AWS Secrets Manager with AWS Config: `https://packt.link/3k5AJ`

Exam Readiness Drill – Chapter Review Questions

Apart from a solid understanding of key concepts, being able to think quickly under time pressure is a skill that will help you ace your certification exam. That is why working on these skills early on in your learning journey is key.

Chapter review questions are designed to improve your test-taking skills progressively with each chapter you learn and review your understanding of key concepts in the chapter at the same time. You'll find these at the end of each chapter.

> **How To Access These Resources**
>
> To learn how to access these resources, head over to the chapter titled *Chapter 21, Accessing the Online Practice Resources*.

To open the Chapter Review Questions for this chapter, perform the following steps:

1. Click the link – `https://packt.link/SCSC02E2_CH20`

   Alternatively, you can scan the following QR code (*Figure 20.17*):

Figure 20.17: QR code that opens Chapter Review Questions for logged-in users

2.   Once you log in, you'll see a page similar to the one shown in *Figure 20.18*:

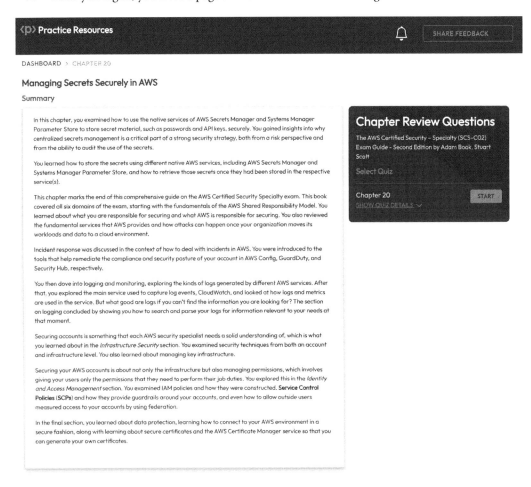

Figure 20.18: Chapter Review Questions for Chapter 20

3.   Once ready, start the following practice drills, re-attempting the quiz multiple times.

Exam Readiness Drill

For the first three attempts, don't worry about the time limit.

ATTEMPT 1

The first time, aim for at least **40%**. Look at the answers you got wrong and read the relevant sections in the chapter again to fix your learning gaps.

ATTEMPT 2

The second time, aim for at least **60%**. Look at the answers you got wrong and read the relevant sections in the chapter again to fix any remaining learning gaps.

ATTEMPT 3

The third time, aim for at least **75%**. Once you score **75%** or more, you start working on your timing.

> **Tip**
>
> You may take more than three attempts to reach 75%. That's okay. Just review the relevant sections in the chapter till you get there.

Working On Timing

Target: Your aim is to keep the score the same while trying to answer these questions as quickly as possible. Here's an example of how your next attempts should look like:

Attempt	Score	Time Taken
Attempt 5	77%	21 mins 30 seconds
Attempt 6	78%	18 mins 34 seconds
Attempt 7	76%	14 mins 44 seconds

Table 20.1: Sample timing practice drills on the online platform

> **Note**
>
> The time limits shown in the above table are just examples. Set your own time limits with each attempt based on the time limit of the quiz on the website.

With each new attempt, your score should stay above 75% while your time taken to complete should **decrease**. Repeat as many attempts as you want till you feel confident dealing with the time pressure.

Accessing the Online Practice Resources

Your copy of *AWS Certified Security – Specialty Exam Guide (SCS-C02) 2nd Edition* comes with free online practice resources. Use these to hone your exam readiness even further by attempting practice questions on the companion website. The website is user-friendly and can be accessed from mobile, desktop, and tablet devices. It also includes interactive timers for an exam-like experience.

How to Access These Resources

Here's how you can start accessing these resources depending on your source of purchase.

Purchased from Packt Store (packtpub.com)

If you've bought the book from the Packt store (packtpub.com) eBook or Print, head to `https://packt.link/scsc02practice`. There, log in using the same Packt account you created or used to purchase the book.

Packt+ Subscription

If you're a Packt+ subscriber, you can head over to the same link (`https://packt.link/scsc02practice`), log in with your Packt ID, and start using the resources. You will have access to them as long as your subscription is active.

If you face any issues accessing your free resources, contact us at customercare@packt.com.

Purchased from Amazon and Other Sources

If you've purchased from sources other than the ones mentioned above (like Amazon), you'll need to unlock the resources first by entering your unique sign-up code provided in this section. Unlocking takes less than 10 minutes, can be done from any device, and needs to be done only once. Follow these five easy steps to complete the process:

STEP 1

Open the link `https://packt.link/scsc02unlock` OR scan the following QR code:

Figure 21.1: QR code for the page that lets you unlock this book's free online content

Either of those links will lead to the following page as shown in *Figure 21.2*:

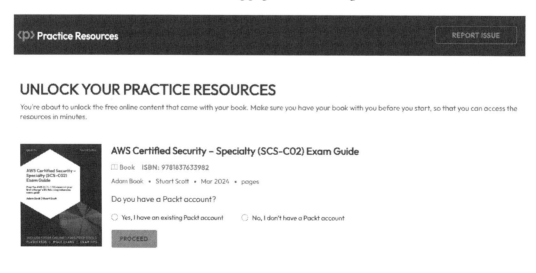

Figure 21.2: Unlock page for the online practice resources

STEP 2

If you already have a Packt account, select the option Yes, I have an existing Packt account. If not, select the option No, I don't have a Packt account.

If you don't have a Packt account, you'll be prompted to create a new account on the next page. It's free and only takes a minute to create.

Click Proceed after selecting one of those options.

STEP 3

After you've created your account or logged in to an existing one, you'll be directed to the following page as shown in *Figure 21.3*.

Make a note of your unique unlock code:

EDG5677

Type in or copy this code into the text box labeled Enter Unique Code:

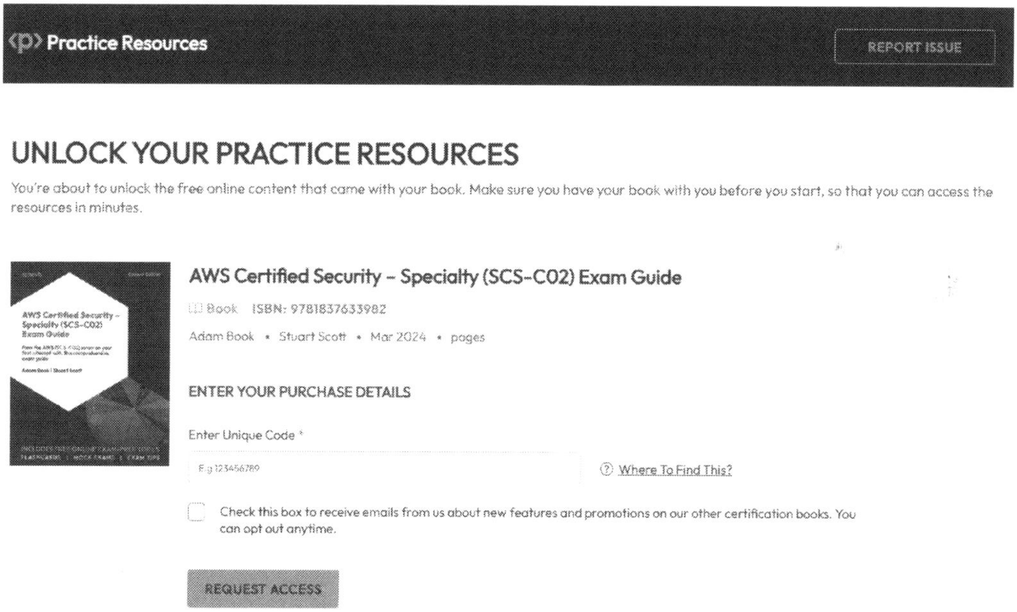

Figure 21.3: Enter your unique sign-up code to unlock the resources

> **Troubleshooting Tip**
>
> After creating an account, if your connection drops off or you accidentally close the page, you can reopen the page shown in Figure *21.2* and select Yes, I have an existing account. Then, sign in with the account you had created before you closed the page. You'll be redirected to the screen shown in *Figure 21.3*.

STEP 4

> **Note**
>
> You may choose to opt into emails regarding feature updates and offers on our other certification books. We don't spam, and it's easy to opt out at any time.

Click Request Access.

STEP 5

If the code you entered is correct, you'll see a button that says, OPEN PRACTICE RESOURCES, as shown in *Figure 21.4*:

PACKT PRACTICE RESOURCES

You've just unlocked the free online content that came with your book.

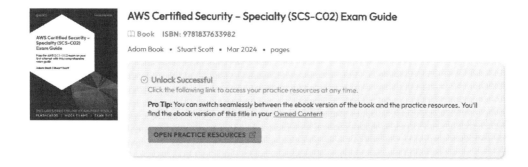

AWS Certified Security – Specialty (SCS-C02) Exam Guide

Book   ISBN: 9781837633982

Adam Book • Stuart Scott • Mar 2024 • pages

⊘ Unlock Successful
Click the following link to access your practice resources at any time.

Pro Tip: You can switch seamlessly between the ebook version of the book and the practice resources. You'll find the ebook version of this title in your Owned Content

OPEN PRACTICE RESOURCES

Figure 21.4: Page that shows up after a successful unlock

Click the OPEN PRACTICE RESOURCES link to start using your free online content. You'll be redirected to the Dashboard shown in *Figure 21.5*:

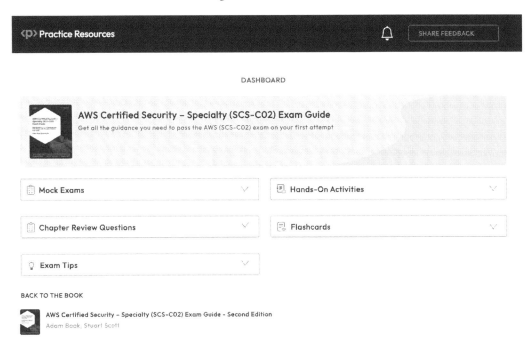

Figure 21.5: Dashboard page for practice resources

> **Bookmark this link.**
> Now that you've unlocked the resources, you can come back to them anytime by visiting `https://packt.link/scsc02practice` or scanning the following QR code provided in *Figure 21.6*:

Figure 21.6: QR code to bookmark practice resources website

Troubleshooting Tips

If you're facing issues unlocking, here are three things you can do:

- Double-check your unique code. All unique codes in our books are case-sensitive and your code needs to match exactly as it is shown in *STEP 3*.

- If that doesn't work, use the Report Issue button located at the top-right corner of the page.

- If you're not able to open the unlock page at all, write to customercare@packt.com and mention the name of the book.

www.packtpub.com

Subscribe to our online digital library for full access to over 7,000 books and videos, as well as industry leading tools to help you plan your personal development and advance your career. For more information, please visit our website.

Why subscribe?

- Spend less time learning and more time coding with practical eBooks and Videos from over 4,000 industry professionals

- Improve your learning with Skill Plans built especially for you

- Get a free eBook or video every month

- Fully searchable for easy access to vital information

- Copy and paste, print, and bookmark content

At www.packtpub.com, you can also read a collection of free technical articles, sign up for a range of free newsletters, and receive exclusive discounts and offers on Packt books and eBooks.

Other Books You May Enjoy

If you enjoyed this book, you may be interested in these other books by Packt:

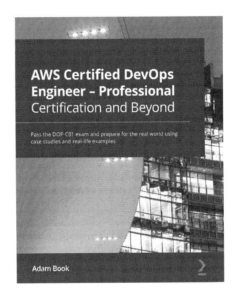

AWS Certified DevOps Engineer - Professional Certification and Beyond

Adam Book

ISBN: 978-1-80107-445-2

- Automate your pipelines, build phases, and deployments with AWS-native tooling
- Discover how to implement logging and monitoring using AWS-native tooling
- Gain a solid understanding of the services included in the AWS DevOps Professional exam
- Reinforce security practices on the AWS platform from an exam point of view
- Find out how to automatically enforce standards and policies in AWS environments
- Explore AWS best practices and anti-patterns
- Enhance your core AWS skills with the help of exercises and practice tests

AWS for Solutions Architects, Second Edition

Patrick Sard and Yohan Wadia

ISBN: 978-1-80181-313-6

- Design and deploy fully secure, dynamically scalable, highly available, fault-tolerant, and reliable apps on AWS
- Integrate on-premises environments seamlessly with AWS resources
- Select appropriate architecture patterns and AWS services for designing and deploying complex applications
- Continuously improve solution architectures for security, reliability, performance, operational excellence, and cost-efficiency
- Plan and execute migrations of complex applications to AWS
- Implement cost-control strategies to deliver cost-effective solutions on AWS

Share Your Thoughts

Now you've finished *AWS Certified Security – Specialty (SCS-C02) Exam Guide, Second Edition*, we'd love to hear your thoughts! Scan the QR code below to go straight to the Amazon review page for this book and share your feedback or leave a review on the site that you purchased it from.

https://packt.link/r/1837633983

Your review is important to us and the tech community and will help us make sure we're delivering excellent quality content.

Download a Free PDF Copy of This Book

Thanks for purchasing this book!

Do you like to read on the go but are unable to carry your print books everywhere?

Is your eBook purchase not compatible with the device of your choice?

Don't worry, now with every Packt book you get a DRM-free PDF version of that book at no cost.

Read anywhere, any place, on any device. Search, copy, and paste code from your favorite technical books directly into your application.

The perks don't stop there, you can get exclusive access to discounts, newsletters, and great free content in your inbox daily.

Follow these simple steps to get the benefits:

1. Scan the QR code or visit the link below:

https://packt.link/free-ebook/9781837633982

2. Submit your proof of purchase.
3. That's it! We'll send your free PDF and other benefits to your email directly.

Index

W

Made in the USA
Middletown, DE
11 September 2024

60784845R00340